BOMBING HITLER

BOMBING HITLER

One man's war with Bomber Command

T. I. STEEL

Matador
9 Priory Business Park,
Wistow Road, Kibworth Beauchamp,
Leicestershire. LE8 0RX
Tel: (+44) 116 279 2299
Fax: (+44) 116 279 2277
Email: books@troubador.co.uk
Web: www.troubador.co.uk/matador

ISBN 978 1784620 448

British Library Cataloguing in Publication Data.
A catalogue record for this book is available from the British Library.

Typeset by Troubador Publishing Ltd, Leicester, UK
Printed and bound in the UK by TJ International, Padstow, Cornwall

Matador is an imprint of Troubador Publishing Ltd

This book is dedicated to all the aircrew, ground staff and W.A.A.F's of R.A.F. Bomber Command and to the Firefighters of the world.

CONTENTS

FOREWORD

The Second World War was, and will almost certainly remain, the single most destructive conflict in mankind's entire history. The amount of subjects and events worthy of being recounted is vast, covering theatres of war as diverse as the North Atlantic to the African desert and from the rolling countryside of Britain to the volcanic islands of the Pacific. The title of World War truly applied to the conflict as almost every nation on earth was involved in some way or another and countless numbers of people played their part.

The amount of books written on the subject is also massive and most areas of the war have been covered somewhere, so what is this one about? This book is the story of one tiny part of what was the single most destructive force created by man before the advent of the Atomic Bomb; Royal Air Force Bomber Command. The story covers one man's journey from civilian non-combatant, through each of his phases of training until he finally became a pilot of one of the mighty Avro Lancaster bombers which pounded Nazi occupied Europe night after night.

The central subject of the book is one man, Bernard Frank Steel, my Grandfather, and a man I had the honour of knowing extremely well, spending several years living with him and his wife, my Grandmother, Ellen. The idea for the book was born out of his own operational flying log books which he 'accidently' forgot to hand over when he was de-mobbed and which have been a superb source of information; however they did bring their own problems.

As with everything Second World War, one tiny piece of information leads to another and before you know it the whole thing becomes organic and takes on a life of its own. When I embarked on this venture I envisaged it taking about six months to complete with perhaps a fifty page commentary resulting; but as you can see, the project decided where it was going to go all on its own; in fact I had to force myself to curtail its expansion in certain areas as things were beginning to get out of hand.

As well as the wealth of factual literature available on the Second World War there are many fantastic works of fiction written about this period of history, many of which have almost become accepted as fact, usually with the help of Hollywood, but even many of the factual stories have been tinged with a little extra colour.

This book contains some tiny elements of licence which have only been employed for the benefit of making the book readable and have been kept deliberately to an absolute minimum. There are only two areas which may not be 100% accurate, although even they are as close as can be known this long after the event. The only two areas where inaccuracy may have been allowed to creep in (as far as I am aware) are the dates of some of Bernard's leave periods and the exact wordings of some of the conversations; although most of those are direct recollections of real conversations from Bernard himself and the gist of each conversation is accurate.

Everything else in the book actually happened and has been researched over a five year period using such fantastic sources as the R.A.F. Museum archives at Hendon and the National Archives at Kew, along with Bernard's own papers, log books and his own first hand recollections. The latter stages are reported from family members and my own experiences of Bernard and should, I hope, give the reader a true sense of what it was like to be a part of Bomber Command through those dark days. With all things of this size and covering events which occurred up to seventy years ago, there are almost certainly some omissions and I can only apologise for them.

Although the story gives the account of just one man's journey, it was a journey familiar to many thousands of brave young men who fought and died in huge numbers in the skies over Europe.

CHAPTER ONE

'No Such undertaking'

The Phoney War. 3ʳᵈ September 1939 to 2ⁿᵈ September 1940.

At 11.15am on Sunday 3ʳᵈ September 1939, in the front room of his rented home at 67 Honeywell Road, Battersea, Bernard Steel leant forward and turned up the volume of his wireless. The broadcast he was listening to was originating from just a few miles away but its effect would reverberate around the world. His wife of less than fourteen months, Ellen, stood beside him, the look of nervous anticipation on her face bordered upon fear, and rightly so.

As the valves warmed the wireless crackled into life and the strained tones of the Prime Minister, Neville Chamberlain, filled the room.

"This morning the British Ambassador in Berlin handed the German Government a final note, stating that unless we heard from them by 11 o'clock, that they were prepared at once, to withdraw their troops from Poland, a state of war would exist between us.

I have to tell you now, that no such undertaking has been received and that consequently this country is at war with Germany."

Neither Bernard nor Ellen knew the extent to which their lives would change or just how close they would both come to death in the coming years; at that moment the future must have seemed very uncertain. No one knew if Britain would be able to stand alone against the growing military might of the German Reich and the threat of invasion of the British Isles was only too real as Britain's own military capability had been massively reduced at the end of the Great War with only the Navy maintaining any real power. At that moment the prospect of a long and happy life lived in freedom, which had been promised at the end of the First World War, seemed very bleak indeed.

The R.A.F. was the first of the British armed forces to go into action on that first day of war and did so twice. Bomber Command launched the first action as a Blenheim reconnaissance aircraft from 139 Squadron, along with eighteen Hampdens and nine Wellingtons, took off at mid-day to search for German naval vessels. Although the Blenheim managed to photograph some ships to the north

1

of Wilhelmshaven, neither of the bomber groups managed to make contact with the enemy and they all returned safely to base.

The Blenheim of 139 Squadron had been the first British aircraft of the war to cross the German frontier, that night it was followed by three Whitleys from 51 Squadron and seven from 58 Squadron who carried thousands of leaflets and dropped them over Hamburg and Bremen. Once again there were no losses of British aircraft but that would soon change as the air war rapidly intensified. The very next day, fifteen Blenheims and fourteen Wellingtons were dispatched to attack the ships which had been discovered by the reconnaissance aircraft the previous day. Although ten of the aircraft failed to find their targets due to low cloud, some of the Blenheims found and attacked the pocket battleship Admiral Scheer and managed to hit it with several bombs, all of which bounced off the ships armour plating and fell harmlessly into the sea. Five of the Blenheims were shot down by anti-aircraft fire, with 107 Squadron losing all but one of the five aircraft it sent on the raid. The first British casualties of the war were the crew of Blenheim N6184 of 107 Squadron consisting of the pilot, Flight Lieutenant W.F. Barton, the navigator, Flying Officer J.F. Ross, and Wireless Operator, Corporal J.L. Ricketts, who were shot down by anti-aircraft fire from the ship Admiral Hipper; they would turn out to be just the first of very many. The raid showed just how difficult the air war was going to be as the loss rate for the raid was seven aircraft, a staggering percentage of 23.3%.

The day after the declaration of war, Monday morning, Bernard and Ellen made their way to the office as they did every morning, but that day there was electricity in the air, a sense of anticipation. Every commuter bustling to their place of work had the same topic of conversation on their lips. London was the capital city of a country at war, everyone knew that it would bear the brunt of German aggression at some point; very few would have guessed just how severe it would be.

Bernard and Ellen's destination was just a few yards from the Palace of Westminster where the country's politicians were in fervent discussion as to what should be done. It seems strange to us now with the benefit of hindsight but there was, at the time, a not inconsiderable lobby who wished to strike a peace deal with the Germans. The fear of another long war of attrition, with its huge losses of both personnel and finance, was the last thing the British Empire needed, they argued.

The office of Cluttons, where Bernard had worked as an Estate Agents Clerk since 1929 and Ellen as a Telephonist, was located at 5 Great College Street near to Westminster Abbey. Its position between the policy makers in Parliament and the final resting place of many a British hero has a certain irony that neatly fits Bernard's position. He didn't know it yet, but exactly a year to the day of the outbreak of war he would commence his service with the Royal Air Force; a service he hoped at that moment would not be necessary, after all it would all be over by Christmas, wouldn't it?

The early days of the war saw no fighting on the home front and very little elsewhere for the British. As a result, for most people, life went on almost as if nothing had changed and in time this early period earned itself the nickname the 'Phoney war.' For Bernard and Ellen their routine was similarly unaltered. Bernard was 27 years old when war broke out and had married Ellen the previous June after having met at work. With no children they were free to enjoy the fruits of their labours and had made a comfortable home for themselves in their rented, two bedroom, Battersea home from where it was only a short commute to their office where they arrived promptly every day.

By today's standards Bernard would be considered as short, measuring 5 feet 4 ½ inches, but back in the thirties he was firmly in the average category. His black hair was always well kept, with a ruler straight left hand parting, as was the vogue of the day, and it was never allowed to get long enough to trouble his collar or need more than the most gentle of trims. He was of medium build, his R.A.F. record gives a chest measurement of 30 ¼ inches (deflated), with strong arms and a handsome, smiling face that would not have gone amiss in the realms of the matinee idol. His nose was not inconsiderable but not large, unlike his brothers and especially his sisters, with a strong set jaw which was complemented by his greyish, blue eyes. Whether at work or at home his appearance was always immaculate, his shoes were cleaned every day, including the insteps, and every pair had Blakey's fitted to both heel and toe; his shirts had neat creases and his suits fitted exactly. He gave the impression of a man who was doing rather well for himself and could afford to have his suits made at the best tailors. The truth of the matter was that he liked to do things properly and maintained standards to such a level that his off the peg suits belied their origin. He was a man who possessed great dignity and respect for both himself and others and as a result of that, coupled with his personal pride and humorous nature; he had about him the air of a proper British gentleman.

Christmas 1939 came and went with the only change to Bernard and Ellen being the introduction of meat rationing on 28th December. 1939 became 1940 and the couple saw it arrive together in blissful ignorance of the changes the

Ellen and Bernard's portrait photos taken in 1937

New Year would bring. Ellen was four months older than Bernard and coincidently four inches shorter. She had a simplistic attractiveness about her that when combined with her gentleness formed a magnetism that had drawn Bernard to her. Her hair was light brown and wavy, sometimes unruly, but could be kept in check with a well placed hair grip and her eyes were dark brown and smouldered from beneath neatly plucked eyebrows. Throughout her life Ellen was slim, maybe bordering on thin, and looked as if a good gust of wind would blow her over but her appearance belied her strength both physically and mentally and she would prove her mettle many times in the years to come. She had had an unconventional childhood which had taught her a personal, mental toughness but ironically gave her the ability to worry about other people on an industrial scale. She could work like a Trojan all day without flagging, despite never appearing to eat, and could turn her hand to almost anything; all in all, this was one tough little lady.

Bernard and Ellen's relationship had built slowly from nervous smiles snatched as they passed one another in the office. The smiles led to small, trembling chats and then finally to proper courting, culminating in their marriage in Worcester Park, where Ellen lived at the time, on 11th June 1938.

On the night of 15th/16th May 1940 Bomber Command launched its first raid of any notable size. Ninety-nine aircraft, made up of thirty-nine Wellingtons, thirty-six Hampdens and twenty-four Whitleys, headed to the heavy industrial area of the Ruhr. There were sixteen different targets identified for the night but none of

The RAF Hendon Wellington, one of just two surviving

them were seriously damaged and just one aircraft, a Wellington of 15 Squadron, was lost when it crashed into high ground near Rouen in France.

From the skies over Britain, the Luftwaffe was beginning to give the British population a taste of what was to come. As summer began to arrive so did the German bombers and from the 18th June onwards considerable numbers would cross the Channel almost every night, it was as if the Germans were counting guns, much as the Zulu's had done at Rorke's Drift. The purpose of their probing would soon become apparent.

Battersea had been a relatively peaceful haven up to that point and the new organisations and defences springing up around them had little effect on Bernard and Ellen. However, Bernard was an intelligent man and realised that call up papers would soon be arriving in large numbers on doormats across the country. Ellen's father, Oswald Sims, who had been a railway station worker at Ashtead in Surrey and had served in the trenches during the Great War, urged Bernard not to get himself caught up in any modern day equivalent of that madness. Bernard agreed and thought that the best course of action, not having any knowledge of the sea, was to join the Royal Air Force.

There were many reasons a man would choose the junior service, it was dashing with technical, modern equipment, or at least the R.A.F. told the public that, but that did not sway Bernard. They were the only service capable of taking the fight to the Germans and were bombing targets nearly every night, so the papers exclaimed; that didn't sway him either. (In reality their slow, outdated, light bombers were being swatted from the sky and often when they did drop their bombs, they would fall miles from the target). "They come back to a base in England and you get to sleep in a proper bed." Oswald Sims declared; that convinced Bernard. As a result, sometime in June or July 1940, 28 year old Bernard Steel volunteered for service with the R.A.F; the R.A.F. duly accepted.

By July 1940 the Germans had the vast majority of mainland Europe under their control and with the European peoples subjugated, could focus their attention elsewhere. With the fall of France, most of mainland Britain fell within range of the Luftwaffe and they launched their first large scale raid on 10th July with a force of seventy aircraft attacking the South Wales docks area. Hitler was drawing up plans for operation Seelowe (Sealion) which was to be the invasion of Britain, despite warnings to the contrary by many of his senior military advisors. General Jodl correctly advised Hitler that air superiority would be vital to allow an invasion and that the R.A.F. would need to be wiped out as a precursor. In response Hitler issued Directive 15 which decreed that the air offensive, with the aim of wiping out the R.A.F., would begin on 5th August. He didn't know it but Hitler had just arranged the greatest air battle in history; the Battle of Britain.

Eleven Hampdens of 49 and 83 Squadrons were ordered to attack the Dortmund-Ems canal near Munster on the night of 12th/13th August 1940. Their target was a pair of viaducts that carried the canal over the River Ems which were heavily defended with anti-aircraft positions following an earlier, unsuccessful attack. The German flak barrage that night was intensive during the raid and two Hampdens were shot down. A third, piloted by Flight Lieutenant R.A.B. Learoyd of 49 Squadron, suffered numerous hits by flak but despite the damage he put in a 'determined attack' which damaged but could not destroy the aqueducts. For his courage in the face of stiff opposition, Learoyd became the first member of Bomber Command to receive the Victoria Cross.

With the Luftwaffe having regularly bombed British cities for some time, the War Cabinet finally sanctioned the first raid on the German capital, Berlin. On the night of 25th/26th August around fifty Hampdens and Wellingtons were sent to the capital but discovered on arrival that the city was covered with low cloud (a situation that would prove a regular feature of raids on Berlin) and as a result the bombing was extremely inaccurate. Due to the poor visibility the only damage to the city was a rather unfortunate summer house in the garden of a suburban home of which the two occupants were slightly injured. The rest of the bombs fell in the fields of the farms that surrounded the city. Although the raid was ineffectual, the fact that the R.A.F. had managed to drop bombs anywhere on their capital after Hermann Goering had declared that it would never happen, so embarrassed Hitler and his hierarchy that they were unable to control the urge to take retaliatory action. That retaliation would become known as the Blitz.

CHAPTER TWO

Donkeys and Towers

No.9 Reception Centre, No.1 Receiving Wing, No.3 Initial Training Wing,
No.50 Group Pool & No.22 Elementary Flying Training School (R.A.F.
Cambridge). 3rd September 1940 to 21st May 1941.

Bernard's first day in Royal Air Force blue came on 3rd September 1940, exactly a year after the declaration of war, with his arrival at No.9 Reception Centre (Blackpool). For a young man in 1940, Blackpool must have seemed a far off, almost exotic location. In a time when only the rich owned motor cars and air travel was almost unheard of, a journey from London to Blackpool entailed a considerable train journey. Travel, especially abroad, was the preserve of the rich and out of the reach of a lower, middle class man like Bernard.

His parents, Walter and Lily, had five children of which Bernard was the youngest boy and they were all born and raised in a Victorian, terraced house at 41, Caxton Road, Wimbledon; a suburb of south-west London. Bernard had two older sisters, Eileen born in 1906 and Dorothy born in 1909 and a younger one, Elsie, born in 1916. His older brother, Walter, who was born in 1908, was one of the most naturally funny men you could wish to meet and was probably the only owner of a pushbike that was capable of doing 'half hour in twenty minutes' as he described it. With the seven of them packed into a three bedroom house, both space and money were tight but they were not poor by the standards of the day. The house is still standing and is probably worth a fortune in our modern, property obsessed world, but back then it was basic with an outside toilet and no proper bathroom.

Young Bernard proved himself to be an intelligent lad and as a result ended up being schooled at the renowned Rutlish School in Merton by virtue of a scholarship. The well rounded education he received there, coupled with the same ready wit as his brother and his relative maturity (he was 28 and married with his own home when many men joining the forces were as young as 18) made him well suited for the training that lay ahead. There would be hundreds of hours of theory work alongside the practicalities of learning to fly, all coupled with coming to terms with military life and separation from his wife and family. This was a daunting time.

On arrival at 9 Reception Centre, Bernard, along with all his fellow cadets, was endowed with the rank of Aircraftman 2nd class and the trade title of Aircrafthand under training (pilot) which was immediately abbreviated to U/T Pilot. Along with their exceedingly long titles and job descriptions they received their pay of the not so large sum of two shillings per day (10 pence).

The reception centre (one of many dotted around the country) was located at Blackpool for several reasons. Firstly it had a large number of rooms available in the bed and breakfast hotels situated around the town in which to billet the new airmen and also it had vast open spaces on the beach and promenade upon which the men could be given hours of drill instruction and physical training. As well as learning how to march and salute, the Recruitment Centre taught all the rudimentary skills required for military service. The men (they were all men then as political correctness had yet to be invented) were issued with their uniforms and boots along with a basic cleaning kit. They had to polish every hard surface, buttons, buckles and boot caps to near destruction and put straight creases into every item of clothing in exactly the right place. People then, as now, question why such emphasis was put on what seem to be pointless tasks, the answer to that is simple. The recruits were not taught to polish and launder to such high standards in order that they would make pretty corpses on a battlefield but to instil a sense of unquestioning discipline that, by following orders immediately they were given, would hopefully prevent them from becoming a corpse in the first place. If you can polish a button for two hours without argument you will get your head down in the face of enemy fire when your senior officer tells you to.

The grind of cleaning, kit inspection and lectures on rank marking recognition was broken only by a physical training session on the beach or a squad march in full uniform along the promenade. The squad marches in the waning September sun were looked forward to by most of the men as a little light relief. As they smartly made their way in step along the promenade, crowds of people would stand and watch them pass by. Old veterans would watch the young men and remember when they had marched off to the slaughter fields of the Great War just twenty-five years before and wonder if the same fate would befall these brave souls. Alongside the veterans would be young girls (see the group in the left foreground of the following photograph) who would smile and wave flirtingly and occasionally shout a risqué advance or blow a wolf whistle or a kiss. The men were fast learning that being in uniform, despite its many drawbacks, had many advantages too.

Bernard's R.A.F. service began during the height of the Battle of Britain as

9 R.C. recruits march down Blackpool Promenade, September 1940

Fighter Command struggled to keep the Luftwaffe at bay. On 4th September 1940, an increasingly irate Hitler declared that his Luftwaffe would 'erase' British cities as a reprisal for the R.A.F. bombing of Berlin on the night of 25th/26th August. The tactical switch from attacking Fighter Command airfields and infrastructure to cities would prove fatal to German attempts to achieve aerial superiority. Two days later the Luftwaffe attacked a series of Channel ports and south coast towns prompting the invasion alert to be raised to its second highest level; on the night of 7th September the Luftwaffe sent some 300 bombers to attack the London docks, dropping over 340 tons of bombs in the process. The fires that raged through the warehouses were huge and more than 450 civilians were killed and 1,300 injured. As a result of the previous nights raid on London, at just after 0800 hours on 8th

September, the codeword 'Cromwell' was issued to all British authorities. That meant, as far as the British government was concerned, the invasion of Britain was expected to take place within 24 hours.

Although the invasion itself did not materialize, over the next few days the Luftwaffe did. Each night they re-appeared over London and on the night of 11th September managed to hit Buckingham Palace. With only a few days left for the Luftwaffe to achieve their aim of aerial superiority, which would allow Operation Sealion to go ahead, Hermann Goering launched his most concerted effort yet. On 15th September wave after wave of German aircraft swept over the south-east of England with London and Southampton bearing the brunt. Elsewhere, Liverpool, Manchester, Bristol and Cardiff were also hit. During the battle the Luftwaffe lost 56 aircraft and the R.A.F. 25 but even this last throw of the dice had failed to destroy the R.A.F. and as a result, on 17th September, Operation Sealion was postponed indefinitely, although the Luftwaffe bombing raids continued. The London Blitz had been a costly affair for both sides; since the Luftwaffe had concentrated their efforts on London, starting on 7th September 1940, the R.A.F. had lost 247 fighters while the Germans had lost a combined total of 433 fighters and bombers. More tellingly the British public had lost a total in all towns and cities of 6,950 dead and 10,600 injured; total war had well and truly arrived.

The night of 15th/16th September saw 155 Bomber Command aircraft strike back at the Germans, carrying out raids on a wide ranging set of targets. At that stage of the war, although relatively high numbers of Bomber Command aircraft were being dispatched, they were generally split between large numbers of targets and therefore the bombing was not concentrated. One of the targets for that night was the German invasion barges in the docks of Antwerp and it was to there that eighteen year old Sergeant, John Hannah, found himself sent as a wireless operator aboard a Hampden of 83 Squadron. During the attack his aircraft was hit by flak and caught fire. Instead of baling out, Sergeant Hannah stayed aboard and although he was badly burnt, managed to extinguish the fire enabling the Hampden to return safely to base. For his actions Hannah was awarded Bomber Commands second Victoria Cross of the war.

At home in London, St. Paul's Cathedral was continuing its charmed existence. Having survived the Blitz of August and September 1940, in October it took a direct hit from a high-explosive bomb which crashed through the roof and landed on the high altar, reducing it to a heap of rubble. However, God was looking after one of his favourite houses that day and ensured that the bomb did not detonate, so preventing extensive damage. The Luftwaffe continued their raids during

October and the British civilian casualty figures showed 6,334 killed and 8,695 injured including 643 children under the age of sixteen.

Bernard's initial training at Blackpool lasted for six weeks and was immediately followed with a week of home leave. With the lowly rank of Aircraftsman 2nd class and a smart, new R.A.F. uniform, he headed back to Battersea and the waiting Ellen. Their time together would be brief as his week of leave would end with the young couple saying goodbye to one another at Lords Cricket ground on Friday 25th October. Having said goodbye to his wife, Bernard was collected by a Sergeant in a commandeered bus and driven off to the next stage of training at No.1 Receiving Wing, based in Torquay. Once at the Devonshire resort, the training would continue in much the same way as at Blackpool with more physical training and lectures, with some recruits spending up to ten weeks at a Receiving Wing before being deemed suitable to move on to the next training stage, which would be at an Initial Training Wing.

Bernard's stay at No.1 R.W. lasted just two weeks after which he was sent on to 3 Initial Training Wing on Saturday 9th November. The I.T.W. was based at St. Leonards in East Sussex (near Hastings) and was basically a ground school for would be aircrew. At that point in their training the recruits did not know what job they were to be trained for and the role of the I.T.W. was to find out which role they were best suited to. The training at St. Leonards still contained all the usual drill and P/T but also had an increased level of classroom work. The I.T.W. was designed to be a twelve to fourteen week course with lessons on meteorology, flight theory, engine theory, signals, revisionary mathematics, aircraft recognition and navigation. Along the way the men were subjected to psychological and aptitude tests which culminated in final exams on each subject. Once the results were collated and a suitable role was found for the new airman, he was then posted to another unit for further ground instruction which would be more specific to the job he would finally be doing.

Although the Battle of Britain had been won by Fighter Command in the summer, the Luftwaffe had not been deterred from launching large raids against British cities. On 14th November waves of German bombers flew over Coventry throughout the night, dropping hundreds of tons of high-explosives and incendiary devices. The 14th century cathedral was reduced to ruins along with a large industrial area and a considerable number of residential homes, killing 550 civilians in the process. To this day the ruins of Coventry cathedral stand as a memorial to that horrific night. Coventry wasn't the only town to suffer under the new Luftwaffe tactics. 19th November saw a large scale raid on Birmingham while the R.A.F. retaliated with an attack on the Skoda works in Pilsen, Czechoslovakia on the same night. The force consisted of a total of 63 aircraft made up of Hampdens, Wellingtons and Whitleys but only seventeen reported bombing their primary target and there were no details of the amount of damage inflicted, although Bomber Command lost one Wellington and one Whitley in the raid. 23rd November saw Southampton hit again and the following night the Luftwaffe decided to visit Bristol. The R.A.F. were doing their best to reply to the constant Luftwaffe raids and sent 42 aircraft, comprising Blenheims, Hampdens, and Wellingtons, to Hamburg on the night of 24th/25th November followed the next night by a force of 36 aircraft, made up of Hampdens, Whitleys and Wellingtons, to Wilhelmshaven. In contrast to the devastating Coventry raid, Bomber Command could only manage to raise four fires in Hamburg with just two deaths and in Wilhelmshaven only managed to hit an empty air raid shelter. The R.A.F. was having real difficulty in locating their targets at that point of the war, due mainly to poor technical equipment and aircraft that were rapidly becoming outdated. Radar was still in its infancy and satellite navigation hadn't even been dreamt about. Navigation was still mainly carried out by a process of dead reckoning, using a map and compass with some applied mathematics to take account of wind direction and the occasional star position reading; as a result, at night, without visual references, a crew was doing well to get within several miles of its target. It was becoming obvious to those at the top of the R.A.F. that improvements needed to be made, but even they could not have dreamt of the devastating power and accuracy the R.A.F. would eventually wield.

With November drawing to a close the Luftwaffe's raids showed no sign of letting up as Liverpool was attacked again on 28th and Southampton suffered the same fate two days later. London had continued to receive regular visits from the Luftwaffe and right across the country the home front was becoming a very dangerous place to see out the war as British civilian casualties for November stood at 4,588 killed and 6,202 injured.

The night of 16th/17th December 1940 was to see a complete change of tactics by the R.A.F. In response to the recent bombing of British cities and increasing civilian casualties, the War Cabinet authorized, for the first time, an attack on a city as opposed to a specific military target. The target chosen was Mannheim and a force of 200 aircraft was selected to attack under the codename Abigail Rachel. Worsening weather forced the number of aircraft to be cut to 134, made up of 61 Wellingtons, 35 Whitleys, 29 Hampdens and nine Blenheims. The weather over the target was reported by the returning crews to be clear of cloud and 102 of the aircraft claimed to have bombed the target. Despite their claims the raid was not a great success as the first wave, who were detailed to mark the city centre with incendiary bombs, were not accurate and the following crews bombs were scattered. A report by the Mannheim authorities stated that mainly residential areas were hit with 476 buildings being destroyed, including thirteen commercial premises, one school and two hospitals. The casualty list read 34 dead and 81 injured; the R.A.F. lost two Hampdens and one Blenheim with another four aircraft crashing while landing back in Britain. The raid was significant because it was the first time the R.A.F. had adopted area bombing as a tactic, but it certainly would not be the last and they would eventually hone the technique to near perfection; the Germans had another term for the tactic, they called it terror bombing.

Somehow Bernard passed all that was set before him at the I.T.W. and his psychological profile summed up his character as 'very good', as a result he was selected for Pilot training on 29th December 1940 and received his first promotion to the rank of Leading Aircraftman on New Years Eve. By that point in the war the R.A.F. had set up the Empire Air Training School which saw most would be pilots sent abroad to be trained. Many were sent to Canada and the United States as well as to South Africa. There were many advantages to training in such places with better weather being the main one. In addition there was a smaller chance of a trainee pilot being caught in the air by a marauding German Fighter. However, there were exceptions to the rule and Bernard would be one of those exceptions. Cadets over the age of 26 and those who were married (Bernard qualified on both counts) were not allowed abroad and would be trained in the damp and dangerous world that the skies over Britain had by that time become.

On the home front the air raids on London reached a new ferocity on the night of 29th December as a Christmas lull in activity was broken with a night of intensive bombing over the capital. St. Paul's cathedral once again escaped relatively unharmed but had spent the entire night silhouetted by flame. The Fire Service, along with the Police and other civil defence workers, excelled themselves in both bravery and work rate to keep the damage to a minimum, losing several lives in the process. Among the notable landmarks damaged were the Guildhall and eight churches built by Sir Christopher Wren. It seems a little ironic that they could hit almost everything he built with the exception of his great cathedral and landmark, St. Paul's'. The end of 1940 saw the British civilian casualties for December stand at 3,790 killed and 5,250 injured.

Portsmouth was the next major city to suffer Goering's wrath on the night of 10th January 1941 and Plymouth was to suffer the same fate just three nights later resulting in multiple civilian deaths with many hundreds more being made homeless. The Luftwaffe's air attacks on Britain had been scaled back during February, partly due to adverse weather, and as a result the respite showed in the casualty figures with a marked drop to 790 killed and 1,070 injured. After the lull of February the Luftwaffe stepped up its bombing campaign on cities across Britain with concentrated raids which hit Merseyside on 12th and 13th March and Clydeside being hit on 13th and 14th. A week later on 20th and 21st March, Plymouth was in the Luftwaffe's sights with the destruction caused being officially described as 'heavy as any provincial city had so far sustained.' The raid of 21st March saw more than 20,000 incendiaries dropped alongside hundreds of high explosives.

Bernard in uniform; taken sometime during his initial training

Meanwhile Bernard's training continued at No.3 I.T.W. until March of 1941 when, following another spot of leave, he was posted to 50 Group Pool to await his posting to an Elementary Flying Training School where he would finally get his hands on a real aircraft. When the posting ultimately came, it was to be to No.22 Elementary Flying Training School based at Cambridge with effect from 15th March 1941. After seven months of theory work, P/T sessions, drilling, ditching drill, marching and endless tests, Bernard was finally going to get his hands on a real aircraft.

The Airfield.

R.A.F. Cambridge was located on the eastern outskirts of the historic, University City next to the village of Teversham and became home to 22 Elementary Flying Training School on the day war was declared. The airfield itself was no more than a large expanse of flat grass, which was the norm at most R.A.F. fields of the time as the aircraft of the thirties were mainly light bi-planes that did not require proper concrete runways as we know them today. There was one other good reason for a grass strip at an E.F.T.S. The idea of an E.F.T.S. was to take a trainee who had never touched an aircraft and instruct him to a standard where he was able to do a solo circuit; that is to say, take off, gain altitude (typically 1,000 feet) circle the airfield and land safely on his own. An E.F.T.S. was the R.A.F. equivalent of your father letting you drive around the car park in the family car for the first time. The grass strip was ideal as it gave a wide area to land upon so taking the pressure off the trainee on landing as opposed to trying to set down their aircraft on a thin concrete strip. The site is now the Cambridge City Airport which handles executive traffic and provides initial pilot training by Marshall's group, the same company that provided the training for the R.A.F. pilots when No.22 E.F.T.S. was initially set up back in 1939. It seems very little has changed in Cambridge.

The trainee pilots were billeted in Nissen and Laing huts located just to the south of Greenhouse Farm and on the northern side of the Newmarket Road which ran along the northern edge of the airfield proper. The Nissen huts were constructed of curved, corrugated, iron sheets buried in the ground to form a half pipe shape and were sealed at each end (apart from the door of course) either by bricks or concrete. They were heated by a single cast iron boiler in the centre of the room and as a result were freezing in winter and boiling in summer as the Sun beat down on the metal roof. The Laing hut was made up of standard, prefabricated, lightweight, timber wall sections which were bolted together with the ends made of two eight feet, three inch corner sections and a central two foot, six inch door section, making the hut nineteen feet wide. The sides were usually made of ten, six foot sections, each containing one side of a steel window frame. The walls were lined with plasterboard and the outside covered with felt while the roof was made of corrugated asbestos sheets.

The Aircraft.

The aim of the E.F.T.S. was to take a complete novice and turn them into a pilot capable of taking off, completing a circuit of the airfield and landing again without killing himself or anybody else in the process. In order to achieve that aim the R.A.F. needed an aircraft that was simple to operate, sturdy, stable and responsive in flight. They found these qualities in the iconic De Havilland DH.82 'Tiger Moth'. The Tiger Moth was a 1930's bi-plane which evolved from the earlier DH.60 'Gypsy Moth' and first flew on 26th October 1931, entering service with the R.A.F. at the Central Flying School in February 1932. Orders rolled in from the R.A.F. to such an extent that by the outbreak of World War II they had 500 of them in service and by the end of the war over 7,000 had been built with more than 4,000 of those being destined for the R.A.F.

Nearly half of the total numbers produced were made under license by the Morris Motor Co. with others being built as far apart as Norway, Portugal and Canada. The Tiger Moth was typical of the bi-planes of the time in that its wings were constructed of wood with a fabric covering but its fuselage was a rectangular, steel, tube structure which was in turn fabric covered. Its wings spanned 29 feet 4 inches (8.98m) and it was 23 feet 11 inches (7.3m) long, weighing in at 1,115 lbs (507kg) when empty with a maximum weight of 1,825 lbs (830kg). Power was supplied by one, 130 hp Gipsy Major, four cylinder, air cooled engine mounted in the nose which delivered a maximum speed of 109 mph, which is slower than nearly all modern cars can travel today. The climb rate was a sedentary 670 feet per minute with a service ceiling of 13,600 feet and a range of 300 miles, which was more than enough for any lesson to be completed before fuel ever became a worry.

There are many preserved examples left today and no aircraft museum worth its salt is without one, but more tellingly there are still many flying worldwide and a joy ride in one of these fine old birds can be bought for less than £200.

Tiger Moth T6296 which can be seen on display at the R.A.F. Museum Hendon

22 Elementary Flying Training School, Sunday 16th March 1941.

Seven months after pulling on the light blue of the R.A.F. Bernard was finally going to get 'hands on' with an aircraft. A Sunday may seem a funny day to be starting training but two things make the day of the week irrelevant. Firstly there was a war on and secondly this was military life where every day is the same, Sunday is just another day, just any one of seven.

With sweaty palms and butterflies in his stomach, Bernard made his way across the airfield with his instructor, Flying Officer Fowler, who was trying to convince him that there really was nothing to this flying lark and that the parachute really was only a precaution. Tiger Moth N6927 was the aircraft that was to take him skyward for the first time and was only 21 months old and in peak condition, she would continue to train nervous young men throughout the war and beyond; only ending her service when she was struck in mid-air by a jet engine powered Gloster Meteor in September 1948. It seems as if N6927's story is a metaphor of aviation history, the stick and string bi-planes of a bygone age being swept from the sky by the arrival of fast, sleek and noisy jets.

The first lesson was a simple one. F/O Fowler ran through the cockpit controls and dials slowly and methodically in order that Bernard could familiarize himself. He was shown how the various controls, adjusting devices and fire appliances were operated along with the fuel and ignition systems. Most importantly he was shown how to abandon the aircraft should it all go wrong while simultaneously being re-assured that it wouldn't.

With familiarization out of the way, lesson two consisted of flight preparation. As this was to be Bernard's first flight, F/O Fowler mainly paid attention to his personal comfort, checking his helmet, goggles and parachute and assisting him to get into the cockpit and settle down comfortably. Once in, he had to learn to adjust his harness straps properly (vital as they would prevent him falling out in a roll as the Tiger Moth had an open cockpit) then how to use the inter-com system.

Having shown his pupil how to get comfortable and safe in the cockpit, F/O Fowler got him out again to take a general look over the aircraft. Firstly he checked that it was in a suitable position to start up, well away from other aircraft or open office windows and had plenty of room to taxi out. Next they checked the tyres were inflated, the chocks in place and that the Pitot head was uncovered (the Pitot head is a hollow tube which measures and then displays the airspeed on a gauge in the cockpit). Already Bernard was becoming overwhelmed with the amount of information he was expected to absorb and found himself nodding and grinning in agreement to F/O Fowlers every word without actually knowing what it was he was agreeing to.

Just as he thought the ground checks were complete, F/O Fowler moved on again, this time to check that the brakes were fully on and that the tail trimming control, whatever that was, was set to fully heavy tail position. With all this done they got back in the cockpit and strapped themselves in. At last, thought Bernard, turn her on, rev her up and let's get into the air; how wrong he was. The checks had only just begun as now they had to start the engine and keep it ticking over at a steady 900 to 1,000 rpm while it warmed up for at least four minutes. While the engine warmed they ran through a whole new series of checks for the instruments. First they had to check all the instruments were reading correctly with the oil pressure displaying 35 psi followed by checking that the altimeter was reading zero and that all the switches and controls were set to the right position; once that was done the flying controls had to be run through to ensure they all worked easily and freely and in the right direction. Having completed this latest round of checks they waited for the required temperatures to be reached and then at last they could finally think about moving. Bernard had always considered himself to be reasonably intelligent and able to take on new information with relative ease, but at that moment he had never felt more inadequate as he could not recall a single thing he had been told over the last few minutes. The tidal wave of information that had come his way, coupled with nerves of his first flight and all that lay ahead had completely overwhelmed him; he didn't know it of course but almost every trainee pilot felt that way on their first familiarization, he was by no means in the minority.

With the basics covered it was time to take to the air. The first flight was little more than a joy ride to get the trainee used to the alien experience of being in the air as very few of the men would have ever flown before. The open cockpit, with its inherent noise and wind buffeting, could be disconcerting and a view of the world from high above was one that few men had seen in the early 1940's. Throughout the flight Bernard was encouraged to keep his hands resting lightly on the controls in order that he could feel the small adjustments his instructor made as he moved through the air. Fowler pointed out identifying landmarks and asked simple questions such as 'What is our height?' or 'What is our airspeed?' to encourage Bernard to read the cockpit instruments. The exhilaration of being so high off the ground for the first time in his life, watching the land slip away beneath him, filled him with a sense of how small he really was in the scheme of things; the world just looked so much bigger from up there. After just twenty minutes in the air Bernard's first flight was over. It is not recorded how he took to it or whether the exhilaration he felt equated to enjoyment but one thing is for certain, he would become good at it.

The next five days passed slowly in the classroom with the only break in the monotony coming from a gas exercise on the Tuesday, when all ranks had to wear respirators for a period of thirty minutes. The wait for Bernard's next flight was becoming intolerable by the Friday following his aerial debut, as he longed to experience that feeling of freedom and excitement again. Friday the 21st was to provide plenty of relief from his frustration with two flights in the day during which he finally got his hands on the controls for real. Taking to the air again under the instruction of F/O Fowler, the lesson for the morning was firstly flight preparation. This time, as F/O Fowler repeated all those instructions he had given Bernard on his debut flight, he was pleasantly surprised by how much of the information he had actually retained. For the first time it was Bernard who was carrying out all the checks on the aircraft before taking off, such as a look over the general condition of the aircraft and seeing it was in a suitable position before starting the engine. He even remembered that to start up in front of an open office window was not a suitable place and considered bad form, even though his mischievous nature thought it might be good fun!

Once Bernard and his instructor were in the air his first proper flying lesson began. Effect of Controls as it was known, showed the trainee what effect each individual control surface had on the aircraft in flight. With ailerons (wing control surface), elevators (tail plane control surface) and rudder (tail control surface) to contend with, plus of course their combined effects, this was quite some subject and one that was always covered on several occasions. If the trainee could not get to grips with both the theory and practice of that first lesson then his pilot's career would be over before it began. That first proper lesson lasted for 35 minutes and in the afternoon it was repeated for another half an hour with a little taxiing thrown in, Bernard was on his way to his wings.

The next week saw a growing intensity to Bernard's air instruction time. With the weather holding fair F/O Fowler took him up seven times in the next six days. By the time the Sun set on the 27th March 1941, he had taken to the skies ten times and had flown for a total of four hours 45 minutes. In that time he had undergone lessons encompassing effect of controls, flying straight and level, climbs and descent, stalling, take off, gliding and climbing turns, spinning and most importantly of all, approach and landing. The information load was formidable and while the theory was already learnt the current goal was to make all those procedures second nature in the aircraft itself. The aim was not to make the trainee a pilot that steered an aircraft through the sky but to become a vital component of it. The pilot was to be the last piece the machine required to make it fly; he was not to be the master of the aircraft but an essential part of its mechanics. By nightfall on that Thursday Bernard had covered all the points he would need to master in order to 'go solo'; the next phase was to polish his skill to the level where Fowler would allow him up alone. The pressure to solo was high as any trainee who failed to do so within a relatively short space of time would be taken off pilot training and sent to a navigator or bomb aimers unit instead; the clock was ticking.

Sunday the 30th saw two more skill honing flights followed by a further three on the last day of March 1941. Bernard didn't fly on the 1st of April as the unit was buzzing with rumours concerning a Court of Inquiry hearing that was taking place concerning a trainee pilot who had gone absent without official leave. He was found guilty, not surprisingly, in his absence, and his conviction was followed the next day with the same verdict for the same crime being handed to an Aircraftsman attached to the Defence Staff. With the excitement of the court cases out of the way, Bernard took to the air again for a further 35 minutes on 2nd April, this time focusing on his takeoffs, stalls and approaches and landings. The 4th April saw two flights of 35 minutes each, covering everything he'd gone over two days before with a few turns thrown in for good measure, by the end of the day Fowler was nearly convinced.

As Bernard worked steadily towards his wings, Bomber Command sent a force of 54 aircraft comprising 39 Wellingtons, eleven Hampdens and four Manchesters to the French port of Brest on the night of 4th/5th April where the cruiser Gneisenau was in dock. The raid itself caused little damage but the following day an unexploded bomb was found in the bottom of the dock and so as a precaution the captain of the ship decided to head out and moor in Brest Harbour while it was defused. Later the same day a Bristol Beaufort of Coastal Command attacked the ship in daylight and scored a direct hit with a torpedo causing serious damage which took over six months to repair. The Beaufort, piloted by Flying Officer K. Campbell, was shot down in the attack and the entire crew were killed. For his bravery in crippling the mighty ship, Campbell was posthumously awarded the Victoria Cross.

For the trainee pilots, as well as the classroom theory and time in the air, there would be time spent in a contraption known as a Link trainer. The Link was a forerunner to today's multi-million pound, computer laden flight simulators and proved itself to be a very effective tool throughout the training of the R.A.F.'s wartime pilots. The Link was invented in the late 1920's by an American organ maker by the name of Edwin Link who had a love of flying. The trainer was obviously not computer driven but was a mechanically operated, darkened box in the shape of a tiny aircraft. Inside was a full cockpit layout with the full array of working instruments and controls where the pupil sat and reacted to the changes he saw before him which were manually manipulated by the instructor from the outside. Once again it may have been crude but it proved to be an effective tool in learning the art of instrument flying and of course eradicated the danger of a pupil killing himself by misinterpreting his instruments.

On 6th April 1941 Bernard had his first experience of the Link with his familiarization 'flight' of thirty minutes, which showed him the basics of how to use the contraption. Before he left Cambridge he would visit the Link eleven more times spending a total of six hours inside the claustrophobic box. The first six exercises covered courses (being able to hold a prescribed course just using his

The Link trainer cockpit and top the navigation table from which the operator could manually adjust the pilots instruments. Note the cockpit canopy which closed over the 'pilot' to isolate him from the outside world.

instruments) and then the last five increased in complexity, still tasked with maintaining his course the operator introduced turns as well while allowing Bernard the use of only a limited amount of the flight panel to simulate the difficulties created by a malfunction. For a little wooden box the Link was a highly adaptable training tool.

Monday 7th April dawned bright and crisp; a perfect flying day and a day which Fowler had decided should, barring any large faux pas, take Bernard a giant step towards that elusive solo. A short flight in the morning of twenty minutes duration re-affirmed Fowler's confidence. A second flight, also of twenty minutes, covering stalls, turns, straight and level flight and descents and landings confirmed his progress. Fowler approached the Flight Commander, Flight Lieutenant Porter, and asked him to carry out his own test of Bernard's ability. The dangers of sending up a trainee pilot alone before he was ready are obvious and therefore two instructors had to agree that the trainee was ready before he was allowed to go solo. Late that afternoon Bernard took to the sky with Flt/Lt Porter watching his every move. Twenty minutes later they were back on the ground and Flying Officer Fowler had permission to send his protégé solo. As Bernard woke the following morning filled with nervous excitement, he fully expected to have 'gone solo' by the days end. However, his heart sank as he looked out of the hut window to see low cloud and drizzle; his solo would have to wait for another day.

The R.A.F. was beginning to show signs that it could become a force capable of delivering meaningful blows to Germany by that point of the war. As an example of their growing effectiveness they launched the largest raid on a single target so far on the night of 7th/8th April 1941. That night a total of two hundred and twenty-nine aircraft, 117 Wellingtons, 61 Hampdens, 49 Whitleys and two Stirlings, attacked Kiel in a raid that lasted for over five hours. The raid inflicted widespread damage, especially around the docks area which manufactured U-boats and 88 people were killed with a further 184 injured for the loss of two Wellingtons and two Whitleys. Not satisfied with their nights work, Bomber Command sent a further 160 aircraft, 74 Wellingtons, 44 Whitleys, 29 Hampdens, twelve Manchesters and a solitary Stirling, back to Kiel the following night. This time the majority of the bombs fell in the town centre causing severe damage to a wide range of buildings including the gas works. The resulting death toll was 125 killed and 300 injured. Two Wellingtons, one Hampden and a Manchester were lost in the raid but a further nine assorted aircraft crashed on return to England. Despite the losses, the two raids had been the most successful and effective of the bombing campaign so far. With increasing confidence the night of 9th/10th April saw the R.A.F. mount their largest attack yet on the German capital with a force of eighty bombers made up of 36 Wellingtons, 24 Hampdens, seventeen Whitleys and three Stirlings; five aircraft failed to return.

After two days of poor conditions at Cambridge, 9th April provided better weather and so without delay Fowler took Bernard up for one last polish of his skills before setting him free. With a perfect circuit executed, he allowed Tiger Moth T5636 to gently kiss the grass and come to a smooth stop. Impressed by what he had seen from the rear seat, Fowler climbed out of the cockpit and over the roar of the engine told Bernard, with just nine hours 45 minutes flying time under his belt, to go up and do exactly the same again but this time alone.

Fowler retreated to the northern edge of the grass covered airfield and watched his pupil take off eastward. With a hollow feeling in the pit of his stomach, Bernard set the throttle to full power and released the brakes, letting the aircraft gently accelerate across the grass. The Tiger Moth left the ground smoothly and climbed steadily at an air speed of 70 m.p.h. until she reached a height of 200 feet where he throttled back to 2,050 r.p.m. and the textbook climbing speed of 66 m.p.h. A minute or two later the aircraft had reached the desired 1,000 feet and he throttled back again to 1,950 r.p.m. As the aircraft leveled out from her climb she sped up slightly to her preferred cruising speed of just over 75 m.p.h. Having guided T5636 to her cruising height and speed, Bernard leaned out over the port side of the cockpit and saw the village of Teversham passing beneath him. For the next few minutes he and his 'Moth' flew straight and level at 1000 feet until he checked over both shoulders for traffic. With the airspace around him free of other aircraft, he put the Tiger Moth into a gentle left hand bank and began to turn through 90 degrees until he faced due north. Regaining level flight and maintaining his altitude, he flew on over the airfields natural boundary of the Newmarket Road and once across it, he again banked the aircraft left and turned another 90 degrees until he faced due west. Looking around him Bernard could see the grass airstrip down to his port side (left) and cruising at between 75 and 80 m.p.h. he flew directly over his barrack hut and Greenhouse Farm. By keeping a straight course he and his Tiger Moth flew on as one, passing the airfield buildings on a heading for Cambridge itself. Once above the open fields of Elfleda Farm he began his third 90 degree turn and headed south until he crossed Coldhams Brook where he made his final 90 degree turn and onto a heading straight back to the airfield.

With the take off, ascent, turns, navigation and straight and level flight aspects of his solo complete, and satisfactorily so Bernard thought, all he had to do now was a controlled descent and landing and his solo was in the bag. Closing the throttle down so that the engine was at 1,100 r.p.m. he reduced speed and began to descend. Once his speed had dropped off to around 65 m.p.h. he unlocked the automatic slots (moveable surfaces on the wing which allow the aircraft to fly at slower speeds without stalling) and pushed the stick gently forward to aid his descent. As his speed dropped slowly so did his height, 900 feet passed as did 800 and 700 while he was still over Coldhams Common. Another 100 feet had been lost by the time he reached the back gardens of the semi-detached houses to the west of the airfield and the altimeter was reading 400 feet as he crossed the airfield perimeter. Facing directly into the wind as he had been instructed, the Tiger Moth lost another 200 feet by the time it was into the grassy area of the landing strip and was then at the perfect approach speed of 55 m.p.h. Fowler looked on impressed by his pupils' performance when inexplicably the aircraft dropped suddenly. In the cockpit Bernard had suffered a common problem with first time solo pilots in that he suddenly had so many things to do at once he'd run out of hands, feet and eyes to do them with. Having forgotten to check his altimeter, as he was busy looking at the rapidly rising ground, he had allowed the aircraft to increase its rate of descent, once he realized the problem he pulled back a little on the stick which brought the nose up slightly but the aircraft lost its final few feet of altitude too quickly and the undercarriage hit the ground hard and bounced the Tiger Moth back into the air. Recovering his composure and realizing his mistake, Bernard put her down safely 100 yards further along the grass strip and brought the sturdy old girl to a stop before turning and taxiing to the edge of the field. As he made his way across the grass he cursed himself for missing his opportunity and for allowing his nerves to muddle his actions; by the time he parked up he'd convinced himself that navigator's school was the best he was going to do now.

Fowler arrived by T5636's side just as Bernard climbed out and was sheepishly removing his leather flying helmet. With a straight, unemotional face Fowler looked him in the eye and said "Any landing you can walk away from is good enough for me, but you'll do it perfectly this afternoon."

That afternoon, true to Fowlers prediction, Bernard executed the perfect solo. He wouldn't be visiting navigator's school after all.

As he dressed the morning after his successful solo, Bernard was feeling very self satisfied. This flying lark appeared to come naturally and the rest would be a relative breeze he thought, along with the few others who had gone solo on his course so far. By lunchtime they would all have had a reality check that this 'flying lark' wasn't a breeze or a bit of fun, this was serious stuff and if you didn't treat it with respect it would turn round and bite you in the backside. Leading Aircraftman Walford found out the hard way as he crashed near the village of Quy but luckily escaped with comparatively light injuries and was admitted to the R.A.F. hospital at Ely. Walfords mishap served as a timely reminder to all the pupils who, in the exuberance of youth, had been in danger of becoming over confident.

With the basics of solo flying having been mastered, the rest of Bernard's flying time at Cambridge was devoted to more advanced skills which included such topics as Sideslipping (descending through the air broadside), Instrument flying, Low flying, Forced landings, Action in the event of fire, Aerobatics, Night Flying, Pilot navigation and Formation flying, a work load which was intense both physically and mentally. When the weather allowed flying time was maximized and he took to the air on the 12th April twice, once on the 13th and 14th, three times on the 16th and twice more on the 17th. The weather provided an enforced break from flying over the weekend but on Tuesday 22nd April Bernard took to the air twice to re-cap on his basics; that was the start of three weeks of intensive flying the likes of which he had never experienced before but would certainly see again and more.

The 23rd April gave a hint of what was to come. Five times Bernard took to the air covering Stalls, Take-offs, Turns, Approach and landing and Sideslipping during his twenty minute first flight. The second lasted 35 minutes and encompassed the same areas as the first with a third flight also of 35 minutes to polish his performance. The afternoon consisted of flights four and five, which as well as those areas covered in the morning, took in Take-offs and landings out of wind and lasted for fifteen and 45 minutes respectively. NB: Take off and landing is usually carried out into the prevailing wind if possible as this enables the aircraft to have a slower ground speed on take off and touch down as the wind blowing over the wings provides additional airspeed and lift.

Thursday 24th consisted of just two flights, mainly due to the visit of the much loved Duke of Kent who came to inspect the base and serve as a morale booster for the airmen. He was to become a symbol of the dangers of flying himself as his life of privilege and excess would be ended in an air crash on 25th August 1942 at the age of 41. The Duke was traveling to Iceland on official R.A.F. business when the Short's Sunderland flying boat he was traveling in crashed killing all on board near Dunbeath in Scotland.

Bernard's course assessment form for his time at
No. 22 Elementary Flying Training School

The base was again graced with visiting dignitaries on the Saturday when the Secretary of State for Air, Sir Archibald Sinclair, accompanied by Sir Louis Greig and Sir Hugh Seeley, flew in to discuss the possibility of accelerating the flying training programme. One look at a trainee pilots log book would have told them that they were already pushing their luck.

With four more flights on Monday 28th covering Turns, Spins, Sideslipping, Low-flying, Take-off and landing out of wind, Forced landings, Fire drill and Aerobatics and Stalls, the pressure was beginning to mount up. With over three hours spent in the air, Bernard's brain was on the verge of overdosing on all aspects of aviation but there was to be no let up in the pace. The following day saw four more flights and another three hours in the air and then on the last day of April he took to the air no fewer than six times and flew for over four hours. As April turned to May he had flown for 23 hours and fifty minutes with eleven hours of that solo. The 59 men of Bernard's course (No.22) finished on 30th April although they would not leave Cambridge until 17th May due to a lack of places for them to continue their training at more advanced units. In the meantime they would continue to practice all they had learnt and revel in the fact that they had set a school record with the highest average for their ground instruction at 86.05%. They had achieved the required flying standards with an average of 24 ½ hours dual flying and 29 ½ hours solo. Bernard had done it in 19 hours 25 minutes dual and just eleven hours solo.

While the men of No. 22 Course awaited their next posting, they took to the skies whenever possible and continued to improve the skills they had learnt over the previous six weeks. On the 4th May 1941 Bernard was set the task of his first solo cross country flight. His brief was to leave Cambridge and to navigate approximately forty miles west to the grass strip of Sywell aerodrome which is about eight miles north-east of Northampton and is still a private, grass strip aerodrome to this day. Taking off from Cambridge in N6595 he successfully found Sywell and touched down at 1040 hours with his landing being described as 'good' on the form 1415 (Cross Country Flight Assessment) which only had the highly descriptive terms of good, medium and bad available to the assessing ground instructor. The return journey was the third flight of five he took that day, his confidence growing with every minute in the cockpit and a growing sense that things were becoming second nature.

On the moonlit night of 10th May 1941, London endured its most intense air-raid of the war so far. The raid lasted for several hours with countless numbers of incendiaries being dropped along with a huge tonnage of high explosive bombs. The city suffered many casualties, including two borough mayors, along with considerable building damage. Among the notable buildings hit were the House of Commons, (causing parliament to relocate to Church House in Westminster which had been prepared for such eventualities) Westminster Abbey, The British Museum, five hospitals, several churches and many public and commercial buildings along with numerous private dwellings. However, the Luftwaffe didn't have it all their own way that night. The R.A.F. had started to fit radar into its night-fighters and as a result, Luftwaffe losses began to climb.

The fitting of radar to British aircraft had no effect on one German pilot who flew un-molested through British airspace on the night of 11th May. In one of the strangest, and to this day, mysterious episodes of the war, Hitler's deputy, Rudolf Hess, landed by parachute in the village of Eaglesham in Lanarkshire after flying solo from Germany in a Messerschmitt Bf110. There are many un-answered questions and conspiracy theories concerning his arrival which pervade to this day but the official line is that he believed he could negotiate peace with the Allies which would then free up German forces for the coming invasion of the Soviet

Union. Unfortunately for Hess, instead of being treated as a peace envoy he was taken prisoner for the rest of the war after which he was tried at the war crimes trials at Nuremberg and sentenced to life imprisonment. He served his time in Spandau prison in Berlin alongside Albert Speer and Baldur Von Schirach until they were released in 1966. From then on he was in effective solitary confinement until he died in August 1987 aged 93, allegedly from suicide but many believe he was murdered. Hitler, upon hearing of Hess' flight, immediately claimed that he had gone insane and had Hess' entire staff arrested. Whatever the truth is, Hess' mission, trial, imprisonment and death are a story in their own right.

Finally the time came for Bernard to leave Cambridge on Saturday 21st May 1941 for two weeks well deserved leave. On the train heading back to Ellen in Battersea he must have looked over his form 414(A) and wondered just how he had managed to be only rated as average. He would soon realize when he arrived at his next unit that everyone who passed the course was 'average.' By the time the war ended these men would prove to be anything but, these men were exceptional.

CHAPTER THREE

Tricky little blighters

No.2 Service Flying Training School. R.A.F. Brize Norton, Oxfordshire.
22ⁿᵈ May 1941 to 9ᵗʰ August 1941

The Airfield.

R.A.F. Brize Norton was the home of No.2 Service Flying Training School when Bernard arrived on 1ˢᵗ June 1941. The airfield was, and still is, located to the north of the A4095 midway between the towns of Carterton and Witney, approximately twelve miles west of Oxford. Work began on the airfield in 1935 and it finally opened in August 1937 when No.2 Flying Training School arrived with their complement of Airspeed Oxfords and North American Harvards. Brize Norton remained a training base until July 1942 when it changed role to the Heavy Glider Conversion Unit and remained so until December 1945. Since then it has had a variety of roles and is today the largest operational airbase in the R.A.F. Brize Norton is presently (2014) home to several squadrons, 99 Squadron flying their fleet of eight Boeing C-17 Globemaster transport aircraft, 10 and 101 Squadrons flying the Airbus Voyager K2/K3 tanker, 216 Squadron flying a fleet of nine Tristars and XXIV, 30, and 47 Squadrons flying twenty four G-130J Hercules transports. The base currently employs some 5,800 uniformed and 300 civilian staff as well as 1,200 contractors and provides support for all three arms of the military around the world. As Brize Norton is still an active R.A.F. base there are no site plans available for security reasons.

The Aircraft.

Having learnt the basics of flying at Cambridge the role of No.2 Service Flying Training School was to teach Bernard and his fellow trainees to become proper pilots. Completion of the course at Brize Norton would result in the awarding of their wings and an automatic promotion to the rank of Sergeant. The aircraft chosen to fulfil that role was the Airspeed Oxford. The R.A.F. was already flying twin engine bombers such as the Vickers Wellington and even more advanced four engine 'heavy' bombers were being designed and built. As a result of those advances, a trainer with a degree of technical difficulty was deemed necessary and the Oxford fulfilled the criteria having been deliberately designed as 'a tricky little bugger' to fly.

Airspeed Oxford MKII at R.A.F. Hendon

The Oxford's prototype flew at Portsmouth on 19th June 1937 before full production began on the two variants. The two types were to be the Mk1 which was a general purpose training aircraft and could have a dorsal turret fitted for the training of air gunners and the MkII without a turret but with dual controls for advanced pilot, navigator and radio operator training. The initial order was for 136 aircraft but that was soon increased with a further order for 100 of both marques. Airspeed, unable to fulfil the order alone, sub-contracted the order to deHavilland at Hatfield and further orders were sub-contracted to a third company, Percivals of Luton. The aircraft were made from a wooden frame with a stressed steel skin and were assembled from four main components which could be manufactured at separate locations and then brought together for assembly, which made the aircraft very quick to build. The average production time at Airspeeds Christchurch factory was just three weeks.

The Oxfords main role was in the advanced training of pilots but was also extensively used in Beam Approach Schools, (Beam Approach was an early form of navigation aid which allowed a pilot to lock on to a radio signal and be navigated into an airbase) as well as being used as 'hacks' in station flights for general transport duties. The Oxford proved to be extremely successful with over 8,500 individual aircraft being produced by just five factories. Oxfords saw service until October of 1956 with the R.A.F. and until September 1957 with the Fleet Air Arm, a total service life of twenty years which was almost unheard of at the time as aviation was advancing then at the rate with which computers seem to do so today.

The wingspan of the Oxford was 53 feet 4 inches (16.26m) and it was 34 feet 6 inches (10.52m) long and weighed in empty at 5,380 lbs (2,445 kg). The power was supplied by two, Armstrong Siddeley Cheetah X, seven-cylinder, radial engines that produced 375 hp each on take off and 355 hp in flight. This resulted in a maximum speed of 188 mph at 8,300ft (303 kph at 2,530m) and a stall speed as low as 67 mph (108 kph). For its day the Oxford had an impressive service ceiling (maximum flying height) of 19,500 feet (5,945m) and a range of 925 miles (1,490km).

Having been designed specifically to be tricky to fly, any pilot who mastered the Oxford should be able to handle any other multi-engine type confidently, which of course was the idea. It was generally accepted that at least 150 hours on Oxfords were required before a pilot was deemed proficient, as the aircraft required that extra bit of skill. The aircraft was instrumental in producing pilots of great skill and competency and more importantly, it enabled those who trained in it to have confidence in their own ability.

Bernard arrived at Brize Norton on 1st June 1941 and was immediately acquainted with the Oxford in a familiarization flight that afternoon as Flying Officer Arundel took him up in L9646 for a thirty-minute flight around the airfield. The following day the same pair took Bernard's first two training flights in V3585 totalling one and a half hours airtime and covering flight preparation, air experience, effect of controls, straight and level flight and climbing and descending. With a few flights in the Oxford under his belt Bernard could not help but feel a little disappointed. Not because of any faults with the aircraft, in fact he felt quite affectionate towards the little machine. The disappointment came from the fact that he was no longer exposed to the elements, the whole flying experience seemed somehow to have been sanitised by the enclosed cockpit and in that, somehow the romance and freedom of open cockpit flying had been lost.

The Link trainer would be omnipresent throughout any R.A.F pilot's career and Bernard found himself in Brize Norton's for the first time on the 4th June and by the end of the month he had completed fourteen general exercises in the simulator.

The early onslaught of airborne training did not last and for the next nine days, due to a combination of bad weather and intensive ground instruction, Bernard's feet stayed firmly on the ground. The 12th June saw the airborne action resume with four flights, two of twenty minutes and two of one hour each, covering the basics of straight and level flight, climbing and descending. It was becoming clear to him that these Oxfords really were tricky little beasts and even the simple things required a lot of practice. This fact was driven home to all the under training pilots on the base that afternoon when news came through from Nottingham that one of their Oxfords, T1334, had collided with a Wellington bomber, crashed and burst into flames killing u/t pilots Newton and Parkinson. War was proving to be dangerous even when people were not shooting at you.

14th June saw more training of the basics but this time with the added drama of action in the event of fire and abandoning the aircraft thrown in. An engine fire was to be dealt with in the following order of actions, firstly turn off the petrol to the affected engine and then open the throttle fully to quickly use up the remaining fuel in order to prevent an explosion. Once the engine had finished firing and hence used up all the fuel, it should be switched off. If the fire had failed to go out then sideslipping sharply was to be employed in order to try and blow out the flames; if that failed to work then the fire extinguishers should be operated. If after all that the fire continued to burn then a steep dive could be employed assuming enough height was available; if that failed it was time to abandon the aircraft.

More flights covering the same subjects followed over the next few days culminating in Bernard's first flight on one engine in this twin engine aircraft. With one engine out the Oxford became a real handful. Even by fully opening up the throttle on the remaining engine it was difficult to maintain height and usually the fuel mixture would have to be changed to the richer take off setting. The aircraft would also try to bank and so constant aileron input (wing surface controls) would be needed to keep it level while also applying constant rudder input with the foot pedals to prevent the power of the one engine creating a turn. An airspeed above 85 m.p.h. was also needed otherwise the aircraft would steadily lose height and so the pilot was fully occupied just keeping the stricken aircraft in the air and on course even before he thought of carrying out a landing. Having successfully completed his first one engine flight, F/O Arundel decided that it was time for Bernard to go solo on the Oxford for the first time and so, after just eight hours and ten minutes experience on the type, in fine weather and good visibility, he took a fifteen minute solo circuit of Brize Norton on 17th June.

Once a pilot had proved himself competent in the basics he almost became his own teacher. Bernard would take to the air alone and practise the skills he had learnt while his instructor busied himself with another pupil so allowing the school to maximise the number of pilots they could train. After a couple of flights practising what he had been taught, the instructor would go up with him again and move his training on to the next level. Throughout the rest of June Bernard used this method to cover subjects such as low flying, one engine flight, map reading and navigation, and instrument flying. By the end of the month, he had racked up 26 hours and twenty minutes on Oxfords and was beginning to get the first hint of confidence. The latter part of June had been blessed with hot, dry weather with superb visibility and as a result, the u/t pilots had been able to advance their skills with no interference from nature; with hopes of more of the same, June slipped away and became July.

On the night of 27th/28th June, Bomber Command sent a force of 73 Wellingtons and 35 Whitleys to attack Bremen. The mission was dogged by difficulties from the outset as the aircraft ran into storms and icing conditions and then for the first time 'intense night fighter attacks'. As a result the force failed to find its target and bombed Hamburg some fifty miles away instead, killing seven and injuring a further thirty-nine. The night fighters took a huge toll shooting down eleven of the Whitleys, a staggering 31%, and three Wellingtons. The raid exposed just how outdated the Whitley was becoming and Bomber Command realized that its days as a frontline aircraft were numbered.

The first days of July brought foggy and hazy mornings to Brize Norton that gradually cleared as the Sun grew stronger, they also brought a new instructor for Bernard. Sergeant Birley took him up on the afternoon of 2nd July in N6262 to recap on his straight and level flight and descent and climbs. The early part of the month saw a change of emphasis in his training with a move away from the constant repetition of basic flying and a move towards learning how to navigate. Considerable time had already been given over to the theories of navigation during lessons on the ground and now the u/t pilots had to put it into practice in the air. In addition the Link trainer lessons changed too, beginning to encompass various navigation and V.H.F. radio exercises as well. In total, throughout July, Bernard underwent eleven Link exercises with four of them coming on the 29th July. In total, during his time at Brize Norton, he spent more than eleven hours in the simulator and with it successfully passed the General Instrument Flying Course.

All the u/t pilots would have completed a basic navigation flight at their

Elementary Flying Training School, but at Brize Norton it would become more complex. With four navigation flights under his belt, including one navigation test, Bernard was ready for the flight on 7th July that would see his airborne training intensify to previously unknown levels. The morning of the 7th dawned with fine weather, good visibility and light winds. Mother nature had provided the right environment and the training staff were to provide the workload. In the morning, after a good breakfast, Flight Lieutenant Elliott took him up for a navigation flight that lasted for two hours and ten minutes, eventually landing at the relief landing ground at Akeman Street, during which time Bernard solely filled the role of navigator. With a change of aircraft, he was airborne again, this time with Flight Lieutenant McDougall taking the controls and Bernard acting as co-pilot and navigator as they made their way back to Brize Norton. Once there, Flight Lieutenant McDougall got out and left him alone to fill the dual roles of pilot and navigator and make his way back to Akeman Street. With the to-ing and fro-ing of the morning over, the afternoon saw a single flight of fifty minutes with Flight Lieutenant McDougall instructing in the dangerous art of low flying (below 400 feet). As if the day's exploits had not been enough, there was to be a new element thrown at Bernard that day. With good weather available to them, airtime was being maximised and that night he was going to get his first opportunity at night flying. This element would be of extreme importance as the operational work of Bomber command was mainly carried out during the hours of darkness and as a result this was a skill that would need to be mastered.

Flight Lieutenant McDougall took Bernard up twice that night, the first time to complete six circuits of the airfield in a flight lasting an hour, and a shorter second flight of two more circuits lasting half an hour. By the time he slumped, exhausted, in his bed that night, Bernard had completed six flights totalling five hours. At that rate those 150 hours for competency would soon mount up.

As Bernard slept, exhausted from his days training, the operational crews of Bomber Command launched four attacks on the towns of Cologne, Osnabruck, Munster and Monchengladbach with much improved success. On the return from the raid on Munster, a Wellington from 75 Squadron was attacked by a night fighter and a fire broke out on the starboard wing. With the flames threatening to engulf the engine, Sergeant J.A. Ward, a New Zealand second pilot, climbed out of the aircraft and onto the wing making holes in the canvas covering in order to gain a hand hold. Ward managed to beat out the flames before climbing back inside the aircraft enabling it to return safely to England. For his selfless and daring action that night, Sergeant Ward was awarded the Victoria Cross.

The R.A.F. had been launching bombing raids whenever possible over occupied Europe and between 12th March 1941 and 7th July 1941 had launched raids on 106 days and 87 nights. In total the R.A.F. had carried out 12,721 sorties dropping 11,850 tons of bombs. We now know that although bravely carried out in outdated, slow aircraft (mainly Blenheims, Hampdens and Wellingtons) the effect on the German war machine was negligible, mainly due to the inaccuracy of the bombing caused by the use of primitive navigation equipment. However, the effect upon German morale, and more importantly the British public's morale, was incalculable. Unfortunately the morale boost came at a high price for the aircrews with 321 aircraft being lost during that period.

The 9th July once again brought an early covering of cloud to Brize Norton but the summer sunshine and a steady breeze from the North soon turned the day into a good flying one with fair weather and excellent visibility. The level of vision was to be extremely beneficial to Bernard that day, as for the first time he would practice the very thing he was being trained for; dropping bombs. The unfortunately named Sergeant Sleep took him aloft for a mammoth two hours 45 minutes of instruction and followed it up with a further one hour and fifty minute flight with Bernard at the controls. That night saw no let up in the pace of training either as he took to the skies three more times to practice night circuits for another two hours and ten minutes of airtime. With six hours 45 minutes airborne that day, as well as ground instruction, the strain was beginning to take its toll. The level and intensity of the instruction was relentless and mirrored the urgency and seriousness of the war in general. He now found that his final thought each day, as his head settled into his pillow, was not of flying theory or the Airspeed Oxford but of some precious leave and a chance to be with Ellen. The thought though was always fleeting as sleep enveloped him quickly as his fatigued mind seized on its chance to recharge its batteries.

July provided the u/t pilots with a mixed bag of weather but the instructors made sure that the trainees took advantage of the situation and gained as much experience as possible in all conditions. While adverse weather may have provided vital opportunities for gaining experience, it undoubtedly contributed heavily to the tragic death of u/t pilot Leading Aircraftman Chambers. Flying in Oxford T1384 on 16th July 1941, Chambers lost control while practising low flying at night and in cloud to the south-east of the relief landing ground at Akeman Street, his aircraft hit the ground and he was killed instantly.

The shock of the death of Leading Aircraftman Chambers concentrated the minds of the remaining trainees as they pressed on with their relentless regime. Just as the u/t pilots were beginning to put the death of Chambers to the back of their minds, the war once again came rushing up to meet them. The war finally arrived for the trainees at 0330 hours on the morning of 28th July when Leading Aircraftman Smith, practising night flying two miles north-east of Akeman Street, was shot down and killed by a roaming enemy night-fighter. It seemed the Luftwaffe could not yet distinguish a trainee from a combat pilot and from then on, the trainees would have another danger to watch out for.

Year	Aircraft		Pilot, or	2nd Pilot, Pupil	Duty
Month · Date	Type	No.	1st Pilot	or Passenger	(Including Results and Remarks)
—	—	—	—	—	— Totals Brought Forward

Qualified for award of FLYING BADGE under K.R. & A.C.I.'s para. 811 Clause 5.

on 9th Day of Aug. 1941.

Chief Flying Instructor, for, Officer Commanding No. 2 Flying Training School, Royal Air Force.

PROFICIENCY AS PILOT ON TYPE. — *Average.*

To be assessed :— EXCEPTIONAL; ABOVE THE AVERAGE; AVERAGE; BELOW THE AVERAGE.

Any special faults in flying which must be watched :—

Officer Commanding No. 2 S.F.T.S. ROYAL AIR FORCE

Date 9/8/41.

The awarding of Bernard's 'wings' in true understated R.A.F. style on 9th August 1941

With no let up in the training programme, Bernard racked up another 23 hours flying time in the remainder of July and was becoming increasingly confident at the controls of the Oxford. August would see more of the same but would ultimately be the month when he would earn his wings. The early part of the month saw a concentration on instrument flying while still practising the basics and in addition the u/t pilots were instructed in the art of formation flying which would be vital during the huge bomber raids that would come later in the war. On 7th August 1941 Bernard flew for the last time under the title of u/t pilot and on 9th August qualified for the award of his Flying Badge with the usual proficiency rating of average, followed by his promotion to the rank of Sergeant on New Years Eve. Eleven months after joining the R.A.F. and with 146 hours and 35 minutes in the air, he had finally earned his 'wings' and could call himself a pilot; but at that moment the most important award was a spot of well earned leave.

CHAPTER FOUR

In the dark

No.2 Central Flying School, R.A.F Church Lawford, Warwickshire.
10th August 1941 to 15th October 1941

Bernard was awarded his flying badge on 9th August 1941 and with the gold braid, embroidered, cloth wings safely tucked away in the inside pocket of his tunic, he boarded a train and returned to Battersea and the waiting Ellen. His ten days of leave were a precious break from the relentless pressure of flying training and the mental load of theory work. As time passed, and he gained more experience, his confidence grew but every so often that confidence would be dented as another pilot was killed or injured in yet another flying accident. The men undergoing their flying training around the country, and the many more, who were being trained abroad in Canada and South Africa, knew that even before they undertook an operational mission they were putting themselves at considerable risk. Flying in the 1940's was not the safe experience it is today even without people trying to shoot you down. The ten days respite passed in a flash and soon enough Bernard was on his way to his new posting, once again leaving Ellen alone in an increasingly war torn London. His next posting saw him once again heading north, this time to Church Lawford in Warwickshire, the home of No.2 Central Flying School, where he would undergo an instructors training course. It appeared that the pupil was soon to become the master.

On the 16th August, Bernard began to pack his kit ready to head off to his new posting. His freshly acquired 'wings' had been expertly attached to the left breast of his uniform tunic by his skilled wife, and he felt that he had finally left the tag of u/t behind him. By the time he completed the instructor's course at Church Lawford he would be firmly established within the R.A.F. structure, he thought. It was not the posting he had hoped for, as he had joined to fly operational missions, but he was able to see the benefits he would reap and he knew that the extra experience he would gain before he had to pilot a crew over occupied territory could well prove to be the difference between life and death. It is likely that Bernard was selected to train as an instructor due to his relatively advanced age. His maturity would instil confidence in new u/t pilots and would probably give the impression that he had been a pilot for far longer than he actually had. Whatever the politics behind the decision, Bernard was off to instructor's school. Church Lawford was home to No.2 Central Flying School which was dedicated to the training of instructor pilots. No.2 C.F.S. was first formed in November 1940 at Cranwell when it was realised that the existing Central Flying School would not be able to produce the large numbers of instructors that would be required. The unit relocated to Church Lawford in June 1941 and it was there that Bernard reported for duty on the morning of 17th August 1941.

The Airfield.

The airfield of R.A.F. Church Lawford in Warwickshire was located approximately seven miles east of Coventry and four miles west of Rugby to the southern side of the modern A428 which links the two towns. Located in an area of open, sparsely populated countryside near the eponymous hamlet, the base was purpose built and opened in April 1941, boasting three concrete runways along with all the relevant support buildings. The site was relatively compact with only two dispersed barrack sites, which were themselves only a few hundred yards from the main airfield.

Today the site gives tantalising insights to its previous use with several of the original buildings surviving. The main hanger and maintenance site to the north of the road is now an industrial estate with the Bellman hangars surviving and being used as industrial units, and they still bear their 1940's camouflage paintwork. The runways have now disappeared, as the area has been excavated for gravel with the rest of the area being returned to farmland. Most people passing by would never guess what an important site this had been just 65 years ago but the clues are there for those with time to look.

The Aircraft.

Church Lawford operated two types of aircraft for its training, the Airspeed Oxford, which is described in the previous chapter, and the Avro Tutor Bi-plane. The Tutor was a British built, pre-war trainer of steel tube construction with fabric covering and had been introduced to replace the Avro 504, which had been in use since the Great War. From a distance the Tutor looked similar to the Tiger Moth

41

with its twin, open cockpit layout. Power was supplied by a single 215hp Armstrong Siddeley Lynx, seven cylinder, radial, air cooled engine which gave a top speed of just 116mph. The maximum service ceiling was 14,800 feet (4,940m) with a range of 250 miles (400km). The Tutor's wings spanned some 34 feet (10.36m) and the aircraft had an overall length of 26 feet six inches, standing nine feet seven inches tall. The lightweight construction gave an unladen weight of 1,686lbs and contributed to the relatively good climb rate of 800 feet per minute.

Pill box just south of the main entrance

Church Lawford Watch Office

The Avro Tutor was built in several different specifications, originally being simply titled the 621. 381 actual Tutors were built at A.V. Roe in Manchester with the main batch being produced in 1933; however, by the outbreak of war they were already out of date and although the Central Flying Schools kept some on charge, they were steadily replaced by more modern aircraft and very few saw out the war. Today, only one remains, K3241 is preserved in full flying condition at the Shuttleworth Collection housed at Old Warden in the UK.

The only surviving airworthy Avro Tutor owned by the Shuttleworth collection

Bernard passed through the gates of Church Lawford early on the morning of 17th August 1941 and spent his first two days settling in and attending ground instruction lectures alongside the 29 officers and thirteen other sergeants who made up Number 16 (War) Flying Instructors Course. The morning of 19th August began with the sight of dozens of Firemen dashing around the place, shouting orders and rebukes to one another in that semi-military, down to earth way they have about them. The cause of all the commotion was a Rugby Fire Brigade exercise that was simulating a fire on the airfield following an air-raid, which had also taken out the water mains. As a result water was being pumped from local static supplies and natural sources (there are a number of ponds within the airfield) with the pumps producing a deafening noise and Bernard looked forward to getting airborne to escape their drone. That afternoon his wishes were fulfilled as he took to the sky but he had not managed to escape any of the din created by the Fire Brigade. Their exercise had finished by lunchtime with the results being described in true wartime fashion as 'satisfactory'.

Pilot Officer Collett took Bernard up that afternoon for his first two familiarization flights in an Avro Tutor and after taking the controls of K3428 he felt satisfied with the aircraft after just about an hour in the air and delighted to be back in an open cockpit. The following day P/O Collett went through the same procedures but this time in the Airspeed Oxford. Although these flights were described as refresher flights, they were really assessments of Bernard's ability on the tricky little blighter. Having satisfied P/O Collett of his ability after just two flights totalling 65 minutes, that same afternoon P/O Sleep took him up for his first lesson in becoming an instructor.

Elsewhere on the airfield other pilots were not having the same straightforward sort of day that Bernard was enjoying. While Bernard was airborne with P/O Sleep, another pilot landed in Oxford N4579 and taxied to his dispersal spot. Unfortunately he hit a tree stump on the way and damaged the aircraft but fortunately not himself. Just over a year later on 28th August 1942, while attached to the Empire Central Flying School, the same aircraft spun into the ground while carrying out spinning tests over Wiltshire killing its crew.

The following day, 21st August 1941, No.2 Central Flying School suffered its own fatal accident. During the afternoon P/O Sharp and P/O Candler had been on a training flight and landed at the satellite airfield at Sibson, Leicestershire, approximately fourteen miles north-west of Church Lawford. That night they took off in the dark to carry out a night flight return to Church Lawford but Oxford T1050 failed to climb on take off and struck a water tank. The aircraft crashed and burst into flames killing P/O Sharp and badly injuring P/O Candler; T1050 was completely destroyed.

In an amazing coincidence, just eight days after the fatal accident involving T1050, T1051, the consecutive Oxford to the ill fated T1050, suffered exactly the same accident, striking an object on night time take off from Sibson and diving into the ground. Thankfully, neither of the crew were killed, although Sergeants Rawthorne and Lipkin were seriously injured.

It appeared that the Airspeed Oxfords were living up to their reputation as being tricky to handle, but between the twin disasters of T1050 and T1051, Bernard continued his training without a hitch. By the time T1051 dived into the ground on the evening of 28th August, he had racked up four hours and forty minutes in the Avro Tutors and seven hours and ten minutes in Oxfords, covering nearly all the manoeuvres required including the more risky tasks of spinning and low flying.

The 29th saw two flights, one in the Tutor and one in an Oxford, but also saw

Bernard's first visit to the Link trainer while at Church Lawford, where he spent an hour and a half carrying out three navigation exercises. The following day was the most intense day of flying that he was to experience while at No.2 C.F.S. The flying day began after breakfast with the wonderfully named Flight Lieutenant Banning-Lover taking him up for a flight lasting two hours fifteen minutes, covering ascent, descent and low-flying. On his return, Bernard switched from Oxford AB701 to P1070 where firstly Sergeant McCoy took him up for an hour and then Sergeant Holtom repeated the exercise for another hour. Both those flights covered the same subjects that Banning-Lover had started the day with and confirmed that Bernard was achieving the required standards. Although he had already spent three and a quarter hours in the air that day, there was plenty more to come and that night would see him tackle one of the most important manoeuvres a pilot had to master; no flaps, night time landings. With the majority of Bomber Commands operations taking place at night, the art of landing in the dark was an essential one to master and with the chances of returning from an operation with damage to your aircraft being high, it was important to be able to land without the use of the flaps. The flaps are moveable surfaces on the wings which allow the aircraft to fly at a lower speed without stalling, without them the landing had to be done at a much higher speed so making the manoeuvre much more difficult and dangerous. In addition the airfields were not well lit as they are today, as the enemy would be easily able to identify and attack them, and there was little by way of electronic aids to help the pilot; although a system was being steadily introduced, but more on that later.

Flying Officer England took Bernard up for his first experience of this manoeuvre with a flight lasting an hour and a half and involving no less than seven landings. Once F/O England was satisfied that he had grasped the principles, he stepped out of the aircraft and sent Bernard up again to do a solo circuit and a no flaps night landing which he executed to the satisfaction of his on-looking instructor. With nearly five hours in the air already, Bernard could be forgiven for thinking that his work for the day was over, but nothing could be further from the truth. Late in the evening, as darkness cloaked the Warwickshire countryside, accompanied by Sergeant McCoy, he climbed into Oxford P8995 and took off to practice more night flying landings in the now pitch dark. One and a half hours later, and with nine landings behind them, they parked P8995 up at dispersal and returned to the flight office. His airtime for the day stood at six hours and 25 minutes but the fun wasn't over yet. No sooner had Bernard entered the flight office to the East of runway 3 than F/O England nabbed him to act as his navigator for a night time navigation flight to the satellite at Sibson, the scene of the recent accidents; by the time they returned the Sun was already coming up. Finally, after a seventy minute, uneventful roundtrip, he was at last allowed to remove his flying boots having clocked up a total of seven hours and 35 minutes in the air. The training was intense but then it had to be as some operational bombing missions, especially later in the war, could last for anything up to ten hours. This was already shaping up to be a long war.

September began with a visit from the top brass to Church Lawford as Air Marshal Sir W.L. Welsh, KCB, DSC, DFC and Air Vice Marshall Keith Park, CBE, MC, DFC came to inspect the airfield. Thankfully they had left by the time P/O Curtis overshot the flare-path while carrying out a night landing and crashed his Oxford into the fence on the aerodrome boundary; mercifully only his pride was injured in the incident.

The training continued with Bernard spending his flying time almost equally split between the Oxford and the Tutor and between a variety of instructors. As time passed it was becoming increasingly apparent to him how dangerous this flying game was becoming. As pilots became more experienced they were increasingly asked to perform more dangerous tasks and manoeuvres and as a result accidents seemed to be more prevalent. 7th September saw yet another fatal crash, when Flt/Lt Reader was killed and P/O Mudd was injured in an incident which this time didn't involve one of the tricky little Oxfords, but one of the slow and steady Tutors. The following night saw the Oxfords regaining their trickiness title as two crashed on night landings. The first caused no deaths or injuries but the second resulted in facial injuries to Sergeant Kimber as the starboard undercarriage of his aircraft collapsed on landing.

Later that same night the R.A.F. sent its heaviest force yet on a raid to Berlin. By September 1941 the R.A.F. had begun to receive four engine bombers in the form of Shorts Stirlings and Handley Page Halifaxes into its frontline squadrons and that night, under bright moonlight, the force sent to Berlin included a token number of these new 'heavies'. As a reminder of the first German raid on London exactly a year before, Bomber Command sent a total of 197 aircraft made up of 103 Wellingtons, 43 Hampdens, 31 Whitleys, ten Stirlings, six Halifaxes and four Manchesters. 137 of the crews reported good bombing results with the Berlin authorities reporting that most bombs fell in the north and eastern districts of the city. Damage was reported as totalling four war industry factories, ten transport targets, thirteen public utilities, two public buildings, sixteen farms, 200 houses and a Zoo. 36 people were killed and a further 212 injured. The R.A.F. lost eight Wellingtons, two Hampdens, two Whitleys, two Stirlings and a Manchester, an expensive total of fifteen aircraft.

Having not flown for four days, two of which had been a very welcome 48 hour pass, Bernard embarked on another one of those intensive flying days on 9th September. The day's entertainment began with a low level navigation exercise with him playing the role of navigator and co-pilot, while his instructor, P/O Collett, filled the left hand pilots' seat. After an hour and 25 minutes in the air they landed and switched from Oxford P8995 to R6034 and headed off to Sibson. The flight to Sibson was for a specific purpose; it appears that although Bernard's overall flying was excellent, as had been borne out by his progression so far, it seemed that there was one aspect he was struggling with. That day was designed to be 'kill or cure', unfortunately if he got it wrong it was much more likely to be kill. Bernard's nemesis it appeared was the no flaps, night flying landing.

As a satellite airfield, Sibson was slightly quieter than Church Lawford and therefore would allow Bernard more opportunities to land and take off again. P/O Collett took the controls for their first circuit and showed him how it was done before putting down and sending him off to Join Sergeant Nicholls in W5649 for some intensive practice. For the next two hours and five minutes in the gathering darkness they flew non-stop circuits and landings; by the end of the flight he had completed fourteen but had still not mastered the art. This was becoming a problem for the instructors as they would not want to lose a pilot who showed so much promise in all the other aspects of the job. As a result, after a break for a cup of tea, Bernard took to the skies once again, this time with P/O Tasker. An hour and a half passed and he made ten more landings before Tasker decided to call it a day. Tasker led Bernard to the flight office where P/O Collett and P/O Sleep, his main instructors, were waiting for him. The sense of relief was palpable, not only to Bernard but to all the instructors as Tasker announced that the last five landings had been acceptable and that he at last seemed to have mastered it. For now at least the dreaded no flaps, night flying landing seemed to have been mastered.

The following week was spent covering a variety of topics in the air alongside the usual ground theory and several more trips to the Link trainer then, on the 17th September, the old nemesis of no flaps, night flying landings came back to haunt Bernard. On spec, Flt/Lt Banning-Lover decided that he would check out his abilities with the infamous landings as his instructors had briefed him that he had now mastered it. A knot formed in Bernard's stomach as he took to the air and performed the required landing. It is not known what Banning-Lover said to him after they landed but the fact that he was immediately sent up with an instructor for another five attempts at it speaks volumes. It looked like his nemesis was back.

The following night the Oxfords were back in the wars again. P/O Ball took off in darkness and immediately found himself in trouble as one of his cylinders cracked. Showing considerable skill he controlled the aircraft and gained enough height to complete a circuit of the airfield and land safely. The night after, Sergeant White wasn't quite so fortunate. The undercarriage of his Oxford collapsed during a heavy landing and slid to a stop across the airfield, thankfully White was uninjured. It seemed that Bernard wasn't the only one having trouble with his landings.

Another week passed without any more no flaps, night flying landings until, on 25th September, P/O Collett decided it was time to carry out a spot check on Bernard. From start to finish a circuit of the field, including the take off and landing, took around fifteen minutes, but it had probably seemed like an eternity to Bernard as he began his descent. As the aircraft came to a stop at the dispersal he got the nod of approval from Collett and a wave of relief swept over him, finally he felt he was getting this particular monkey off his back; Flt/Lt Banning-Lover however had different ideas. Two days later Bernard had spent an hour and twenty minutes with P/O Collett practising medium turns, taking off and landing out of wind and precautionary landings in a Tutor, when Banning-Lover summoned him for an air test on his favourite manoeuvre. Once the skies had darkened enough, Bernard and Banning-Lover took off in Oxford AB703 and once again Banning-Lover was not impressed with what he saw and ordered Sergeant McCoy to take him up and drill it into him. After an hour and a half and six successful landings, McCoy handed him over to Sergeant Bartrum to confirm his own assessment. Bartrum called it a day after four landings and concurred with McCoy that he could see nothing wrong this time. Having witnessed the last ten landings for himself and being informed by two of his instructors that their charge was fine as far as they could see, Banning-Lover had to finally concede that Bernard had reached the required standard; it appeared that his R.A.F career was back on track.

As the Flying Instructors course neared its end, each flight became more intensive in its content. Just one flight, on 29th September, included the following subjects; effect of controls, taxiing, straight and level flight, climbing, descending, approach and landing, spinning, sideslipping and low flying. Virtually every flight now covered at least five separate subjects as the final assessments approached. There was just two weeks of course 16 left, and every move from there on in was scrutinised and judged.

With the final accident of the month resulting in another Tutor being written off, after crashing in to a parked Oxford on the 28th, the hectic month of September came to a close. The station war diary shows the strength at Church Lawford as follows, 116 officers, 44 Sergeant Pilot Pupils (of which Bernard was one), 45 Senior N.C.O.'s, 660 Airmen, five W.A.A.F. Officers, 82 Airwomen and 66 Corporals. A total of 1,018 personnel to train and be trained on just 56 Airspeed Oxfords and 29 Avro Tutors; it took a lot of people to win a war.

The first week of October was filled with theory and brushing up on all aspects of flight instruction in the air. Finally, the moment of truth arrived as the assessments began with the Flight Commanders test on 8th October. Bernard climbed into Oxford R6022 alongside Flt/Lt Banning-Lover who would play the role of Bernard's pupil while assessing his instructing skills, delighted no doubt that it was daylight and the night flying landing would play no part in the test. For 55 minutes he was put through his paces in the air, his performance was assured and professional as he executed each manoeuvre and demonstrated to his pretend 'pupil'. Finally Bernard instructed Banning-Lover to turn the Oxford onto a heading of 270 degrees, true west, and line up on runway no.1. With the main body of the airfield buildings lying off to port he began his instruction, talking Banning-Lover through each tiny stage of their descent from 1000 feet. The rate of descent was spot on all the way; with small rudder adjustments for wind effect they maintained the perfect line for the centre of the runway. Bernard's demeanour was calm and assured as he kept Banning-Lover steady at the perfect air speed of between 80 and 85 mph. As the ground came up to meet their wheels, he instructed Banning-Lover to flatten out and hold the Oxford off the ground just long enough to show he was fully in control, the main undercarriage wheels touched down a fraction of a second before the rear wheel and without any bounce they were down. With small adjustments to his rudder Bernard helped his 'pupil' keep the Oxford along the centre line of the runway and steadily brought R6022 to a halt, as they did so even Banning-Lover had a tiny hint of a smile rising from the corner of his mouth.

The relief at his success had lifted a weight from his shoulders and Bernard noted that he grinned to himself on several occasions that afternoon; even being collared to carry out a taxi cab flight to and from Sibson that evening couldn't dampen his spirits. The course was nearly over; he had three more tests to pass, of which he was more than confident, and then he would be enjoying a spot of leave with Ellen back in London, even in wartime life could still be good.

Bernard's next major flying test came on 10th October as Squadron Leader Carey-Foster took him up for a 55 minute Certified Flying Instructors test which he again completed competently. The following day saw him breeze through his navigation test as well as his cross-country flight, and with that behind him all the flying tests were complete. The final four days saw theory tests interspersed with practice flights, where Bernard continued to play the role of instructor while his instructors pretended to be his pupils. As 15th October came to an end, along with course 16, he had amassed 254 hours and fifteen minutes total airtime and awaited his results which would come in the morning.

Bernard's 414a detailing his Flying Instructors Course

Wing Commander Wallace handed over Bernard's 414a form with a brief smile and the fine words of 'Congratulations Steel.' On initial inspection Bernard's heart sank as he saw the assessment of 'below the average'. As he settled into the train journey back to London from Rugby, he studied the 414a in more detail. As he did so his initial despondency lifted as he realised that he was still qualified to instruct on both elementary and multi-engine aircraft, even if it was under supervision. He knew that the 'supervision' would last for a minimal period as the pressures of the war would take their toll on valuable instructor's time. With an air of self assurance, he tucked the form inside his logbook and dozed off as the train rattled its way south towards home and the waiting Ellen.

CHAPTER FIVE

The Next Generation

No.3 Service Flying Training School. R.A.F. South Cerney, Gloucestershire &
No.1 Beam Approach School. R.A.F. Watchfield, Oxfordshire. 16th October 1941
to 17th October 1942.

Bernard's leave, which he had hoped for on completing his instructors' course at Church Lawford, only turned out to be a very disappointing 48 hour pass. Before leaving he had been handed his next posting which was to be No.3 Service Flying Training School based at South Cerney, Gloucestershire, approximately nineteen miles south-east of Gloucester itself, where he would take up the post of an instructor. Having left Church Lawford on 16th October, he found himself arriving at the gates of South Cerney on the morning of the 19th; by the 20th he was back in the air but this time he was doing the teaching, we'll never know if Sergeant Hawkins ever realised he was Bernard's first 'customer'.

Unaware of the horrors unfolding in Stalingrad as the Russian and German forces fought each other to destruction, Bernard felt a little low as he arrived at South Cerney having only had a couple of days break since finishing his instructors' course. At the Service Flying Training School he would be taking u/t pilots who had just completed their elementary flying training and developing their skills to the point where they would become pilots and receive their 'wings'; just seven months since he first took to the sky Bernard had become an instructor. War, it seemed, was fought at a frantic pace.

The Airfield – R.A.F. South Cerney, Gloucestershire.

South Cerney is located in the Gloucestershire countryside just three miles south-east of Cirencester, heading north-west on the modern A419 the airfield is located to the west of the road just beyond the town of Cricklade. South Cerney opened in August 1937 as a Flying Training School and by June 1940 it had become a training centre exclusively for multi-engine aircraft and in September 1940 had 108 Airspeed Oxford's on its establishment. The base maintained the same role for the duration of the war, changing its title to No.3 (Pilots) Advanced Flying Unit on 1st March 1942. The airfield is still partially used by the military as a Joint Air Mounting Centre where three large hangars are used for processing up to 1,500 troops before they are despatched abroad for exercises or as more recently for combat operations. The unit is now known as the Duke of Gloucester Barracks and military units report there for processing, baggage checks and feeding before being moved to either R.A.F. Brize Norton or R.A.F. Lyneham for onward flights to combat zones. Many of our troops who have served in and continue to serve in Iraq and Afghanistan have passed through here. As well as its continued military use the base maintains an airstrip which is still used occasionally and a skydiving school operates from within its boundaries.

The Aircraft.

The role of the Service Flying Training School, as it was named when Bernard joined it (later becoming a (Pilots) Advanced Flying Unit), was to teach the u/t pilots fresh from elementary training to the standard where they would become fully qualified pilots. No.3 S.F.T.S. was attached to Bomber Command which was planning for four engine heavy bombers to replace the twin engine aircraft which were currently the mainstay of the bomber force. The first four engine bomber was the Handley Page Halifax which first arrived at squadrons in late November 1940. It was soon accompanied by the Shorts Stirling which first saw operational combat in February 1941. The Lancaster began to arrive in small numbers by September of 1941 and these arrivals began to spell the end of the twin engine bombers such as the Wellington, Hampden and Blenheim whose crews had fought bravely in those underpowered and outdated aircraft. As a result of the sophistication of the new 'heavies' most bomber crew training was by that point being carried out on the tricky little Airspeed Oxford with which No.3 S.F.T.S. was exclusively equipped.

Just seven months before arriving at South Cerney, Bernard could not even drive a car let alone pilot an aircraft; in fact he could barely ride a bicycle. Now he was taking to the air as an instructor, passing on the knowledge and skills he had gained over that intensive period. A certain Sergeant Hawkins was his first pupil and they spent 55 minutes aloft practising straight and level flight, ascents, descents and even a few steep turns. Later the same day it was Leading Aircraftsman Kuzminski's turn, but this time they substituted the steep turns for some low-flying.

If Bernard had thought the flying intensity would ease up now he was an instructor, he was to be sorely disappointed. The fact of the matter was that the need for pilots was urgent enough that the training schedule had already been cut by two weeks and the pressure on the few instructors the R.A.F. had was immense. As an example, on 22nd October, just three days after arriving at his new posting, he took six training flights with six different pupils; on 23rd he took five flights with four different pupils and on the 25th he took another seven flights with six pupils.

The 25th October turned out to be a day of calamity for No.3 S.F.T.S. with no less than five flying accidents. The day started badly when the port undercarriage of an Oxford, piloted by Leading Aircraftman Read, collapsed on touchdown and resulted in serious damage to the aircraft but thankfully none to Leading Aircraftman Read. Things got more serious from that point on as Oxford L4636 was destroyed by fire after spinning into the ground near Cricklade in Wiltshire, fatally injuring the pilot, Corporal Hodkinson. As darkness fell, Acting Pilot Officer Ejbich lost his way and crashed while trying to land, injuring himself and seriously damaging Oxford N6267 in the process. Then, just when everyone thought the day couldn't get any worse, it did. Two Oxfords coming into land collided with one another killing the pilots of both aircraft, Leading Aircraftman Baker and Leading Aircraftman Griffiths, and damaging both aircraft beyond repair. Bernard certainly hoped that the unit had managed to get all its accidents out of the way in one hit but unfortunately time would prove the opposite to be true.

The 26th saw another five flights for Bernard with four different pupils, all of which involved low flying. It appeared that either he was particularly good at the daredevil stuff and was therefore asked to pass on his skills or more likely he was given the rather hazardous job as he was the new boy on the training staff. Whatever the reason, the 48 hour pass that Bernard received for 27th and 28th allowed him some welcome relief from the stresses of low level flying and allowed him to spend some time in the surrounding towns of Swindon and Gloucester, where no doubt he found a decent pint of beer or two.

While Bernard was away enjoying the delights of the English countryside, No.3 S.F.T.S. was suffering further mishaps. Flight Lieutenant McAllen struck a hedge on approach resulting in a heavy landing which seriously damaged his aircraft but not himself on the 27th October, the same day as Leading Aircraftman Skrzypek, a pupil pilot, and Leading Aircraftman Janowicz, his safety pilot, were killed after they hit a tree and crashed while practising low flying near Oldbury-on-Severn, Gloucestershire, in Oxford V3644.

With his batteries partially re-charged, Bernard returned to the air on 29th October with more low flying training for the Polish pilots under his charge and finished the day with a fifty minute flight instructing Sergeant Topham in the difficult art of no-flap landings. Also that day Bernard underwent a Beam Approach exercise in the Link trainer as he had to maintain his own skills as well as teach his pupils. In total he would make eighteen separate visits to the Link during his year at South Cerney, most of them covering Beam Approach and instrument navigation exercises.

November arrived almost without Bernard noticing as he was airborne at least three or four times a day by then. However, the life of an instructor wasn't so bad, he thought, as he settled into his new role. Just as that thought entered his head he was told he was to attend a course in Beam Approach at Watchfield in Oxfordshire; it appeared that feeling settled was not to be encouraged by the R.A.F.

The Airfield – R.A.F. Watchfield, Oxfordshire.

Beam Approach was a new navigation aid that was being used by the R.A.F. to allow aircraft to find their airfield more easily in the dark or in bad weather. A fixed transmitter was located on the airfield and a receiver in the aircraft told the pilot where he was in relation to the beacon through a series of audible dots and dashes. It may have been crude, but it was effective and was the forefather of the modern beacons that guide jetliners into every airport in the world today.

R.A.F. Watchfield was located in Oxfordshire, approximately seven miles north-east of Swindon and to the west of the modern A420 road. It was built specifically for the war effort and the site only remained in service for the duration of the war, closing in 1946, but in that short space of time it played not only a pivotal role in the war but its legacy lasts to this day in civil aviation. It is estimated that nearly 90% of all bomber command pilots passed through there at one point in their career. Built on open farm fields on the outskirts of Shrivenham, the airfield never had a proper runway and only ever used a grass strip. Despite that, the airfield was often the only one flying in bad weather due to the nature of its activities. Watchfield was the home of No.1 Beam Approach School which was using the innovative method of navigation that allowed a pilot to land even in the thickest fog by homing in on a radio signal emitted from a stationary beacon on the airfield. Although the system was basic by today's standards this apparatus was a great leap forward for the time and undoubtedly saved the lives of many bomber crews who had become lost on their way home from a raid. This embryonic system has since developed into the sophisticated guidance system that allows modern airline pilots to navigate around the world without ever having to look at a map and even to land their aircraft without touching the controls.

Today, very little remains to indicate that this site was ever such an important part of the Allied war machine, with just a few lumps of concrete scattered about which would only be identifiable by those in the know. The site itself, like so many old airfields, is now an industrial estate and its illustrious past is all but forgotten, but when Bernard arrived as part of course No 56 on 4th November 1941 it was a hive of aerial activity.

The Aircraft.

No.1 Beam Approach School used two types of aircraft, the Airspeed Oxford, which has already been described and which was by now very familiar to Bernard, and the Avro Anson which he had yet to encounter.

Avro Anson of the Shuttleworth Collection

The Anson had started life as a six-seat passenger aircraft designed by Avro's genius designer Roy Chadwick in June 1933. The prototype took to the air on 7th January 1935 and the first military variant entered service with 48 General Reconnaissance Squadron in March 1936. The Anson rapidly became outdated in the reconnaissance role and was switched to training duties as early as the end of 1936, a role in which it excelled. In the spring of 1939 an order was placed for 1,000 of the training variant and they became widespread through the training units of the R.A.F. Production finally ended in May 1952 by which time 8,138 had been produced in the UK along with a further 2,882 being built in Canada.

The Anson continued to fulfil its training role so well that it remained in service with the R.A.F. until 28th June 1968, an incredible service life in excess of 32 years.

The Anson was 42ft 3in long with a wingspan of 56ft 6in and stood 13ft 1in high. Power was supplied mainly by two Armstrong-Siddeley Cheetah engines, although several other types were used depending on the variant. There were many marques to the Anson family and performance varied accordingly. Top speed ranged from 171mph at 5,000ft for the T.20 to 202mph at 5,000ft for the Mk.V. The range was equally widespread varying between 580 miles to 790 miles and a service ceiling spread of between 14,000ft and 21,500ft. All in all the Anson was an adaptable and capable little aircraft that supplied a considerable range of abilities and performance depending on the marque.

Bernard set off from South Cerney in a transport lorry and travelled the sixteen miles to Watchfield on the afternoon of 3rd November 1941 to settle in for the start of a two week course beginning the following morning. The first day of his membership of course No.56 involved two flights in an Oxford with Sergeant MacDonald. The first was a familiarization flight of just over an hour followed by a further training flight of another hour. Bernard, alongside the other twelve men who made up the course, would spend a lot of time in the classroom as well as in the air to come to terms with this new technology and as well as the theory there would be plenty of time spent in the link trainer which was ideally suited for this type of training.

The airfield thronged with pilots and instructors of the various courses that were on the base at any one time, each at a different stage of their two week duration. Often there would be flights for 23 hours a day as the whole idea of the Beam Approach system was that flying could be achieved in any conditions. From day one of his course Bernard took to the air at least twice a day and visited the link trainer at least once a day for the next week. In total he spent over seven hours in the Link that week and completed thirteen exercises, most of which involved locating the beam and then landing.

At that point of the war Bomber Command was the only tool available to the British with which to strike back at the Germans and the night of 7th November 1941 saw them launch their largest raid of the war so far. Recent poor weather had frustrated the Commander in Chief, Sir Richard Peirse, so he decided to send his main force to Berlin that night despite the predicted bad weather of thick cloud, icing and hail over much of the required route to the target. Along with the Berlin raid there would be two further raids that night, one to Cologne and another to

Mannheim. A force of 169 aircraft was sent to Berlin consisting of 101 Wellingtons, 42 Whitleys, seventeen Stirlings and nine Halifaxes although only 73 aircraft reached the city and bombing was scattered resulting in just eleven German deaths with a further 44 injured. The losses for bomber command however were huge with ten Wellingtons, nine Whitleys and two Stirlings being lost; a massive 12.4% of the strike force. As a result Berlin would not be attacked again until the beginning of 1943.

Cologne saw 61 Hampdens, and fourteen Manchesters attack with little damage and only five fatalities and five further injuries on the ground. Mannheim was attacked by 53 Wellingtons and two Stirlings with 43 crews claiming to have bombed the target, however no bombs actually fell on the town that night and no one actually knows where they did land. Although the attack on Cologne saw all its aircraft return safely, the Berlin raid saw the loss of 21 aircraft while the Mannheim raid saw seven Wellingtons fail to return. The cost in men and machines to the R.A.F. was far outweighing the German losses they were inflicting and the air ministry was beginning to realise it needed to react and as a result changes in Bomber command were about to start arriving thick and fast.

On the 9th November Bernard took to the air in an Anson for the first time as Flight Lieutenant Morton took him up in R3586 for an hour and forty minutes of circuits and bumps. With the exception of two flights in Oxfords, the rest of his flying at Watchfield was completed in Ansons including his final flight on 15th November. The statistics for the course show the thirteen pupils all completing successfully with an average of 22 hours day flying, 45 minutes night flying and six hours fifty minutes in the link trainer. Bernard spent 21 hours fifty minutes day flying, no night flying and 7 hours 15 minutes in the link. Not surprisingly he once again achieved the assessment of average.

With the course successfully completed Bernard left Watchfield on the 16th November and was back in the air at No.3 Service Flying Training School on the 17th taking Leading Aircraftman Pankiewitz on a forty minute, low level flight. By then he was beginning to feel the effects of constant flying both as an instructor and as a pupil, which had been compounded by the mental strain of the coursework and the fortnight at Watchfield. With great relief he almost immediately received a week's leave and left South Cerney on the morning of 18th November and headed back to Battersea.

Seven days leave swept past, as it always did, and almost without realising it Bernard found himself sitting in the cockpit of Oxford V3642, alongside Leading

Aircraftman Gmiter, early on the morning of 26th November 1941. Gmiter, another Pole, was staring intently through the windscreen silent in his concentration as he strained to keep his place in the formation. Bernard was a little more wistful and was pondering where the last week had gone and just how many more it would be before he had another opportunity to go home again.

The leaden grey skies of November over Gloucestershire soon gave way to the leaden grey skies of December. Bernard had been back at South Cerney for almost a week and was by then fully immersed in his task of pilot training. The yearning for home he felt when he first returned to the base soon passed, as it always did, only to re-emerge in moments of boredom or discomfort. As he racked up ever more hours in the air, he became more and more at ease with his job and more proficient at it too. Flying had quickly become second nature to him, much as riding a bike does for a schoolboy. The constantly changing faces appearing in the pupils' seat kept things interesting, especially when it was coupled to one of the determined Poles who passed through in great numbers. After Bernard's third and final flight of 30th November, his flying hours totalled over 313 and the intensity was showing no signs that it was about to drop. December saw a further 41 flights, twelve of those on one day, the 7th, adding another 25 hours to his total. Meanwhile the base continued to suffer flying accidents, most of which saw the pilots walk away uninjured, but Leading Aircraftman E. McAllister and Sergeant E.W.J. Hunter were December's fatalities. On the evening of 23rd Bernard took the train back to London and spent a quiet Christmas at home with Ellen but he was back at South Cerney in time to be back in the air on 27th. The 48 hour pass he had managed to wangle for himself for New Year was put to good use with some revelry in the bar and local pubs; 1942 arrived with hopes and fears aplenty.

At 0755 hours local time on 7th December 1941, Hawaii saw possibly the most momentous and far reaching event of the entire war. At that point the Americans, separated from the war by the vast Atlantic Ocean, still maintained their stance of isolationism despite their increased assistance in the supply of materials of war. As dawn broke across the island that December morning, the American stance would be drastically and dramatically changed as the Japanese Imperial Navy launched an unprovoked attack on the American Naval base at Pearl Harbor in the Pacific and changed the course of the war and of history.

The attacking Japanese fleet consisted of six aircraft carriers, Soryu, Shokaku, Zuikaku, Hiryu, Akagi and Kaga, along with two battleships, two heavy cruisers, nine destroyers, three submarines (carrying mini-subs) as well as assorted supply ships and had taken up a position some 250 miles north of Hawaii. On board the carriers were nearly 400 aircraft with a mixture of high level bombers, dive bombers, torpedo bombers and fighters. At 0600 hours the first wave of 180 aircraft took off for the island to attack the American Pacific fleet which slumbered, unaware, at anchor in the natural port at Pearl Harbor. Two hours later the Japanese aircraft arrived over the island and took the Americans completely by surprise. By 0840 the second wave of attacking aircraft had arrived, made up of some 135 bombers and 35 fighter escorts, and continued to wreak havoc. By the time the last of the Japanese raiders had completed their work and peeled away to head back to their carriers, two American battleships, the Oklahoma and Arizona, had been sunk at their moorings along with six others severely damaged. Three cruisers, three destroyers, two auxiliary ships and a minelayer had also been sunk along with nearly 200 aircraft damaged or destroyed on the ground at the islands airfields. Official figures compiled after the war put the human losses at 2,330 Americans killed with another 1,350 injured. The Japanese lost just 29 aircraft and five midget submarines, a total of 64 dead. The following day America and Britain declared war on Japan and sealed what would become a mighty alliance. Three days later the Germans and Italians declared war on America and so finally brought all the players to the table. It was then just a question of who would hold their nerve and which way the cards would fall.

The World situation at the end of 1941 saw the German advances in Russia halted and the Russians starting to push them back while the Japanese were beginning to dominate in the east. The British were under threat in Malaya while the Americans were struggling to keep a foothold in the Philippines. In addition the Japanese were occupying every little island they could find that stuck its head above the vast Pacific surf. Back in Britain the Luftwaffe still paid regular visits, while Bomber Command responded in kind at every available opportunity. Ironically, while the British were struggling against the Japanese in the east, every passing day saw the British forces at home grow stronger, producing more and more war materials in order to one day take the war fully to the Axis powers. However, the Americans with all their industrial might were fully involved in the war and only time would tell which way the war would develop. In Britain, with the majority of the action being fought in far off exotic places, the British civilian casualty figures for December 1941 fell to 34 killed and 55 injured.

One officer who obviously didn't have a good New Year's Eve was Air Marshall

Sir William Welsh K.C.B., D.S.C., A.F.C. Commander-in-Chief, Headquarters, Flying Training Command, who arrived at South Cerney on New Year 's Day to inspect the station despite many of its personnel still nursing hangovers. The following day saw the first crash of the year as Pilot Officer R.P. East made a heavy landing, seriously damaging the aircraft and injuring both East and his passenger, Sergeant Regnault. 3rd January sent a shock through Bernard as he heard the news that Leading Aircraftman Gmiter, the trainee pilot who had concentrated so hard on his formation flying the day Bernard returned from his weeks leave, had been killed after losing control in a turn and diving into the ground near Shorncote, Gloucestershire. The day after that Sergeant Cowan and his pupil, Flight Sergeant Hewlett, were also fatally injured following a mid air collision; the start to the year did not bode well. The weather wasn't helping matters and was harsh throughout January with temperatures regularly below freezing, turning any rut on the airfield into a solid obstacle to catch out the unwary. No.3 S.F.T.S. saw eleven accidents that month, mainly during landings, in addition to the two fatal accidents of 3rd and 4th. However, Bernard's record continued to be exemplary with a further 47 flights totalling 33 hours and covering just about every manoeuvre in the book, along with some exotic trips to such far flung destinations as Dorchester and Grantham.

February began with Bernard back in London on a four day pass which history proves he obviously made full use of. As he sat on the train heading back to Gloucestershire on the 4th, he was blissfully ignorant of the fact, but he had just changed his life forever, no matter what the war would bring. Ellen didn't know it either yet but she would soon realise that she was pregnant.

February continued to provide the freezing temperatures that January had brought but the training schedule continued regardless. Bernard was back in the air on 5th and would fly relentlessly for the remainder of the month with only a 48 hour pass to provide some respite on the 9th and 10th. The training school continued to suffer the usual accidents but thankfully none of the fourteen in February proved fatal. Despite two short leave periods, Bernard still managed to accumulate a further 63 flights totalling 45 hours, taking his overall total to 397 hours in the air.

Elsewhere in the R.A.F. a small change in the structure of Bomber Command took place on 22nd February when, without fanfare, a new Commander was appointed by the name of Air Marshall Arthur T. Harris. Harris, who would come to be known as 'Bomber', was destined to end up as one of the most controversial figures of the war, but would also lead changes in Bomber Command that would transform it from a buzzing annoyance to the enemy into the most potent weapon of war ever seen in the pre-nuclear age. At the time Harris took over, the strength of Bomber Command was still relatively small. As at 1st March 1942 he had 221 Wellingtons, 112 Hampdens, 54 Whitleys, 29 Stirlings, 29 Halifaxes, twenty Manchesters and four Lancasters in the night force, backed up by a further 56 Blenheims and 22 Bostons from the day force; a total of just 547 aircraft, most of which were already outdated.

Following the realisation that Bomber Commands efforts in the early stages of the war were extremely inaccurate, the government had set up the Butt report to look into the matter. The report realised how difficult it was for crews to find specific targets in the dark let alone attack them, (bear in mind there were no guided bombs or electronic navigation aids then) Bomber Command under Harris took the decision that area bombing of cities and industrial centres was to become their new modus operandi rather than trying to pinpoint military targets. They could never have dreamt at that stage just how effective and proficient at it they would become.

Almost as a rejection of the criticisms of the Butt report, Bomber Command carried out one of its most accurate missions of the war so far on the night of 3rd/4th March 1942. The attack was on the Renault factory which was producing lorries for the Germans in the town of Boulogne-Billancourt to the west of the centre of Paris. 235 aircraft, consisting of 89 Wellingtons, 48 Hampdens, 29 Stirlings, 26 Manchesters 23 Whitleys and twenty Halifaxes, attacked in three waves with the first wave consisting of the most experienced crews who attacked at low level dropping flares as well as bombs to mark the target. 232 aircraft claimed to have attacked the target, dropping some 450 tons of bombs in just under two hours. This was the highest number of aircraft to attack a single target so far and the official report from Boulogne-Billancourt reported that 300 bombs hit the factory destroying some 40% of it in the process. French civilian casualties were high (367) due both to the proximity of the factory to apartment blocks and the French taking no notice of air raid sirens as bombers often flew over while heading into Germany. The accuracy of the raid led to the development of the highly skilled and effective Pathfinder force which would allow Bomber Command to wreak so much havoc later in the war.

With 'Bomber' Harris in firm control of Bomber Command, the first in a series of steps forward in the art of navigation took place on the night of 8th/9th March 1942. For the first time a raid was carried out, this time on the Krupps Steel works in Essen, using the 'Gee' system. Gee worked by sending out radio pulses which were picked up by an oscilloscope aboard the aircraft and operated by the navigator. The pulses were sent from known bases in England and therefore the navigator could work out his position relative to the transmitting stations. Over long distances the Gee system had an accuracy of about one mile and so could assist attacking aircraft to the right area from which point they would have to bomb by sight. 211 aircraft, consisting of 115 Wellingtons, 37 Hampdens, 27 Stirlings, 22 Manchesters and ten Halifaxes, set off for the notoriously difficult target in the heart of the Ruhr. The night was a fine one but the heavy industrial haze which hung over the area prevented accurate bombing and the Krupps works were not hit. However, the new Gee system proved that as a method of navigation to an area of town size it was most effective. In total eight aircraft were lost during the raid.

March saw not only a change in the weather but also a change in the name of the school. No.3 Service Flying Training School became 3 (Pilot) Advanced Flying Unit on 14th March and provided a more descriptive title for the role the unit carried out. On the flying front, March was beginning to look as if it would pass without a fatal accident as by 23rd the unit had only suffered minor incidents. Then, Flight Sergeant Tobias, an instructor, struck a wall causing the undercarriage to collapse. The aircraft was seriously damaged but both Tobias and his pupil, Sergeant Sowa, walked away uninjured. Unfortunately, Flying Officer Stefanus (Polish), who was acting as the Aerodrome Control Officer, was struck by the crashing aircraft and received fatal injuries.

On 29th March 1942, after having made a bit of a mess of things the night before while attempting to support the daring Commando raid on St.Nazaire, which had seen British Commandos and Naval forces successfully destroy the huge dry dock in the French port so denying an Atlantic base to the German battleship Tirpitz, Bomber Command were back in action at Lubeck in what would turn out to be their most effective raid of the war to date. 234 aircraft, 146 Wellingtons, 41 Hampdens, 26 Stirlings and 21 Manchesters, attacked in three waves from as low as 2,000 feet. With only light flak and a bright, full moon, along with the help of Gee, which helped the navigators most of the way to the target (Lubeck was just outside Gee's effective range) more than 400 tons of bombs were dropped, two thirds of which were incendiaries. 191 crews reported successful attacks, a claim backed up by various reports which stated some 190 acres of the town were destroyed. This equated to nearly a third of the towns area with 1,426 buildings destroyed and another 10,000 damaged (62% of all the buildings in Lubeck!). The human cost amounted to 320 killed with 780 injured, the highest toll in a German raid so far. Area bombing had well and truly arrived.

The end of March saw a ten day leave for Bernard, which he joyfully spent with Ellen in Battersea, during which she broke the happy news of her pregnancy. Having returned to the air on 10th April, by the end of that month his air time had reached 468 hours and the list of trainee pilots that he had played a part in training was growing steadily. The improved weather saw a drop off in the number of flying accidents with just fourteen for March and April combined. Unfortunately the spectre of fatal accidents returned when, on 5th April, Sergeant B. Jeffery, flying Oxford V3869, spun and hit the ground while attempting to recover from a dive near Lechlade, Gloucestershire. A second fatal accident claimed the lives of Sergeant Bilton (pilot) and his passenger, Aircraftman 1st Class A.N. Tracey, on the 18th when Oxford AS477 hit a tree while low flying at White House Farm in Brinkworth, Wiltshire and was destroyed by fire.

The mighty Avro Lancaster was beginning to arrive at front line squadrons by the spring of 1942 and at 1500 hours on 17th April Bomber Harris launched an experimental raid consisting of just twelve Lancasters. Six from 44 and six from 97 Squadron headed for Augsburg, some 500 miles inside German held territory, to attack the M.A.N. diesel engine factory. The aircraft were due over the target at 2000 hours but four were shot down by anti-aircraft fire outside Paris en-route. Squadron Leader John Dering Nettleton had taken his section of three 44 Squadron Lancasters all the way to the target at extreme low level, sometimes down to as little as fifty feet. One of the aircraft in Nettleton's section was shot down near the target but the other two swept over the factory under heavy anti-aircraft fire and dropped their delayed fuse bombs which later detonated causing considerable damage. Both aircraft were hit by anti-aircraft fire but because of their extremely low altitude most of it fired straight into the surrounding buildings. As the aircraft turned for home, the second aircraft in the section caught fire and crash landed leaving Nettleton to fly his badly damaged aircraft home alone, once again at tree top height. After a nine hour flight he finally touched down back at base, one of just five of the twelve to do so and was subsequently awarded the Victoria Cross for his actions. He was posted missing after a raid on Turin in July 1943.

From the skies over Britain, the Luftwaffe launched reprisal raids for the R.A.F. attacks on the Baltic ports of Rostock and Lubeck. Between 24th April and 3rd May the Luftwaffe hit Exeter, Norwich, Bath and York, some more than once, causing heavy damage. Amazingly these towns were selected not as military targets but randomly from a list of recommended towns to visit in a German tourist guide.

May was another intense month for Bernard, as the Unit tried to make the most of the improving weather, with 63 flights totalling 62 hours. With the welcome news of his impending fatherhood, he found himself contemplating his mortality a little more often than he had in the past and found the constant stream of accidents was beginning to niggle in the back of his mind. To be shot down by a German night fighter would be one thing but to die in a crash caused by an inexperienced pupil would be hard for him to take. The improved weather had all but eliminated taxiing accidents as the ground improved, but in the air the task of pilot training was continuing to prove hazardous. There were fifteen minor accidents in May, which is not surprising as for the first time a total of 1,000 hours night flying was achieved in a single month. 22nd May saw a horrific accident which claimed the lives of pilots Pilot Officer E.F. Gregory and Pilot Officer C.D. Rutherford. Flying in Oxfords R6321 and W6555. The two pilots were part of a formation above the airfield when, while changing formation, they collided and both aircraft dived into the ground. Two days later the unit lost another instructor and his passenger when Oxford BF939 struck a tree while low flying during a night flying test at Cirencester Park, Gloucestershire, killing Sergeant S.G. Haines and Aircraftman 2nd Class T. Smith, a fitter, instantly.

The rapid development of Bomber Command under Harris became evident on the night of 30th May when they pulled out all the stops to launch a 1,000 bomber raid on the Reich. Harris took crews and aircraft from training units to link up with the frontline squadrons in order to make up his goal of 1,000 aircraft and launched them mercilessly on Cologne. In total 1,047 aircraft were dispatched, made up of 602 Wellingtons, 131 Halifaxes, 88 Stirlings, 79 Hampdens, 73 Lancasters, 46 Manchesters and 28 Whitleys. Of that total, 898 aircraft claimed to have bombed the target dropping 1,455 tons of bombs. The German records reported the damage to have been; 2,500 separate fires, 3,330 buildings destroyed, 2,090 seriously damaged and 7,420 lightly damaged. Of these 2,560 were industrial buildings with 36 large firms losing complete production. Other classes of building lost included seven official administration buildings, fourteen public buildings, seven banks, nine hospitals, seventeen churches, sixteen schools, four university buildings, ten postal and railway buildings, four hotels, two cinemas, two newspaper offices and six department stores. The bombing lasted for over one and a half hours and some 13,010 houses and flats were destroyed with casualty figures somewhere between 469 and 486 killed, 5,027 injured and 45,132 bombed out. The R.A.F. losses were also high that night with 41 aircraft; 29 Wellingtons, four Manchesters, three Halifaxes, two Stirlings and one each of the Lancasters, Hampdens and Whitleys, failing to return; a total loss rate of 3.9per cent. As Harris had stated, the Germans had sown the wind and now they were reaping the whirlwind.

One of the four Manchesters lost that night was piloted by twenty year old Flying Officer Leslie Manser of No. 50 Squadron. His aircraft was met with heavy anti-aircraft fire as he approached the target and sustained damage but Manser pressed on and made a successful bombing run from 7,000 feet. On his return the aircraft was once again hit by heavy flak despite having dived down as low as 1,000 feet. At that height the port engine began to overheat but Manser managed to coax the aircraft to 2,000 feet before the engine burst into flames. As the aircraft began to lose height again, Manser ordered his crew to bale out, refusing to leave the controls until the last man was out. Almost immediately after the last crew member had left the aircraft it spun out of control and crashed killing Manser. For his bravery and selflessness in saving the lives of his crew, Flying Officer Leslie Manser was posthumously awarded the Victoria Cross.

June began with Bernard's annual flying assessment which revealed that after 530 hours in the air he had achieved the predictable rating of average. No one could ever accuse the R.A.F. of being over descriptive. Later that month, despite receiving the usual assessment rating, Bernard's instructors rating was upgraded to allow him to instruct on all types of aircraft unsupervised. Apart from his upgrade, the month passed much as the previous eight had and a sense of monotony was beginning to creep into his mind. He was a sensible and logical man and knew that at some point he would be posted to an operational squadron. Part of him wanted to get on with it and be able to attack the enemy, after all that was the reason he had joined up in the first place. However, another part of him enjoyed the relative safety of the instructor's role, especially as Ellen was by then five months pregnant. Another four months as an instructor would do him nicely he thought, as then at least he would get to see his child before being thrown into the maelstrom of combat where he knew the chances of survival were slim. On the afternoon of 8th June he headed home on another 48 hour pass, which in reality meant just 24 hours at home. He was back at South Cerney by late evening of 9th June and wrote to Ellen the following day putting his feelings down on paper in typically understated 1940's fashion.

> My Darling Ellen,
>
> How are you today, Dear? I hope you are still keeping well and that you got back home without any trouble yesterday evening. Thank you very

much for coming to the station with me again, and for buying me that glass of beer. I had quite a comfortable journey down and was fortunate enough to catch the 9.30 pm bus as usual. I found some supper in the mess on my return and added a pint of beer to it, so I think I did quite nicely, don't you? I suppose you kept yourself busy again when you got home, or did you spend the evening with Louise?

I was up at 5.30am this morning and did some flying and one or two other odd jobs that required finishing up. I think I shall go to the pictures this evening to see The Corsican Brothers with Douglas Fairbanks Junior. I understand it is pretty good so I hope to enjoy myself. I saw Bob this morning and he enquired after you, and at the same time invited me to tea tomorrow, so I am going. I shall telephone you during the evening though darling, don't you fret!

Which brings me to tomorrow. By the time you receive this letter we shall have been happily married for four years. It doesn't seem all that time and that lovely Saturday when we stood side by side in St. Philips church, does it? And even now I can picture the scene, and most particularly that vision of you looking very lovely, and making me feel very proud to be your bridegroom. A lot has happened since then, but we have been extremely happy despite the war separating us. We shall have many more anniversaries, darling, when we can quietly celebrate with our baby, who will be quite grown up by this time next year, won't he? Perhaps I shall be back in civilian clothes by the time our fifth anniversary arrives, I hope so anyway.

I hope you have a nice time tomorrow darling, and try to go out for a little while, won't you?

I expect you are getting a little nervous now about leaving the office and no doubt you will feel a little upset at first, but you will soon get used to it dear and Baby will keep you busy. I expect he has been kicking since I left you yesterday?

Well darling, I want to wish you many; many happy returns for tomorrow and God bless you and keep you safe always.

I love you darling, and send all my love and kisses to you. Please take care of yourself for your ever loving and devoted husband, Bernard. xxxxxxx

X for baby from Daddy.

Despite his fears that he would never get to see his own child, Bernard kept his thoughts to himself as he returned home to Ellen again on 27th June for a weeks leave and made no mention of the accidents and fatalities which had become a matter of course to him.

He returned to duty on 4th July with the prospect of long, sunny days flying in blue summer skies. It all sounded idyllic but the realities of the training regime shattered the illusions. The fatalities continued as the unit capitalised on the decent weather with ever more intense flying programmes. On 15th July Pilot Officer S.E. Godwin and his pupil, Pilot Officer K. Halstead, were killed when Oxford ED115 hit an obstruction and crashed while low flying one mile east of Aston, Gloucestershire. A second double fatality followed the next day when Oxford BF940 lost control at night half a mile south-west of Ashton Keynes, Wiltshire, with Flying Officer A.K.C. Holder and his pupil, Sergeant D. DePodesta, the unfortunate victims. Sadly this was not to be the end of the tragedies for the month as Pilot Officer K.T. White and his pupil, Sergeant A.H.S. Henderson, were killed on the night of 21st July after hitting trees on take-off from the relief landing ground at Southrop and crashed at Homeleigh Farm in Oxford AT603. There were a further nineteen accidents of varying severity that month, the most notable of them coming on 23rd when Sergeant G.F. Disbury excelled himself by making a safe landing despite one of his engines and its mountings falling out while in flight.

Throughout July Bomber Command had continued to launch major attacks on German cities with raids in excess of 250 aircraft on Bremen twice, Wilhelmshaven, Saarbrucken, Duisberg four times and a further two raids on Hamburg, one of which consisted of over 400 aircraft. Almost as if to finish the month on a high note they sent 630 aircraft to Dusseldorf on the last evening of the month. The force, made up of 308 Wellingtons, 113 Lancasters (this was the first time more than 100 Lancasters had been sent on a single raid), seventy Halifaxes, 61 Stirlings, 54 Hampdens and 24 Whitleys, dropped more than 900 tons of bombs in the attack, although some of that tonnage fell in open country. However, the official reports from the town authorities stated that most areas of the town were hit with 453 buildings destroyed and a further 15,000 damaged. Some 954 fires were started (67 of them classed as large) with 279 people killed. The loss rate overall was not outstanding for the R.A.F. with 29 aircraft being lost (4.6%) but the toll on the inexperienced crews from 92 Operational Training Unit was a staggering 10.5% and clearly unsustainable. The practice of using crews who had yet to fully complete their training for full operations was, as a consequence, under very serious review.

Bernard received welcome news on 1ˢᵗ August 1942 as he was promoted to Flight Sergeant, the highest of the non-commissioned ranks, and received the much needed pay rise to 10 shillings a day (50p) that came with the rank. It was becoming increasingly rare for a month to pass without a fatal flying accident and that pattern of events was not only being played out at 3 (P) A.F.U. but at all the training units throughout the commonwealth. The R.A.F.'s death toll was high even without taking into account those operational crews who were being lost carrying out the tasks the rest were training for. August was not going to be one of those death free months either. This time, at 0100 hours on 12ᵗʰ August, Oxford AT738 struck the quarters of Flying Officer McTurk and exploded. The house was completely burnt out and the pilot, Sergeant D.C. Collins, suffered multiple injuries and burns resulting in his death. The second 'fatal' of the month came on the 14ᵗʰ when Oxford ED133, flown by Flying Officer B. Wykes and his pupil, Sergeant A.V. Langridge, dived into the ground while carrying out an overshoot at about thirty feet. For the first time in his flying career Bernard too blotted his copybook. On 18ᵗʰ August he managed to clip another aircraft while taxiing causing minor damage to both aircraft. For his misdemeanour he received a permanent endorsement in the back of his log book. Despite his little mishap he still racked up 68 flying hours that month, 55 of those at night and took his total air-time to over 732 hours. September followed the same pattern with 71 flying hours, 66 of which were night flights. Once again the month took a toll on young airmen's lives as, on 22ⁿᵈ September, Pilot Officer N.L. Casely and his pupil, Sergeant J.N. Harvey, flew into a tree near Lulsgate Bottom in Oxford W6610, both men were killed instantly.

On the night Bernard was crashing into other aircraft while taxiing, Bomber Command saw two new milestones. That night a raid of 139 aircraft launched an attack on Osnabruck which in itself was of little note except that it was the last attack to take place without the benefit of Pathfinders to mark the target for the oncoming crews. From that point on the effectiveness of Bomber Command was to improve dramatically. Also that night saw the last operational sorties carried out by Bristol Blenheims, as the aircraft had become obsolete and the last attack was made by aircraft of 18 Squadron, based at Wattisham, who made intruder raids on a variety of air bases.

Following several unsuccessful raids using the Pathfinders since their inception, Bomber Command changed its tactics on the night of 4ᵗʰ/5ᵗʰ September during an attack on Bremen. That night, for the first time, the Pathfinders were split into three main groups. First came the 'illuminators' who lit up the area with white flares, followed by the 'visual markers' who came in and used the artificial light to identify their target and then dropped their coloured flares and finally the 'backers-up' who dropped all incendiary bomb loads on the coloured flares. This method would remain much the same for the rest of the war and would also prove to be most successful. That night the Pathfinders were accurate and well backed up by the main force which consisted of 98 Wellingtons, 76 Lancasters, 41 Halifaxes and 36 Stirlings. The Bremen authorities confirmed that the raid had been accurate with 21 industrial units being destroyed along with 149 more damaged and 460 houses destroyed with 8,900 damaged. 124 people were killed in the raid and the report poignantly notes that the flak defences were unable to protect the town. The attacking force lost twelve aircraft that night, seven Wellingtons, three Lancasters one Halifax and a Stirling.

Bernard's 414a for his time with 3 (P) A.F.U. at South Cerney

The early days of October finally brought welcome news for Bernard. With just a month to go before his child was due to be born he was to be transferred to

1525 Beam Approach Training Flight as a beam instructor. His final official day as an instructor at 3 (P) A.F.U. would be 25th October meaning that he would have completed exactly a year at South Cerney. He was relieved that a change of scenery was on the cards and that, with a bit of luck, he would get away from the constant accidents and fatalities. He also appreciated the fact that he would get to see his child before being sent on to an operational squadron. As it turned out Bernard's last day at 3 (P) A.F.U. would be 17th October as he would take a weeks well deserved rest before joining his new unit. His final pupil at South Cerney was a Sergeant Heath who, after a fifty minute flight, helped take Bernard's flying time to 832 hours and thirty minutes. Unfortunately October was unable to give the unit a fatal free month. The last man to be killed in a flying accident at 3 (P) A.F.U. while Bernard served there was Sergeant S.F. Smith, who was killed in Oxford AP401 after losing control during a night-time overshoot at Bibury relief landing ground. The aircraft was destroyed by fire after crashing. He was the thirtieth young airman to die at 3 (P) A.F.U. during Bernard's year at South Cerney.

CHAPTER SIX

Owner of a Son

1525 Beam Approach Training Flight, R.A.F. Docking, Norfolk.
18ᵗʰ October 1942 to 11ᵗʰ September 1943.

As Bernard relaxed at home before heading to his new posting, which would be in the relatively tranquil surroundings of the Norfolk countryside, elsewhere in the world the Russians and Germans continued to engage in increasingly bitter fighting at Stalingrad and, as he enjoyed another night in his own bed anticipating the arrival of his child, the British Eighth Army in North Africa, under the command of General Bernard Montgomery, began their offensive on the night of 23ʳᵈ October 1942 at El Alamein.

Since leaving South Cerney Bernard had enjoyed a ten day leave back in Battersea with his heavily pregnant wife. It was a huge wrench when he had to report to his new posting at Docking in Norfolk, as Ellen was by then well into the final fortnight of her pregnancy. The new posting was with 1525 Beam Approach Flight where Bernard would be instructing pilots on the navigation system he had learnt about just ten months before at Watchfield. The thought of a long posting there was not one he relished as the system was relatively straightforward and therefore his instructing would have little variety and plenty of repetition; three months would be about his limit he thought. As he arrived at the olive green gates of Docking on 26ᵗʰ October 1942, he found himself to be one of four new instructors to arrive that day. The other three, Acting Flight Lieutenant Parry, Sergeant Locatelli and Flying Officer Buckland, all came from No. 6 (P) A.F.U. with just Bernard coming from No. 3 (P) A.F.U.

The Airfield.

R.A.F. Docking was opened in July 1940 and fulfilled various roles while under the control of both Bomber and Coastal Commands. 1525 Beam Approach Flight was based at Bircham Newton from 13ᵗʰ July 1942 but actually operated from its satellite airfield which was Docking. The airfield was located in Norfolk approximately fourteen miles north-east of King's Lynn and just three miles north of its main airfield at Bircham Newton, with the expansive beauty of The Wash just seven miles to the west. Just a few hundred yards north of the village of Docking, off of what is now the B1454 road, the airfield boasted a grass strip, with the control tower (watch office) to the north of the crossing point of the two designated 'runways'. 1525 Beam Approach Flight was disbanded on 26th June 1945 but the airfield continued to be used until it eventually closed down in 1958. Today the sight has been reclaimed for agricultural use with the land mainly being turned over to potato production but some of the old buildings still survive such as the Control Tower/Watch Office.

The Aircraft.

The aircraft operated by 1525 Beam Approach Flight were exclusively Airspeed Oxfords. However, the base at Docking/Bircham Newton saw a vast array of aircraft types over the war period including Bristol Blenheims, Lockheed Hudsons, Vickers-Armstrong Wellingtons, Gloster Gladiators, Handley Page Hampdens, Supermarine Spitfires, Bristol Beaufighters, Armstrong Whitworth Whitleys, Grumman Avengers and Lockheed Venturas.

The Beam Approach system was a relatively new technology in 1942 and was still very much under development. The whole idea of it was to guide tired and often injured crews, who may well have damaged aircraft, safely onto their runway in the dark or reduced visibility such as fog. By the standards of today's sophisticated, satellite assisted systems, it was extremely primitive but without a doubt it saved the lives of many crews who would have otherwise missed their runways or made a crash landing.

The principle was relatively simple but as with all things aviation the details were somewhat more complicated. A basic explanation of how it worked is as follows. On each airfield there were usually three runways but the Beam Approach (B.A.) system would be installed only on the main runway. The system consisted of two main beacons, the inner and the outer, which transmitted signals to a receiver set in the aircraft. The ground beacons were often mobile units fitted to Austin Vans but increasingly became permanent fixtures as the war went on. The beacons emitted three different tones, dots, dashes and a constant tone, and each one told the approaching crew where they were in relation to the runway. If the aircraft was to the left of the runway the receiver in the aircraft would pick up dots,

RAF Docking Control Tower / Watch Office

1ˢᵗ Floor Control Room of the Control Tower

to the right it would receive dashes and a constant tone would be heard if the aircraft was accurately flying down the beam.

The system could be initiated by two methods, wireless transmission request (radio) to the station control operators at least half an hour before expected arrival, or by prior arrangement before leaving base. The first stage of the process consisted of the station control operators simply guiding the aircraft towards the airfield by telling the crew to turn "left, left" or "right" and adding the distance to the airfield in miles. The instruction for left was always repeated while right was said only once in order that the crews would know which way to turn even if the radio reception was poor. Once within ten to fifteen miles of the airfield the Beam Approach set was turned on in the aircraft and the guidance system would begin.

Using the inner marker as a guide the aircraft would fly down the beam and over the airfield at a height of 1,500 feet to point 1 shown in the diagram below. As it was unlikely to be flying directly down the beam the aircraft would most likely be either receiving dots or dashes and in the diagram below we have an aircraft flying slightly to the right of the runway and therefore the receiver would be receiving dashes. Once beyond the airfield the pilot would turn right (if hearing dashes and left if hearing dots) away from the QDR line in a level one turn (gentle) onto a bearing adjusted by thirty degrees to the QDR line. Here for example, if we assume the runway runs exactly east to west the pilot turning right would add thirty degrees to his westerly course of 270 degrees so making it 300 degrees on his compass or subtract thirty degrees if turning left so making it a course of 240 degrees. Once on the course the pilot would maintain that course for sixty dashes (or dots) until he reached point 2. At point 2 he would then make a rate one turn to the left until he regained the constant beam note of the QDR and then settled on that course. In our example that should now tally with a heading of 90 degrees (the reciprocal (opposite) of the desired direction of landing). QDR stands for direction reciprocal. Our pilots direction of landing would be exactly west (270 degrees) therefore the opposite direction is east at 90 degrees. The dotted line shows what happens if the pilot doesn't turn sharply enough. He should not increase his rate of turn but maintain it until he regained the beam slightly further down. Once the constant beam note was heard at point 4 the pilot then turned onto the beam.

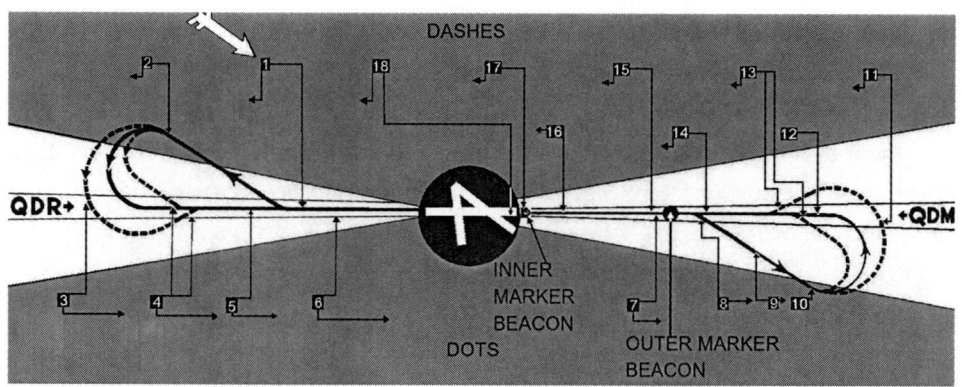

Adapted from Air Diagram 3966 (1944) Crown Copyright. Reproduced with kind permission of the Trustees of the R.A.F. Museum Hendon

With a constant note the pilot would check at point 5 that his heading was correct, in this example it should be 90 degrees. By point 6 he should be at an airspeed of no more than 120 mph and a height of 1,000 feet. Maintaining his course the pilot would fly over the airfield and the inner marker until he reaches the outer marker (about five miles from the runway) at point 7. Once the receiver picked up the outer marker, the pilot lowered his undercarriage. Once past the outer marker the pilot began another 180 degree turn as he had done before. Here, at point 8, he turned to the right off of his 90 degree heading onto one of 120 degrees. Once he had heard sixty dots he would begin to turn left (point 10) until he regained the constant beam of the QDM (direction magnetic) at point 12. Point 11 once again shows the path to take if the aircraft did not turn quickly enough. The other dotted line shows what would happen if the aircraft turned too quickly. At point 12 the pilot should lower his flaps for landing maintaining an airspeed of 100 mph and losing height at a rate of 500 feet per minute until he gets down to 600 feet. This should be about seven miles from the airfield. By point 13 the pilot should be on the required heading (270 degrees in our example) and holding the constant tone of the beam. As he passed through point 14 he should have been at 600 feet and 100 mph and on the beam, making corrections as he goes. If he was receiving slight dots then he knew to correct slightly to the right and if dashes slightly left. All the systems emitted dots if you were to the left of the runway while heading in the direction of landing and dashes if you were to the right.

As the aircraft passed over the outer marker at point 15, the pilot would reduce the throttle to reach an airspeed of 90 mph and begin to lose height at 500 feet per minute until he reached 150 feet. By point 16 he should have achieved 90 mph and 150 feet, while on the constant beam note or hearing slight dots or slight dashes. If any one of those criteria was not met then the aircraft should follow the overshoot procedure and accelerate and climb and go through the whole procedure again. If everything was looking good then the aircraft would touch down using the assistance of the airstrip landing lights. What could be simpler!

On arrival at Docking Bernard was given his responsibilities as an instructor, which being one of the most junior instructors on the staff, in terms of rank anyway, were the most repetitive and tedious ones. He was responsible for one Airspeed Oxford, DF280, planning of flying times and a practice known as compass swinging. For the Beam Approach system to work properly it was essential that the magnetic compasses were accurate, obviously that's good practice all the time.

Compass swinging was the method by which the aircraft's compass was set accurately and each pilot must be taught the correct method; that was Bernard's job alongside his general instructor's duties.

Compass swinging was carried out on the ground and was performed under the following circumstances; every two months, whenever the Navigation Officer decided, when any doubt over the compasses accuracy was raised, after any major inspection, service, engine change or modification or when the aircraft had been standing for a long time on the same heading, such as in a storage unit.

The method of compass swinging was long and laborious and involved a degree of mathematical ability to get it right, bear in mind that there was no such thing as a calculator in those days. Firstly the aircraft was carefully aligned on a due magnetic north heading and the deviation of the compass was noted (degrees by which the compass was inaccurate). This was then repeated on a due south heading and a correction factor was calculated using the formula C = (North − South) divided by 2 and the compass was then adjusted. This process was then repeated on headings of east and west and another calculation made using the formula (East − West) divided by 2 and the compass adjusted again. The aircraft was then placed on a series of eight headings; north-west, north, north-east, east, south-east, south, south-west and west and the deviation on each heading noted. A final correction factor was then calculated using the formula, (NW + N + NE + E + SE + S + SW + W) divided by 8. The compass was then adjusted using the adjustable correctors in the compass mechanism and the compass was then re-sealed. This was a vital but tedious job and so it is no wonder it was given to a junior instructor.

Bernard first took to the air from Docking on 27th October in Oxford DF279 with Flight Sergeant Whetton alongside him for a quick recap. The following day he took a further three refresher flights before taking up his own pupil, one Flying Officer Brandon-Tyre, to practice homing on the beacon from the front on dots, i.e. to the left of the runway. Many of his subsequent flights involved not one but two pupils, taking turns to carry out the various training drills. By the end of October, he had already instructed six separate pupils.

November began with Bernard once again taking up two students, Sergeants Dunlop and Bartlett, for three flights, the first of which lasted for two hours and involved flying the whole B.A. circuit at a constant height and then, once that had been achieved successfully, doing the same thing again but this time hooded. Hooding actually involved the instructor, Bernard in this case, pulling a canvass hood over the pilot in the cockpit so that he had no external visual reference and had to rely entirely on his instruments and the instructions from the B.A. equipment. The following two flights, which lasted an hour each, involved more of the same but this time bringing the aircraft as low as 200 feet while still hooded. The 2nd November continued in the same vane as Dunlop and Bartlett were taken aloft twice more, recapping their instruction from the previous day. At just after 1000 hours on 2nd November, Oxford DF278 came to a halt at its dispersal point and was met by a runner from the Watch Office. Once the engines had stopped and the runner could finally hear himself think, he shouted up to Bernard that he was to report to the Watch Office immediately. Promising Dunlop and Bartlett that he would be back to debrief them, he made his way across the damp grass to the Watch Office. On arrival at the first floor control room (see photo above) he was greeted by the Officer in Charge with a big smile and an outstretched hand. "Congratulations Steel. You're the proud owner of a bouncing baby boy! Here's a 48 hour pass, get going."

Bernard clenched both fists and emitted a strange "Waayhaay!" as he shook the OiC's hand and headed off as quickly as he could for London. Dunlop and Bartlett never got their debrief.

Late that afternoon Bernard arrived at the Maternity Home that was then located in Alexandra Road, Epsom, Surrey. His baby son had been born late the previous evening and was almost twenty-four hours old by the time his father laid his eyes on him. However, by the standards of the day that was pretty quick, even if the father had been at home. Ellen, who was a naturally slim woman and always seemed to look as if a slight breeze would blow her over, was naturally exhausted following her labour but perked up at the arrival of her husband; probably due in no small part to the fact that he would have looked extremely dashing in his R.A.F. blue, pilots' uniform. He gently picked his son from his crib for the first time and smiled that new father smile that is a mixture of elation and fear and welcomed Douglas Bernard Steel to a very uncertain world.

The two days in Epsom passed like a shot, lost in a blur of visiting trips to the maternity home and before he knew it, Bernard was arriving back at Docking late in the evening of the 4th. The next two days saw him return to the air but his thoughts were in Epsom with his wife and newborn son. His commanding officer had pulled some strings and on the afternoon of the 6th he found himself once again on the L.N.E.R. branch line that passed to the south of the airfield, beginning his journey back to London with two weeks leave in his pocket.

Caring for a newborn child, especially your first, is hard enough in the pampered times in which we live today, the difficulties in war torn Britain of 1942 can only be guessed at. However, Bernard and Ellen made the most of their two weeks together with Douglas, while Ellen recovered her strength at her parents house at 1 Ingram Cottages, Albert Road, Epsom. When his leave all too quickly came to an end, Bernard was disappointed at having to head back to Norfolk despite the appealing prospect of a decent nights sleep.

Arriving in Docking during the evening of 22nd November he was immediately marched the mile or so down the road from his quarters to Docking village for a few celebratory glasses of beer at the Railway Inn. With a slightly fuzzy head he found himself back in the air the following day. The 24th November proved that the Beam Approach system was far from being perfected. While landing during abysmal weather with zero visibility (exactly the circumstances Beam Approach was designed to overcome) Oxford DF282 suffered Category B damage (beyond repair on site but repairable at a Maintenance Unit) luckily there were no injuries to the crew.

Italy had become a regular target for the growing might of Bomber Command and on the night of 28th/29th November 1942 a force of 228 aircraft consisting of 117 Lancasters, 47 Stirlings, 45 Halifaxes and nineteen Wellingtons, was launched against Turin. One of the Short Stirlings was piloted by Flight Sergeant Rawdon Hume Middleton of 149 Squadron. The Australian took off at 1814 hours from Lakenheath and headed over the Alps where they experienced difficulties in getting over the peaks and as a result used too much fuel. However, once they had crossed the mountain range, Middleton spotted flares being dropped on the target of the Fiat factory and decided to press on. Middleton made three runs over the target before he was satisfied they had identified the right building using up even more valuable fuel in the process. As they made their bombing run the aircraft was hit by anti-aircraft fire with one shell shattering the windscreen wounding both pilots. Middleton lost the sight in one eye and also received wounds to his legs and body and subsequently lost consciousness. The second pilot, despite suffering injuries himself, took over the controls and regained altitude and successfully bombed the target.

Middleton regained consciousness and took control again, ordering his co-pilot to get medical treatment while he headed for home. After a further eight hours of flying in considerable pain and still losing blood, they crossed the French coast with their fuel at a critical level. Realising that they would not make safety, Middleton flew along the south coast of England and ordered his crew to bale out. With the crew all out, the aircraft finally ran out of fuel and crashed into the sea at 0255 hours. Two of the crew landed too far out to sea to be rescued and drowned but the others were picked up safely while Middleton remained at the controls as the aircraft crashed into the sea, his body being washed up between Dover and Folkestone some two months later. For his numerous acts of courage that night and his ultimate self sacrifice, Middleton was posthumously awarded the Victoria Cross.

Having just had two weeks leave, Bernard only received one more 48 hour pass (16th and 17th December) before Christmas. With flights on both Christmas Eve and again on 27th December he had to spend his sons first Christmas separated from him and consoled himself with a couple of other instructors back at the Railway Inn. As it turned out, he was to have something else to celebrate as, on the last day of 1942, almost as if it was something the Air Ministry had forgotten to do, Bernard was promoted to the rank of Flight Sergeant. The first month of 1943 saw awful weather which prevented flying even with the aid of the Beam Approach system. Heavy snow prevented any flying on 5th, 6th and 7th and on the 8th there was still enough snow lying to conceal a hole which Oxford DF281 dropped into and sustained damage.

As 1942 came to an end, the Allies around the world were beginning, slowly, to make inroads. The Germans were under extreme pressure in the southern sector of the Eastern Front and in North Africa, while the Japanese were struggling to contain the Americans on Guadalcanal. 1943 was looking like it may become the vital year of the war, however long the conflict was to last and whoever was going to win.

On the 11th January 1943 President Roosevelt of the United States and Winston Churchill met at Casablanca. During their conference they agreed to Stalin's demands for a second front to be opened up in Western Europe in order to stretch the German military by splitting their forces in two. Churchill suggested an attack on Italy, which he described as the 'soft under-belly of Europe' while Roosevelt wanted an attack in France. Churchill agreed to support an attack in France as long as it was put off until 1944 to give the Allies more time to train and build up their forces while in the meantime appeasing Stalin by carrying out his plan for an attack on Italy. The two leaders agreed and plans were begun for a landing in Sicily. At the same meeting the two leaders decided that German occupied northern Europe, including Germany itself, should be softened up for the 1944 invasion by intensive aerial bombing by both day and night with the aim of totally destroying the German centres of production. The directive was signed and passed to the head of R.A.F. Bomber Command, Sir Arthur (Bomber) Harris for implementation.

It seemed as if Bomber Harris had been waiting for the instruction to go, and as a result Bomber command launched their first major raid on Berlin for fourteen months on the night of 16th/17th January. As an example of how far Bomber Command had progressed, this would not only be the first operation in which proper target indicators (coloured flares dropped by the highly skilled Pathfinder force) were used, but also the first raid in which all participating aircraft were four engine bombers. The aircraft had advanced so quickly that even the four engined Shorts Stirlings were deemed out of date. The force consisted of 201 aircraft, 190 Lancasters and 11 Halifaxes, being drawn from the Pathfinder squadrons and 1, 4 and 5 groups. Despite the advances in aircraft technology, this particular raid still encountered problems. Because Berlin was so far away the Gee and Oboe navigation systems were of little use and the more traditional methods of navigation were hindered by thick cloud en route. Berlin itself was covered with thick haze and bombing was scattered across the south of the city. In an organisational faux pas more akin to modern Britain, most of the German flak gunners happened to be away on a course that night and so the flak barrage was very light and as a result only one Lancaster was shot down. The Germans suffered 198 killed.

On 27th January Bernard headed back home to Ellen and Douglas again for another weeks leave, not returning to Norfolk until the evening of 3rd February. As March came to an end, he had not had any further leave with the only breaks being supplied by adverse weather. By the time April arrived he had clocked up over 1,082 hours in the air and was beginning to feel as comfortable amongst the clouds as he did on the ground.

Meanwhile, back in Europe, the combined air forces of Britain and the United States declared a new air offensive on 25th February based on the decisions taken by Churchill and Roosevelt at Casablanca. Vowing 'round the clock' aerial bombardment the Americans would be bombing by day and the Royal Air Force taking the night shift. Almost as confirmation of that declaration, Bomber Command launched its heaviest raid of the war so far on Berlin during the night of 1st/2nd March 1943. 302 aircraft took part, 156 Lancasters, 86 Halifaxes and sixty Stirlings, with bombing photography showing the attack to be spread over an area of 100 square miles. Concentrated bombing had proved difficult as the Pathfinders had not been able to mark properly, as their H2S (early ground reading radar) sets could not distinguish individual landmarks in the built up area. Most of the bombing was in the south-west of the city with 22 acres of workshops at the railway repair depot at Tempelhof burnt out, along with twenty other factories damaged and 875 further buildings destroyed. The death toll on the ground that night stood at 191 while the R.A.F. suffered the loss of seven Lancasters, six Halifaxes and four Stirlings; 5.6% of the bomber force.

The next night Bomber Command launched 417 aircraft against Hamburg but due to an error in marking by the Pathfinders, managed to bomb the town of Wedel some thirteen miles to the south. Even so the raid took out a naval clothing depot and several industrial buildings around the harbour area which backed up 'Bomber' Harris' belief that bombing was always useful; even if you hit the wrong target. Losses for the raid were four Lancasters, and two each of the Wellingtons, Halifaxes and Stirlings. With the relative failure of the raid of the 3rd March still fresh in their minds; Bomber Command launched a fresh raid on the night of 5th /6th March, this time on the industrial centre of Essen. 442 aircraft, comprising 157 Lancasters, 131 Wellingtons, 94 Halifaxes, 52 Stirlings and eight Mosquitoes, were launched at the target although for some reason a disproportionately high percentage, 13% or 56 aircraft, turned back before bombing due to some form of technical defect.

The eight Mosquitoes on the raid were all Pathfinders and despite three of them being among those to turn back early, the remaining five marked the target perfectly. The bombers attacked in three waves with the Halifaxes in the first wave followed by the Stirlings and Wellingtons in the second leaving the Lancasters to roll in and finish the job. Two thirds of the bomb load took the form of incendiaries, with one third of the remaining high explosive bombs being set on delayed fuses. After forty minutes of consecutive bombing, 160 acres of Essen had been destroyed with the vital Krupps works alone suffering damage to 53 of its buildings. A local report stated that 3,018 houses were destroyed with a further 2,166 seriously damaged with deaths being reported as between 457 and 482 including ten Firemen; the previous highest loss in a raid was 469 in the 1,000 bomber raid on Cologne in May 1942. The R.A.F. lost fourteen aircraft, four Lancasters and Wellingtons and three Halifaxes and Stirlings; a loss rate of 3.2%.

In the skies over Europe, Bomber Command had continued to do their best to fulfil the promise of a relentless bombing campaign. The night of 29th/30th March saw 329 aircraft bomb Berlin, 348 had attacked Essen on 3rd/4th April, 577 had attacked Kiel on 4th/5th, 392 attacked Duisberg on 8th/9th, 502 went to Frankfurt on 10th/11th and 462 hit Stuttgart on 14th/15th. The raids were coming thick and fast, hitting their targets with much improved accuracy but at a high cost. In these few raids alone, Bomber Command had lost 119 aircraft.

Although his personal life had been punctuated with real excitement with the arrival of Douglas, it only served to add to the boredom that Bernard was beginning to feel at the repetitiveness of his role at 1525 B.A.T. Flight. With only nine different drills for the trainee crews to undertake, and all of those being done within a ten mile radius of the airfield, his instructing role had very quickly descended into tedium. The training lacked variety and there was a seemingly endless supply of courses flowing through the flight. Course no 43, which had arrived at Docking on 30th March, was the eighteenth Bernard had seen. The monotony continued to grow and was only relieved by the occasional leave period. He had predicted to himself that three months would probably be enough at a B.A.T. flight and he had already been there for nearly double that. Although he desperately wanted some relief from the repetitiveness, he was beginning to dread a new posting. Part of him desperately wanted to fly operationally, even though he was fully aware that the odds were against him surviving as they were for all bomber crews, but increasingly his heart was telling him the only important thing was to see his son grow up. The decision as to which scenario was to unfold would be made well above his head, and in any event he would almost certainly be the last to know. In this war he knew his life was no longer his own, it firmly belonged to the nation.

On 3rd May a small daylight force of twelve Lockheed Venturas from 487 (New Zealand) Squadron were despatched to attack a power station in Amsterdam. Unfortunately, on the same day, some 69 highly experienced German fighter pilots were attending a conference at Schiphol airport in the city. The pilots were scrambled to intercept the Venturas and nine were shot down with one more damaged which managed to escape back to England. With one more having already turned back early due to technical problems, there was just one aircraft left, piloted by Squadron Leader L.H. Trent. Finding himself all alone, Trent pressed on and bombed the target causing some damage before being shot down himself. Squadron Leader Trent and his navigator survived and were taken prisoner for the duration of the war. In recognition of his courage in pressing home his attack in the face of overwhelming odds, Trent was awarded the Victoria Cross in 1946.

The R.A.F. was not to be outdone by the Army's stunning victory in North Africa where the British had pushed Rommel's Afrikakorps from the continent in the early months of 1943. On the night of 16th/17th May 1943 the R.A.F. mounted their most daring raid of the entire war and one which has gone down in history as the Dambusters Raid. The idea had been conceived by Barnes Wallis, a scientist who worked for the Vickers aircraft company at Brooklands near Weybridge in Surrey and who was already famous as the man who had designed the Wellington Bomber. His plan was to destroy the three main dams, the Sorpe, Eder and Mohne, which supplied water and hydroelectric power to the industrial Ruhr Valley.

On the night of 16th May 1943, nineteen Lancasters in two waves and a reserve force, took off from R.A.F. Scampton and flew at extreme low level (between sixty and 100 feet) all the way to their targets. The Mohne and Eder dams were successfully breached causing huge damage and massive loss of life on the ground but at a considerable cost to 617 Squadron. In total the raid cost the lives of 53 men with three more taken prisoner. The effectiveness of the raid has long been debated but what is not in question is the courage of all involved and at the very least it proved to the Germans that the R.A.F was finally capable of hitting any target they chose. The number of bravery awards made following the raid tells its own tale, not least that of Guy Gibson's Victoria Cross. Even though Gibson's crew survived this most hazardous of raids, it is interesting to note that not a single one of them survived the war; a sure sign of just how dangerous being part of a bomber crew really was.

On 11th June 1943 Bomber Command launched a huge 783 aircraft raid on Dusseldorf with a force made up of 326 Lancasters, 202 Halifaxes, 143 Wellingtons, 99 Stirlings and thirteen Mosquitoes. The Pathfinders marked perfectly until one Mosquito accidently dropped its marker flares to the north east of the city causing part of the force to waste their bombs in open country. However, the main body of the force accurately hit the centre of the city and destroyed an area covering 130 acres. The Dusseldorf authorities reported the fire area measuring eight kilometres by five with over 8,800 individual fires reported; 1,500 of them classified as large. 1,292 people were killed and 140,000 were rendered homeless. The raid would turn out to be the heaviest of the war for Dusseldorf but was still a long way from the peak of Bomber Commands' destructive power. The Allied losses totalled 4.9% with 38 aircraft failing to return home.

As an example of how ruthlessly efficient Bomber Command was becoming, a further raid on the night of 28th/29th June 1943 on Cologne, saw 608 aircraft attack, resulting in the loss of 6,500 buildings with another 15,000 damaged and with a new peak in single raid deaths of 4,377 killed and a further 10,000 injured. Even this terribly large figure was soon to pale into insignificance with what was to come.

Hamburg had been attacked by Bomber Command on the night of 24th/25th July 1943 by 791 aircraft resulting in some 1,500 deaths. But worse was to come for the city as the bombers returned two nights later with a force of 353 Lancasters, 244 Halifaxes, 116 Stirlings and 74 Wellingtons. The Pathfinders marked the target well and the force accurately dropped 2,326 tons of bombs. The situation on the ground was primed for disaster with higher than usual air temperatures and a prolonged period of dry weather leaving the city parched. With most of the fire service still away to the west of the city dealing with the aftermath of the previous raid, Bomber Command chose that night to produce their most accurate effort yet with an estimated 600 bomb loads falling within an area measuring just two miles by one. As a result huge fires broke out and eventually joined up causing a massive demand for oxygen. The raging fires produced a firestorm which sucked the air through the densely built up streets destroying some 16,000 buildings in the process. Almost all the people in the area were killed, many of them suffocating in their basement shelters as the firestorm ripped the very air from their lungs; the total death toll could not be accurately recorded due to the numbers involved but is reliably put at a staggering minimum of 30,000.

Back at Docking the months slowly ticked past and still Bernard received no news of another posting although he finally got some good news in the form of a promotion. On 1st August 1943 he received his commission and became a proper officer with the rank of Warrant Officer. Despite his promotion he was beginning to think that he had been lost somewhere in the bureaucracy of the Air Ministry as summer drew to an end, until finally he received news in the early days of September.

With the pressure mounting on the Italians, 112 Stirlings, 34 Halifaxes and six Lancasters attacked Turin on the night of 12th/13th August. A Stirling of 218 Squadron, piloted by 21 year old Flight Sergeant Arthur Louis Aaron, was hit by gunfire from a tail gunner of another bomber while approaching Turin. The navigator was killed and Aaron was hit in the face by a bullet which shattered his jaw and ripped away part of his face, as well as receiving injuries to his chest and right arm. Unable to continue flying, the flight engineer and bomb aimer took over control from Aaron and set course for North Africa to make an emergency landing. As the Stirling reached North Africa, Aaron insisted on helping the crew to land. He tried to take over the controls on two occasions but was unable to do so. Unable to speak, he had to resort to writing down instructions left handed and successfully assisted in making a wheels up landing. Nine hours later Flight Sergeant Aaron died of his wounds and was posthumously awarded the Victoria Cross for his bravery.

Throughout the war the Allies possessed a superb intelligence network which provided them with vital information on all aspects of the conflict. One of those vital pieces of information alerted the Allies to the fact that the Germans were developing long range, unmanned weapons, which would be capable of striking at mainland Britain. The first was the V1 or 'Doodlebug' as it became known in England and was a type of pilotless aeroplane carrying a high explosive warhead. The second was the V2, a ballistic missile against which there would be no defence once it was launched. The intelligence services identified the research and development site for these two weapons as being located at Peenemunde on the Baltic coast and had no difficulty in convincing Churchill that it should be attacked by Bomber Command at the earliest opportunity.

On the night of 17th/18th August, a force made up entirely of four engine bombers, consisting of 324 Lancasters, 218 Halifaxes and 54 Stirlings, headed for the target. The night was specifically chosen as it was brightly moon lit and would assist the force in identifying the relatively small target. The Pathfinders duly identified the base with ease and the first two waves attacked accurately, dropping some 1,800 tons of bombs. The third and final wave, although again accurate, was unlucky enough to be set upon by German night fighters who had been kept occupied for the first two waves by a diversion raid to Berlin which had been carried out by a handful of Mosquitoes. Bomber Command lost forty aircraft that night, 23 Lancasters, fifteen Halifaxes and two Stirlings, mainly during the final wave; a loss rate of 6.7%. Although the loss rate was high, the cost was deemed worthwhile for what turned out to be such a successful attack on a vital target. 180 Germans were killed, many of them key technicians, and estimates state that the programme was put back by at least two months and also reduced the size of the attacks when they did eventually come. Many of the Bombers shot down that night would not have known what hit them as that night was the first time the Germans used 'Schrage Musik' which was the name they gave to their new upward firing canons fitted in the cockpit of their Messerschmitt Me110's. With none of Bomber Commands aircraft having a belly turret, the Me110's could simply fly undetected below the bomber and shoot it from the sky with no danger of being shot at themselves. The bomber boys' already dangerous lives had just become even more dangerous.

ON POSTING.

(*4690—117) Wt. 51983—5030 48,500 4/40 T.S. 700   FORM 414 (A)

SUMMARY of FLYING and ASSESSMENTS FOR YEAR COMMENCING 1st *11 SEP 1943* *19

[*For Officer, insert "JUNE" ; For Airman Pilot, insert "AUGUST."]

| | S.E. AIRCRAFT | | M.E. AIRCRAFT | | TOTAL for year | GRAND TOTAL All Service Flying |
	Day	Night	Day	Night		
DUAL						
PILOT			628·40			
PASSENGER	—	—	—			

ASSESSMENT of ABILITY

(To be assessed as :—Exceptional, Above the Average, Average, or Below the Average)

(i) AS AN *J.A.A. INSTRUCTOR* †PILOT *Above Average*

(ii) AS PILOT–NAVIGATOR/NAVIGATOR

(iii) IN BOMBING

(iv) IN AIR GUNNERY

† Insert :—"F.", "L.B.", "G.R.", "F.B.", etc.

ANY POINTS IN FLYING OR AIRMANSHIP WHICH SHOULD BE WATCHED.

Date 11 SEP 1943   Signature *R.W. Knight* S/Ldr.

Officer Commanding O.C. No. 1525 BAT. FLIGHT

Bernard's Flight Assessment on leaving 1525 B.A.T. Flight September 1943

On 11th September 1943 Bernard's tedium was finally relieved as he was posted to No. 6 (Pilots) Advanced Flying Unit based at Windrush in Gloucestershire. In a way all his wishes had been answered. Although he still wanted to fly on operations, he was delighted that by undergoing a second stint as a flying instructor he would get away from the tedium of the B.A.T. flight and still be around to see his son grow. However, he was fully aware that as every day passed the inevitable operational posting was drawing nearer. His eleven months at Docking had been heavy going mentally and physically; his flying hours stood at a staggering 1,441 and fifteen minutes and his own flying ability had improved immeasurably. Evidence of his improvement is shown in his 414(A) form, Summary of Flying, which shows his assessment as 'above average'. That may sound tame now but in the language of the day, and bearing in mind that nearly all 414's were completed as 'average', it was praise indeed.

CHAPTER SEVEN

The last refuge

No. 6 (Pilots) Advanced Flying Unit. R.A.F. Windrush, Gloucestershire. 12ᵗʰ
September 1943 to 17ᵗʰ November 1943.

The never ending monotony of Beam Approach training had finally reached its end for Bernard. Eleven months of repetition had pushed him to the point where any change was as good as a rest but at last his final day at Docking, 11ᵗʰ September 1943, arrived and after a 48 hour pass he reported to his new posting of 6 (Pilots) Advanced Flying Unit based at Little Rissington in Gloucestershire. As it turned out Bernard would not actually spend much time at the main base of Little Rissington but at a satellite airfield named R.A.F. Windrush just four miles to the south.

The Airfields.

Little Rissington was opened in August 1938 as a grass strip with three concrete runways being added later. Across the northern end of the airfield were, and still are, an impressive array of four 'C' type hangers, each measuring 152 feet wide and 300 feet long, with huge 35 feet high steel plate doors. The airfield was used as a training base throughout the war and survives in amazing condition today. The concrete runways are still in place with the southern section of the airfield being used by a Glider school. The northern section, from the control tower and 'C' type hangers upwards, is now an industrial estate with nearly all of the airfield buildings surviving intact, including all four of the 'C' type hangers. Little Rissington is located approximately fifteen miles east of Cheltenham between the modern A429 and A424 roads with Windrush being four miles south of Little Rissington adjacent to the A40.

Windrush was a satellite of Little Rissington to take the overflow of pilots undergoing training. The airfield was specifically built for the war effort and opened in June 1940 serving as a training base throughout the war and being closed down in 1945 at the end of hostilities. The two runways were constructed from

Somerfield Tracking, a form of pre-fabricated wire mesh, while the hangers were one T1, a metal 'transportable' hanger of 90 feet by 240 feet, and ten 'blister' hangers, six of which were of the 'extra over' type. Blister hangers were made of wooden arched ribs covered with corrugated iron and could be erected just about anywhere without foundations or hard standing. They had a span of 45 feet and came in sections 45 feet long so that as many lengths as required could be joined together. The 'extra over' type was the same but had steel ribs and a span of 69 feet.

After closing in 1945, the airfield at Windrush was returned to agricultural use and remains farmland today. Several of the buildings survive intact with hangars being used as storage sheds by the farmer and the control tower has been fully restored. The northern perimeter fence would have run alongside the modern A40 where foundations of some of the huts and buildings can still be found.

Bernard arrived at Little Rissington early on the morning of Tuesday 14th September 1943 to be immediately told to report down the road at Windrush, the base he had just been driven past. The initial confusion as to where he was supposed to be posted was soon cleared up, and by the early afternoon he found himself airborne over the rural Gloucestershire landscape in Oxford MP358. His first flight at 6 (P) A.F.U. was an assessment of his abilities with Squadron Leader Danby and took some 45 minutes. Bernard guided the aircraft deftly through the sky completing each of the required manoeuvres skilfully, effortlessly and silently. Danby spoke only to order a new manoeuvre and Bernard only replied with an assured 'Yes, Sir'. The hundreds of hours he had now amassed on the tricky little Oxford allowed him to fly her almost without thought; he knew the types every foible and knew every little trick to get the best from the aircraft. By the end of the test, Danby was suitably impressed to the point of envy; however 1940's England was not a place for gushing enthusiasm and backslapping, so Danby let Bernard go with a grumbled 'You'll do'. That afternoon he was aloft with his first 'customer', Pilot Officer Ray, in Oxford Y3847, teaching him the finer points of going round again (aborting an approach to landing and going round the circuit again before attempting to land for a second time). It was still training but at least here there was variety in what he could teach. This of course was his second stint at a (P) A.F.U. after having spent a year at 3 S.F.T.S. (renamed as 3 (P) A.F.U.) at South Cerney but it was welcome relief to the monotony of Norfolk and Bernard felt a happier man for it.

One element that he had not missed while at Docking was the amount of accidents that seemed to occur at (P) A.F.U.'s. At Docking Bernard had been

Little Rissington Control tower

One of the C type hangars

training already experienced pilots and as a result accidents were a rarity, unfortunately the same could not be said at (P) A.F.U.'s where the pilots were fresh from basic flight training and it was only four days before the first accident occurred at Windrush. On the evening of 18th September 1943, Sergeant D.H. Collings took off from the airfield in Oxford LX157 and immediately encountered difficulties. The aircraft crashed near the airfield and was destroyed by fire, Sergeant Collings

91

suffered a broken right wrist and ankle and extensive burns from which he died. Bernard was no longer sure which was the lesser of two evils.

The weather for September was surprisingly good with fair to good visibility and any fog restricted to the early mornings. The wind had been moderate and generally from the west, with the only downside being lower than average temperatures, especially towards the end of the month; on the night of 26th/27th the mercury dropped as low as 34 degrees F (1C). As a result of the relatively good weather, the pilots and instructors could take advantage and maximise their time in the air, Bernard took a total of forty flights by the end of September and added another 38 hours to his tally.

October arrived with low cloud and drizzle and only light winds which seemed incapable of pushing the clouds away. Despite the miserable conditions, the flying continued unabated with Bernard taking up Sergeants Berry and Barker on the 1st, Gingrich and Brettel on the 2nd and Barker, Dainty and Warrant Officer Whetton on the 3rd. The subjects covered contained the variety he had craved with take offs and landings prominent among night flights, no flaps landings and navigation exercises.

The 6th saw a court martial take place which held interest for every pilot and instructor at the two bases. Sergeant R.G. Browne was court martialed for 'so negligently performing his duty as a pilot as to cause His Majesty's Oxford LW790, when taxiing, to collide with His Majesty's aircraft PG260, which at the time was also taxiing, and thereby causing damage to both the said aircraft.' Browne was found guilty and sentenced to be severely reprimanded. Bernard thought back to his own taxiing accident and considered himself lucky to have escaped the stress of a Court Martial. However, the punishment for Sergeant Browne was minimal, it seems as though a valuable pilot could not be lost for simply crashing a couple of the King's aircraft.

The night of 8th October saw a tragedy of larger proportions than Bernard had witnessed so far. Up to now airmen had died in ones and twos but that night would see the deaths of five in one hit. Wellington R1028 from 21 Operational Training Unit based at Moreton-in-Marsh, crashed at Great Rissington (between Little Rissington and Windrush airfields) and burst into flames. Flight Sergeant Hazeldene, Sergeant Jones, Sergeant Cox, Sergeant Johnson and Sergeant Rees all suffered multiple injuries and extensive burns and died at the scene. Sergeant Smith, who is believed to be the rear gunner, survived but suffered severe head injuries. The body of Flight Sergeant Hazeldene, an Australian, could not be repatriated due to the restrictions the war imposed and was laid to rest in Little Rissington churchyard on 12th October.

Elsewhere Bomber Command continued to keep up the pressure on the Germans and Hannover was their target on the night of 8th/9th October with 504 aircraft, 282 Lancasters, 188 Halifaxes, 26 Wellingtons and eight Mosquitoes, making up the force. The skies over the city were clear that night and the Pathfinders marked accurately and were followed up by an extremely concentrated attack. Extensive damage was caused to the centre of the city with a large fire area developing. 1,200 people were killed with 3,345 injured and some 4,000 buildings destroyed with a further 30,000 damaged. Fourteen Lancasters were lost along with thirteen Halifaxes but almost as if in tribute to their superb work, all of the Wellingtons returned safely on what would prove to be the last raid in which the old stalwart would take part.

Not all accidents at that time proved fatal. Sometimes due to the skill and training of the crews, the attendance of the emergency teams, or more often to blind luck, many aircrew walked away from serious accidents. On 17th October another Wellington, this time belonging to 82 Operational Training Unit based at Ossington, Nottinghamshire, attempted to make an emergency landing at Little Rissington having lost an engine. As the aircraft made its circuit the good engine also failed while on the southern leg and the Wellington rapidly lost height and crashed at Windrush airfield where it burst into flames and was completely destroyed. Incredibly Sergeant Kirkland and his crew of six all escaped unhurt although it was beginning to seem as if this little corner of Gloucestershire was no place for a Wellington.

That same day Bernard left to start one weeks leave and headed back to Battersea to be with Ellen and Douglas, who was now nearly a year old. In his absence the accidents continued when on 20th October two Oxfords, LX178 and W6586, collided at Windrush. W6586 was destroyed by fire and its pilot, Sergeant M.C.R. Lang, suffered a fracture to his left leg, one to his jaw and another to the base of his skull which resulted in his death.

Hannover was attacked again on the night of 18th/19th October by a force of 360 Lancasters, eighteen of which failed to return. The raid itself was of little real note but one of the Lancasters shot down that night became the 5,000[th] bomber lost by Bomber Command in the war so far. The statistics show that by the end of that raid Bomber Command had flown 144,500 sorties and lost a total of 5,004 aircraft. They had averaged 96 sorties every 24 hours at an overall loss rate of 3.5%.

With yet another leave period over, Bernard arrived back at Windrush on the frosty evening of 24th October and the following morning was back in the air with Sergeant Dainty in Oxford EB701, running him through aircraft familiarization and circuits. He spent 1st November; his sons first birthday, stuck on the ground at a fog bound Windrush. The lack of activity only made him long for home as he stared into the white blanket that blocked out all views of the Gloucestershire countryside. The 2nd was no better and he eventually got back into the air on the 3^{rd,} not instructing this time but carrying out flying tests on Oxfords MP358, BG548 and T1209. With improving weather he was airborne nearly every day up to and including the 16th when he received news that he was to be posted yet again. This time however, it was not to another training unit as an instructor but to an Operational Training Unit; this was the first step to converting to heavy bombers and a posting to an operational squadron. Three years and two months after joining the R.A.F. and with 1,548 flying hours under his belt, it was time for him to go head to head with the Nazis. For Bernard the war was about to truly arrive.

In the meantime Bomber Command continued its assault on occupied Europe as, on the night of 3rd/4th November, they unleashed their might against Dusseldorf with 344 Lancasters, 233 Halifaxes and twelve Mosquitoes, a total of 589 aircraft. One of the Lancasters, piloted by Flight Lieutenant William Reid of 61 Squadron, was attacked twice by night fighters while en route to the target and suffered serious damage. Most of its guns were knocked out and both the navigator and wireless operator were killed as well as Flight Lieutenant Reid being injured in both attacks. Reid pushed on for the remaining 200 miles and the crew even managed to take an aiming point photograph. The return journey was filled with further problems as the oxygen supply failed and the windscreen was shattered. Reid slipped in and out of consciousness but recovered enough to make an emergency landing at Shipdham in Norfolk. For his courage in carrying out his attack and bringing the remainder of his crew back, Reid was awarded the Victoria Cross.

CHAPTER EIGHT

And then there were five

81 Operational Training Unit. R.A.F. Tilstock, Shropshire. 18ᵗʰ November 1943 to 31ˢᵗ December 1943.

As 1943 came to its conclusion the worldwide intensity of fighting reached its crescendo. In the skies over Germany 'Bomber' Harris unleashed his forces for the first of a series of raids over the next four months, which would come to be known as the 'Battle of Berlin'. In total Bomber Command would launch thirty two raids on large German cities in that period and exactly half of those would be on the German capital. The first was on the night of 18/19ᵗʰ November 1943 with a force of 440 Lancasters and four Mosquito's being despatched. The raid was seriously affected by complete cloud cover over Berlin resulting in the Pathfinder Mosquitoes having to mark the target blind and the Lancasters of the main force bombing in a similar fashion. As a result, the bombs were scattered across the city causing the destruction of four industrial premises and damage to twenty-eight others. Casualties on the ground amounted to 131 killed and 391 injured. As time progressed the raids would grow in both intensity and their destructive power; at last the world had found a way of taking the war directly to Hitler's front door and it's method of delivery was none other than R.A.F. Bomber Command.

Bernard left Little Rissington on 18ᵗʰ November 1943 and took a few days leave before beginning his posting to 81 Operational Training Unit at Tilstock with effect from 23ʳᵈ November 1943. However the dates here become a little cloudy as he didn't take to the air again until 13ᵗʰ December so his arrival date at Tilstock is a little uncertain.

The Airfield.

Tilstock is located in Shropshire, approximately twenty miles south-west of Stoke-on-Trent, and sixteen miles south-east of Wrexham. The actual airfield site lies in the triangle made between the junction of the A49 and A41 at Prees Heath, with the village of Tilstock about one mile to the west. Tilstock was a wartime airfield and was constructed by the McAlpine Company with three concrete runways and four T2 hangars. T2 hangars were transportable (hence the T) metal buildings with open spans of 97 feet 2 inches and a length of 239 feet 7 inches. The maximum door height was 25 feet as standard but all measurements could be varied slightly for local requirements.

The airfield was opened on 1ˢᵗ August 1942 and became home to 81 O.T.U. flying Armstrong Whitworth Whitley's in September the same year. 81 O.T.U. remained at Tilstock under Bomber Command until 1ˢᵗ January 1944 when it was transferred to No. 38 Group to train Horsa glider pilots for Special Forces operations, namely Operation Overlord or D-Day. In January 1945, 1665 Heavy Conversion Unit, flying Halifax's and Stirling's, moved in and the airfield played host to various training units until it was closed in March 1946. The airfield has now been returned mainly to agricultural use but several buildings remain, mostly in a poor state of repair.

The Aircraft.

The aim of the Operational Conversion Units was to prepare the pilots for the rigours of handling a large, multi-engine bomber. Up to this point, most pilots would have flown nothing larger than an Airspeed Oxford (wingspan 53 feet 4 inches, 16.26 metres) but were now being readied to handle one of the four engine 'heavies' such as the Avro Lancaster with a wingspan of 103 feet (31.1 metres). The first step towards this conversion required a large twin engine aircraft with reasonably benign handling characteristics and the Armstrong Whitworth Whitley fitted the bill perfectly.

The Whitley had its origins in Air Ministry specification B3/34 issued in July 1934, which called for a bomber capable of carrying a bomb load of 2,500lbs over a distance of 1,250 miles and at a height of 15,000 feet. The speed was bizarrely set at a maximum of 225 mph and the aircraft was to have an easily adaptable bomb bay and defensive armament in the nose, tail and amidships. The wingspan was to be restricted to 100 feet, as at the time that was the standard width of an R.A.F. hangar, and should have accommodation for a crew of five.

Several aircraft manufacturers looked at the specification but decided it was too expensive to fund a prototype alone and requested funding from the Air Ministry. In true government style, the Air Ministry would fund only one prototype and chose the Armstrong Whitworth design, designated the A.W.38. John Lloyd was the designer and produced a prototype with a new light alloy wing construction, made up of a torsion box design as opposed to the traditional rib design. On 17th March 1936 the A.W.38 flew for the first time, just eighteen months after the Air Ministry issued its specification. Due to pressure for the R.A.F. to expand and modernise, the Air Ministry had taken the unprecedented step of ordering eighty A.W.38's before the prototype had even taken to the air. Further expansion led to another 240 being ordered just two months after the A.W.38's first flight, by which time it had been allocated the name Whitley after the companies works site near Coventry.

One of the Whitley's design features was a maximum flaps angle of sixty degrees which gave a slow approach and landing speed as well as take off speed. This suited the airfields of the time, which were still mainly short, grass strips. The power was supplied initially by two 795hp Armstrong Siddeley Tiger IX radial engines which were later replaced by Rolls Royce Merlin X's producing a much improved 1,145hp. The Whitley boasted a wing span of 84 feet (25.6 metres) with a total wing area of 1,232 square feet. The fuselage measured 69 feet 3 inches (20.5 metres) and stood 15 feet high (4.57 metres). Maximum speed was just 186 mph for the MK.I but rose as high as 245 mph for the MK.IV, with a service ceiling ranging from 16,000 feet for the MK.I to 26,000 feet for the MK.V. Climb rates were slow in the early aircraft at just 550 feet per minute but following the engine upgrade this rose to 900 feet per minute and range peaked at 1,500 miles. The aircraft changed considerably over its seven incarnations and the extent of the change is evident in the dramatic rise in its weight from 14,275 lbs unladen for the MK.I to 19,605 lbs for the MK.VII. In total 1,737 Whitley's were produced, of which 1,466 were MK.V's, with the last one rolling off the production line in June 1943 as production focus was switched to the mighty Avro Lancaster.

The first squadron to be equipped with Whitley's was 10 Squadron at Dishforth, where the first arrived on 9th March 1937. In the early days of the war the type was involved in propaganda leaflet drops but as the fighting intensified the leaflets were soon replaced by real bombs. The Whitley took part in its last raid in significant numbers on the night of 29th/30th April 1942 with a raid on Ostend but continued to operate and helped to make up the numbers during the thousand bomber raids on Essen and Bremen. Its final operational sortie took place on the night of 15th/16th July 1944, when four carried out a leaflet drop over enemy territory. The aircraft saw service in a variety of roles such as with Coastal

Command and as a troop carrier for airborne forces as well as a tug for gliders and for dropping agents behind enemy lines.

Charles Turner Hughes, the chief test pilot at Armstrong Whitworth's, described the Whitley as 'a pleasant, easy aircraft to fly with no serious vices' and in all its formats, was described as a docile old lady with more good points than many later aircraft and boasted formidable structural integrity, being able to sustain considerable battle damage, a feature much sought after by all aircrews. Unfortunately this unglamorous old girl has been all but forgotten in the shadow of its more illustrious descendents, but the importance of its role and its place in the evolution of the heavy bomber should not be forgotten. The Whitley became obsolete during the war when resources were scarce and the remaining aircraft were broken up for scrap, with the exception of one which survived at Armstrong Whitworths until 1947 when that too was scrapped. By 1950 there was no complete Whitley left in the world.

The Operational Training Units were a complete departure from all the other units Bernard had been taught in or had been an instructor in himself. Up to then all efforts had been focused on simply producing competent pilots but the aim of the O.T.U.'s was to produce a competent bomber crew. The main drawback on arriving at the O.T.U. for a pilot was that he didn't have a crew; a problem that was soon to be solved. Most O.T.U.'s operated either Wellingtons or Whitleys, both of which had space for a crew of just five, but by that time the front line bombers, the Lancaster, Halifax and Stirling, were crewed by seven. As a result most crews formed into fives at an O.T.U. consisting of a Pilot, Navigator, Wireless operator, a Bomb Aimer (who doubled as front gunner) and a tail gunner. The other two, Flight Engineer and another Gunner, would join the crew later, usually at a Heavy Conversion Unit.

As you would expect the process of creating crews who would need to work together so closely and efficiently under extreme stress in order to keep themselves alive, while operating state of the art technical equipment, was highly evolved. For most crews the process involved all the men, whatever their role, being put in a hanger together with the door closed behind them and only being let out when they had formed a crew! It seems that the R.A.F. put little faith in any form of compatibility testing or psychology; it does seem however that human nature triumphed more often than not, creating crews that became like brothers and worked together like Swiss watches. There were, obviously, crews that didn't work well together but they seem to be the exception rather than the rule; maybe we could learn a lesson or two today from these simpler times.

Bernard leant against the wall of the hangar at Tilstock with his right hand thrust deep in his trouser pocket and drew regularly on the Players in his left. Within minutes two men sidled up almost ashamedly, probably attracted by Bernard's casual air and mature age which radiated a sense of reliability and inquired if he had 'crewed up' yet. The two men were a navigator, by the name of Jack MacDonald and Len Symmons, a wireless operator. Jack was a huge Canadian Sergeant, standing over six feet tall which was exceptional for the time. He had dark, wavy, unruly hair with deep set eyes and had a look of serious determination about him while Len appeared to be his polar opposite. Len Symmons was much younger than both Jack and Bernard and if anything was slightly shorter than Bernard. He was a youthfully handsome man reminiscent of a young Tom Cruise, with black, Bryl creamed hair parted immaculately on the left. Bernard looked them up and down, flicked his dog end on the hangar floor and beamed a warm smile across his mischievous face as he extended his hand to Jack and said, "I've just started to, welcome aboard."

Within a short time a bomb aimer in the form of Sergeant Jock Walker and a rear gunner named 'Doc' Boyd, had formed the main body of Bernard's Crew. Jock Walker stood around five foot five and as was the vogue of the day sported slicked, dark hair. He was a rugged man with a stocky, broad frame and a thick set, strong jaw, big hands and a mischievous grin. 'Doc', another Canadian, was quite large for a rear gunner, standing around five feet seven inches and had a youthful, studious look hence the nickname. Gordon Cardew the Flight Engineer and Les Bignell, the mid-upper gunner, would not join the crew until they arrived at their Heavy Conversion Unit. However, the 'crewing up' process would once again prove itself effective as the crew was to remain unchanged from that day on.

The newly formed crew took to the air together for the first time on the 13th December 1943. The sky was mainly cloudy with poor visibility and a light easterly wind but their instructor, Flying Officer Trotman, was more than satisfied that the weather was suitable enough for a brief familiarization flight. The fifteen minutes they had in the air certainly qualified as brief, whether it qualified as a familiarization is a matter for debate.

Ground instruction took precedence over the next few days and it wasn't until the 19th that the crew was airborne again. The early morning drizzle was soon replaced with a cloudy day interspersed with the odd, bright period and supplied good visibility accompanied by a 10-15 mph wind from the south-west. Flying Officer Dunlop took the men aloft for ninety-five minutes of circuits and landings and was satisfied with what he'd seen. The following day, with the weather continuing to play ball, Flying Officer Dunlop took full advantage and ran the crew through circuits and landings, overshoots, single engine flying, emergency landings, prop feathering, steep turns, evasive action and the tricky flapless landings in a flight that lasted an interminable three hours and ten minutes. On 21st December, Dunlop took them up again in unseasonably good conditions, for a half hour recap on circuits and landings, overshoots and emergency landings before declaring his satisfaction with them and hopping out of Whitley T4177 and letting them go off to practice on their own. The good weather continued and those pilots and crews who were deemed to be making satisfactory progress honed their skills unaccompanied by instructors. Earlier that day Bernard had turned his attentions to home and wrapped his Christmas presents for Ellen and Douglas which he sent home with an attached note.

My Darlings,
Here are my Christmas presents to the two dearest people in the world and with the presents go my very best wishes to you both for a very happy Christmas and a bright, peaceful New Year. God bless you, my darlings, and all my love to you.
Your ever loving and devoted Husband and Daddy.
xxxxxxx xxx

P.S. £2 enclosed for rent and £1 towards your outlay for Christmas presents. Just received your letter dear, and have to collect parcel this afternoon. Thank you darling and I will be writing tonight and tomorrow.
Bern.

On the 23rd December Bernard took to the sky for a further hour and twenty minutes, without his crew but with two other Sergeant pilots, Braid and Stecyk to practice circuits and landings, overshoots, single engine flying, steep turns and evasive action.

There was no leave for any of the crew that Christmas and Ellen and Douglas would be without their Husband and Father. Although there is no record of the days celebration, a clue can be found in the units official Operational Record Book which states; 'Christmas Day was observed as is customary in the R.A.F. Despite the restrictions and difficulties of supply an excellent day was had by everyone.'

Despite the previous days festivities it was back to normality on Boxing Day as the crew took to the air with fuzzy heads and dry mouths for a two hour practice of circuits and landings, overshoots, emergency landings, steep turns and evasive action. After discussion on the ground about their own performance they determined they could do it better and decided it was necessary to take to the air again on the same afternoon for further practice on their steep turns and evasive action. Whatever had not been right in the morning was rectified to their own satisfaction after another thirty-five minutes in the air.

The intensity of training continued as, on 27th December, in continued good weather, the crew were taken aloft by Pilot Officer Webb for instruction on high level bombing, beam approach and emergency landings which lasted an hour and a quarter. After dropping Webb safely back on the airfield, they headed off alone for another hour and forty minutes self practice until their own high standards were satisfied. The crew was by then beginning to knit together nicely as they honed their newly acquired skills and meshed each mans individual tasks into a team performance. On 29th December, Flying Officer Eastwood took the crew for an hour and a quarter's instruction on instrument flying in formation and single engine landings. Despite the steady drizzle over the Shropshire countryside, Flying Officer Eastwood supervised them on what would turn out to be their final flight at 81 Operational Training Unit, despite them not having yet completed their course.

On return to the airfield at Tilstock, the crew, along with all the other pupils of 81 O.T.U., were told to report to various new units around the British Isles. No reason was given to the men for the sudden change of plans and it is unlikely that any would have asked, after all, they knew they would not get an answer and in a war situation you did what you were told and that was that. Bernard's crew had been relocated to 28 O.T.U., at Wymeswold in Leicestershire, to complete their course and were due to report on New Years Day 1944. None of the aircrew leaving 81 O.T.U. would have known why at the time and probably never did; the reason as it turns out was that the unit had been transferred to 38 Group which had been set up specifically for training related to the upcoming D-Day landings of operation Overlord which would take place in June 1944. 81 O.T.U.'s role would be to train the tug pilots who would tow the Horsa gliders to such famous D-Day battles as the taking of Pegasus Bridge.

As the freshly formed crew headed off to their new home at Wymeswold, Bernard's promotion to the officer ranks, which he had received back in August, was published for the world to see in the London Gazette. Bernard officially became a Warrant Officer on the last day of 1943; he was no longer an enlisted man but an officer which fitted neatly alongside his long held position as a gentleman.

CHAPTER NINE

Toilet roll taxi

28 Operational Training Unit. R.A.F. Wymeswold, Leicestershire.
1ˢᵗ January 1944 to 19ᵗʰ March 1944.

Berlin continued to receive the undivided attention of Bomber Command as 1944 started with a 421 Lancaster raid on the night of 1ˢᵗ/2ⁿᵈ January followed by a 383 aircraft raid the following night. The city then received a much welcome respite until Bomber Command returned on the night of 20ᵗʰ/21ˢᵗ with a huge force of 769 aircraft. During that period the German night fighter force was taking a heavy toll of the attacking R.A.F. crews. The raid on 1ˢᵗ/2ⁿᵈ lost 28 Lancasters with a further 27 being lost the next night. In the following days a raid on Stettin on the night of 5ᵗʰ/6ᵗʰ accounted for fourteen Lancasters and two Halifaxes with the Berlin raid of 20ᵗʰ/21ˢᵗ suffering the loss of 22 Halifaxes and thirteen Lancasters. As bad as these figures were they were nothing compared to the disastrous night of 21ˢᵗ/22ⁿᵈ January which saw a force of 648 aircraft attack Magdeburg with a staggering loss of 57 aircraft. Twenty two of those were Lancasters making a loss rate of 8.8% but for the unfortunate Halifax crews the night was much worse with 35 aircraft lost at an unbearable loss rate of 15.6%. The beginning of 1944 was no time to find yourself in a bomber over Germany.

Christmas had passed at Tilstock in a haze of beer and cigarette smoke in the bawdy confines of the Sergeants mess. The contrast was striking as New Year was spent quietly and soberly at home with Ellen and the now fourteen month old Douglas toddling around and into everything. Both methods of celebration had been thoroughly enjoyed bringing Bernard much welcome relief from the pressures of flying training and keeping his mind from what he knew was to come. His newly formed crew was ordered to report to their new unit, 28 Operational Training Unit, based at Wymeswold in Leicestershire, with effect from 1ˢᵗ January 1944 in order to complete their half finished O.T.U. course, however they were not expected to turn up until Monday 3ʳᵈ January.

The Airfield.

R.A.F. Wymeswold was located in the Leicestershire countryside immediately west of Wymeswold village and north of Burton-on-the-Wolds, with its southern most extremity immediately north of the modern B676 road and most of the base's dispersed sites scattered around the village of Burton-on-the-Wolds itself. Loughborough is located just three and a half miles to the west and Nottingham eleven miles to the north.

Wymeswold was one of the many Bomber airfields built specifically for the war effort and was opened on 16th May 1942 with three concrete runways, two of 1,250 yards in length and one of 2,000 yards. It boasted one B1 hangar of Steel construction, with an open span of 120 feet and 227 feet 6 inches in length, with a door height of 27 feet, and four T2 types as described in the previous chapter. From the day it opened Wymeswold played host to 28 O.T.U. initially equipped with Vickers-Armstrong Wellingtons MkIII and MkX but later with Short Stirling's, Handley-Page Halifax's and also Avro Lancasters, before being transferred into the control of Transport Command on 15th October 1944 with 108 (Transport) O.T.U. taking over. The airfield was finally closed sometime in 1957 and has today, in part, been returned to agricultural use, with some of the existing buildings forming an industrial park.

The Aircraft.

At the time Bernard and his crew arrived, 28 O.T.U. was still equipped with the Vickers-Armstrong Wellington Ic. The Wellington was born out of response to Air Ministry specification B.9/32, issued in 1932, which requested a bomber capable of carrying a 1,000lb bomb load (454kg) over a range of 720 miles (1,160km). The aircrafts designer was the brilliant Barnes Wallis of bouncing bomb fame, who came up with a twin engine aircraft constructed from the now famous 'geodetic' construction. This meant that instead of the usual ribs and spars, the wings and fuselage were made of a metal lattice work which was then covered in doped fabric. This construction method made the aircraft light and flexible, a characteristic which took some getting used to, and most importantly made the Wellington capable of taking very high levels of battle damage and being quick and easy to repair.

The prototype, powered by two 850hp Bristol Pegasus engines, took its maiden flight on 15th June 1936 and considerably exceeded the requirements of the Air

Ministry's specification, being capable of carrying a 4,500lb (2,040kg) bomb load over a range of 2,200 miles (3,540km). When war broke out the Wellington was being produced in its Ia variant with powered front and rear turrets and improved 1,000hp Pegasus engines. The main factory was in Weybridge in Surrey, located inside the perimeter of the world famous Brooklands racetrack where Barnes Wallis was based and lived nearby in Fetcham, but production was further enhanced by two more factories in Chester and Blackpool. The airframe was upgraded and fitted with various engine types to fulfil a multitude of roles throughout the war and beyond. In total there were sixteen different marques, some of these with subdivisions of their own, with the MkIII being the main Bomber Command variant.

The Wellington was of similar size to the Whitley, upon which Bernard's crew had begun their O.T.U. course, with a wing span of 86 feet 2 inches (26.26m), length of 64 feet 7 inches (19.68m) and standing 17 feet 6 inches (5.33m) high. Empty, the MkIc flown by 28 O.T.U., weighed in at 18,556lb (8,417kg) and could reach a top speed of 235mph (379km/h), climb at 1,050feet per minute (320m) and reach a service ceiling of 22,000 feet (6,710m). Some later variants could reach 256mph (410km/h) and a ceiling of 38,000feet (11,600m).

The first Wellington entered service in October 1938 and the last would be delivered on 13th October 1945, after the war had finished. The aircraft made its last operational Bomber Command sortie on the night of 8/9th October 1943 but continued fulfilling vital secondary roles while still carrying out full operational missions in other theatres, such as the middle east and south-east Asia. In total 11,461 Wellingtons were built and it continued to see service as a trainer until 1953. Today there are very few examples remaining with only two complete aircraft in existence. One is located at the R.A.F. Museum Hendon and the other, which was discovered in Loch Ness whilst a hunt for the fabled monster was taking place, is on display at its birthplace at Brooklands where the museum is carrying out a complete restoration.

Bernard and his crew had been looking forward to their chance of getting airborne in the Wellington but poor weather with bad visibility prevented any flying for their first nine days at Wymeswold and it would be nearly three weeks before they could get off the ground. In the meantime their days were filled with ground lectures, wet dinghy drill training and physical training. Finally, on the afternoon of 21st January 1944, Flying Officer Muggeridge got them into the air in Wellington DV805 for a forty minute familiarization of circuits and landings.

The same was repeated by Pilot Officer Phillips for an hour and a half on the 23rd and when Phillips started with circuits and landings again on the 27th, the crew thought they would be bored to death. They were soon to be wrenched from their complacency as Phillips cut an engine and had them labouring to keep the Wellington aloft on the power of just one. Worse was to come as he demonstrated the single engine landing, with all the power on one wing the aircraft just wanted to turn and so had to be held steady with considerable corrective rudder and of course no power reserves to call upon if it all went wrong. Finally, just to put the cherry on the icing, Phillips took them through the overshoot procedure, which was basically how to pull out of a landing at the last minute if something went wrong and go round again to make another landing. With close proximity to the ground, low air speeds, running out of runway and then maximum power being applied, along with a fairly hefty pull back on the controls to climb away all thrown in, there was a high risk of the manoeuvre ending up as a large pile of scrap at the end of the runway, and it frequently did. Two hours and forty minutes after leaving the ground, Z1162 touched down safely and the exhausted crew staggered away vowing never to complain about circuits and landings again.

The skies over Berlin were becoming used to the sight and sounds of constant streams of Allied aircraft overhead unleashing their destructive power in the ongoing Battle of Berlin. The first raid of this epic aerial battle had been on the night of 18th/19th November 1943 and by the night of 20th/21st January the raids had grown in size from the 440 of that first raid, to a force of 769 aircraft made up of 495 Lancasters, 264 Halifaxes and ten Mosquitoes. However, despite the size of the attacking force there is a mystery surrounding the raid. As usual Berlin was completely cloud covered but the sky markers dropped by the Mosquito's appear to have been dropped correctly and the Lancasters fitted with H2S radar, which could see through cloud to identify landmarks on the ground, indicated that the force had mainly bombed the eastern area of the city. With no aerial reconnaissance possible, due to the cloud cover on the night, the R.A.F. had to wait for the usual German damage reports which they received via a series of reliable sources in the city. However, no reports came and when aerial reconnaissance was possible it showed little damage. What happened to the vast tonnage of dropped bombs was unknown but what they did know was that the German fighter defences were still very effective and as a result they had lost 22 Halifaxes (seven from 102 Squadron alone) and thirteen Lancasters; a loss rate of 4.6%.

The afternoon of 27th January was spent in the classroom and all the gathered aircrew were steeling themselves for another lecture on theory of flight or flaps, slats and air brakes. However their interest was guaranteed when they found out that the day's instructor was not one of 28 O.T.U.'s resident staff but a certain Flight Lieutenant Durnford. Durnford was attached to M.I.9 the organisation responsible for trying to assist Allied airmen to evade capture or to escape from prisoner of war camps. He briefed his hushed, transfixed audience on previous escapes, both successful and failed, and the lessons to be learned, along with the ingenious gadgets and aids that M.I.9 could supply.

Bomber Command continued the Berlin onslaught on the night of 27th/28th January with 515 Lancasters attacking and 33 of them failing to return home. Undaunted by the losses they were suffering in their attempt to destroy the German capital, they went back the following night with a force of 432 Lancasters and 241 Halifaxes. This time the losses were 26 Halifaxes and twenty Lancasters. With just one nights respite from the bombing, Bomber Command returned again on 30th/31st with 440 Lancasters and 82 Halifaxes; this time 32 Lancasters and a solitary Halifax were downed.

On 29th January, Bernard's crew was deemed competent enough to deal with the basics of flying the Wellington alone and 'soloed' that afternoon, performing circuits and landings, overshoots and single engine landings under the beady eye of Flying Officer Muggeridge, who, perhaps wisely, watched them from the safety of the control tower.

The weather in February showed no improvement over that of January with the conditions on fourteen days preventing any flying at all at 28 O.T.U. However, between 2nd and 8th February the crew managed to complete five flights totalling an amazing eighteen and a quarter hours, the longest of which was five hours forty minutes, by far the longest time any of them had spent in the air at one time. These long hours were put to good use where circuits and landings, overshoots, single engine flight and landings, cross country navigation exercises, high level bombing practice (above 10,000 feet) and fire drills were all honed. A lecture on the 10th brought home to all the pupils at 28 O.T.U. just how serious this flying lark really was, as Flight Lieutenant Boning from A.I.D.K.2 (a unit of Aerial Intelligence) gave a talk and showed a film on how to deal with interrogation at a German prisoner of war camp; it was moments like these that brought the young airmen down to earth with a bump and reminded them that this wasn't some big boys jolly paid for by the taxpayer.

DeHavilland Mosquito at R.A.F. Hendon

Having been pounded by Bomber Command, Berlin had been enjoying a fortnight of peaceful nights until on 15th/16th February they returned; launching what would be their final attack of the 'Battle of Berlin'. 823 aircraft; 561 Lancasters, 314 Halifaxes and sixteen Mosquitoes, made up the largest four engine bomber attack (the twin engine Mosquitoes were Pathfinders) of the war and dropped a record 2,642 tons of ordinance. Berlin, as usual, was cloud covered but damage in the city was extensive. Over 1,000 separate fires were reported with many war industries being hit. 26 Lancasters and seventeen Halifaxes were lost in the raid, but with the end of the 'Battle of Berlin' the bomber crews could breathe a collective sigh of relief as they would, from then on, only occasionally be required to fly the vast distance to the enemy capital.

The weather intervened again from the 9th and the crew would not return to the air until 16th February, but when they did it was to be at night. By the 21st they had spent eight hours twenty minutes night flying and were proficient both by Sun and Moon light. Much of the rest of February was lost to the weather but any 'airtime' was spent concentrating on high level bombing; the crew were beginning to feel like a tight knit unit as each exercise had become second nature and most importantly they were looking like the finished article to their instructors.

The first night of March again proved a sobering experience for the trainee crews. It was common practice for crews who were deemed competent enough, to be sent out on leaflet dropping (codenamed Nickel) raids over 'soft' targets in preparation for the real bombing missions that were to come. That night a Wellington from 28 O.T.U. was briefed to drop leaflets over Northern France and then to return and land at Lichfield. After successfully dropping its payload it crash landed at Cranfield after both engines cut out and one of the propellers dropped off. Thankfully all the crew survived, but the incident proved to the O.T.U. crews that there was no such thing as a 'soft' target or an easy mission.

The early days of March were taken up with fighter affiliation exercises before a few days leave came their way but the crew were back in the air for a final polish of skills on 10th March with a three hour night flight. The 12th saw a practice of Beam Approach, at which Bernard obviously excelled, and it was instantly decided that there would be little point revisiting that particular skill. Three more lengthy night flights followed in the next four days by which time the crew had proved themselves to be one of the best on the Unit. As a result they were shocked, if not surprised, to be chosen on the 16th March to take part in a Nickel raid. The feelings of apprehension can only be guessed at as they lifted off into the darkness of the Leicestershire night, unsure if they were ready, not knowing what lay ahead, or if they would meet the same fate as the Wellington that had crashed on its way back from France just a fortnight before. Despite the doubts they headed off on their first raid of the war ready to do their best no matter what. Unfortunately or fortunately, depending on the point of view, they soon hit a bank of cloud which steadily thickened to ten tenths cover at which point the bomb leader called the operation an abort and they all turned for home. Less than two hours after taking off, Bernard and his crew were back at base, relieved, disappointed, thrilled and a multitude of other emotional states all at once. Their life as a bomber crew had begun.

The next step on their operational career was only two days away. On the night of 18th March 1944, Bernard's crew, in Wellington X9936, along with two others from Wymeswold and three more from Castle Donington, took off on a Nickel raid (leaflet dropping) or bumph bombing as the aircrews called it, to northern France. Climbing into the night sky they headed due south over Reading having linked up with the Castle Donington aircraft on the way. At Reading they altered course slightly to the east and crossed the English coast above Selsey Bill. The Channel below would have appeared black and oily as they flew the route to the town of Ouisterham on the French Normandy coast. The unwelcoming sea had still not given way to French soil when one of the Castle Donington aircraft developed engine trouble and had to turn back, making a safe landing at Middle Wallop. The five remaining aircraft crossed the coast just west of Ouisterham and continued on with a slight course adjustment to the French town of Alencons, some 65 miles south-south-east of Ouisterham.

Over the target all five aircraft spilled out their bundles of leaflets, scattering in the air like confetti. The R.A.F. dropped many different leaflets throughout the course of the war and which ones were dropped that night is unknown, what is certain is that the vast majority of them would have been used by the locals as toilet paper. Having taken their 'bombing' photographs, which were later developed and proved the 'attack' to be accurate, the five turned for home following the same course they had flown out on. Having been in the air for five and a quarter hours Bernard touched X9936 down gently back at Wymeswold and successfully completed their first operation over enemy territory. The flight would not count towards their operational sorties tally but for the men of Bernard's crew, the knowledge that they had been good enough to successfully carry out their mission was reward enough.

At Wymeswold, with the instruction staff suitably impressed, the crew was graduated the following day and posted to 1656 Heavy Conversion Unit where they would learn to handle one of the mighty four engine heavy bombers and receive the final two members of their crew. Bernard received his usual assessment rating which simply stated; 'Assessment as a heavy bomber pilot: – Average.'

COURSE

SUMMARY of FLYING and ASSESSMENTS FOR ~~YEAR~~ COMMENCING 21st. JANUARY *19 44

[* For Officer, insert " JUNE " ; For Airman Pilot, insert " AUGUST. "].

		S.E. AIRCRAFT		M.E. AIRCRAFT		TOTAL for year COURSE.	GRAND TOTAL All Service Flying
		Day	Night	Day	Night		
DUAL				6·50	3·20	10·10	
PILOT				31.55	32.20	64.15	
PASSENGER		—	—	—	—	74.25.	

ASSESSMENT of . ABILITY

(To be assessed as :—Exceptional, Above the Average, Average, or Below the Average)

(i) AS A...HB...: † PILOT ......Average..............

(ii) AS PILOT–NAVIGATOR/NAVIGATOR.............

(iii) IN BOMBING ....

(iv) IN AIR GUNNERY.............

† Insert :—" F.", " L.B.", " G.R.", " F.B.", etc.

ANY POINTS IN FLYING OR AIRMANSHIP WHICH SHOULD BE WATCHED.

NIL

Date...19 - 3. 44

Signature.................

Bernard's 414A form for 28 O.T.U

CHAPTER TEN

Big Boys Toys

1656 Heavy Conversion Unit. R.A.F. Lindholme, Yorkshire & 1 Lancaster Finishing School. Hemswell, Lincolnshire. 20ᵗʰ March 1944 to 25ᵗʰ May 1944.

With the exploits of their Nickel raid still vivid in their minds, Bernard's crew dispersed for leave from 28 O.T.U. on 19ᵗʰ March 1944 with orders instructing them to report to 1656 Heavy Conversion Unit, based at R.A.F. Lindholme in Yorkshire, on 16th April. The role of the H.C.U. was to complete their transformation to a full bomber crew, firstly by adding their final two crew members and then teaching them how to operate one of the huge four engine 'heavies'.

The Airfield.

R.A.F. Lindholme was opened in June 1940 and was originally named Hatfield Woodhouse as it was near the village of the same name before being re-named in August 1940. The site is located to the west of Scunthorpe on the A614 between the junction of the M18 and M180 which of course did not exist during the war. The airfield consisted of three tarmac runways and was equipped with five 'C' type hangars as described in Chapter 7.

The first unit to be based at Lindholme was 50 Squadron, equipped with Handley-Page Hampdens, who arrived in July 1940 and stayed for a year. They were replaced by 408 Squadron, also with Hampdens, before 304 Squadron followed by 305 Squadron, both equipped with Vickers-Armstrong Wellingtons, succeeded them. 1656 Heavy Conversion Unit took over at Lindholme in October 1942 and stayed until the end of the war, being initially equipped with Avro Manchesters before upgrading to Handley Page Halifax Mk II and V's and ending with Avro Lancaster I and III's. 1656 H.C.U. left the site in November 1945 and the airfield was immediately closed. Today the old airfield is home to H.M. Prison Lindholme but several of the original buildings survive.

The Aircraft.

When Bernard arrived with his crew, 1656 H.C.U. was still equipped with the four engined Handley Page Halifax. It seems that most winning formulas are made up of partnerships, Laurel and Hardy, Fred and Ginger, Hurricane and Spitfire and of course Lancaster and Halifax. What? Halifax? Never heard of it would be most people's response, after all it was the Avro Lancaster that won the bomber war, wasn't it? No it wasn't, well not alone anyway. The Halifax played a huge role and made up a large percentage of the R.A.F's heavy bombers during the Second World War.

Both the Halifax and the Lancaster were born out of the Air Ministry directive 13/36 issued in September 1936, which called for a bomber capable of carrying an 8,000lb bomb load at over 200 mph. Strangely both companies set about building a twin engine bomber. Avro produced the ill fated Manchester, which later evolved into the superb Lancaster once two more engines had been bolted on, and the same happened at Handley-Page when designer, George Volkert, realised that a twin engine bomber would be hopelessly inadequate and opted to build a four engine bomber which would become the Halifax. The development of the Rolls-Royce Merlin engine was a godsend to both Avro and Handley Page and the first prototype Halifax took to the air on 25th October 1939 at Bicester. The second Halifax, fully equipped with working turrets, (the prototype did not have any turrets) took a further ten months to get airborne but the production line was already in full swing. As a result the first operational Halifax arrived at 35 Squadron on 23rd November 1940, daylight missions began in 1941 but the first night raid, which was against Le Havre, did not take place until 11th March 1942.

The Halifax was 70 feet one inch long (21.36m) with a wingspan initially of 98 feet ten inches (30.12m) which grew to 104 feet 2 inches (31.75m) as the aircraft was developed. The Halifax's height remained steady however at twenty feet nine inches (6.32m). The four Rolls-Royce Merlin's or Bristol Hercules engines produced a top speed of between 265mph and 312mph dependent on the marque, with a service ceiling between 22,800 feet (6,950m) and 24,000 feet (7,315m). The range also varied from marque to marque with a fully laden Mk I capable of a range of 980 miles and the Mk III capable of a range of 1,260 miles. The bomb load totalled 13,000lb and defensive armament consisted of a nose turret with twin .303 Browning machine guns, a mid-upper turret with a further two and a rear turret equipped with four. In total 6,176 Halifax's were produced compared to 7,377 Lancasters. The Halifax served under a variety of roles until it was finally phased out of service in 1952.

The night of 30th/ 31st March should have been a quiet night for Bomber Command as the Moon was full. However, meteorological reports suggested that high cloud would provide cover on the outward leg with clear skies forecast over the target of Nuremberg which would allow accurate ground marking. A reconnaissance flight, made by a met office Mosquito, reported that the conditions were in fact the exact opposite with clear skies on the approach but a cloud covered Nuremberg. Despite the risks the conditions posed, the raid went ahead with a large force of 795 aircraft made up of 572 Lancasters, 214 Halifaxes and nine Mosquitoes. The German night fighters were well controlled and accurately guided on to the bomber stream, falling on their prey as the bombers reached the Belgian border. In the ensuing battle 82 bombers were shot down on the outward journey alone. In total that night, Bomber Command lost 95 aircraft, 64 Lancasters and 31 Halifaxes, 11.9% of the force. That infamous night would turn out to be numerically Bomber Commands worst of the entire war.

During the raid, 22 year old Pilot Officer C. J. Barton, flying a Halifax from 578 Squadron, found his aircraft under night fighter attack from a Ju88 during which his aircraft was severely damaged. Following a communications mix up, three of his crew, the navigator, bomb aimer and wireless operator, all baled out but despite losing vital members of his crew, Barton decided to continue on to the target. Having dropped his bombs as best he could, he turned and headed in the general direction of England, even though the aircraft was by then flying on just three engines. With no navigator and a steady cross wind he was blown off course but managed to spot the English coast around the area of Sunderland. As the aircraft crossed the English coast it was running desperately low on fuel and lost power to two more engines leaving Barton no choice but to carry out a rather hurried crash landing. His three remaining crew walked away from the wreckage but Barton was killed in the crash. For his tenacity and bravery, Pilot Officer Barton was posthumously awarded the Victoria Cross.

Within days of arriving at Lindholme the skeleton bomber crew of Steel, MacDonald, Walker, Symmons and Boyd were added to with a Flight Engineer by the name of Gordon Cardew and a Mid-upper Gunner named Les Bignell. Gordon Cardew stood about five foot nine inches tall and had a youthful, studious, round face which was usually filled with a grin that involved all his features. He had an athletic build and was topped off by light, wavy hair which could not be tamed with Bryl Cream, so he never bothered trying. Les Bignell too had a round, youthful face but instead of a studious look he had the appearance of a bon vivant, usually clothed not with a collar and tie but with a cravat instead. He was a handsome man of around five foot seven with the slicked, dark hair common in the forties and an air of relaxed confidence about him. With their arrival the five had become the full complement of seven and would remain so until fate determined otherwise.

After nearly four weeks leave, the crew had to blow out a few cobwebs as well as integrate two new members and get to grips with a Halifax for the first time. As a result the first 'flying' Bernard undertook at Lindholme was in the Link trainer on the 19th April when he carried out a Beam Approach exercise. His performance in the Link must have impressed someone as two days later he was promoted again, this time to the rank of Pilot Officer. He finally got into the air for real on 23rd April, but even then he was without his crew. His first flight in a Halifax took place in the early afternoon when Flying Officer Pickles took him up in DT552 for a familiarization flight which lasted fifty minutes. Two more Beam Approach exercises in the Link came his way, one on the 26th and another on the 27th before the whole crew finally got airborne together on 29th April when Flying Officer Pickles took all seven of them up, this time in BB269, for two hours of circuits and landings. Once Pickles was satisfied, he let them loose on their own for another hour and thirty-five minutes of circuits. As their confidence rapidly grew and the crew meshed, they set forth for the third time that day but had to cut their practice short as BB269 developed a fault and had to land being declared U/S (unserviceable).

The night of 26th/27th April 1944 saw two raids by Bomber Command, with 493 aircraft attacking Essen and a further 215 Lancasters attacking Schweinfurt. During the Schweinfurt raid, a Lancaster of 106 Squadron was hit by a night fighter and a fire started in the starboard wing between the fuselage and the inner engine. Warrant Officer Norman Cyril Jackson had been wounded in the right leg and shoulder during the attack but as the Flight Engineer he took it upon himself to tackle the fire. As he crawled out of the cockpit escape hatch above the pilots head, his parachute opened and he was left dangling on the parachute lines as the crew held on to the canopy inside the cockpit. As he made his way towards the fire Jackson slipped and fell into the flames. Seeing that he was being burned the crew released his canopy and Jackson slipped off the wing and disappeared into the night sky with both his clothes and his parachute canopy alight. The pilot, realising that the fire would prove fatal to the stricken Lancaster, ordered his men to bale out and four of them landed safely, but the pilot and the rear gunner failed to escape and died as the aircraft crashed. When Jacksons crew mates were released from their prisoner of war camp at the end of the war, they recounted his tale of selflessness little knowing that he had actually survived his fall, despite landing heavily and shattering an ankle as well as suffering severe burns. In October 1945 Warrant Officer Jackson received the Victoria Cross for his actions.

The problem of faulty aircraft was a common one at conversion units as the aircraft were invariably old Squadron aircraft with plenty of hours on the clock, and more often than not had been battle damaged or suffered minor accidents. This, coupled with inexperience and lack of familiarity with the type of aircraft being flown, made the training for aircrew inherently dangerous. As if to prove the point, Halifax BB264 made a heavy landing on the intersection of the runways and crashed with the Pilot and Flight Engineer being admitted to hospital with minor injuries. A second accident followed on 29th April when Halifax E9437 crashed on take off to the north of the aerodrome inflicting minor injuries on all the crew. Once again these incidents served as a warning to the trainee crews and Bernard's crew wisely took them on board.

The following day was one of mental strain for Bernard by the end of which he was sick of the sight of the Link trainer and beginning to wish he had become an air gunner instead. The day was taken up with periods of ground instruction interspersed with three visits to the claustrophobic Link. The first half hour stint was an instruments exercise followed by two more Beam Approach exercises, each of forty-five minutes. As the day drew to a close and the crew gathered together, Bernard was looking forward to getting back into the air for real but mostly looking forward to his bed.

The weather at the beginning of May was fine and bright and allowed plenty of flying. The 1st of May saw the crew aloft again, firstly under the supervision of Pilot Officer Wellham, as he checked their progress with twenty-five minutes of circuits and landings. Once he was satisfied, Wellham set them free for a ninety minute local area flight. After lunch the crew swapped aircraft, leaving BB267 behind to be serviced, and took W7860 aloft under the guidance of Flying Officer Crawford. Once again the ageing H.C.U. Halifax let them down and they had to land after just twenty five minutes and once again declare the aircraft U/S.

3rd May was a sunny, clear day with near perfect visibility and the crew took to the air immediately after breakfast in W7860, which had by then been patched up from two days before. Their task for the day was a long duration cross country, navigating from point to point around the British Isles until they reached a pre-determined 'target' where they would practice bombing before returning home. The flight was the first real test of the crew, both in their compatibility and in their endurance and by the time they landed back at Lindholme nearly six hours later, they had at the very least proved that they had the latter.

The crew. Left to right, Jack MacDonald, Gordon Cardew, Bernard Steel, Jock Walker, Len Symmons, Les Bignell and 'Doc' Boyd

As if to further prove their endurance capabilities, the crew would be airborne again that evening. Flying Officer Pickles decided that a night flight was the order of the day and he seemed intent on tempting fate. Having flown an aircraft that morning that they had previously declared U/S, that night they would fly another that they had declared U/S, as they took up BB269 which was fresh from the repair hangar. For two and a half hours they performed circuits and manoeuvres, including three landings, before BB269 once again developed a fault and had to return to base to be declared U/S yet again. The early landing came as a relief for Bernard and his men after the longest day they had experienced so far with a total of eight hours and twenty minutes aloft. For once the unreliability of the ageing aircraft had worked in a crews favour.

The coming days would see more long duration exercises as the instructors prepared the crews for the long hours they would have to spend in the air while on operational duties. 5th May saw two night flights, the first under Flying Officer Brown, which lasted an hour and thirty-five minutes, followed by an instructorless cross country flight of a further two hours twenty-five minutes. The 6th saw their longest night flight to date with a six hour cross country which was a fair representation of an operational mission. Their final night flight at 1656 H.C.U. was a marathon six hours forty-five minutes at the end of which they were diverted to Blyton in Lincolnshire. The return from Blyton the following day would turn out to be their last under the umbrella of 1656 H.C.U. as the instructors were satisfied that the seven men who had been complete strangers just five months before had transformed into a functioning and able crew.

The crew had only one hurdle left between themselves and an operational squadron and that was a conversion course onto Avro Lancasters. The 11th May saw them leave Lindholme for a weeks leave and Bernard received the customary Form 414a Flying Assessment, upon which the pilots were invariably marked as average for ability. Bernard tucked the form inside his kit bag without even looking at it and got aboard the transport to take them to the railway station. An hour into the journey home boredom overcame him and he took the 414a out of his bag and read its assessment. A self satisfied grin slowly spread over his face and without saying a word he slipped it back into his bag. Noticing the little grin from across the carriage compartment Gordon Cardew piped up "What's tickled you then, Skipper?"

"Nothing much, it just never ceases to amaze me how few officers can spell average."

SUMMARY OF FLYI… AND ASSESSMENTS FOR COURSE COMMENC…

FORM 414 (A) 1943.

	S.E. AIRCRAFT		M.E. AIRCRAFT		TOTAL	GRAND TOTAL
	Day	Night	Day	Night	for course	All Service Flying.
DUAL	—	—	4·10	4·30	8·40	
PILOT	—	—	12·30	15·00	27·30	
PASSENGER	—	—	—	—		

ASSESSMENT OF ABILITY.
(To be assessed as – Exceptional, Above Average, Average, or Below Average)

(i)   AS A ....*H.B.*......... + PILOT .....*ABOVE AVERAGE.*

(ii) AS PILOT-NAVIGATOR/NAVIGATOR .....*NOT ASSESSED*

(iii) IN BOMBING .....*— "—*

(iv) IN AIR GUNNER .....*— "—*
      + Insert 'F' 'L.B.', 'G.R', 'F.B', etc.

ANY POINTS IN FLYING OR AIRMANSHIP WHICH SHOULD BE WATCHED.

NIL.

Date ....*11/5/44*.........   Signature .... w/c

                                     Officer Commanding ...*1656 H.C.U.*

Bernard's 414a from 1656 H.C.U. showing the rare assessment of above average

Once again Bernard's week of leave passed all too quickly and before he new it he was headed to No.1 Lancaster Finishing School based at R.A.F. Hemswell in Lincolnshire. The entire crew arrived on 19th May knowing that this was to be the final leg of their individual and joint training odysseys before their operational careers began.

The Airfield.

R.A.F. Hemswell was a pre-war airfield which opened in January 1937 and boasted three concrete runways and five main hangars, four 'C' types and a solitary T2. The airfield was located immediately to the east of the Lincolnshire village of Hemswell on the eastern side of the B1398 and on the northern edge of the modern A631 between Market Rasen and Gainsborough. Lincoln itself is eleven miles to the south with Doncaster 25 miles to the north-west. The first occupants were 61 Squadron and 144 Squadron who arrived together on 8th March 1937 and shared the airfield whilst flying a variety of aircraft including Avro Ansons, Bristol Blenheims, Handley Page Hampdens and Avro Manchesters before they both departed on 17th July 1941.

1 Group then took over the airfield and posted 300, 301 and 305 Squadrons to Hemswell in July 1941, all three of which were equipped with Vickers Armstrong Wellingtons. By the end of June 1943 all three had been posted elsewhere and the base had no permanent unit until 1 Lancaster Finishing School moved in during January 1944 and stayed until November. 83 Squadron came to keep them company in April 1944 and were subsequently partnered by 150 and 170 Squadrons until the end of the war with all three squadrons flying Avro Lancasters.

83 Squadron remained at Hemswell after hostilities had ceased, re-equipping with Avro Lincolns, the Lancasters successor, and stayed until January 1956. The airfield was eventually closed in 1967. Today the majority of the airfield has been returned to agriculture although stretches of two of the runways survive and the main body of buildings including the 'C' type hangers remain and are an industrial estate with other derelict buildings still scattered around the area.

The Aircraft.

The Avro Lancaster was not created but evolved though a series of design changes to its predecessor, the Manchester, as that aircrafts shortcomings were gradually identified one by one. The story begins with the same air ministry specification, P13/36, which gave rise to the Handley-Page Halifax, which called for a twin engine bomber capable of carrying an 8,000lb bomb load. Avro's answer was the Avro type 679 of which two prototypes were ordered. The first, which was designated the Manchester, was allocated the serial number L7246 and first flew on 25th July 1939. The aircraft was initially fitted with twin Rolls-Royce Vulture engines but they proved to be underpowered and unreliable. The engine problems were coupled with handling difficulties which led to an increase in wing span and the addition of a central tail fin in an attempt to overcome them.

The need for rapid re-armament to meet the growing German threat seemed to cloud air ministry thinking at the time and two hundred Manchester's were ordered before the prototype testing had been completed. As a result, although production began in August 1940, delays due to design modifications meant that the first examples did not arrive at squadrons until the end of November. The Manchester made its operational debut on the night of 24th/25th February 1941 during a raid to Brest but the shortcomings of the type were soon borne out by its losses as sixty eight were lost on operations and a further sixty three crashed; a shocking one hundred and thirty one out of just two hundred built.

However, the losses were not as a result of Roy Chadwick's design but mainly due to the shortcomings of the Rolls-Royce Vulture engine. The loss of one of the two engines meant that the other could not provide enough power to maintain height and a crash became almost inevitable as the above statistics show. Handley Page had already reacted to the shortcomings of the Vulture and as a result had fitted four Merlin's instead to produce the Halifax. The logical course of action for Avro was to follow the same route and following a minor change to the airframe, four Merlin's were fitted to the Manchester and the aircraft underwent a metamorphosis into the Lancaster prototype BT308 which had its inaugural flight on 9th January 1941.

The initial trials proved to be an unqualified success and with immediate effect the Air Ministry ordered that production of Manchester's should be swapped to Lancasters. The first operational squadron to receive Lancasters was 44 (Rhodesian) Squadron who took delivery on Christmas Eve 1941 and they flew their first bombing mission, to Essen, on the night of 10th March 1942. From then on production intensified and in total 7,377 were built. By the wars end Lancasters had carried out 156,000 sorties and dropped 608,000 tons of high explosives along with 51,500,000 incendiaries. 3,349 Lancasters were lost on operations. Although statistics can be manipulated to prove almost anything, one which illustrates the effectiveness of the Lancaster is that the tonnage of bombs delivered per aircraft lost for the Short Stirling was 41 tons, for the Handley Page Halifax 51 tons but for the Lancaster it was an astounding 132 tons.

The attributes which made the Lancaster such a formidable aircraft are demonstrated in its specifications. The size and strength of the aircraft are truly staggering even by today's standards. Its wingspan was 102 feet (31.1m) with a fuselage length of 69 feet six inches (21.2m) and a height of 19 feet seven inches (6m). Unladen the Lancaster weighed 36,500lb (16,700kg) with an all up weight of 68,000lb (30,800kg) with the bomb load alone being typically 14,000lbs but loads as high as the 22,000lb Grand Slam could also be delivered. As a comparison the Boeing B-17, the mainstay of the USAAF, could only cope with a normal bomb load of 6,000lbs.

The huge 22,000lb 'Grand Slam' bomb

Maximum speed was 287 mph at 11,500 feet with a cruising speed of 234 mph at 20,000 feet and a stall speed as low as 95 mph. The Lancasters versatility was also evident in its range, with 2,500 miles possible with a reduced 7,000lb bomb load but a more normal 12,000lb load gave a range of 1,750 miles at a service ceiling of 23,000 feet. This amazing performance was possible due to the combination of Roy Chadwick's superb airframe and the engine that won the war, the Rolls-Royce Merlin. The four units that powered the Lancaster produced various levels of horse power dependent on the variant fitted but typically gave 1,620 hp each on the Mk1. The combination of airframe and engine produced not only the most famous bomber of the Second World War but also the most effective and it is a prime example of necessity being the mother of invention. It was an aircraft loved by those who flew it and one that proved to be reliable and most importantly rugged. The Lancaster was capable of bringing its crew home when other aircraft would not and when it had no right to either.

The Lancaster continued in service after the war in a variety of roles and the last, in a maritime role, left service in 1956. However, officially it remains in service to this day with the Battle of Britain Memorial flight which still draws huge crowds wherever it appears.

The 'City of Lincoln' Lancaster of the Battle of Britain Memorial Flight

The crew settled in to their new home at Hemswell knowing, barring disasters, their stay there would be short and sweet. They had already completed their training at 1656 H.C.U. and were competent on most of the systems in a modern four engine bomber, the task in hand at 1.L.F.S. was simply to assimilate them with the mighty Lancaster. After a couple of days ground school and static familiarization, the crew finally took a Lancaster off the ground on the morning of 22nd May 1944 aboard W4859, under the supervision of Pilot Officer Adams, for a two hour familiarization flight. The morning was fine and bright with cloud at three to 4,000 feet and the crew seemed to take quickly to the Lancaster. With the initial flight having passed without a hitch, they were sent up in the early afternoon haze to practice alone for an hour which included several circuits and landings. As the day drew to a close, Pilot Officer Adams rejoined them for their third and final flight of the day to check on their progress and within twenty-five minutes declared himself satisfied.

The following morning was cloudy with 9/10ths cloud cover above 3,500 feet but proved no bar to an early re-cap flight. Having satisfied themselves with their progress, the crew spent the afternoon undergoing ground instruction in preparation for their first night flight which would follow that evening. As the light faded, the crew took up their positions around the aircraft almost as if acting out a dress rehearsal for the main event that was to come. Bernard took W4264 into the air under the supervision of Flying Officer Rees for a further hour and ten minutes exploring the darkness. Once again their instructor was soon satisfied with their progress and allowed them a further hour and a half to experience a Lancaster in the dark for themselves.

The evening of the 24th May brought fair conditions with small amounts of cloud at 3,000 feet and above. Two short flights, both of under an hour, were enough to convince the instructors that they were the finished article. After just three days, and nine hours flying time in a Lancaster, the crew was finally deemed ready to take on the Germans in a frontline, operational squadron.

Bernard had been in the R.A.F. for three years and nine months and had flown eight types of aircraft, either as a pupil or as an instructor, in ten different units. His flying time totalled 1,795 hours and many of them had been extremely difficult but without a doubt the most difficult were about to come, and this time they would be over enemy territory.

CHAPTER ELEVEN

Into the Reich

*166 Squadron, R.A.F. Kirmington, Lincolnshire. 26ᵗʰ May 1944
to 25ᵗʰ June 1944.*

Bernard and his crew arrived at Kirmington on 26ᵗʰ May 1944 and were taken to their quarters at No.7 Dispersed Site, which was just about as far from the airfield as you could get. Located away from the main site to the east, the collection of 22 buildings was an array of construction styles including Laing huts, Nissen huts and the more luxurious temporary brick constructions. The crew drew the short straw and found themselves in a Nissen hut, which were notorious for being unbearably hot in the summer and equally as cold in the winter. With the month of May not yet bringing the hot temperatures of high summer, their accommodation was enjoying a rare spell of comfort but that would inevitably change. As it turned out their particular dispersed site suffered more than most as the flies and midges, attracted to the pond located behind the trees to the back of their site, infested the huts if the windows were left open.

With the joys of the local wildlife yet to be experienced, Bernard and his crew took to the air the very next day aboard Lancaster LM388 for a cross country and bombing exercise. Over the next four days they carried out a further three cross countries before being declared ready for operations; the training had finally ended; the time had come for the real thing.

The Airfield.

R.A.F. Kirmington was located in the Lincolnshire countryside adjacent to the eponymous village and midway between Scunthorpe, twelve miles to its west, and Grimsby to the east and lies today adjacent to the A18. The airfield was purpose built for the Second World War and was opened in October 1942 sporting three concrete runways, all three of which were extended from the standard length before the station was opened. The main runway length was increased from 1,450 yards to 2,000 yards, which involved the diversion of the A18 road to the north, while the other two were increased from 1,100 yards to 1,400. As well as the usual array of dispersed sites spread around the surrounding countryside and in the village of Kirmington itself, the base was equipped with two T2 Hangars and a single B1 type. The B1 hangars were bigger than the T2's with an open span of 120 feet, 227 feet long with a door height of 27 feet and were constructed using a steel frame which was then usually clad with corrugated steel sheets.

The first unit to occupy the base was 150 Squadron flying Wellingtons who arrived on its opening but only stayed until the end of 1942. They were then replaced by 142 Squadron who stayed for even less time, lasting just 39 days before being replaced by 166 Squadron on 27th January 1943. 166 Squadron stayed put for the duration of the war and finally left on 18th November 1945 when the squadron was disbanded. The station was mothballed in February 1946 with only a skeleton staff remaining to maintain the site until it was finally handed over to the Ministry for Agriculture in 1953. Some small aircraft continued to use the site and in the late 1960's a charter service began to operate and the seeds of change were sowed. In 1970 it was decided the site should be developed to become Humberside airport and the runways were refurbished resulting in the A18 being restored to its original route which now leaves a small section of the original runway cut off to the north of the site. The new airport finally opened in 1974 and today operates passenger and cargo flights right across Europe and handles up to 500,000 passengers a year.

Having spent nearly four years in the R.A.F., Bernard's baptism into the world of combat operations finally came on 2nd June 1944. At 1430 hours that afternoon, the station teleprinter rattled into life and began to print out Form B, the instructions and details for that night's raid. The order of battle, a list of the crews who would be taking part, had been posted earlier in the day and he saw that he was to ride along with an experienced crew, piloted by Pilot Officer Boles, in Lancaster NE647. His first operational mission, as was usual, was to be an experience gathering one where he would do little more than observe from the Lancasters foldaway, co-pilots seat. The briefing room was a cacophony of chatter, nervous laughter and the sound of scraping chairs with a heavy atmosphere of anticipation mixed with tobacco smoke. By the time Wing Commander Garner walked in accompanied by the intelligence officer, which immediately hushed the men and caused them to stand to attention almost as a reflex action, the rumours of the target for the night had travelled several times around the room and its possible location had changed as many times.

As the sheet covering the map was pulled away, there was an audible sigh of relief as the red ribbon denoting the route led to the realisation that their target was to be a short run to the French coastal batteries around Calais, which meant only the briefest of time to be spent over enemy occupied territory and not some lengthy trek into the heartland of Germany. The briefing covered the raid in every detail from fuel and bomb loads to navigation and rendezvous points, down to the colour of marker flares to be used by the Pathfinders and the code words for the Master Bomber, main force and various possible eventualities, such as abandoning the mission. By the time it was over, Bernard was pleased to have had the opportunity to get some experience of the whole process without having to bear the burden of responsibility.

As darkness began to close in across the airfield, the twenty crews of 166 Squadron were ferried out to their dispersal points and their waiting aircraft. The ground crews were busily finalising their preparations with each Lancaster having 1,265 gallons of fuel pumped into its tanks and a bomb load made up of eleven 1,000lb and four 500lb high explosive bombs, making a total bomb load of 13,000lb. Although the coastal guns of Calais were considered an easy target by the crews, as Bernard climbed into the aircraft he could not help but feel emptiness in the pit of his stomach, similar to the feeling you get when you think you're going to fall off the back of a chair. With all the checks out of the way, Pilot Officer Boles started each of the mighty Merlin engines in turn and waited for them to reach the correct temperature. Eventually the time came for NE647 to taxi towards the runway and after holding station at the end for a brief time, at 2305 hours, the green light flashed at them from the black and white signal van prompting Boles to push forward the throttles allowing the Lancaster to begin its acceleration down the runway and into the air.

Once they were airborne Boles climbed steadily and his navigator, Flight Sergeant Hughes, gave him a heading for the first rendezvous point, which was to be over Orford Ness on the Suffolk coast to the east of Ipswich. When they arrived at the prescribed point they were in the company of 62 other aircraft who then headed directly to their target. From the rendezvous point, the force of Lancasters maintained a direct route southward for 75 miles taking them to the east of the Strait of Dover. As they crossed the coast into ever thickening cloud, Boles ordered his gunners to test their weapons and Hughes gave Boles a new heading of 170 degrees (south-easterly) onto which he turned and began to cross the dark Channel waters. By then the aircraft were at between eight and ten thousand feet and once they came to within twelve miles of the French coast they began regularly ejecting bundles of 'window' (metallic strips which confused the German radar) which they would continue to do until they were heading home, back across the Channel. The Lancaster powered on toward the enemy coast where the German flak defences had begun firing but the crew had no choice other than to continue on their course as they were effectively on the bomb run. Just before they reached the coast Bernard saw a Lancaster just above and in front of them take a hit from flak, it steadily began to fall away from the bomber stream until, after a few minutes, he lost sight of it altogether in the darkness of the night.

The target was being marked that night by four Mosquitoes from the Pathfinders of 8 Group who were using the OBOE navigation system and at 0027 hours, in the distance, Bernard saw the glow of red and green flares as the Mosquitoes dropped their first target indicators. The orders for the night specified that the first 25 aircraft to bomb were to be manned by the best crews available, with particular attention being paid to the quality of the bomb aimers. Sergeant Dickinson, the bomb aimer for Boles' aircraft, more than qualified for that accolade and so, at 0030 hours, NE647 began its bomb run. Below them was a covering of 8/10ths thin cloud which allowed the glow of the target indicators to still be clearly visible. The first aircraft began bombing at 0031 hours and Bernard could see the flashes through the cloud as the bombs exploded. Immediately there was one huge explosion, probably an oil store, which sent a thick black plume of smoke skyward which eventually reached their altitude at 10,000 feet and within moments, a similar explosion added to the smoke and cloud that covered the target. The ground defences were still mercifully light, with only the odd burst of flak, which made the sight of the Lancaster being hit earlier on even harder to take. Moments after the second huge explosion had begun sending its smoke plume skyward; it was their turn to bomb as Boles received instructions from his bomb aimer, Sergeant Dickinson. The moments as the Lancaster headed into the fray seemed to last forever and although the flak was still relatively light, Bernard could not help but feel even more vulnerable than he had when he witnessed the unfortunate aircraft being hit as they approached the coast. Eventually Dickinson was happy he was in the right place and at 0032 hours, from a height of 8,000 feet, announced 'bombs gone' and as he did so the aircraft simultaneously leapt upward as it was relieved of its 13,000lb load. With the bombs gone and the obligatory photograph taken, Hughes issued another course change instruction to his skipper and Boles turned the aircraft towards the town of Ardres, about seven miles to the south-east of Calais.

The home leg of the journey had to take into account the three other raids going on in the same area and also had to avoid known flak battery sites along the coast and around other towns. No sooner, it seemed, than Boles had changed onto his new course as instructed by his navigator; he was being issued with yet another.

"New course, Skipper. 045 degrees." Instructed Dickinson.

"045 degrees." Repeated Boles as he banked to port (left) onto his new heading which would take him and his crew to the coastal town of Gravelines. The speed that the crew worked at without a hint of being in any way flustered and the sheer economy by which they operated impressed Bernard while also causing him to wonder if he and his crew would be anywhere near as slick when their turn came.

After just over thirteen miles on the 045 degree heading, Dickinson piped up again. "New course, Skipper. 344 degrees." And with that Boles again banked to port and onto a north-westerly heading which would take them over the French coast and all the way back to Orford Ness where they would make the final course adjustment to take them back to the safety of Kirmington.

As Bernard saw the eastern English coast emerge from the gloom, his nerves began to leave him for the first time that night. Hopefully, he thought; when he was actually busy flying he would be too preoccupied to feel nervous. As the Lancaster touched down at 0150 hours on the morning of 3rd July, he felt a mixture of relief, excitement and satisfaction that at last he had been part of an offensive operation but he realised that soon he would not just be observing but actually doing it himself; a realisation that both scared and excited him.

The raid itself had been relatively inaccurate, mainly due to the cloud cover which had worsened as the raid went on and only thirteen of the twenty aircraft that set out from 166 Squadron actually dropped their bombs, but the main aim of the operation was really to convince the Germans that the invasion, which would take place just three days later, was to be launched at Calais and not Normandy, and in that it succeeded. The aircraft that Bernard saw being hit by flak belonged to 166 Squadron and was Lancaster ND651, piloted by Pilot Officer G.D. Jones. All seven of the crew were killed and are buried in Marquise Communal Cemetery.

Bernard hardly had time to draw breath before the Order of Battle was posted for the following day, 3rd June, and this time he and his crew were selected as the twentieth and last crew on the list of the selected primary crews and had been allocated Lancaster X–X-ray, LM581. The briefing had helped to set the men's nerves at rest as their target was revealed as being the Wimereux coastal gun battery, just two miles to the north of Boulogne, and, as an added morale boost, Wing Commander Garner would be piloting C-Charlie, ME746. If the boss was going, they reasoned, the powers that be must be confident it was a simple to find and lightly defended target, not too far into enemy territory.

The early summer sun had already disappeared and been replaced with the cloak of darkness as the men were dropped off at their dispersal point. Bernard knew exactly how each of his men felt at that moment, as he had experienced it the night before. By comparing how he had felt the previous night, he knew that nothing would ever feel like the moments before that first operation. He was keen to encourage and support all of his men as they found previously dextrous hands reduced to clumsy paws and their voices hinted at the tiniest touch of vibrato. Bernard, who had felt exactly the same way twenty four hours earlier, now exuded, outwardly at least, an air of calmness and confidence. Inside he was still nervous and fearful but he had eradicated the fear of the unknown at least. Each of the crew climbed into the aircraft in what was that night a purely random order, but that order would not change for their entire time together in deference to the gods of chance. Bernard wandered around the outside of the Lancaster, peering up at her huge form and checking that all was in order while all the time the ground crew bustled around him. Standing beneath the starboard wing he lit one last Players and watched the smoke dissipate into the night before throwing it, half smoked, on the ground and grinding it out with his left foot. Gently and subconsciously he patted the huge tyre of the right undercarriage and with that, he became the seventh and final man to climb aboard.

He made his way along the cramped fuselage and climbed over the bulkhead of the main spar and settled himself into the pilot's seat, then called up on the intercom and requested that everyone check in to confirm their intercom was working. 'Doc' Boyd in the rear gunner's seat, Les Bignell in the mid-upper gunners, Len Symmons the wireless operator, Jack MacDonald the navigator, Jock Walker the bomb aimer and Gordon Cardew the flight engineer all confirmed they were present and correct, and, after replying to Bernard, busied themselves with their own specific pre-flight checks and tasks.

In the cockpit, Bernard and Gordon Cardew ran through their checks together, the engine booster pumps all showed over the required 130lb psi and the ground/flight switch was flicked over to flight. Bernard prepared to start up by setting the Master Engine cocks to off, opened the throttles by half an inch and set the propeller controls to fully up. The supercharger settings were set to the M ratio, air intakes to cold and the radiator shutters to automatic. Gordon selected no.2 fuel tank as was required for take off and turned on the Master Engine cock for the first engine to be started, along with the ignition and booster coil, and then pressed the starter button on the right hand side of the instrument panel. The propeller slowly turned with the whine of the electric starter motor before the cylinders began to fire in what seemed to be a random order, until eventually, the beast of the Merlin engine finally leapt into life with a huge discharge of exhaust fumes as if it had belched after enjoying a big meal. Once all four engines were running smoothly, Gordon turned off the booster coil switch and Bernard slowly increased the rev's on each engine to 1,200 r.p.m. at which speed he left them to warm up while he checked temperatures, pressures and the hydraulic system by lowering and raising the flaps. Finally he opened the radiator shutters, checked the magnetos and the operation of the constant speed propellers and once he was satisfied all was in order, settled back to await his instruction to taxi.

At just after 2330 hours, the crew of LM581 were ordered to begin taxiing to the end of the runway. Bernard carried out the final few checks, navigation lights on, altimeter set, and the correct vacuum readings on each pump before giving the signal for the ground crew to remove the chocks and releasing the brakes. The roar from the four Merlin's obliterated all other sounds as he pushed the throttles forward and the lumbering Lancaster began to inch forward. Eventually the aircraft was manoeuvred around the perimeter track towards the end of the runway, the last in a line of twenty, where he brought her to a halt and awaited the signal to go. He ran through the final list of checks, compass setting to normal, Pitot head heater on, trimming tabs correctly set and Gordon checked the fuel tanks and their settings one final time as Bernard set the flaps to twenty degrees down. By the time he had done all that, at 2341 hours, he looked up just in time to see the black and white van flash its green light at him and signal the start of their first sortie.

Bernard released the brakes and eased the throttles gently forward with the port side engines being revved slightly higher to compensate for the Lancasters tendency to swing to port. The aircraft accelerated down the runway until the tail lifted and he got a clear view ahead of him for the first time. The speed gradually climbed until, when the gauge showed 100 mph, he eased the aircraft off the ground and began a steady climb. As he raised the undercarriage the aircraft dipped its nose slightly and he readjusted as he gained airspeed and height and then the first instruction from another member of the crew came through his headphones. "168 Degrees skipper, we're heading for Brentwood". Declared Jack MacDonald.

"Good, I've always wanted to bomb Brentwood! 168 Degrees". Bernard confirmed, injecting a touch of humour. The little ripple of laughter and the accompanying grin which spread through each of the crew was just enough to break the tension and went a long way to easing each of the men into their tasks. From there on in they would find that for the vast majority of the time they would be too busy to even think about being nervous.

The twenty Lancasters of 166 Squadron which were heading south to Brentwood, made up part of a total force of 61 primary bombing aircraft that would be attacking the gun battery at Wimereux along with four Pathfinder Mosquitoes from 8 Group to mark the target. As they arrived at between 8,000 and 9,000 feet in the skies over Brentwood, the force formed up and changed course to head for Tonbridge in Kent. Making their way over the blacked out landscape of southern England, Bernard gently, slowly and deliberately manoeuvred his aircraft until he formed up just to the rear of, and slightly below one of the other Lancasters in the bomber stream. Conventional thinking would say that the safest place to be from night fighters would be above and in front of any other aircraft, but Bernard's logical mind reasoned that he was more likely to be shot down by flak than a night fighter and that the flak gunners would always start firing at the lead aircraft and probably over estimate height. His theory was nonsense and he knew it, but that would be his answer should anyone inquire. The real reason was that the night before he had seen another crew from 166 Squadron be hit and killed from a position above and in front of him while he had survived. Tempting fate was not a pastime he intended to start dabbling in now; if it had worked once, then it was good enough for him.

By the time the aircraft passed over Tonbridge and made their port turn towards Hythe on the Kent coast, Bernard had secured himself in the position he had desired. The clouds were providing 10/10ths cover over England reaching to a height of 12,000 feet and the aircraft was behaving perfectly as was confirmed by the occasional broad grin and thumbs up from Gordon Cardew his Flight Engineer. In addition the rest of the crew seemed to be operating as efficiently as he had hoped. Jack MacDonald called out the course directions and changes at regular intervals and informed Bernard to turn onto a bearing of 105 degrees just as the aircraft in front of him began to turn. The confidence in his crew, which he had built up over the previous few months, was already proving to be well founded he thought, and he allowed himself a little smile in recognition of the fact.

"Crossing the English Coast at Hythe, Skipper. New bearing of 130 degrees. That should take us straight to the target". Informed Jack.

For the second time in twenty four hours Bernard found himself leaving the safety of England and heading across the inky black Channel below to drop tons of bombs on something he couldn't see. 'Funny old world' he thought. The short, thirty mile hop over the water passed in a flash and at 0112 hours the three remaining Mosquitoes (one had returned home with a technical problem) began to drop their red and green markers, which they repeated just one minute later. At just after 0115 hours the first of the primary aircraft arrived over the target and began dropping their deadly load. As they neared the French coast the heavy flak guns, both on shore and on flak ships, unleashed their shells at the bomber stream and four of 166 Squadrons aircraft received hits. The gunners, Les Bignell and 'Doc' Boyd, scanned the night sky, expecting to see night fighters everywhere in the moonlight but saw nothing. They were pleased at the time, for obvious reasons, to draw a blank but became somewhat more apprehensive and concerned at their own abilities when they later discovered that there were at least four formations of six enemy aircraft lurking out there somewhere who were spotted by other crews.

Towards the back of the 61 aircraft, Bernard began to take his instructions not from his navigator but from his bomb aimer, Sergeant Jock Walker. As the first main force aircraft began to drop their bombs, Bernard and his crew found themselves on the final stages of their bomb run with the bomb bay doors open ready to unleash their load. The thick cloud through which they had flown over England had gradually dissipated as they crossed the Channel and over the target there was only a 2/10ths covering of thin cloud which gave them near perfect visibility in the bright moonlight. Jock Walker could see that the target indicators were tightly grouped together and so should have resulted in a good concentration of bombing. As the markers came into his bombsight Walker held the brown, Bakelite bomb release button in his right hand with his thumb poised on top of the spring loaded button. With Bernard keeping the aircraft as steady as he possibly could, the rest of the crew peered through the darkness to see the brightly burning fires caused by the early bombers, which appeared to be tightly grouped around the target indicators.

As Jock stared through his bombsight the smoke below was beginning to obscure the markers but eventually he satisfied himself that he was in the right place with his crosshairs on a cluster of red target indicators that were burning on the ground. At 0118 hours and from a height of 9,000 feet, Jock Walker firmly depressed his thumb, bringing his fist down at the same time as if he were thumping an imaginary table, and called over the intercom, "Bombs gone!" The aircraft lurched upwards as one huge 4,000lb 'cookie' and sixteen 500lb high explosive bombs left the bomb bay and within a few seconds of their exit the bomb bay doors had been efficiently closed. The Lancaster maintained its course long enough to take the required bombing photograph and then, back under the instructions of Jack MacDonald, headed out into the French countryside. Just seven miles further on Jack called a new heading of 206 degrees and Bernard threw the aircraft into a sharp starboard (right) turn, deliberately losing height as he did so. Within moments Jack barked through another course change to 292 degrees and again Bernard threw the Lancaster into a starboard turn. By the time he had completed the first sharp turn, he had dropped his height to below 7,500 feet, as instructed at the briefing, in order to avoid aircraft attacking other targets in the area. With the second turn safely negotiated the crew had just a few miles of enemy territory left to fly over before crossing the French coast and heading for the relative safety of the English coast, which they would cross just to the east of Hastings.

With more and more of the Channel slipping beneath them, the crew began to slowly relax while all the time remaining vigilant for night fighters and also for other bombers so as not to have a mission spoiling collision. As the English Coast passed beneath them and they turned towards Reading, the rest of the crew felt that air of relief that Bernard had felt the night before. The flight up from Reading across England to Kirmington became increasingly lonely as various aircraft peeled away to their own bases until, eventually, at 0310 hours, Bernard too gently landed LM581 back on the tarmac at Kirmington, three and a half hours after they had left it. As the engines came to a stop he called up his crew on the intercom, "Well done men, a job well done." he congratulated, and with that they had successfully completed their first sortie.

The night of 3rd/4th June had been a good one for Bomber Command. 100 aircraft, 96 Lancasters and four Mosquitoes, had attacked and completely wiped out a German signals station at Ferme-d-Urvile, while two other raids, one of which was the one Bernard's crew was on, totalling 127 Lancasters and eight Mosquitoes, successfully attacked the Wimereux and Calais coastal batteries, all without the loss of a single aircraft.

By 4 o'clock on the morning of 4th June they had successfully completed their first operation and Bernard was delighted with their performance, despite it being a straightforward mission. For a first run out he felt they had performed confidently and calmly and was reassured that his crew would turn out to be one of the best. He was not alone, throughout the war virtually every aircrew member was convinced that his crew was the best; it was just as well they did, as they probably would never have got into the aircraft if they felt any other way.

The 4th June saw 166 Squadron being stood down from operations which gave

Bernard and his crew time to reflect on their first sortie. However, the 5th saw the Order of Battle being posted again and once more the crew were one of the 25 aircraft that 166 Squadron would have in action that night. The crews were not aware of the magnitude of the events in which they were about to play a part, even during the briefing they were not told exactly what that nights operation was really about, just that it was a vital part of the war effort and that every effort should be made to press home their attacks and to make them accurate. The reality was that this was D-Day and the men of Bomber Command were to be the opening salvo in what would go down in history as the Longest Day.

During the afternoon and evening of 5th June 1944, a huge armada of ships left the shores of England and headed towards the Normandy coast of France. For months, thousands of troops had been gathered together and trained to their peak in the southern countryside of England and the time had come for them to be unleashed on the German defensive positions along the French Channel coast. Having already been delayed by poor weather, General Eisenhower took a gamble and decided that D-Day would be 6th June 1944. The operation, codenamed Overlord, began at just after 2200 hours on 5th June as British and American parachutists and glider borne troops took off from airfields across southern England. By midnight the first of the aircraft were beginning to arrive in the skies over Normandy which was well lit by bright moonlight. Meanwhile the vast naval fleet was heading across the Channel made up of over 2,700 ships carrying or towing another 2,500 landing craft and escorted by 700 warships including five battleships, 25 cruisers and over 100 destroyers. Their destination was five beaches along the Normandy coast; the British beaches were codenamed Sword, in the area around Ouistreham, and Gold around Arromanches. The Canadians were to land on Juno beach, around Bernieres, while the Americans landed at Utah beach near La Madeleine on the Cotentin peninsular and Omaha beach around St. Laurent and Colleville.

At 0000 hours on 6th June the first parachutists of some 20,000 to drop that night, began to fall through the skies. There were three airborne divisions in total; two American, the 82nd and 101st Airborne and the British 6th. Their aim was to support the landings by knocking out enemy communications, gun batteries and to secure vital bridges before the Germans could destroy them. By dawn the first French village, St Mere Eglise, had been liberated by the Americans while the British Parachute Regiment had taken, and were continuing to hold, the vital bridge over the River Orne at Caen; the bridge that would famously be renamed Pegasus Bridge in their honour.

As an example of the planning that had gone into the operation, following the huge armada, the Allies would tow huge concrete caissons across the Channel which would be flooded off the French coast to form two harbours, known as the Mulberry Harbours, as well as a fuel pipeline which started from the southern coast of the Isle of Wight and was codenamed PLUTO, pipeline under the ocean.

At 0630 hours the first American troops set foot on Utah beach while the first British troops landed on their beaches at 0730 hours. Wave after wave of troops were put ashore until, by the end of the day, some 155,000 men had been landed and so the largest seaborne invasion in history had truly begun.

While the Allied invasion force steadily made its way across The Channel to the beaches of Normandy, Bomber Command sent a huge force of 1,012 aircraft, 551 Lancasters, 412 Halifaxes and 49 Mosquitoes, to bomb ten different coastal batteries which were defending it. All but two of the targets were cloud covered and bombing was carried out using OBOE marking. In total 5,000 tons of bombs were dropped which set a new single night record for the war so far and Bernard and his crew were to play their part in it.

In addition to the direct attacks on the Normandy installations, Bomber Command sent a further 110 aircraft in support operations, such as jamming night fighter radar. A further 58 including the aircraft of 617 Squadron, the Dambusters, dropped a trail of window (foil strips which showed up on enemy radar as contacts) steadily across the Pas de Calais as a decoy to simulate a large convoy of ships approaching the enemy coast far to the east of the real invasion beaches. In total Bomber Command carried out 1,211 sorties during the night which would see the greatest invasion force in history and amazingly, lost just eight aircraft in the process.

Being a new crew, Bernard and his men had yet to earn the right to always use the same aircraft and at that stage had to take whatever was available. The Order of Battle showed them as being assigned Lancaster Y-Yankee, ND628, and their briefing, making no mention of the invasion, filled them in on the details of their target. Their destination was a gun battery at St. Martin-de-Varreville in Normandy which was located to the rear of what would become known as Utah Beach. Armed with all the information they needed and no more, at just before 2100 hours they found themselves being dropped off at the dispersal where their aircraft had been readied for them. The crew settled in and completed their checks, each man not daring to deviate from the method he had employed two nights before, and at 2125 hours they were in the air and on their way. Heading south-west, the sixteen aircraft of 166 Squadron who had been assigned to attack the gun battery at St. Martin de Varreville, the other nine were attacking a similar emplacement at Crisbec, steadily climbed until they reached 8,000 feet. By the time they arrived at Upper Heyford in Oxfordshire, they were at the required height where they rendezvoused with the other seventy eight aircraft who had been assigned the same target. With the force assembled, they turned onto a new heading and ploughed on in a south–westerly direction to their next navigation point which was to be the Dorset coastal town of Bridport. On board ND628, the men quietly went about their tasks, all of them were considering the importance of the night's raid and the speculation that had followed the briefing had thrown up the possibility that tonight would see the start of the invasion, although none of them new for sure. Even those who had convinced themselves that it was the invasion believed that their target was just a diversionary raid and that any invasion would be across the Pas de Calais; an indication of just how complete and effective had been the Allied deception plans. Little did they know just how vital their target really was.

As was already becoming the norm, Jack MacDonald called up just before they arrived at their next navigation point over Bridport and gave Bernard a new heading of 172 degrees, just as the aircraft ahead began to turn. Bernard eased the aircraft into a gentle port turn and kept his height and distance from the Lancaster ahead and above him. As he levelled off, the aircraft slipped over the coastline and out into the blackness of the Channel. While the bomber stream passed over the choppy waters below, they climbed steadily to ten thousand feet with what had been patchy cloud beneath them gradually thickening as they headed south. By the time they reached the French coast, they had 10/10ths cloud beneath them rising to a height of about six thousand feet. The weather had been unseasonably poor for the time of year and the invasion had already been delayed once because of it. After covering some twenty five miles, the force made another turn, once again to port, and on to a south-easterly track. So far the night had gone smoothly but from there on in they knew that things were likely to start getting a little bumpy.

"173 degrees, Skipper. This is the heading to target." Informed Jack MacDonald.

With the usual simple acknowledgement, Bernard made the small adjustment to starboard and headed towards the French coast. Below them the cloud was thick and nothing could be seen through it. At the briefing the primary crews had been informed that the Pathfinder Mosquitoes would be navigating using OBOE and that the main force was to bomb on the target indicators regardless of the level of visibility.

Above the cloud, which topped out at 6,000 feet, and with the moon ahead of them and off to starboard, the visibility was remarkably good and Bernard could see many of the aircraft around him. At 2345 hours, and at a height of 10,000 feet, the aircraft had just levelled out from their turn when suddenly the relative peace of the trip so far was shattered by 'Doc' Boyd from the rear gunner's position. "Corkscrew right! Bandit five o'clock high!"

Instantly he heard the instruction from his rear gunner, Bernard slammed the yoke forward and to the right and put the Lancaster into a dive, meanwhile the single engine fighter, which was picked out clearly by the moonlight against the dark sky, dived after them in response to Bernard's evasive manoeuvre.

"Where is he, Doc?" Cried Les Bignell from the top of the fuselage in the mid-upper turret.

"500 yards off our starboard quarter and high!" Came the curt reply from 'Doc'. With that 'Doc' opened up at the gaining fighter with the chatter of the Browning machine guns echoing throughout the fuselage, the sound of his guns instantly tightening the stomachs of all the other men aboard. Almost instantly Les Bignell locked his sights on the aircraft and fired too. The fighter turned away sharply to its port side, flying across the rear of 'Doc' Boyd's turret and then dived away to the rear, port quarter of the Lancaster and disappeared into the gloom.

As both Les and 'Doc' confirmed that the fighter had thought twice about his attack and had left them, Bernard pulled the huge Lancaster out of her twisting dive and began the slow process of regaining height. Both Les Bignall and 'Doc' Boyd had loosed off around 150 rounds at the attacker, finally stopping their fire when the German had opened a gap of about 400 yards from them. Despite their 300 rounds, they could not be certain of making any hits and didn't claim to do so.

"Excellent work, men." Praised Bernard through the breathlessness of wrestling with the aerobatics of the Lancaster. "Keep a good look out in case he decides to come back." He instructed almost pointlessly. 'Doc' was already well ahead of his skipper on that point and was staring intently into the darkness, he would later tell the tale that he was convinced he didn't blink again for the rest of the night.

Still out over the Channel, the rest of the force flew past the northern end of the French Cotentin peninsular, some twenty five miles off the coast and made their final turn for the target. Meanwhile, a little further back Bernard and his crew were playing catch up, trying to regain height and distance on the rest after their encounter with the fighter. Over the target, only two of the Pathfinder Mosquitoes from the five despatched had made it to their destination, the other three having to turn back with technical problems. At 2350 the two stalwarts began dropping their target indicators and within two minutes of that, the main force began to arrive and unleash their destructive payloads. Below was the gun battery of St. Martin de Varreville, positioned on the east coast of the Cotentin Peninsular, between the town of St. Mere Eglise and the beach which would be forever known as Utah. There, in just seven hours time, the first Allied soldiers would set foot on occupied soil in what would be the largest and greatest seaborne invasion in history.

As the aircraft approached the coast near Cherbourg, a few puffs of flak burst in the sky around them from a flak ship in the Channel, but the fire was inaccurate and not heavy enough to trouble the crews. At just after 2350 the first of the primary crews began bombing and a few minutes later Bernard and his crew, having finally regained their composure, found themselves on the final approach to the target with Jock Walker guiding them in. Below him Jock could see the glow of the red markers through the clouds and guided Bernard smoothly onto the main concentration. At 2354 hours, as he had done two days before, Jock released his bombs and announced their departure, handing full control back to Bernard as he did so. Eleven 1,000lb and four 500lb high explosive bombs fell towards their target, just a small proportion of the 545 tons of bombs dropped on that one target that night. Immediately they had taken their bombing photograph, which would prove to be useless through the cloud, they turned to starboard towards the town of Carentan, where they turned again onto a north-westerly track and headed back out over the French coast at Les Pieux on the western coast of the Cotentin Peninsular and into the Channel. Seventy miles later, Jack MacDonald called through another course change, onto 334, degrees which took them directly back to the English coast, which they crossed at Sidmouth, and where they altered course again, turning to starboard onto a north-easterly track. Once over England, the crew felt confident enough to relax sufficiently to enable themselves to discuss the fighter attack as they headed back towards Upper Heyford. Once again the accompanying aircraft gradually dissipated into the night and at Upper Heyford Bernard made his final turn and headed back towards Kirmington where they landed safely at just after 0215 hours on the morning of D-Day itself. By the time the crew climbed out of the Lancaster and headed to their interrogation with the intelligence officer, the first airborne troops were already in action on French soil and the bulk of the beach landing troops were well on their way across the Channel.

By the following day, 7th July, the British had established considerable bridgeheads following successful landings on their two beaches, while the Canadians had done the same from their beach, Juno. The Americans too had secured a small bridgehead but their progress had been restricted by the difficulties they had encountered in securing their beaches, Utah and Omaha. The fighting on Omaha beach had been particularly difficult, mainly due to the loss of all their floating tanks which had sunk in the heavy seas after being launched too far out to sea. The loss of American life on Omaha led to it earning the unenviable name, Bloody Omaha.

The night of 12th/13th June saw 671 Bomber Command aircraft attack various communications targets in support of the invasion force. One of the targets was the railway at Cambrai and during the attack a Lancaster of 419 Squadron was attacked and set on fire by a night fighter. The pilot ordered the crew to abandon the aircraft and as crewman Pilot Officer Mynarski was about to bale out of the rear door, he saw that the tail gunner was trapped in his turret by the flames. Mynarski went through the flames to try and release him but the turret was jammed and the trapped gunner, realising that the situation was hopeless, waved Mynarski away. Mynarski managed to leave the aircraft but both his clothing and his parachute were alight and he suffered severe burns from which he died shortly after landing. The tail gunner miraculously survived the crash and reported Mynarski's courage for which he was posthumously awarded the Victoria Cross.

With just two complete operations beneath their belts, the vagaries of the R.A.F. leave system threw up a weeks leave for the crew and they duly headed to their respective homes. Arriving back at Battersea, Bernard was desperate to tell Ellen of the part he had played in the only talking point in town, the invasion. However, he was sworn to secrecy and even telling his wife the details of his actions was strictly taboo so he kept counsel. He made the most of his time with his family, especially enjoying his time with his son who was by then beginning to toddle around on his own. However, even away from the Squadron and back home with his family, Bernard could not entirely escape the war, as he was at home to witness the first flight of V1 flying bombs over London in the early hours of his last day of leave, little realising how soon they would have a direct impact on his and his young family's lives. All too soon he found himself back at the gates of Kirmington and returning to the duties which seemed so far removed from his life at home.

The 13th June saw the arrival into the war of the first German 'V' weapon and the air raid sirens woke Bernard earlier than he had hoped on his last morning of leave. At 0330 hours the first V1's were launched towards England from launch pads on the Channel coast. The V1 was a small, pilotless aircraft with a seventeen foot six inch wingspan and 27 feet four inches in length and carried an 850kg Amatol high explosive warhead. The V1 could fly at 3,000 feet at a speed of 375 mph and was powered by a pulse jet engine which made a very distinctive drone. Once it had reached its destination, determined by a preset timer, the engine cut out and the craft plummeted to earth where it detonated. By the end of the war the Germans would have launched over 10,000 of these indiscriminate vengeance weapons towards London.

V1

While he had been away 166 Squadron had continued to be active and had taken part in raids to Acheres twice, Versailles, and to Gelsenkirchen. The reality of how tenuous the grasp on life was for a Bomber Command crew hit him as he realised how many of the faces had changed in less than a week. During the raid to Versailles on the night of 7th/8th June, two of 166 Squadrons Lancasters, DV367 and LM126, were shot down by night fighters with all hands lost. On the second raid to Acheres on 10th/11th June another Lancaster, LM135, crashed in France, once again killing all aboard. Finally, on the night of 12th/13th, as Bernard was returning to base, the crews of ME777, LM581, which Bernard's crew had flown on their first operation, and ND399 were all shot down, once again with complete loss of life. In total, while he had been away, in just under a week, the Squadron had lost six aircraft and forty two men.

The crew had little time to dwell on the squadron's losses as on their return they found themselves immediately listed on the Order of Battle for 14th June. The raid for that day was classed as a daylight raid, which Bomber Command had not embarked on since the end of May 1943; Bomber Harris considered daylight raids to be extremely risky and hence was reluctant to commit his crews. However, the actual moment of bombing was to be at 2235 hours, late dusk, and as a result at least the journey home would still be under the cover of darkness. Even so, the thought of a 'daylight' coupled with the losses the Squadron had suffered while they had been away, did little to fill the still inexperienced crew with confidence.

The target was to be the docks at Le Havre, where the Germans had a fleet of fast motor torpedo boats, known as E-Boats, along with other light naval craft, which directly threatened the Allied shipping around the Normandy beachhead just thirty miles away. The raid was to take place in two waves with the 26 aircraft from 166 Squadron being in the first wave, followed by a second wave, made up of 100 aircraft from 3 Group, attacking two hours later. The operation was to begin with 617 Squadron (The Dambusters) attacking with some 22 Lancasters, each loaded with a single 12,000 lb 'Tallboy' bomb, with which they hoped to break through the concrete E-Boat pens allowing the main force to follow on and destroy the boats themselves.

With the time of the attack set for 2235 hours, Bernard and the crew found themselves at JB649, Z-Zulu's dispersal point by 2000 hours and still in broad daylight, even though there was a full 10/10ths cloud cover. On board, the armourers had installed eleven 1,000lb and four 500lb high explosive bombs which were to be dropped by Jock Walker once he had a visual confirmation of his target. The Pathfinders were to drop green target indicators to identify the aiming point but the final target identification on this particular raid was to remain the responsibility of the individual bomb aimers. The men's fears of carrying out a daylight attack were calmed a little by the news that they were to be escorted to and from the target by six squadrons of Spitfires, each sporting the distinctive invasion colours of black and white stripes on the wings and fuselage, along with a further six squadrons who would be patrolling off the French coast, hunting for German fighters.

The calmness of the ground crew around Z-Zulu belied the fact that they had been worked hard. A late change to the bomb load had caused them to remove one load and replace it in its entirety. As usual, they had performed admirably and all of 166 Squadrons aircraft were ready to go in time with the correct load safely aboard.

At 2035 hours Z–Zulu became airborne with Bernard entirely reliant on his instruments as he climbed through the cloud, heading due south to the rendezvous point over Gravesend on the Thames Estuary. The 'Tallboy' bombs which were to be dropped by 617 Squadron were required to be dropped from above 18,000 feet in order that they would gain enough speed (above the speed of sound) to become effective on impact. As a result the Lancasters of 1 Group had to achieve the same height so as to avoid the risk of having a huge 12,000lb bomb dropping on them. At that height, even in summer, it was bitterly cold and the men were heavily wrapped up against the elements and would have to be breathing oxygen once they rose much above 10,000 feet. By the time they reached Gravesend they were halfway to their required height but had to maintain their climb rate in order to top 18,000 feet before they crossed the coast at Beachy Head.

Steadily Bernard added to the height, watching the needle on his altimeter gradually rotating clockwise as the other members of the crew began to complain of the increasingly bitter cold and to fumble around in thick gloves and leather flying gear, while all the time keeping vigilant to the possibility of another Lancaster coming at them through the thick cloud. At just above 10,000 feet, they broke through the top of the cloud and by the time the Lancaster was above the Channel and Jack MacDonald had called a new course to the south-west, the crew had reached 19,000 feet with Bernard settled into his usual position in the bomber stream. Today was an altogether different experience, as they broke through the cloud with 198 other 1 Group Lancasters clearly visible in the daylight around them, interspersed by dozens more Spitfires, it made for a truly awe inspiring show of strength. Somewhere out ahead of them were the Lancasters of 617 Squadron with their huge bombs and to come behind were another 100 Lancasters of 3 Group. Bernard consoled himself in the thought that, no matter how dangerous this bombing game was, he would much rather be where he was at that moment than sitting, unaware of what was about to come, in the port of Le Havre.

As they headed across the Channel, the thick cloud steadily began to break up and by the time they reached the enemy coast it had vanished altogether, giving perfect visibility and allowing the crew, especially Les Bignell in the mid-upper turret, a perfect sight of the entire attacking force.

At 2230 hours a Mosquito of 617 Squadron dropped a cascading, red target indicator to signal the start of their part of the raid and almost immediately they started dropping their huge weapons. Several of the 'Tallboys' found their mark and the roofs of the E-Boat pens were seriously damaged in several places. Every five minutes after that, the Pathfinders of 8 Group took over the marking and remarked the aiming point with a cascading, green target indicator. In the seven minutes which followed, the first section of 65 Lancasters made their attack and then peeled away, aware that two more sections were following closely behind.

Bernard's crew were in the second section, which comprised some 66 Lancasters, the first of which dropped its load at 2243 hours. At that time Z-Zulu was nicely on her bomb run and Jock Walker peered down through his bomb sight and the bulbous, Perspex nose of the Lancaster at the carnage which was developing below him in the port. To the eastern end of the deep water quay, Jock could see a huge fire blazing, combining the smoke it gave off with that from the many smaller fires which straddled the aiming point and threatened to obscure the target altogether. Enemy fighters were nowhere to be seen and the heavy flak, which had been sporadic at best between fifteen and 20,000 feet on the approach, had begun to fade in its intensity and was virtually non existent by the time the third wave came in. Of the 198 aircraft of 1 Group who had taken off to attack Le Havre, 195 managed to successfully drop their bombs while two could not get their bombs to release over the target and a third had to return to base with a defective starboard outer engine.

Ahead of him, Bernard saw the bombs fall away from the bay of the Lancaster he had been following and fall at a safe distance past the nose of Z-Zulu on their way to the target. As soon as the bombs had passed from his sight and beneath the nose of his aircraft, Jock saw his cross hairs line up over a vessel below and at 2247 hours released his load from a height of 20,000 feet. With their payload gone, Bernard closed the bomb bay doors and continued on in the bomber stream out to a position above the Seine Estuary. Once above the waters of the river he was instructed by Jack to make a sharp turn to port and head back to the English coast on a bearing of 005 degrees. He banked the aircraft sharply until he settled on his required bearing and in the rapidly dimming light began to lose height at a rate of 1,000 feet per minute, pushing his airspeed ever upward until he topped out at nearly 220 mph. The crew crossed the north French coast just to the west of the town of Fecamp and headed back across the Channel, constantly losing height as they did so. Bernard maintained the same heading right across the Channel and finally levelled out from his dive at just above 6,000 feet, which he maintained as they passed over the Sussex coastal town of Bexhill and continued on the same

005 degree bearing until they reached the southern bank of the Thames Estuary. From there Jack calculated their final course change and they headed for home.

After four hours and five minutes in the air, Bernard deftly touched JB649 down at Kirmington at 0040 hours while simultaneously the next wave of 3 Group Lancasters was hitting Le Havre again. In total, of the 335 Lancasters sent to attack Le Havre, 329 managed to attack dropping some 1,778 tons of bombs including the 22 massive 'Tallboys'. The bombing had been extremely accurate and very few of the E-Boats escaped damage, effectively removing their threat. Some areas around the port were inevitably hit with 76 civilians being killed and some 150 injured. Bomber Command lost one Lancaster of 15 Squadron.

The following day, once again, saw the Order of Battle posted with Bernard and his crew listed to fly. Bomber Command had requested that 166 Squadron provide 23 aircraft for the night's attack on an oil plant at Sterkrade in the Ruhr and passed through the details of the bomb load which the armourers set about installing. However, at 1340 hours, the mission was cancelled and all the crews stood down at 1845 hours which gave them the opportunity to head into the village of Kirmington for a pint or two at the Marrowbone and Cleaver, or 'The Chopper' as the crews referred to it. The pub looked large from the outside but inside was compact and cosy. The two bars were packed with men of varying ranks and trades shrouded in cigarette smoke, while even more spilled outside in the warm summer temperatures. Throughout the war, this little haven of normality would play host to many hundreds of aircrew and ground crew alike and for many of the aircrew it would sadly be the last pub they would ever have the pleasure of drinking in.

The morning of 16th June 1944 saw the crew climbing into V-Victor, LM386, soon after breakfast and heading east over the Lincolnshire coast and out over the North Sea where they practised air to sea firing. For once it was a relief to be in the air without the pressures and dangers of an operation but as with all things in this war, they had to maintain their vigilance for marauding German fighters. After seventy five minutes in the air, the crew returned to the Watch Office to find the Order of Battle for the day had them allocated to Z-Zulu, JB649, for the second successive raid.

The relief from the day before, as their raid to the deadly Ruhr area had been cancelled, was soon shattered as the map curtain was removed and revealed that they were being sent to the same place; Sterkrade. The Ruhr was, and still is, the industrial heart of Germany in an area around Cologne, Dusseldorf and Essen near to Germany's western border with Holland. There, oil and steel were produced and in turn transformed into many of the essential war materials the Germans relied on, including tanks and aircraft. As a result the area was extremely well defended with night fighters, flak batteries and bands of searchlights. The prospects for surviving the night, as all the crews in the briefing room knew, were not good.

At 2220 hours, as the sky was beginning to darken over the airfield, the crew arrived at JB649's dispersal and began their by now familiar routine. Bernard looked up into the bomb bay and cast his eye over the deadly pay load they were to carry. Suspended above him was one huge 4,000lb 'Cookie' high explosive bomb, which looked like two oil barrels welded together, and arranged around it were sixteen assorted 500lb bombs, each of which had the capacity for severely ruining your day. Amongst the sixteen 500lb bombs were four fitted with delayed action fuses which were set to detonate for anything up to six days later. With each aircraft carrying four of these delayed action bombs and over 320 aircraft attacking, the Germans would have to contend with nearly 1,300 un-exploded bombs while also trying to deal with the damage caused on the night, so tying up valuable resources as well as coping with continual detonations of those bombs that had not been found and defused. The effects of bombing raids were designed to last for more than just one night.

At 2240 hours the first aircraft began to take off from Kirmington and fifteen minutes later Bernard took off, the penultimate 166 Squadron aircraft to leave the ground. Jack MacDonald gave him the first bearing which was on a south-easterly track to the Norfolk coast above the town of Sheringham. Bernard steadily gained height and settled on his course while at the same time feeling the tightening in the pit of his stomach that he hadn't felt since his first mission. He may not have been there himself yet, but a trip to the Ruhr had that effect on a person.

Crossing out into the North Sea, the crew could see a few of the other 171 aircraft who were to make up their wave of the attack, with a second wave of 150 aircraft attacking using a more southerly route to the target and to attack just minutes later. Mixed in with the fifty 1 Group Lancasters, were 99 Halifaxes from 4 Group and six Lancasters and sixteen Mosquito Pathfinders from 8 Group. As the massed aircraft headed for the Dutch coast, they climbed steadily to 22,000 feet, and once they were within 45 miles of the coast each aircraft started to drop bundles of the tinfoil strips known as 'Window' to confuse the German radar. Les Bignell stuffed the bundles of foil down the chute in the rear of the Lancaster, unable to feel his chilled fingers, but fully aware that these simple little strips could keep the dreaded night fighters away from the bomber stream.

"Enemy coast ahead, Skipper." Called Jack as the aircraft approached the Dutch coastal town of Wassenaar just north of The Hague but from the cockpit Bernard could see nothing of the coastline below. The cloud topped out at 10,000 feet, some 12,000 feet below him, and lay like a thick impenetrable blanket, while above in the clear night sky, the bomber stream was clearly visible.

The stream ploughed on navigating a route between the cities of Rotterdam and Utrecht, before turning to port, on to a course which took them very nearly due east and to the south of Arnhem. As they passed the city, Les Bignell called up on the intercom from the mid-upper turret to tell the crew he had seen a night fighter attack off to port and well ahead of them. The realization that night fighters were amongst the bomber stream intensified their already considerable concentration as they peered with unblinking eyes into the night sky. Unfortunately their vigilance would only serve to show them the carnage that was to be wrought that night.

With Arnhem just behind and to the port side, Jack called a new bearing of 124 degrees and informed Bernard that this was the bearing for the target, which was just fifty miles away. As they ate up the ground to the target, more and more flak started to penetrate the cloud below, bursting randomly around the bombers threatening to end their night at any moment.

At 0115 hours on the morning of 17th June, the Pathfinder Mosquitoes began to lay their red target indicators in the face of intense heavy flak and just over five minutes later the first of the main force, unable to see through the cloud, bombed on the markers. Over the next few minutes the pathfinders re-marked with both red and green indicators and at 0125 hours, from a height of 21,000 feet, Jock Walker released his bombs into the mix of target indicators and the heaviest concentration of fires, cloud and smoke. With the load gone and the Lancaster jumping and bouncing in the air as it was buffeted by the concentration of the flak explosions, Bernard banked hard to port and began their attempt at escape. The flak was beginning to take its toll on the bomber stream and the crew called out several times as they witnessed aircraft being hit, the resulting fires showing clearly in the clear night air above the cloud. As if the high concentration of heavy flak was not enough, the fear and danger levels were added to by a constant and strong night fighter presence. The German fighter controller that night had picked the night-fighter beacon at Bocholt as the point at which to hold his aircraft and this beacon was positioned just ten miles from the bombers route to the target, nestled neatly in the 'v' shape created by the route in and the route out again. As a result the sight of night-fighter attacks was not a rare one. Bernard, as usual, had secured his normal spot in the bomber formation for the route in but as they left the target area the concentration of aircraft thinned out as each crew began effectively flying for itself and the crew found themselves in space of their own.

With every passing moment, Z-Zulu put more and more distance between herself and the target, as a result the flak began to slowly thin out although the night fighters were still making hay. As the crew reached the town of Stadtlohn, thirty miles east of Munster, Jack called a new bearing of 305 degrees and with another bank to port, Bernard felt they were finally on their way home. The night fighters continued to pick at the stream but miraculously none had even come in striking distance of Z-Zulu, although they had seen plenty at a distance. As they crossed a point of longitude six degrees east, fifteen miles north of the Dutch town of Apeldoorn, Jack called up again. "You can begin to lose height now, Skipper. Between twelve and 14,000 feet."

"Thanks, Jack. Let's get out of here." Came the reply of a man who had seen enough for one night. Putting the nose of the Lancaster down a touch, Bernard put the Lancaster into a shallow dive and gained as much speed as he dared until he satisfied himself that 13,000 feet was the right point to level out. Having picked up speed and dived as well, they found themselves only in view of a handful of aircraft as they turned to port once again over the Dutch island of Flevoland in the Ijsselmeer and made directly for the Dutch coast south of Alkmaar. Although still far from safe, the entire crew breathed a sigh of relief as they crossed the coast and headed back across the North Sea on a bearing to take them to Mablethorpe on the Lincolnshire coast, from where it was just a short hop to their base. The sight of the English coast felt like a warm blanket on a cold night as they began to realise that they had survived what they already knew had been a horrific night for Bomber Command. As they touched down at 0350 hours, some of them were even daring to think to themselves that they might just be one of those very rare crews; a lucky one.

The truth about just how bad that night had been would never be known by the crews themselves, Bomber Command didn't voluntarily publicise its losses, and on the face of things Bernard's crew may have thought that the raid had appeared worse than it really was, as 166 Squadron somehow managed to escape unscathed. The rest of the bombing force was not so lucky, with a total of 33 aircraft being lost, 23 Halifaxes and ten Lancasters and a total of 159 men killed and more taken prisoner. At least 21 of those aircraft lost were the victims of night fighters. The raid itself, due to the thick cloud and strong defences, was scattered, although some bombs did fall in the oil plant but had little effect on production.

During the afternoon of 16th June 1944 the Air Transport Corps delivered a shiny new Lancaster to 166 Squadron. Built under licence by Armstrong Whitworths, LM176 was a direct replacement for the latest X-X-ray, LM581, which had been shot down on the night of 12th/13th June by a night fighter during a raid on Gelsenkirchen with the loss of all aboard. As the aircraft was handed over to the ground crew and they were informed of the call sign to paint on its fuselage, the mutterings began. As far as they were concerned, any aircraft at 166 Squadron which was assigned the X call sign appeared to be jinxed, none of them had lasted very long and they couldn't help but to feel sorry for the crews who would be flying her.

The morning after the Sterkrade raid, Bernard was summoned to the squadron office where he was informed that a new Lancaster had been delivered and that his crew would be flying that particular one whenever they were selected to fly. Excited at the prospect of receiving a brand new 'kite', he gathered together the rest of the crew and they headed out across the airfield to look her over. Standing proud, the new Lancaster looked perfect in every way. There were no signs of wear, such as missing paint, dents, scratches to the Perspex or repaired bullet holes as there were in so many of the others.

"You been given this one, Sir?" Inquired one of the ground crew.

"Yes. Doesn't she look good?" Bernard enthused.

"Good luck with her Sir." Smiled the mechanic with genuine sincerity. "You'll need it." He muttered to himself as he turned away.

With genuine fear amongst the ground crew that the aircraft would be jinxed from the start, the armourer piped up with a suggestion. "As it's yours, you ought to personalize it, you know, with a mascot or something." He suggested.

After some deliberation amongst the crew, Jack MacDonald piped up. "Back home in Canada, I've got a dog called Hircleberry, he always gets in scrapes but somehow gets out again; I can draw a mean cartoon of him." The suggestion was met with universal approval by the gathered men and with that Jack proceeded to speedily sketch a cartoon-like dog's face in his note book. The resulting image proved acceptable to the crew and Jack was only prevented from starting work on the aircraft itself by their impending briefing.

The armourers received their bomb load instructions and began to load the required sixteen 500lb high explosive bombs and two delayed action 500lb bombs, set for anything between six and thirty-six hours, little realising that they would be seeing most of this particular bomb load again. The Order of Battle was posted and Bernard's crew were surprised to see they had been allocated JB649, Z-Zulu, as the new LM176 had not been flight tested in time to take part in the raid.

The target for the night was to be the major railway junction at Aulnoye in northern France, close to the Belgian border. The flight and bombing instructions at the briefing were immensely detailed with the bombing height being set as low as 3,000 feet. For Jack MacDonald this was going to be his most testing feat of navigation so far, made especially difficult by the thick cloud which was expected to lie all over northern Europe.

The crew felt disappointed that their new aircraft was not available, as they had all felt that the new Lancaster would be the final piece of the jigsaw that completed the crew. However, they had flown in JB649 on their last two missions and had every confidence in her as they taxied to the end of the runway. At 2330 hours their wheels left the Kirmington strip and as they climbed away, Z-Zulu was steadily enveloped by ever thickening, low cloud and using his instruments, Bernard headed towards Orford Ness on the Suffolk coast, climbing to just over 8,000 feet as he did so. As they crossed the English coast and headed out to sea, Jack called a course change and Bernard turned to port onto a south-easterly course and began to climb again until he was above 14,000 feet. At a point just over halfway across the Channel the crew began ejecting the foil 'Window' strips which they had been instructed to do so until they were well on their way home and back above the waters of the Channel. The cloud began to thin out as they gained height until, through the cloud and the darkness, the crew could see just a few of the 102 other aircraft who made up the bomber stream but unnervingly there were none on which Bernard could take up his usual position. The aircraft crossed the enemy coast just to the east of the Belgian port of Zeebrugge and headed inland until they turned to starboard at a position to the north-east of Gent and on to a southerly course, which was to take them directly towards their target.

"Start losing height, Skipper. 1,000 feet per minute, air speed 200 m.p.h." instructed Jack.

Bernard confirmed Jack's instructions and pushed the nose of the Lancaster forward and back into the thick blanket of cloud, once again they were isolated from the rest of the stream by natures camouflage.

After several minutes Jack piped up again. "Cloud base should be at 3,000 feet, Skipper. We are to bomb as high as possible but below the cloud."

"Roger. Did you get that, Jock?" Bernard inquired of his Bomb Aimer.

"Understood, Skipper." Came the swift and assured reply from the Lancasters rounded, Perspex nose.

As they lost height there was no sign of the cloud thinning and as they slipped below 3,000 feet Bernard called up Jack MacDonald. "We're running out of sky, Jack. We're below 3,000 feet, still ten tenths." Informed Bernard.

"Keep going, Skipper." Instructed Jack.

Meanwhile, ahead of Bernard and the rest of the bomber stream, the Master Bomber was circling the target area at a height of just 1,000 feet but could still not break through the cloud base and as a result could not visually identify the target. Two thousand feet above him, the other Mosquitoes of the Pathfinders dropped their red target indicators at 0134 hours, four minutes before the main force was due to arrive, but the master bomber could not make them out through the thick cloud either. The Master Bomber was tasked with confirming the position of the red indicators by dropping his own green markers which the main force was then to bomb on, but unable to even see the red markers, he could not verify they were correctly sited and could still not get a visual fix. By then the first primary aircraft were arriving on the scene. Their instructions were to bomb on the green target indicators but being only able to see red ones, the first few crews began to bomb on those instead. With the situation becoming dire and with a serious danger of being bombed by his own main force, the Master Bomber called up all the crews in the bomber stream.

"Chugboat 1, Chugboat 1; this is Ghurka 1, repeat Ghurka 1. Lysol, repeat Lysol." The Master Bomber repeated the message over and over, Chugboat1 being the codeword for the main force with Ghurka 1 being his own codename and Lysol the code for stop bombing and go home.

At the wireless operators' station aboard Z-Zulu, Len Simmons received the master bombers signal loud and clear. "Lysol, Skipper. Lysol. Let's get out of here." Len informed, well aware of how dangerous the situation had become.

"Roger, Len. Give me a new bearing Jack." Bernard replied, as he eased the nose up and began to slowly gain height, all the time aware not to make any violent manoeuvres in fear of colliding with another aircraft. All the men's eyes scanned the cloud for any sign of another Lancaster looming out of it, a prime example of just how important each man was and just how they had to work as a team.

Within moments Jack had recalculated the required bearing and Bernard banked gently to starboard, cutting the corner off the final leg of their planned route. The new heading took them just to the south of the towns of Valenciennes and Cambrai, until they regained their planned homeward route and again turned to starboard this time onto a westward heading, which would see them cross the French coast just north of the Somme estuary. As they cut the corner, Bernard steadily climbed, and by the time they had regained the planned homeward course he was at 6,000 feet. After a few minutes on that course and maintaining height, they crossed a point of 2.5 degrees east and Jack informed Bernard that he could begin to climb again to between 8,000 and 10,000 feet. Deciding that as little movement as possible was probably the safest in the conditions; Bernard edged Z-Zulu up to just over 8,000 feet and levelled off.

Some thirty miles off the French coast, the crew could finally stop dropping their window and concentrate on the journey home. Fully aware that the Lancaster had a maximum landing weight of 55,000 lbs the crew jettisoned as many of their bombs into the Channel as was necessary to bring their weight down to a safe level. Still, the entire crew peered into the gloom searching for other aircraft and when they reached a point some 23 miles off the coast of Littlehampton, they turned to starboard onto a north-westerly course and crossed the English coast between Littlehampton and Bognor Regis. With the cloud slowly thinning as they crossed the coast and visibility steadily improving, the crew began to feel a little more relaxed; all except Bernard. He was well aware that they still had several tons of bombs aboard and knew that he had never landed such a heavy aircraft. The controls would be much heavier and the chances of carrying out a successful overshoot if it all went wrong were much reduced.

Near Petworth in Sussex, Z-Zulu turned again, this time to port and headed directly towards Newbury at which point the bomber stream, such as it was since virtually all the crews had had to calculate their own route home, would split up and head for their own bases. At 0445 hours Bernard was lined up on the main runway at Kirmington having completed all his checks. Auto pilot control was out, superchargers were set to low ratio, air intake was on cold and his brake pressure read a re-assuring 280lb per square inch. With his speed below 200 m.p.h. he had already lowered his flaps by twenty degrees while on his circuit and then put the undercarriage down which was confirmed by the indicator in the cockpit and the audible horn, but just to be sure he checked visually as well. The propeller revs were set at 2,850 r.p.m. and the fuel booster pumps were switched on by Gordon Cardew.

By the time the aircraft crossed over the Beam Approach outer marker, they were down to 600 feet, 130 m.p.h. and steadily losing both height and speed. Bernard could feel the aircraft was slightly less responsive than usual but was pleasantly surprised and reassured that it was still nimble enough to respond should anything go wrong. As they crossed the inner marker, they were down to 150 feet and 120 m.p.h. and at 0450 hours drifted lightly onto the concrete, almost as delicately as if they had no load aboard. Once they came to a stop at the end of the runway, Bernard and Gordon shut down the two outer engines and then proceeded to taxi back to their dispersal on the two inner engines alone. Although they had brought most of their bombs back, the crew felt they had done a good job in extremely difficult conditions. Even though there had been no flak or night fighters, it seemed the Germans were too sensible to fly in such conditions; the weather had been a considerable adversary that night and one they had done well to overcome.

In total, 101 aircraft were sent to attack Aulnoye and only seven dropped their bombs, the rest brought them home, as had Bernard and his crew, and thankfully all the crews on the Aulnoye raid returned home safely.

The original pencil sketch of Hircleberry drawn by Jack MacDonald

The thick cloud and rain that had dogged the Aulnoye raid showed no sign of abating over the next few days. The following day saw the squadron being stood down from the planned operation on a V2 rocket site at 1232 hours, which gave

Jack ample time to head across to X-X-Ray and complete his art work. A can of white paint and a brush were rapidly produced by the ground crew and soon after, the pencil sketch that Jack had drawn to show the mixed crowd of air and ground crews had been transferred to the port side of the fuselage, just beneath the pilots' seat. LM176 was now officially X-X-ray but the men who would maintain her and fly her would know her only as 'Hircleberry'.

The mission of 19th June, which was to be to the V2 site they had not managed to go to the day before, was also cancelled at the last minute with twelve of the squadron's aircraft already airborne. The visibility was so bad that one of them had to divert to Linton-on-Ouse.

The 20th saw the mission cancelled again at 1325 hours and the crews stood down, only to be readied again at 1600 hours for a dawn take off, but that too was cancelled at 0135 hours on the morning of 21st. The crews were becoming increasingly frustrated but the weather hadn't yet finished messing around with Bomber Command's plans. The crews were readied again on 21st for take off at 1300 hours which was duly cancelled at 1025 hours, only to be replaced by a new takeoff time for that night which was again, in turn, cancelled.

By the time 22nd June dawned, the crews had just about had their fill of being messed around by the weather, and with a brightening of the skies, it seemed likely they would get airborne again at last. The Order of Battle was duly posted, and for the first time Bernard's crew was allocated LM176 and would, as had been intended, be the first crew to take her into battle. Their ever increasing experience saw them begin to climb up the Order of Battle, and for that days raid they were listed 19th out of the twenty-five crews due to fly.

The briefing took place in the mid morning as the day's raid was to be a daylight one on a V1 site at Marquise in northern France, just south of Calais. By 1345 hours the crew were in position in 'Hircleberry' with all four Merlin's throbbing merrily. Everything about the aircraft felt tight as the vibrations of the engines had not yet shaken the aircraft loose and the crew felt confident in their new Lancaster and had no inkling of the trepidation felt by their somewhat superstitious ground crew and equally worried W.A.A.Fs in the control tower who were fully aware of the X-X-Ray reputation. At 1355 hours 'Hircleberry' took off on her first raid and climbed away to the south, en route to the rendezvous point at Gravesend on the Thames Estuary, climbing steadily to a height of 15,000 feet as she went.

At Gravesend the bomber stream assembled, consisting of 100 Lancasters of 1

Group with the usual Pathfinder Mosquitoes from 8 Group. In the bellies of each Lancaster were sixteen 500lb high explosive bombs with two more delayed action 500lb bombs, set to detonate between six and 36 hours later. From Gravesend the stream turned to port on a south-easterly heading towards Hythe on the English coast. So far 'Hircleberry' was behaving perfectly, her guns proving no exception as they fired for the first time once they had crossed the coast and the gunners loosed off a few rounds to test them. For once, Bernard had been scuppered in taking up his favoured position in the stream even before he had left the briefing room. As the day's raid was in daylight, the crews had been ordered to pair up for mutual protection from fighters and Bernard and his crew had been paired with ME647, piloted by Flying Officer Lewis. The two aircraft held station with one another just 100 yards apart all the way from Kirmington and were further reassured as they began to cross the Channel, where they were joined by a Spitfire escort.

Over the Channel the cloud had cleared away leaving just the odd, sporadic patch and visibility was extremely good with the crew able to see most of the bomber stream, even though they themselves were towards the back. With just the short run across the Strait of Dover to the target, everything felt rather hurried as they seemed to be going in for the bomb run almost as soon as they had left the English coast. As they slipped over the French coast at Cap-Gris-Nez, the flak was considerable and buffeted the aircraft with the black/brown puffs of cordite, which usually remained unseen in the blackness of night, only too visible by day. All of a sudden the aircraft seemed to be filled with a deafening explosion and its port wing was forced violently upwards as a heavy flak shell burst immediately beneath it. Bernard fought with the control column to get 'Hircleberry' back level and while in the process of doing so Les Bignell yelled down the intercom. "Port inner's on fire, Skipper!"

Bernard looked across to his left and sure enough the engine was pouring flames out of its rear and around it he could see damage to the wing and the engines radiator cowling. "Feathering port inner!" He bellowed to Gordon Cardew as he turned off the master fuel cock and Gordon pressed in the feathering button. Bernard completed the process by closing the port inner throttle and turned again to look out the left side of the cockpit and watch the propeller grind to a halt. Gordon was already busy checking his fuel gauges to check that none of the fuel tanks had been ruptured in the strike. As Bernard watched the propeller stop he was delighted, and not a little surprised, to see the fire rapidly die out as the fuel supply was cut to the stricken engine. With the immediate danger having passed, he checked the crew were all okay and then with Gordon's assistance checked that the rest of the aircraft was still functioning. Amazingly their virginal aircraft had proved to be extremely robust and as far as they could tell all the major systems were still fully operational as most of the systems run by the port inner engine were also supplied by the starboard inner. Satisfied that they had enough control of the aircraft, coupled with the fact that they were by then so close to the target, Bernard made the decision to press on. As they moved steadily inland, the flak began to die away and soon they were only a couple of miles from their target.

At 1541 hours the Mosquitoes, who had easily picked out their target visually in the clear conditions, dropped their red, cascading target indicators and re-marked them every two minutes. As the main force arrived they too could easily identify their target, despite being 15,000 feet up, and so had no need to fall back on the Gee or H2S (ground imaging radar) which they had been instructed to use had the cloud obstructed the target and the target indicators. Towards the back of the stream, 'Hircleberry', having recomposed herself, settled onto the bomb run. From their height of 16,000 feet Jock Walker visually identified the target and could see the concentrated bombing around it, happy he was in the right spot, at 1547 hours he released his payload. Bernard held the aircraft steady long enough to take the intelligence photograph before turning slightly to port and leaving the target area.

Seven miles further into the French countryside, Jack gave Bernard the first bearing for the journey home and he banked the Lancaster to starboard onto a southerly course for about ten miles, before banking to starboard again onto a bearing of 270 degrees (due west) and heading back towards the French coast. The Lancaster naturally had a desire to turn slightly to port and with the loss of a port engine the effect was much magnified. In order to keep her heading straight Bernard had to concoct a fine balance of the remaining three engines throttles and apply a constant touch of right rudder. The strength of the aircraft had become apparent to the crew in the last few minutes as she ploughed on despite her injuries and within that short space of time Bernard had taught himself how to fly her effectively under the new flak imposed conditions. But no matter what he did she steadily dropped back from the rest of the bomber stream and was soon alone in the still dangerous sky above enemy territory.

As it had been on the outward journey, the flak around the coast was heavy and the familiar black/brown clouds of cordite began to fill the skies again. Fourteen of the Lancasters had been damaged by flak either on the way in or back out and no less than nine of those damaged were from 166 Squadron. LM388, flown by Pilot

Officer Gibbons, had also been hit on the way to the target but the crew thought they had escaped any real damage. That was until they opened their bomb bay doors and all their bombs just fell out as the flak had damaged the electrical circuits. With no bombs left they had turned early for home and landed safely back at Kirmington. Elsewhere, other 166 Squadron aircraft were suffering too. ND635 saw its bomb aimer, Sergeant Kirkby, hit in the groin by flak and W4994, piloted by Pilot Officer Strath, was hit by two bombs from another aircraft, one of which took its port outer engine clean out of its mounting while the other hit the port side of the fuselage near the mid-upper turret and punched a five foot hole in the aircraft. Despite its battering W4994 and her crew managed to land safely at R.A.F. Woodbridge.

By the time 'Hircleberry' was within a few miles of the French coast she had dropped back enough to be completely alone and the fear was that they were now a prime target for opportunistic German fighters in broad daylight. Just as Bernard was about to issue a call to his crew for vigilance 'Doc' Boyd called up on the intercom to say that a Spitfire had joined them above and to the rear. The sense of relief to the whole crew was tangible but they could not have imagined in their wildest dreams what happened next. Within the next few minutes more and more Spitfires formed up on the stricken Lancaster, each one giving a little wing waggle of acknowledgement as they did so, until she was surrounded by half a dozen of the beautiful, little aircraft.

The modest formation headed across the French coast and in the middle of the Channel Bernard turned to starboard with the Spitfires dutifully following suit, shadowing the stricken Lancaster. They crossed the English coast at Hastings, heading inland to the Sussex village of Heathfield, where the wounded 'Hircleberry' turned slightly to port towards Reading. As the limping Lancaster turned, her escort peeled away with characteristic flair, their job successfully done. 98 of the 100 aircraft sent to attack the V1 site had managed to bomb the target in just eight minutes between 1544 and 1552 hours with the concentration of bombing being very good. Only one aircraft was lost, LL838 of 550 Squadron, piloted by Flight Lieutenant B.J. Redmond, which had been badly damaged by flak over the enemy coast. The pilot managed to get back to England but had to finally abandon the aircraft near Tunbridge Wells in Kent with all the crew parachuting to safety.

At 1730 hours Bernard skilfully landed LM176 safely at Kirmington on her three remaining engines and with her first and her crew's sixth operation completed, the crew breathed a collective sigh of relief. 'Hircleberry' had immediately endeared herself to her crew by bringing them home despite her wounds and the arrival of the guardian angel Spitfires seemed to confirm to the crew that they were one of those rare lucky ones. The aircraft had performed perfectly under the circumstances and Bernard's crew had been exemplary in overcoming its difficulties. Far from shaking their confidence, the dramas of the day had convinced them that their team was now complete and their confidence was building, although they all knew the dangers complacency could bring and were determined to a man that they would not allow that particular evil to take hold. Their ground crew, who had become used to a succession of X-Ray's not making it home at all, were delighted to see this one bring her crew back despite her considerable damage. Perhaps, they began to think, this one might just break the jinx.

Unable to thank their escort of Spitfires personally or while in the air, Bernard and the crew could not impress enough on the intelligence officer during their debriefing how much they appreciated their actions, and influenced by their forcefulness, he duly passed on their comments to Fighter Command.

The 23rd June saw no let up for Bernard's crew, and once again they found themselves listed on the Order of Battle. This time they were listed twentieth out of 27 aircraft who were detailed to attack the Saintes railway marshalling yard to the south of La Rochelle, mid way down the French Atlantic coast. The briefing soon made it clear that this was going to be their longest mission yet, with a long trek south across the Channel, over the Brittany peninsular and down the French Atlantic coast.

By 2130 Hours the crew were at their dispersal checking over every aspect of 'Hircleberry' especially the port wing and inner engine which had been miraculously repaired in double quick time by their highly efficient ground crew. All seven men stared upward at the near invisible repairs, almost in disbelief that this was the same wing that had taken so much damage just a day before. LM176 was to be just one of the 106 aircraft from 1 Group, who would be joined by a further 97 from 5 Group, on the night's operation. The fuel load reflected the length of the flight, with a Lancaster having a maximum fuel load of 2,154 gallons, that night they would be filled with 1,780. At just after 2200 hours, the aircraft of 166 Squadron began to take to the skies and at 2205 hours 'Hircleberry' was in the air and on her way. Bernard pointed her bulbous nose in a south-westerly direction and headed for the first navigation point which was to be over the airfield at Upper Heyford in Oxfordshire. Having climbed to the required height, between eight and 10,000 feet, the gathered force continued on its south-westerly route towards Start Point, the most southerly tip of the Devonshire coastline, before turning slightly to port and heading out over the Channel. From the start of their journey the crew had found themselves in thick cloud which showed no sign of thinning as they reached their correct height, or as they headed out over the Channel. Jack MacDonald called up with the usual "Enemy coast ahead, Skipper." But his declaration was purely academic as none of the crew could make out anything through the cloud which reached up to nearly 10,000 feet.

Ploughing on, 'Hircleberry' cut across the French Brittany peninsular, crossing the north coast near Morlaix and leaving the south coast, and heading out over the Atlantic, at Concarneau. Some forty miles out into the Atlantic, Jack gave a new heading towards the south-east and Bernard duly turned to port and settled on the new track. Their next course change would not come until they were over enemy territory and maintaining their course they left the Atlantic behind them as they crossed the coast at Croix-de-vie. Moving inland the cloud began to rapidly disappear and had completely gone by the time they were within fifty miles of the target. Soon after crossing the coast, the flak, which was mainly of the light variety, began rearing up at them with the aircraft being buffeted by the occasional shell that came a little too close. Before long, at a position to the east of La Rochelle, they made one final turn prior to the run to target, with Bernard banking gently to starboard and heading for the assembly point, losing height to the attack altitude of 8,000 feet as he did so.

At 0149 hours the Pathfinders marked the assembly point with green target indictors and re-marked them every five minutes for the next fifteen minutes. All the main force aircraft had been instructed to fly over the green markers, maintaining their height and with their bomb bay doors open ready to attack the target. Unfortunately a red spot marker had been dropped in error at the assembly point which prompted a few of the earliest aircraft to bomb it but the Master Bomber rapidly corrected the situation by issuing orders to ignore the rogue marker.

Further on, the target area had been correctly marked with red spot flares with the master bomber constantly checking that they were still accurate and ready to change the marking point or bombing instructions at a moments notice. As it turned out, there was no need for any such corrective action, and at 0157 hours the first aircraft began bombing. At just after 0200 hours, LM176 passed over the green markers of the assembly point with her bay doors open to the elements and Jock Walker glued to his bombsight. At 0207 hours he found the red spot markers in his sights and gave his Bakelite bomb button its familiar squeeze. Although Jock had been able to see the red spot flares he could not visually confirm the target as it had become obscured with thick, black smoke from the concentrated bombing. The bomb load for all the primary aircraft consisted of ten 1,000lb and three 500lb high explosive bombs, with 25% of the bombs on delayed fuses once again ranging from six to 36 hours.

Immediately after bombing, as only 30% of the aircraft were fitted with photoflashes and 'Hircleberry' was not one of them, Bernard banked away to starboard towards the south-west for just a handful of miles before turning to starboard again on to a bearing of 289 degrees and heading out towards the coast at Marennes. The flak continued to come up at them all the way back to the coast and reached its highest intensity as they crossed the southern tip of the Isle d'Oleron before finally dying away as they headed out over the waters of the Atlantic. As the Lancaster left the target area, Bernard gradually increased his height until he was back up to 10,000 feet where he would stay for the rest of the journey home. Forty miles out into the Atlantic and free from enemy flak, Jack gave another course change onto a more north-westerly course which took them right across the remainder of the Bay of Biscay and back to the southern coast of Brittany. From that point they virtually retraced their outward route, back across the most western extremity of France and across the Channel back to the English coast at Start Point.

By the time they reached the English coast the long hours aboard the aircraft were beginning to take their toll on the crew and had it not been for the adrenaline still coursing round their bodies, they may well have started to flag. The crew had already been airborne for longer than ever before on a mission and they still had to fly virtually the length of England. Over Upper Heyford the bomber stream began to split and once again they found themselves almost alone over the slumbering English countryside. By the time the wheels of 'Hircleberry' touched the concrete at Kirmington at 0535 hours, the Sun was already coming up and Lincolnshire was being bathed in early morning light; their longest mission so far had lasted for seven and a half hours. The thought of having to go through the process of de-briefing with the intelligence officer was enough to sap them of the final vestiges of energy they had left, but at least they could look forward to a hearty breakfast and then their beds.

The raid had been very accurate; the combination of the clear skies over the target and the concentrated bombing had resulted in the destruction of at least one ammunition train. Of the 203 Lancasters that were sent to attack the target only two were lost, both of them from 12 Squadron. One was lost without trace but the crew of the second aircraft were recovered from the English Channel without serious injury.

The following day Bernard's crew were again listed on the Order of Battle with their names, as was becoming customary, listed alongside LM176. The briefing informed them that they would be once again paying a visit to northern France to attack a V1 site south of Calais.

At 0140 hours 'Hircleberry' was positioned at the end of the Kirmington runway awaiting the green light from the black and white chequered van, and a few moments later she began to gain speed as Bernard accelerated down the runway. Once in the air, they began to climb to the required height of between twelve and 14,000 feet, which they reached by the time they arrived in the sky above Bury St Edmunds, and then continued on to the rendezvous point over the Thames estuary near Canvey. Heading southward, they joined the rest of the 102 Lancasters, all from 1 Group, who were to attack their specific target. For once, the target was not being solely marked by 8 Group Pathfinders, who would still carry out the initial marking using the OBOE system, but the back up marking would be carried out by two, 1 Group Lancasters.

The skies over northern Europe were a confusion of bombing routes that night as Bomber Command was attacking seven other V1 targets as well as carrying out other minor operations and in total had some 820 aircraft in operation. 1 Groups target for the night was a V1 launch site which was still under construction near the tiny village of Flers, some twenty miles west of Arras. As they crossed the English coast at Winchelsea, Jack called out a new bearing of 121 degrees and Bernard banked to port and could see the familiar, inky, black waters of the Channel below him as the 10/10ths of thin stratus cloud, into which they had taken off, had cleared by the time they reached London. Maintaining his height at just below 14,000 feet, Bernard felt comfortable with the sight of another Lancaster just above and ahead of him and from the turn point at Winchelsea, the bomber stream was on a direct route to the target which lay just eighty miles ahead. As they looked down on the surface of the Channel there were only scattered patches of low, thin cloud at heights between three and 8,000 feet but they were not enough to obscure their view and were thinning all the time. Crossing the French coast just to the north of Etaples, the sky seemed filled with groups of searchlights and the flak started up with the familiar bok-bok sound of the shells detonating in the sky around them, but it was not intense and caused little concern to the crew who were becoming used to its presence. Over the target the skies were clear and visibility good as the Pathfinder Mosquitoes marked with red target indicators at 0314 hours and the marking Lancasters backed them up with green markers. The master bomber was obviously happy with the standard of marking as he maintained radio silence, never feeling the need to utter his codename of Coachdoor 1 or the rather un-military main force codename of Cheesecake.

With the target accurately marked, the first of the main force aircraft began to bomb at 0316 hours and soon afterwards 'Hircleberry' had her bomb bay doors open and was waiting for Jock Walker to do his stuff. As the aircraft approached the target they could see the beams of numerous searchlights flicking across the sky, some in groups of up to eight and several times they saw aircraft coned by the beams. Fearful that the next sight would be that of a Lancaster bursting into flames as it was hit by flak or pounced on by a night fighter, they were pleasantly surprised to see each one escape seemingly unscathed. Bernard watched the Lancaster above and ahead of him rear up as she released her load, which he watched fall away in front of 'Hircleberry's' nose and fully expected the call of 'Bombs gone' to quickly follow. He wasn't disappointed and within seconds, at 0321 hours and from a height of 12,000 feet, he found his own aircraft rising as her weight was instantly reduced by 9,000lbs. As Jock's bomb sight lined up over the green target indicators he simultaneously pressed his bomb release button and sixteen 500lb, instantaneous fused bombs and two more delayed action 500lb bombs fell away. As the aircraft ran into bomb some crews saw the distinctive sight of a V1 being launched from one of the ramps below, Flying Officer Savage, the bomb aimer aboard 166 Squadron's ND578, gave a vivid description of one heading off in a north-westerly direction and on the way home the crew of ND635, Piloted by Flying Officer Tutty, saw one attacked and shot down by a fighter in a ball of red flame at a height of two to 3,000 feet.

Bernard maintained his course to take the bombing photograph before banking to port and heading out of the target area. As they left the target, more aircraft were caught in the highly active searchlights but it seemed that although the lights were effective, they were not backed up by force. The flak that night was luckily light and the night fighters were almost entirely absent, with only three combats reported in the whole raid, and all of those were on the journey home.

Having flown for about five miles past the target, Jack MacDonald gave Bernard a new heading and he turned sharply to starboard onto a south-westerly heading for eight miles before receiving a new course of 285 degrees. Once again Bernard banked to starboard and headed back towards the French coast, which they crossed to the north of the Somme estuary. Over the middle of the Channel, off the coast of Eastbourne, they turned to starboard again onto a north-westerly heading and eventually crossed the English coast between Bognor Regis and Littlehampton heading for Reading where, once again, they left the main bomber stream and made their way back to Lincolnshire. Three hours and forty minutes after leaving Kirmington, at 0520 hours, the crew of LM176 arrived home having completed their most uneventful mission to date. Although Bomber Command had lost 23 aircraft that night, mainly to night fighters who had been assisted by the clear skies and bright moonlight, there had only been one Lancaster lost from the raid on Flers as an aircraft of 576 Squadron went missing without trace. For Bernard's crew, the night's action had passed without incident or drama and both crew and aircraft had performed impeccably and as a result they all felt rightfully pleased with themselves. They could not possibly have seen what was coming as they stepped from their aircraft but they were about to be brought back to earth with a rude bump. They had now survived eight missions together but the war was about to hit them from a direction that they never expected and with a certain irony that would bond them even tighter together, but which for the time being at least, would pull them apart.

As soon as the intelligence officer had finished with the crew, Bernard was pulled to one side by Wing Commander Garner, the Squadron Commander, and taken into his office. Still in his flying gear, he slumped in a chair with a feeling of trepidation sweeping through his bowels, not knowing what to expect. His worst fears were soon realised as Garner opened with "I'm sorry to have to inform you, but it's your wife and son."

CHAPTER TWELVE

Striking back

*166 Squadron, R.A.F. Kirmington, Lincolnshire. 26th June 1944
to 25th September 1944.*

Two days earlier, as Bernard had been preparing to take off for the railway marshalling yards at Saintes, Ellen had been at home in Battersea playing hostess to her sister-in-law Elsie, Bernard's youngest sister, and a friend of hers known only as Tam. Having finished their tea and cleared away the dirty crockery, Ellen set about preparing Douglas for bed and had only just got his pyjamas on when the air-raid sirens began their familiar wail. The citizens of London knew that the sirens no longer indicated the arrival of hoards of Luftwaffe bombers but that the threat came in the form of the V1. Sure enough, just a couple of minutes after the siren started, the menacing throb of a V1 could be heard in the skies above Battersea. The sound of the engine meant that the weapon was close enough to be a threat as the engine could cut out at any moment and the huge warhead would then begin its plunge to earth. Ellen called to her guests to get to the shelter, meaning the tin, earth covered Anderson shelter at the bottom of the garden, and Tam scooped up Douglas and hurried out of the back door behind Ellen and Elsie. Ellen reached the shelter and stepped down into it, quickly followed by Elsie who turned and took Douglas from Tam's arms. "I'm going back for the cat." Tam shouted and he instantly turned and headed back the way he had come. Having passed Douglas to Ellen behind her, Elsie heard the V1's engine cut out and she turned back to shout at Tam not to go back but before she could get the words out, the V1 had plunged to the ground and detonated at 1855 hours in a spot between Honeywell Road and Broomwood Road. The blast instantly destroyed the surrounding eight houses, including Ellen's, and severely damaged a further twenty. The blast wave threw Ellen, Elsie and Douglas through the shelter and smashed them into the back wall causing serious facial injuries to Ellen and Douglas and covering all of them with cuts and bruises as well as blasting the clothes off of Elsie's back and rendering them all temporarily deaf. Six people were killed in the blast, including Tam, of whom no trace was found. When the authorities arrived on the scene Elsie had come to but was delirious and stood virtually naked on top of the rubble pile screaming obscenities at Hitler, while Ellen and her young son lay injured and bleeding on the floor of the battered shelter. All three were removed to hospital with Ellen being taken to north London and Douglas ending up at Queen Mary's at Carshalton.

Having explained to Bernard what had happened back at home, Wing Commander Garner gave Bernard a week's leave and he headed back to London to find his war battered family. Unsure what to do first, he headed home to see the devastation and found out from the ARP where his son had been taken but they were unsure where Ellen had ended up. The devastation of what had once been his home was absolute and he found it difficult to comprehend how anyone had survived. With Douglas being cared for in Carshalton, which was still very much in range of the V1's, Bernard decided to head there first. As he gazed down on his little boy, Bernard felt a wave of nausea sweep over him as he saw his battered face and bruised body and wished he could do anything to take the pain away. Being reassured that Douglas' injuries were not life threatening, he refused to leave him in the hospitals care, despite the protestations of the nursing staff. He was petrified that the hospital, which had already been hit on several occasions, would once again find itself in the firing line. Gathering his son up in his arms, he headed off to his parents house in Wimbledon, where he left Douglas while he continued the search for his wife.

Following the chaos of the attack, the authorities were unsure where Ellen had been taken and it took a couple of days of searching before Bernard finally found her, battered, cut, bruised and swollen in a North London hospital. Ellen struggled with the aches and pains for every yard of the journey back to Wimbledon but buoyed by the presence of her husband, she was delighted and determined to get back to her son. Finally, back in Wimbledon, with his precious family all under one roof again, Bernard decided that even there they were not safe enough and arranged with his elder sister, Eileen, for them to see out the war with her in the sleepy Berkshire village of East Woodhey, near Newbury. Together, the three of them headed off for the countryside where Bernard stayed for the last couple of days of his leave to settle them in before heading back to Kirmington. As he sat on the train heading north, he realised that his war had changed yet again. It was no longer a war of good against evil or for freedom; now it had become personal and he was more determined than ever to strike hard whenever he got the chance. You could mess with a man's country, even his ideals, but you should never mess with his family.

With Ellen and Douglas moved to the relative safety of East Woodhey, Bernard arrived back at Kirmington on the 1st July to find that the Squadron had been busy with Operation Crossbow, which ironically was the ongoing battle against the V1's. 166 Squadron played its part in a raid on yet another V1 site on the 27th June, where they lost LM586, piloted by Pilot Officer L. Hunt D.F.C., with all crew members killed, and that was followed up by a daylight attack on another flying bomb site on the 29th and yet another daylight attack on Oisemont on the 30th. As Bernard rolled in through the main gates, the crews were preparing for a planned attack which was to see them taking off at just before 2300 hours, but at 1620 hours the raid was cancelled and the Squadron was readied to take part in another daylight raid on 2nd July instead.

Having filled the rest of the crew in on the details of what had happened back in Battersea, they all declared their renewed determination to give the 'Krauts' what for and were keen to start their work of retribution as soon as possible. They didn't have long to wait as the Order of Battle posted for 2nd July showed Bernard and his crew being immediately thrown back into the fray. 'Hircleberry' was to be reacquainted with its regular crew, having been 'borrowed' by other crews during Bernard's absence, for a daylight raid on the V1 site at Domleger. Bernard's crew was one of 28 put up that day by 166 Squadron, with take off set for 1105 hours but that was eventually put back to 1200 hours. As LM176 left the runway at 1220 hours and climbed away from Kirmington, Bernard steered a course southward towards Gravesend where they rendezvoused with the rest of the force which consisted of some 125 Lancasters. At Gravesend they turned to port, on to a south-easterly heading, and made their way to the south coast which they crossed above the barren shores of Dungeness. By the time the bomber stream arrived over Dungeness they had reached a height of ten to 12,000 feet but the Lancasters continued to climb as they crossed the waters of the Channel until they reached their bombing height of thirteen to 15,000 feet. The cloud cover had varied from eight to 10/10ths all the way from Lincolnshire and reached as high as 10,000 feet but once Bernard broke through the upper reaches of the cloud he emerged into broad, bright daylight, the visibility was perfect and he soon slipped into his usual position. "Enemy coast, Skipper." Informed Jack as they crossed into France above the town of Berck, about twenty miles south of Boulogne. An immediate course change followed from the punctual and efficient Sergeant MacDonald and once again Bernard adjusted 'Hircleberry's' course to port and settled on to the bomb run for Domleger.

As the target grew ever nearer Len Simmons, the wireless operator, called up. "Wormcast's been on Skipper. He's telling us 'squaremile'."

"Did you get that, Jock?" Relayed Bernard.

"Loud and clear, Skipper." Came the prompt response from the Lancasters nose.

The strange conversation aboard 'Hircleberry' was repeated aboard most of the other 124 Lancasters approaching the target and hopefully made perfect sense to all of them. During the briefing for all missions new code words were issued, each with its own specific meaning and it was vital that the crews knew and understood them. In this instance, Wormcast was the codename for the master bomber and squaremile was the instruction to bomb using navigational aids such as GEE because the target was obscured by cloud. Just as the crew had prepared itself to carry out the master bombers instructions, at 1412 hours, the 'squaremile' order was cancelled and the crews were told to bomb on the red target indicators as the cloud had cleared over the target. At 1416 hours, Jock Walker lined up those same target indicators in his bomb sights and right next to them could see the distinctive shapes of the V1 site. Determined to be as accurate as possible, after the misery these weapons had inflicted on his Skipper's family, he waited a fraction longer to line his sight up on the buildings instead of the markers and then released his eleven 1,000lb and two 500lb instantaneous fused bombs, along with two more delayed action 500lb bombs. Beyond the target, with their retribution delivered, Bernard made three successive turns to starboard until he ended up on a bearing of 286 degrees heading back towards the French coast.

Up to then the sortie had passed without any real German resistance, but as the bomber stream reached the outskirts of Abbeville a considerable flak barrage started up and the aircraft were buffeted by the explosions as the brown-black puffs of the exploding shells burst in the skies around them. After a few minutes under fire, the aircraft crossed over the coast at St. Valery-sur-Somme and left the flak behind for the slightly safer skies above the Channel; at least there they only had marauding fighters to worry about. At a point some twenty miles south of Worthing, Jack issued another new bearing and Bernard slavishly steered onto it, taking LM176 across the English coast above Littlehampton and en route to Reading from where they made their final course change for home, touching down at 1605 hours after three hours and forty-five minutes in the air. With the dramas in London behind him, Bernard felt a little more settled to be back with his crew and in more familiar surroundings. It wasn't lost on him how quickly war changed a person and that he felt more at home in the skies over enemy territory than he had done trawling through the streets of London, a city he knew so well in peacetime.

In total, Bomber Command attacked three V1 sites on 2nd July 1944 with a total of 374 Lancasters and nineteen Mosquitoes and all three attacks were highly accurate. Most importantly they only lost one aircraft that day which was wrecked as its undercarriage collapsed on landing at 156 Squadrons base at Upwood causing just two minor injuries.

The 3rd July saw the planned operation to Orleans Marshalling yard being cancelled at 2150 hours and the crew had to wait until the following day to carry out the raid on the same target, some eighty miles south of Paris. At 2205 hours 'Hircleberry' climbed away from Kirmington and headed south towards the Channel but that was to be as far as she would get that night. As they crossed the English coast and headed out over the sea, 'Hircleberry' misbehaved for the first time. Gordon Cardew noticed the oil pressures begin to plummet on the port outer engine and it soon became evident that it needed to be shut down. With only three engines left, a full bomb load aboard and with another 250 miles to the target, as well as the return journey to contend with, Bernard decided that to press on would be foolhardy. With only three engines they would be alone and way behind the rest of the bomber stream by the time they reached the target. An aircraft in that position would be lucky to even make it to their objective, let alone be able to turn around and make it all the way home again without being picked off by a night fighter. With the odds stacked against them, Bernard decided that discretion was the better part of valour and reluctantly turned for home. Having jettisoned enough of their bombs over the Channel to bring them below the safe landing weight, at 0055 hours on the morning of 5th July they safely touched down back at Kirmington having suffered no further dramas but the entire crew were frustrated that their ability to strike another blow against their now personal enemy, for the mean time, had been thwarted.

The remaining twenty aircraft of 166 Squadron helped form a total force of 156 aircraft that took off for Orleans, although only 145 actually reached the target. The raid was an overwhelming success, with highly concentrated bombing which resulted in extensive damage to the railway marshalling yards. 'Hircleberry' wasn't the only aircraft of 166 Squadron to suffer engine trouble that night as ME647, piloted by Flying Officer Lewis, developed a fault and was replaced with the reserve aircraft and crew, ND678 piloted by Flying Officer Welchman. The night was an eventful one for 166 Squadron as LM550, piloted by Pilot Officer Schwass, was attacked by a Focke-Wulf Fw190, which they managed to shoot down without suffering any damage themselves. In another disconcerting incident for the squadron, ND857, piloted by Pilot Officer Blanchard, suffered a 'friendly fire incident' when it was shot at by an unidentified Lancaster causing a fire in the port outer engine which had to be feathered, and a hole in the No.2 starboard fuel tank; thankfully they had no more dramas, friendly or otherwise, and returned safely.

At 1030 hours on 5th July Bernard and his men got their next chance for revenge. The Order of Battle was posted requesting 25 aircraft to be made ready for the night's raid but at 1515 hours that number was reduced to 22 aircraft, of which Bernard's crew was listed fourteenth. His quick decision to shut down 'Hircleberry's' port outer the night before had kept the engine damage to a minimum and as a result the excellent ground crews had her ready to go again just 24 hours later but the same could not be said for 'Doc' Boyd. Doc had fallen ill and had to be replaced in the rear turret by the experienced Sergeant Chalk from Pilot Officer McLaren's crew who had been rested for the night.

The afternoon briefing filled them in on the details of the raid which was to be on the railway marshalling yards at Dijon in the east of France, just seventy miles from the Swiss border. 542 aircraft from other groups were being sent to four V1 sites in a continuation of Operation Crossbow, while Bernard and the rest of 166 Squadron were to make up a force of 154 aircraft, exclusively from 1 Group, which would make the long trek across France to attack Dijon.

At just after 2100 hours the crew were settled into their positions, including their replacement rear gunner and were positioned at the end of the runway. The aircraft was heavily laden with 1,940 gallons of petrol and a bomb load totalling 10,000 lbs, made up of eight 1,000 lb, and two 500 lb instantaneous fused and two 500 lb delayed action fused, high explosive bombs. At 2110 hours the indicator light blinked green from the chequered van; Bernard released the brakes and accelerated away and into the air. Heading initially south-westward towards the rendezvous point, which was once again over Upper Heyford, they climbed towards the required height of between eight and 10,000 feet. From Upper Heyford they continued on to cross the English coast at Bridport where they made a course adjustment to port and headed on a more southerly route across the Channel towards a position off the west coast of the Channel Islands. "118 degrees, Skipper." Called Jack. Bernard glanced out of the port side of the cockpit but could not make out the island of Jersey which he knew to be some thirty miles away through the gathering darkness. He made his gentle turn and the Lancaster slipped on to a direct course to the French coast, which all being well it would cross above Le Mont-St-Michel. By the time they crossed the French coast the visibility was near perfect and in the moonlight they could clearly make out the famous island below them. Once again England had been under 10/10ths cloud with tops up to 7,000 feet but by midway across the Channel it had all but disappeared as if England had been wrapping itself in a protective cloak of cloud. From then on the weather would prove to be perfectly clear and the crew could easily map read their way across France.

As they headed into the interior of the French countryside, the three gunners, (Jock Walker the bomb aimer also manned the nose turret) as well as Bernard and Gordon, continually scanned the sky for the ominous, black outline of night-fighters but so far all seemed quiet. Above him, in his peripheral vision, Bernard could just make out the distinctive tail section of a Lancaster which was unknowingly fulfilling his now superstitious, protective position. Fifty miles inland, Jack turned them onto a new bearing of 155 degrees and Bernard dutifully turned to starboard and headed for the gap between the towns of Angers and Tours. Soon after shooting the gap between the two towns the crew began to jettison the bundles of foil covered Window strips as instructed at the briefing; the sky was filled with thousands of the simple radar jamming devices as each of the 154 aircraft carried out the same detailed order. They ploughed on through the ever darkening night, maintaining the same course for the next 85 miles until they turned again, this time to port, onto a bearing of 99 degrees, which put them on a more easterly track towards their target. Once they had made the turn, Bernard began to steadily lose height until he was nicely within the prescribed six to 8,000 feet which was the set bombing height. Fortunately the skies were clear and the aircraft could maintain a reasonable altitude; at the briefing they had been instructed to drop to as low as 3,000 feet if the cloud obscured their view but thankfully that was not going to be required. They had already been in the air for three and a half hours by the time, at a position to the south-east of Nevers, they made yet another turn; this time quite sharply to port onto a heading almost directly north-east. Their target lay just eighty miles off to the east but the hard work was just about to begin.

To the north-west of Dijon, the bomber stream turned again to starboard and effectively began their bombing run. At 0143 hours, a Mosquito of the Pathfinder Force dropped green target indicators to the north of the target area which indicated the assembly point. All the aircraft had been briefed to cross that point with their bomb bay doors open and at the height and speed at which they intended to bomb. With clear conditions the crews could easily see the markers as well as the details of the ground below and the lack of cloud over the target came as a great relief as there was less chance of them having to go round again in order to accurately identify their target. Ahead of the main force the Deputy Master Bomber, who had arrived before the Master Bomber, dropped one red and one yellow target indicator over the target which the Master Bomber duly assessed as being accurate to within fifty yards of the aiming point. The Master Bomber then backed those markers up himself with red markers which were themselves just 200 yards to the north-west of the aiming point. With such accurate marking and a clear night, all conditions were in favour of the attacking main force. So far the night fighters had stayed away and the flak had been concentrated at lower heights than the main bombing force and only really troubled the Master Bomber who struggled to constantly re-mark the target in the face of considerable light flak (light, medium and heavy flak refer to the size of the shells and not to its intensity). At 0148 hours the first bombers started to unleash their loads and within a matter of minutes 'Hircleberry' swept over the assembly point with her bay doors open and Jock Walkers thumb poised over his trusty button.

As LM176 arrived over the target area, at just before 0200 hours, the red target indicators were clearly visible as well as the marshalling yard itself which Jock could easily make out in the clear night. Already smoke from the bomb blasts was beginning to obscure parts of the ground and several fires were clearly visible to those with the opportunity to look out of a window. At 0201 hours, holding steady at 8,000 feet, Jock could see the yellow target indicators and smoke on which he was to bomb and pressed his bomb release to add 'Hircleberry's' payload to the mayhem below. The whole target area was becoming obscured by smoke but Jock could easily identify it from the distinctive canal and surrounding landmarks. The entire forces bombing appeared to be highly concentrated and as soon as the photoflash had done its work they headed out of the target area to the south-east of Dijon.

Just a handful of miles from the target, Bernard banked to starboard on to a new south-westerly heading and began to climb back towards 8,000 feet. Within a few minutes they had reached the same point to the south of the town of Nevers where they had made their turn on the way to the target and from there they re-traced their route exactly, heading back towards the gap between Tours and Angers and then heading north-west to cross the French coast once again above Le Mont St-Michel. As they crossed the Channel they climbed to 10,000 feet and flew back over the coastal town of Bridport en route to Upper Heyford. Flying above the dark, sleeping countryside of western England, Bernard looked out of the starboard side of the cockpit, knowing that somewhere down there to the east lay his wife and son and hoped that their injuries were healing quickly and painlessly. As part of his personal revenge the night had been a good, effective raid with no dramas or complications, just as he had wanted.

At 0605 hours, just five minutes short of nine hours after they had taken off, Bernard's crew arrived safely back at Kirmington, satisfied that they had played their part in dropping a total of some 625.3 Tons of high explosives on the railway yards of Dijon and without the loss of a single crew. As testament to how accurate Bomber Command had become, subsequent photographic reconnaissance revealed that practically every bomb had fallen within the marshalling yards.

The squadron was in action again the following day with 22 of their aircraft taking part in a raid on yet another V1 site, this time at Foret du Croq. 'Hircleberry's' crew were stood down for the daylight raid and took full advantage of a day of rest, knowing full well that the following day their names would almost certainly once again appear on the Order of Battle.

The 6th July saw Bomber Command attack five separate V-weapons sites using some 551 aircraft, 314 Halifaxes, 210 Lancasters and 26 Mosquitoes. Wing Commander Leonard Cheshire of 617 Squadron (the Dambusters) had led the attack on Mimoyecques that day and on his return was ordered to rest from operational duties. By that time he had completed four tours totalling one hundred operations. Two months later, for his four tours and his courage and skill in developing low level marking techniques, he was awarded the Victoria Cross and never flew on operations again.

Surely as day follows night, the Order of Battle for 7th July showed Bernard's crew listed as one of just ten selected, and to their horror, they saw that they were not to be in 'Hircleberry' but in LM386, V-Victor, instead. At 1020 hours, before they had a chance to question their allocation of aircraft, the raid was cancelled and instead a request was made for twenty aircraft to be made available for a different target, but that too was subsequently cancelled. Just as they were beginning to think they wouldn't be going anywhere that day, at 1302 hours, Group requested, in response to the developing situation in northern France, that all of the squadron's thirty aircraft be made available for an attack on German troops and armour that were holding up the British Army around Caen. As a result of the 'maximum effort', Bernard and his men were delighted to see that after the confusion of it all they had been paired with their beloved LM176.

At 1935 hours 'Hircleberry' left the ground and headed south-west towards Maidenhead, climbing steadily through the reasonably thick cloud to a height of 8,000 feet. The force being assembled for the raid was huge, 467 aircraft, all of them four engine 'heavies' from 1, 4, 6 and 8 Groups, and they gathered over southern England to launch their attack on the German defences that were holding up the British breakout in northern France. The raid needed to be accurate as the British troops were as little as one mile from the Germans and the crews had it impressed upon them at the briefing that under no circumstances were they to bomb through the cloud and that they must visually identify their target. The cloud cover over southern England was at seven to eight tenths and if it didn't clear as they crossed the Channel, the crews would have to drop to as low as 3,000 feet which would be hellish in the face of the concentrated German flak around the area. Bernard banked to port at Maidenhead and turned on to a south-easterly course which would take them across the coast between Littlehampton and Worthing. By the time the force made another turn, this time to starboard in the middle of the Channel, the cloud was showing no sign of thinning and a feeling of foreboding over and above the usual sense of trepidation was beginning to grow in Bernard as he considered the prospect of bombing from low altitude.

Twenty five miles from the French coast they turned again to port onto a bearing of 164 degrees which put them onto their bomb run, the cloud was, at last, beginning to show signs of thinning and as the coast grew ever nearer it dispersed to little more than scattered patches, much to the relief of the attacking crews. As they crossed the coast they could see Juno beach below them where the Canadians had landed on D-Day just a month before. The importance of the raid was self evident as in the month since the invasion the Allies had still not managed to take Caen which was just a dozen miles inland from the invasion beaches and had been intended to be taken on D-Day itself.

As 'Hircleberry' pushed on towards the target the flak defences became intense with the aircraft being buffeted by the explosions and surrounded by the black puffs of cordite hanging in the air. In total eighteen aircraft would be damaged by flak and one of 166 Squadrons aircraft, ND678 piloted by Squadron Leader Weston, was shot down during its bomb run with the loss of the entire crew. At 2146 hours, a Mosquito of the Pathfinders dropped the first red target indicator which was bang on target and the Master Bomber instructed the approaching main force to bomb the markers. The first wave, aided by perfect visibility as the cloud had all but gone, bombed accurately with most of the bombs straddling the markers and by the time Bernard arrived in the second wave, smoke and dust from the explosions had covered the target indicators. The Master Bomber, Wing Commander Pat Daniels of 35 Squadron under the codename 'Chugboat', instructed the force to aim at the southern end of the target and at 2158 hours from a height of 6,000 feet, Jock Walker dropped his bomb load as instructed. Their load, which consisted of eleven 1,000 lb and four 500 lb bombs, joined the misery being rained down on the Wehrmacht and once the photoflash had been taken and 'Hircleberry' had flown out to the south of Caen, Bernard turned sharply to starboard and headed west.

The raid proved to be incredibly accurate and in total some 2,275.7 tons of bombs were dropped on the target virtually destroying the northern suburbs of the town. Leaving the melee behind them, the crew of LM176 turned to the north-west and headed out over the French coast, this time over the top of Gold Beach which had been one of the British beaches on D-Day. Maintaining their height of 8,000 feet they made two course adjustments over the Channel, first to starboard off the north-east coast of the Cotentin Peninsular and then to port some twenty miles off the coast of Littlehampton, finally crossing over the English coast at Bognor before heading back to Kirmington via the outskirts of Reading. Landing safely at 2335 hours, their twelfth mission had lasted just four hours but had seen some of the fiercest flak defences so far. The loss of Squadron Leader Weston and his crew brought it home to them that their growing experience was no defence against flak and even a short trip to northern France could easily prove to be their last.

The British Army in northern France, whom the raid had been in support of, had watched it take place from close range and had been suitably impressed by the power and accuracy of Bomber Command. Their commander in the field, General Bernard Montgomery, sent the following message of thanks to Bomber Harris. 'Again the Allied armies in France would like to thank you personally and Bomber Command for magnificent co-operation last night. We know well that your main work lies further afield and we applaud your continuous and sustained bombing of German war industries and the effect this has had on the German war effort; but we know well that you are always ready to bring your mighty effort closer in when such action is really needed and to co-operate in our tactical battle. When you do this your action is always decisive. Please tell your brave and gallant pilots how greatly the Allied soldiers admire and applaud their work. Thank you very much'.

It seems General Montgomery had forgotten it took seven brave and gallant souls to produce such a mighty effort.

Over the next couple of days, due to a variety of reasons, the squadron was not called upon to carry out any further raids. With his men sitting idly around the station, Bernard found his suggestion of some air firing practice enthusiastically embraced by 'Doc' Boyd and Les Bignell. So, on 10th July, they took to the skies over the North Sea for some practice in Lancaster ND635 and for an hour and a half let off some steam by firing round after round from their Browning machine guns.

On the 8th July the Station had been allotted Airspeed Oxford AB712, to be used as a run around for officers who needed to move between airfields and headquarters. With the tricky nature of the Oxford, some of the older and more senior officers had little or no experience on the type, so Bernard, being by far the most qualified on the Oxford at Kirmington, was given the task of taking Group Captain Carter up for an hour of circuits and landings on the 11th and again for a final circuit check on the 12th before he passed him as competent to fly the Oxford. The irony of the situation appealed greatly to Bernard's sense of humour as the professional airman had to rely on the office clerk for permission to fly!

At 0942 hours on 12th July, while Bernard was still in the air with Group Captain Carter, the Order of Battle was posted for the operation set to take place that night, with all 29 of the Squadron's serviceable aircraft being required.

Once again Bernard's crew and LM176 were paired together and the briefing revealed that they would be heading deep into eastern France for an attack on the railway marshalling yards at Revigny in a raid which would involve 107 Lancasters, all from 1 Group. 'Hircleberry' was loaded with seven 1,000 lb and five 500 lb high explosive bombs and was fuelled with 1,990 gallons of petrol and at 2130 hours took off as part of the first wave of two to attack the target.

Climbing into the darkening sky, the crew could see other 166 Squadron aircraft around them as the skies were clear and visibility was good. By the time they reached Upper Heyford they were already at the required height of 8,000 feet where they would stay all the way to, and back from, the target. Heading relentlessly south-westward, the bomber stream steadily formed and at a point, somewhere between Upper Heyford and Bridport on the Dorset coast, Bernard selected the aircraft upon which he would position himself. By leaving it until the bomber stream had formed he reasoned that at least he wouldn't be forming up behind another crew from his own squadron although he still muttered "Sorry, Chum." under his breath as he slid into his favoured spot. As Bridport slipped beneath them and was replaced by the waters of the Channel, the bomber stream turned slightly to port onto an almost due south heading and out across the sea. Their next turning point was still above the waters of the Channel and some thirty miles to the west of Jersey, where they banked again to port and headed for the French coast which they would cross yet again above Le Mont St. Michel. As ever, Bernard strained his eyes out of the port side of his cockpit in a vain effort to try and catch a glimpse of the German occupied island of Jersey, but as always, the thirty miles distance and the gathering darkness combined to prevent any definite identification.

So far the weather had maintained its clarity but unknown to the crews, both mother nature and sod's law would soon combine to create havoc amongst their number, but for now at least, they were in what seamed perfect conditions. Flying on in a south-easterly direction, they headed into the heartland of France passing between Rennes to the west and Le Mans to the east. Once they arrived at a position to the south of Le Mans, they turned again to port and continued onward passing to the north of Tours until they reached their next navigation point, four miles to the north-west of the small town of Vierzon. There the bomber stream made a sharp change of course, turning off of their south-easterly and onto a north-easterly route which they would maintain for the next 175 miles across central France.

As 'Hircleberry' neared its next navigation point, which was to be to the east of Chavanges, the crew noticed that the cloud was starting to build up giving a five to 8/10ths coverage at between four and 6,000 feet. "033 degrees, Skipper." Called Jack and Bernard once again turned the Lancaster to port and onto the new heading which would take them to the assembly point. As Bernard crossed over the shimmering waters of Lac du Der Chantecoq, ahead of him the raid was beginning to hit problems. The Master Bomber's H2S set (ground reading radar) had failed and he had to mark the assembly point with a green target indicator using the inaccurate dead reckoning method, which he managed to do at 0145 hours. Deprived of his technical aids and with the gathering cloud below him, the Master Bomber called for the other marking aircraft to drop flares over the target area in the hope that he would be able to visually identify and mark the actual target. Both the Master bomber and his deputy were plagued by weak radio signals and even with the flares, were unable to locate the target even after spending some fifteen minutes hunting for it. With Len Symmons only able to pick up patchy radio communications, Bernard found himself over the flares at what should have been the Revigny Marshalling yards. "What do you think, Jack?" he queried of his navigator.

"By dead reckoning, we're over the target, Skipper." Replied Jack.

"What can you see, Jock?" Bernard asked his bomb aimer.

"Loads of flares and some red spots, but I'm not sure if they are target indicators or just fires. It's all a bit hazy, Skipper."

Then Bernard made the decision that all crews dreaded; to go round again.

Banking round in a left hand orbit, he issued his instructions to Jock in the bulbous nose of the Lancaster. "The target is supposed to be illuminated with flares and red target indicators, Jock. If that's what you can see when we go in again, let them go." He instructed.

"OK, Skipper." Replied Jock, and with that 'Hircleberry' was on her second bomb run of the night.

At exactly 0200 hours, having dropped right down to 3,500 feet, Jock could see the flares and the red lights he had seen on the first run and around him other crews were dropping their bombs. Convinced they were in the right place he pressed his bomb release button and their load fell away. "Bombs gone!" He called, closely followed with various derivations of 'thank god for that' from throughout the aircraft. As they moved away from the target area in a north easterly direction, Len Symmons caught a radio transmission from the master bomber. "Skipper, Chugboat 1 has just called Lysol."

To Bernard and the crew that was code for return to base with your bombs, but for the majority of the first wave the call had come too late.

The raid had been blessed with little ground fire and no searchlights but the night fighters, which had so far been conspicuous by their absence, were about to make their presence felt. Eight miles beyond the target area Bernard, under the instructions of his navigator, made a sharp turn to starboard onto a new south-easterly track which took them to the west of Bar-le-Duc. From that point the bomber stream began to be attacked by night fighters and the crew could see the occasional burst of gunfire in the darkness. All available eyes aboard 'Hircleberry' were feverishly scanning the darkness, checking for that ominous dark shape that could mean disaster. All around, the Lancasters of the first wave were beginning to take evasive action or to loose off shots at night fighters, both real and imagined.

Eight miles south of Bar-le-Duc they turned again onto a south-westerly route amid the developing chaos around them. Shortly afterwards the first of 166 Squadrons aircraft to be lost that night was shot down in the most tragic circumstances. In the confusion caused by the night fighters, Lancaster PD202, piloted by Flying Officer E.J. Welchman, and another Lancaster, ND993 of 103 Squadron, Piloted by Flying Officer P.J. Abbott, mistook each other for night fighters and exchanged fire, shooting each other down killing all fourteen men aboard.

Once again 'Hircleberry' ploughed on untouched, her gunners, who had recently honed their skills over the North Sea, not firing a shot. With experience they had learned that the gunners' skill was not in what he fired but what he didn't. The .303 Browning machine guns were not a powerful weapon and were more of a deterrent than anything else. It was better to keep your guns silent and try to get through unobserved rather than to loose off at anything that moved and give away your position with the muzzle flash. Firing at the enemy really was a last, desperate resort. Elsewhere, the bomber stream in general and 166 Squadron in particular, were not faring so well. In the second wave, which was still heavily laden with a full bomb load, three more 166 Squadron aircraft were shot down. LL896, piloted by Flying Officer Banville, came down near Montiers-sur-Sauix to the south of Bar-le-Duc with two fatalities but the other five crew members managed to evade capture and make their way home. JB644, piloted by Pilot Officer J. McLaren, was hit and downed near Chevillon with five killed and a further two managing to evade capture. The final loss for 166 Squadron came 25 miles south-east of Troyes as LM388, piloted by Pilot Officer D.C. Gibbons, was hit by a night fighter and came down with two fatalities. Once again the remaining five crew members, including Gibbons, managed to evade capture.

In total, the semi-abortive raid on Revigny cost 1 Group twelve aircraft, four from 103 Squadron, four from 166 Squadron, three from 550 Squadron and one from 576 Squadron, a huge loss rate of 11.2%.

With the worst of the night fighters behind them, Bernard's crew turned to starboard near the small town of Chateauvillain onto a bearing of 248 degrees and headed south-west back across France to their navigation point to the north-west of Vierzon from where they retraced their outward route all the way back across the Channel to the safety of English airspace. However, the dramas were not yet all over as Kirmington was fog bound and all 25 of 166 Squadrons surviving aircraft had to be diverted to R.A.F. Wittering near Peterborough. At 0637 hours, after nine hours and seven minutes in the air, 'Hircleberry' touched down at Wittering with seven men feeling very lucky to be anywhere near home at all.

Having spent the night at Wittering, all the crews were looking forward to heading back to Kirmington as soon as possible but their optimism was soon dashed as they were told to standby for an operation for which they would take off from Wittering. However, at 1345 hours the operation was cancelled and all the aircraft made the forty minute flight back home at 1800 hours. Bernard's crew found that they had been stood down for the raid on 14th July, which was again to be on the Revigny marshalling yards and proved to be yet another difficult night for 166 Squadron. The raid started badly when Lancaster ME647, the first to take off that night, blew a tyre on the runway causing the starboard undercarriage to collapse and the aircraft to slew off the runway. The aircraft came to rest some 125 yards from the runway and, with no fire or explosion, the rest of the aircraft were cleared for take off. The crew of ME647 thankfully escaped unhurt and the aircraft was later recovered and repaired. The next glitch came when the Master Bomber on the raid was unable to identify the target and aborted the operation. On the way home the squadron lost Lancaster ND621, piloted by Pilot Officer S. Martin D.F.C., over France with all the crew being killed. The final insult came as once again, due to bad weather, all the remaining aircraft had to be diverted, this time to R.A.F Mildenhall in Suffolk.

Bernard and his crew were granted the following 48 hours as leave and left the base for some well deserved rest, which mainly involved drinking beer in Lincoln, as a return trip home would have taken up the vast majority of such a short leave period. As it turned out, their two days off didn't allow them to miss any operations as 166 Squadron was not called upon. However, as soon as they returned to base they found themselves back on the Order of Battle for 17th July. At 1135 hours the Squadron was instructed to provide 24 aircraft for a night operation which was subsequently postponed at 1800 hours. At 2045 hours a new target, Sannerville, was passed with the information that the operation would now take place in the early hours of the 18th July.

As if their job was not difficult enough, the briefing informed them that once again they would be bombing German troop and tank positions which were extremely close to the British troops trying to take Caen. The importance of the mission was emphasised by a message from 'Bomber' Harris which was read out at the briefing.

'The operation in which you are taking part is of major importance and likely to lead to historic results. I know you will realise that it is absolutely essential that your bombing is accurate and that you must carry out the instructions of the Master Bomber implicitly.

The destruction of your targets will be decisive. Inaccurate bombing might be disastrous to our own troops. The results you achieve will be of world wide interest. I know you will do your best.'

No pressure there then?!

At 0300 hours on the morning of 18th July, 'Hircleberry' powered down the runway heading for Sannerville, a suburb of Caen, where the British Army were still being held up by well dug in German units. In total some 942 aircraft were to attack five different villages around Caen in an attempt to blast the Germans out of their defensive positions. The Lancasters of 166 Squadron headed south-west to the rally point to the west of Maidenhead, gradually climbing to between six and 8,000 feet and once there, turned to port onto a south-easterly heading, which took them across the coast at Littlehampton where they were joined by a welcome group of Spitfires from 11 Group. Crossing the Channel, the Sun was beginning to make its presence felt with the skies brightening with every passing minute. Some sixty miles north of Caen, and still over the now shimmering waters of the Channel, the force turned again, this time to starboard and onto a southerly course which would take them directly to their target. By 0540 hours the skies were clear and the targets had been marked using the OBOE system with red target indicators which were subsequently backed up by yellow markers. The Luftwaffe had so far failed to make an appearance and British artillery and naval gunfire helped to subdue the flak batteries in the area. That made for a comparatively quiet run in to the target with only slight heavy and light flak, although the light flak did intensify to some extent as the raid went on. With the British troops on the ground within just a few hundred yards of the German positions, it was vital that the bombing was accurate and although the skies were clear in the dawns light, the target itself was already a mass of smoke. The Master Bomber had confirmed by radio that the red and yellow target indicators were in the correct place and satisfied he was accurately placed on them, at 0550 hours and from a height of 8,000 feet, Jock Walker released his bomb load of eleven 1,000 lb and four 500 lb high explosive bombs, all of which were set for instantaneous detonation. There were to be no delayed action fuses as the British Army did not want to get caught during its advance through Caen by exploding bombs dropped by the R.A.F.

With 'Hircleberry's' bomb load helping to make up the grand total of some

6,800 tons of bombs dropped on the target that day, Bernard turned to port away from the target area and then, just a handful of miles later, turned to port again onto an easterly track. Out over the French countryside to the east of Caen, he banked the Lancaster to port for a third time and turned through ninety degrees onto a due north heading taking them back across the French coast and out into the Channel. Jack MacDonald gave his skipper a course adjustment somewhere over the middle of the Channel and then, heading north-west, they crossed the English coast above Worthing en route to Reading where, as usual, the bomber stream split up and headed for their individual home bases. At last the weather was on their side and there was no need for the aircraft to be diverted to alternative bases and at 0730 hours, with LM176's wheels touching the runway at Kirmington, the crew had their fourteenth operation successfully under their belts.

The operation had proved to be a massive success and highly accurate, causing considerable damage to the embedded German units and giving Operation Goodwood the start it needed. 166 Squadron escaped the morning raid unscathed and with a massive force of 942 aircraft all operating in a small area, it was a near miracle that Bomber Command only lost six aircraft; five Halifaxes and one Mosquito.

With the formalities of the intelligence officer out of the way, the crew managed to get to bed unaware of what was to confront them when they woke. While the crews slept, at 1120 hours the squadron was requested to supply eighteen aircraft for an attack that night and Bernard found himself on the Order of Battle once again. The intensity of the air war soon became apparent to him as he faced his second operation of the day.

As 'Hircleberry's' crew approached the briefing room they had all but convinced themselves that the night's raid would be a nice simple one to somewhere in northern France, as surely they wouldn't be asked to carry out anything more serious having already completed one raid that day. All of their reasoning went out the window when the map cover was pulled back and their hopes were shattered and their stomachs knotted with fear as the tape marking the route took them straight to the heart of the Ruhr.

The danger of a mission to the Ruhr valley came not from its distance, as it was relatively close to home for the bomber crews, but because of what it contained. Being the main industrial area of the German war machine the whole area was swamped with searchlights and flak batteries as well as being supported by night fighters and as a result, made any foray into its airspace a death defying feat.

The briefing filled in the details for the crews, informing them that their specific target for the night was to be a synthetic oil plant located between Schloven and Buer, two suburbs of the city of Gelsenkirchen, in the northern area of the Ruhr. At 2200 hours the crew began to taxi into position ready for take off, the seventh in a line of eighteen aircraft being supplied by 166 Squadron that night. It was becoming self evident to the crew that if you survived a few missions it didn't take long to be promoted up the Order of Battle as you became one of the Squadrons more experienced crews. This was to be their fifteenth raid, and if they completed it successfully they would be halfway through their tour of duty, but at that moment there was not a single one of them that could think any further ahead than just surviving the night.

At 2220 hours 'Hircleberry's' wheels left the ground carrying 1,358 gallons of fuel and her bomb load made up of one 4,000 lb 'cookie' and sixteen 500 lb bombs, of which four were delayed fuses of anything up to 144 hours, that's six days. The relentless pursuit of height began immediately as Bernard climbed steadily, having been set a flight and bombing altitude which was rarely seen in those days. The Avro Lancasters absolute service ceiling (maximum flying height) was 24,500 feet and for that nights raid they were to bomb from 21,000 feet.

The extreme height would bring its own problems, with the aircraft becoming less manoeuvrable in the thin air and the engines struggling for oxygen. The crew too would have to wear oxygen masks the whole time they were above 10,000 feet as well as struggling against the biting cold at such extreme height. The Lancaster, along with all but a handful of aircraft at that time, was not pressurised as today's airliners are but was nothing more than a steel tube with inadequate heaters, meaning the crews had to operate while wearing extremely bulky flight suits and thick fingered gloves. However, not to do so could result in bare flesh sticking to frozen metal causing painful and debilitating cold burns.

Climbing away to the south-east, initially for Mablethorpe on the Lincolnshire coast, Bernard gradually watched the needle of the altimeter rotate clockwise as foot after foot was added to their altitude. By the time they crossed the coast above Mablethorpe, they were only at 5,000 feet and turning to port out across the sea they still had another 12,000 feet to climb in order to be at the correct height for the rendezvous point which was halfway across the North Sea. As they climbed they passed through thin stratus cloud which provided about 7/10ths cover up to a height of 6,000 feet but as long as it didn't thicken further over the target, it shouldn't provide any problems for Jock Walker as he delivered his bomb load.

Sixty miles off the Suffolk coast and at a height of 18,000 feet, they reached the rendezvous point where the force of 153 Lancasters formed up and turned again slightly to port heading for the Dutch coast. For the moment still behind them, but soon to overtake them, and then guide them to the target, was a further force of thirteen Pathfinder Mosquitoes of 8 Group. Having made the rendezvous at 18,000 feet, the force headed on towards the Dutch coast and continued to climb, this time to their bombing height of 21,000 feet and at the same time began to eject the foil strips of 'Window' from their aircraft. The bombing height had been set so high for three main reasons. Firstly, the great altitude would help them keep clear of the light flak which would be intense at a lower altitude, although the heavy flak would still be able to reach them; secondly, as the whole area of the Ruhr was deemed a target, precision was not of the highest importance and finally, below them, some 36 aircraft were carrying out operations in support of the resistance. The force crossed the Dutch coast at Castricum to the north of Amsterdam and soon found themselves over water again as they crossed the Ijsselmeer on a heading of 100 degrees which they maintained to the Dutch/German border. In order to keep the German defences guessing as to their true target, the bomber stream made a late, sharp turn to starboard as they crossed the border into Germany onto a new heading of 183 degrees, almost due south, which left them a straight run in of some 54 miles to the target.

As they approached the Ruhr large numbers of searchlights flicked across the sky, sporadically catching an unfortunate Lancaster who would then be coned by several more lights as it desperately weaved and corkscrewed in an attempt to break free of the beams. All the time the heavy flak was growing in concentration until the barrage reached an intense level and the occasional near miss rocked 'Hircleberry's' wings. Down below the cloud had completely dissipated and was replaced with a light industrial haze but it was not thick enough to interfere with the work of the bomb aimers.

At 0125 hours, the Mosquitoes of the Pathfinders released their first red target indicators and the leading aircraft of the main force started to bomb just a minute later. A few miles back in the first wave of aircraft, Bernard saw a huge, orange explosion on the ground which lit up the area around it as well as the night sky even up to their considerable height of 21,000 feet. He checked the time and saw it was 0129 hours and made a mental note for the intelligence officers benefit when he returned. As it turned out, the explosion had been so large and bright that almost every pilot on the raid did the same thing. As 'Hircleberry' made its bomb run with its bay doors open and Jock Walker giving his running commentary, Bernard could see the huge plume of black, oily smoke from the vast explosion rising to around 10,000 feet and concluded that someone had scored a direct hit on one of the oil storage tanks.

The target had been extremely well marked and with the assistance of the smoke and fires on the ground, Jock had no trouble locating the red target indicators and to the relief of all aboard announced "Bombs gone" at 0132 hours and on their first run. Turning slightly to port, Bernard put 'Hircleberry' onto a due south course for just over three miles to get them out of the immediate target area. Exactly a minute later Jack MacDonald, in order to be heard over the noise of the flak and engines and to ensure he wasn't misheard over the most dangerous place on earth, literally shouted through a new heading of 280 degrees. Bernard, as desperate as anyone else aboard to get out of the Ruhr as quickly as he could, pulled the Lancaster round to starboard in a tight 100 degree turn and onto the new heading which would put them on the shortest route out of the danger zone. As they headed out of the valley, the flak began to lessen in its intensity but around them aircraft were still sustaining damage and others were beginning to be intercepted by night fighters. Thirty miles further on, over the town of Sonsbeck, Jack called another course change and 'Hircleberry' turned again to starboard onto a more north-westerly course towards the Dutch town of Nijmegen. With the intensity of the ground fire dropping off, Jack reminded Bernard of the details of their briefing. "Don't forget to drop down to fourteen to 16,000 feet and slow to 190, Skipper." He prompted.

"Think I'll keep the airspeed for now Jack, quite keen to get out of here." Bernard replied as he started his gradual descent.

Their new bearing of 312 degrees took them directly over Nijmegen, just inside the Dutch border, and on to Amersfoort where they turned to port for the coast, which they crossed above Noordwijk. They knew that they were never safe until the engines had come to a stop back at an English airfield, but every little milestone helped and to cross the enemy coast was always a significant moment, at least from here there was no chance of ground-fire ruining their day, although there were still flak ships dotted along the coastal waters. Out above the North Sea, some 55 miles due east of Southwold on the Suffolk coast, they turned to starboard north-westerly towards the Norfolk coast which they touched upon at Sheringham before turning for the last time to starboard, passing across The Wash and the Lincolnshire Wolds to home.

At 0315 hours the crew touched down and could finally relax as their engines came to a stop on their dispersal point back at Kirmington. The last five hours had once again been a test of nerves but this time at the most extreme end of the scale and all the men were relieved, and probably surprised, to be back home safely. Amazingly, despite the intensity of the German defences, 166 Squadron didn't lose a single aircraft on the raid which turned out to be highly successful and accurate, but on landing back at Kirmington, Lancaster ND614, piloted by Pilot Officer P.H. Allen, suffered a collapsed undercarriage and was seriously damaged in the subsequent crash which left the runway completely blocked from 0406 hours. As a result the remaining aircraft had to land on an alternative runway. Thankfully, all the crew escaped unhurt.

In all, the raid cost Bomber Command just five Lancasters, all of which were brought down by flak. Tragically, Lancaster PB171 of 300 Squadron was lost with its all Polish crew carrying out their 28th mission; just two away from completing their tour of duty. Their aircraft and bodies have never been found.

The following day, 19th July 1944, 166 Squadron was requested to provide nineteen aircraft for an attack that night but the mission was duly cancelled at 1253 hours and the squadron stood down. The 20th saw Bernard's crew being rested and so they took no part in the attack that night on the V1 site at Wizernes, a target they desperately wanted to play a part in destroying, but had to console themselves instead with a night in the 'Chopper' waiting for the operating crews to return, which thankfully they all did. If a crew was not required for an operation they had little else to do on an operational Bomber station and as with all young men boredom could set in quickly. The crew of 'Hircleberry' were no exception and by the end of the second day of inactivity their only source of relief came in a beer glass. Unfortunately things would only get worse for them as the planned raid to Dortmund for 21st July was cancelled and then a raid that was set for St. Nazaire on the 22nd was cancelled too. Even the inside of the 'Chopper' was beginning to become tiresome, so it was with a strange sense of relief that they found themselves back in the briefing room just after lunch on 23rd receiving the details for that nights attack which was to be on the German port of Kiel. The crew's relief at finally being active again was tempered by the news that their wireless operator, Len Symmons, had fallen ill and was to be replaced by another experienced man, Flight Sergeant Wolfe, who usually flew in ND707 under the command of Flight Lieutenant Fleming.

The briefing explained that Kiel was to suffer under four waves of attacking aircraft of which the crews of 166 Squadron would help to make up the second wave. 189 Lancasters from 1 Group, 100 Lancasters from 3 Group, 100 Halifaxes of 4 Group, 99 Lancasters from 5 Group, 42 Lancasters from 6 Group and 90 Lancasters with 9 Mosquitoes from the Pathfinding 8 Group, would make up a total force of 629 aircraft who would pound the target. Bernard's bomb load consisted of one 4,000 lb high capacity 'cookie', eight 500 lb medium capacity general purpose bombs, with assorted fuses of between six and 144 hours, and six 'J' clusters. The 'J' cluster had been introduced in early 1944 and was a bomb containing fourteen 30 lb incendiaries, each of which produced a two foot wide by fifteen foot long white flame which burned for more than a minute. Despite its apparently impressive performance it proved to be less effective per ton than the much smaller 4 lb incendiary and was phased out by the end of August 1944.

At 2245 hours 'Hircleberry' left the ground and headed south-east towards the town of Mablethorpe on the Lincolnshire coast, climbing only as high as 2,000 feet as they had been instructed. With the vast majority of the mission due to be flown above the choppy waters of the North Sea, the rendezvous point was not, for once, to be somewhere over southern England but this time a long way east over the North Sea. As a result, in excess of 600 aircraft made their way at low altitude out over the coast and towards the point where they would form up into their four waves for the attack.

At Mablethorpe Jack MacDonald called up with a course change onto a new bearing of 070 degrees and Bernard turned steadily to port until he settled on the correct bearing, heading north-east out over the coast. For the next 200 miles they maintained the same course and kept their height down to below 2,000 feet in order to avoid radar detection. As they had taken off, the cloud had been thin but with 10/10ths coverage and its base at 2,000 feet. As a result it felt as though they were flying around a room with their heads almost brushing the ceiling as the cloud base was just a few feet above them. However, it allowed them good visibility of the sea below as well as the odd Lancaster scattered around them and also provided a very close bit of cover should any far ranging Germans appear. Finally, as they crossed the four degree east line of longitude, Jack called up a new heading. "072 degrees, Skipper."

"It's hardly bloody worth it!" Joked Bernard, as he made the small adjustment to starboard and watched his instruments settle almost immediately onto the correct course.

"You can start to climb now, Skipper. Up to between seventeen and 19,000 feet." Informed Jack.

"We'll go for the nineteen. Someone told me those Germans have Flak you know?" Bernard joked again as he pulled the nose up and headed into the cloud.

It didn't take long for 'Hircleberry' to break through the top of the cloud which was at 5,000 feet and into the clear night sky above. For the next 125 miles they steadily climbed with more and more bombers becoming visible to them as the force converged on the rendezvous point. Ahead they could just make out a few of the first wave and around them the other 139 aircraft that would attack in their second wave became steadily more and more concentrated.

At a point some 75 miles west of the German coast, Jack informed "This is the rendezvous point, Skipper. You can climb to between twenty and 22,000 feet, new bearing 091 degrees."

As always Bernard did as he was told and took the opportunity to slip into his favoured position in the stream, muttering his apologies to himself as he did so.

The next call from Jack came as he called "Enemy coast ahead." as they slipped over the sparsely populated German coast of the Danish peninsular between the towns of Langenhorn and Bredstedt. At that point, the southern end of the Danish Peninsular (which is part of Germany and not Denmark) is less than fifty miles across and the bomber stream had nearly crossed its entirety before they turned again, this time onto the bomb run for their target. Turning with the rest of their wave onto a new bearing of 149 degrees they were heading south-east and were just 25 miles from Kiel.

As the aircraft approached Kiel the customary flak began to burst in the sky around them but it was described as a 'moderate' amount of heavy flak and so far seemed to have caused the bomber stream few problems. Up ahead, at 0114 hours, the Mosquitoes began to drop flares and sticks of red target indicators which were solely for the benefit of the Pathfinder force. They, under the instruction of the Master Bomber who had checked their accuracy using his H2S ground reading radar, duly backed up the precisely dropped markers with red and green target indicators for the first wave to bomb on. At bang on 0120 hours, as planned, the first bombs began to fall.

Further back in the second wave 'Hircleberry's' stand in Wireless Operator was skilfully picking out the Master Bombers instructions from the German radio jamming and confirmed that the target indicators were in the right place. With everything set, Jock Walker settled into his bomb sight and Bernard opened the bomb bay doors. "There are a lot of red and green markers down there". Reported Jock. As the markers came into his sights they were complemented by an already bright glow from fires caused by the first wave which reflected on the thin clouds; from a height of 22,000 feet at 0127 hours Jock released his bomb load.

Maintaining his course for the obligatory bombing photograph, Bernard took the opportunity to close the bomb bay doors while Jack called up a new bearing of 191 degrees. With the photograph taken they turned to starboard and headed out of the target area to the south-west. Once Kiel was ten miles behind them and with the flak having died away, they turned again to starboard onto a bearing of 286 degrees which took them north-west back across the Danish peninsular where they crossed the west coast at Osterhever and back out into the monotony of the North Sea.

As LM176 arrived at the same point above the North Sea where the rendezvous had been on the route out, Bernard turned her to port and onto a south-westerly heading which would retrace their route back to Mablethorpe and eventually back to Kirmington. Travelling across the North Sea the journey was uneventful with few night fighters being spotted by any of the Bomber Command aircraft much beyond the German coast. At 0350 hours, five hours and five minutes after taking off, 'Hircleberry's' crew touched down safely and taxied back to their dispersal. By the time they had completed all their duties and disembarked the aircraft the time had just ticked past 0400 hours and they watched as ND614, piloted by Pilot Officer Allen, came into land. Everything looked to be fine until his wheels made contact with the runway and the undercarriage, having been damaged by flak, folded up under the aircraft. The fuselage thumped down on the concrete and skidded for what seemed an eternity accompanied by the screeching of metal on stone until finally coming to rest, still on the runway. The watching personnel on the airfield, including the crew of 'Hircleberry', held their breath in anticipation of a fire or explosion which so often accompanied such accidents, but thankfully neither came and all the crew managed to escape safely. It just went to show that at no time could you call yourself safe until you were back in the company of the Intelligence Officer.

The raid on Kiel had been Bomber Commands first major raid on a German city for nearly two months and for a variety of reasons had been an overwhelming success. The German, long range, Freya radar system had been successfully jammed by Mandrel sets carried in some of the attacking aircraft and as a result the defenders were only expecting a handful of aircraft, probably on a mine laying mission, instead of the 629 that had been sent. As a result the German night fighters were ill prepared and Bomber Command lost just four Lancasters on the raid, 0.6 % of the attacking force.

The city of Kiel suffered under its heaviest attack of the war that night. Of the 629 aircraft due to attack, 612 did so and dropped over 2,900 tons of ordinance on the city in just 25 minutes. The bombing was well concentrated in the port area, although all parts of the city were hit, with considerable damage to the U-boat and naval yards. 315 people were killed in the raid and the more than 500 delayed action bombs caused havoc for days to come with there being no public transport for over a week and no cooking gas for three weeks.

The Order of Battle for 24th July, which arrived at just after 1100 hours, found Bernard's crew missing from the eighteen aircraft listed. As it turned out, the squadron's target for the night was to be Stuttgart and of the eighteen aircraft sent, only sixteen would come back. Lancaster ND628, piloted by an Australian, Pilot Officer G.L. Heath, and ND634 piloted by an American, Flying Officer W.G. Shearer, were both brought down near the target to the north-west of Stuttgart with the loss of all their crew.

The following day, 25th July, saw the Order of Battle posted at 1117 hours and required fifteen aircraft for that night's raid with Bernard and his crew being listed at number eight alongside their trusty 'Hircleberry'. The crew were already a little uncomfortable as they settled into the briefing room as their Wireless Operator, Len Symmons, was still suffering from his illness and had been replaced once again by Flight Sergeant Wolfe; their mood was not improved as the target was revealed once again to be Stuttgart. "They've forgotten to change the map." Bernard quipped to Jack MacDonald in the vain hope that he was correct. But there had been no mistake and the target that had claimed two of 166 Squadrons crews the night before was to be hit again and every man in the room was instantly aware of how dangerous the night's mission was going to be.

The first of 166 Squadrons aircraft to take off that night, Piloted by Flying Officer R.J.B. Cann, left the ground at just after 2100 hours and Bernard followed at 2120. The crew was well prepared for what they knew was going to be a very long flight and the first leg took them south-west to Reading before turning towards the south-east and heading out over the English coast at Bognor Regis. Having rendezvoused with the main force 10,000 feet above Bognor, they ploughed on across the Channel. The force continued to climb and crossed the French coast above Houlgate, to the east of Caen, having by then climbed to 12,000 feet. Below them the still German occupied French countryside was blanketed in cloud and gave no assistance to the hard pressed navigators. A few miles inland, Bernard banked to port as instructed by Jack MacDonald and stayed in his favoured position with the tail wheel of another Lancaster visible above him. For the next 125 miles they maintained the same course, with a thick blanket of cloud obscuring the ground the whole time. Nineteen miles to the south-west of the French town of Orleans, they turned on to a course slightly to the north of due east and began the longest leg of the flight. Soon after the 25th had become the 26th July, at 0040 hours, near the town of Courson-les-Carrieres, 166 Squadron suffered its first casualty of the night as Lancaster LM386, piloted by Flying Officer B.T. Singleton, crashed killing all aboard, probably after being hit by flak. The monotony of flying almost blind for the next 250 miles in thick cloud was only made bearable by the fact that it afforded them considerable protection from any German defences, either airborne or ground based until finally, after more than an hour on the same course and nearly at the Swiss border, they turned on to a north-easterly course which would take them past Strasbourg and to the west of Karlsruhe.

As the bomber force passed Strasbourg their route kept the Germans guessing as to where their target might eventually be as Stuttgart lay off to their starboard side and was steadily disappearing behind them. From their current position and direction they could have still been heading for Mannheim, Heidelberg or any one of a dozen other German towns. The force eventually revealed their hand when, at a position fifteen miles north of Karlsruhe, they made a sudden and sharp ninety degree turn to starboard on to a south-easterly track which would have left the Germans in no doubt of their intended target as Stuttgart lay just fifty miles away and was dead ahead. As they neared the city the flak began to build at heights between sixteen and 18,000 feet but probably due to the previous nights raid it never became intense.

The Pathfinders, which were 95 Lancasters from 8 Group, began to mark the target with red and green indicators but had arrived over the target a little early. The allotted bombing time, 'H' hour, was supposed to be 0155 hours but the first crews of the main force began to drop their bombs at 0151. For the next 33 minutes, 138 Halifaxes and 412 Lancasters pounded Stuttgart. Each main force Lancaster was loaded with one 2,000 lb high explosive bomb and twelve 'J' type cluster bombs and at 0204 hours Jock Walker added his bombs to the melee. Through his sight Jock could see a large group of mixed red and green markers and released his bombs over the centre of them noting that the attack seemed to be falling in the centre of the town with a ring of fires surrounding it. As the raid went on, the Pathfinders marking became more scattered until there were several groups of markers which all received a good concentration of bombs. Flying on past the target for some twelve miles, Jack called a course change and Bernard banked to starboard onto a south-westerly heading before turning again to starboard just to the north of Reutlingen and heading north-westward back across the German border.

Once across the German border, Jack gave Bernard a new heading of 253 degrees and he turned 'Hircleberry' to port to begin the long trawl back across France. By then they were some 75 miles to the west of Stuttgart but despite the distance 'Doc' Boyd called up from his rear turret to report that he could still see the glow from the fires. For the next 180 miles they maintained the same course, passing to the south of Nancy and Troyes until finally making another turn, some eighty miles to the south-east of Paris, onto a new north-westerly course. The time in the air was beginning to take its toll and they still had a considerable distance to go before they even got out of enemy territory. The will to survive coupled with the adrenaline coursing through their bodies helped to keep tiredness at bay and each man remained alert, every available eye scanning the dark sky for night fighters while Jack was hunched over his navigators table checking and re-checking his course and calculations. His final course change over France, which came just south of Chartres, took them onto a bearing of 322 degrees and on course to cross the French coast at Villers-sur-mer which would see them bisect the heavy flak concentrations around Caen and Le Havre. As they crossed the coast there were a few distant bursts of flak but their accurate course had kept them out of range of the worst of it and finally they were back above the Channel and heading directly for Reading.

Tired and relieved, the crew of LM176 touched down on the welcoming Kirmington concrete at 0555 hours, having been in the air for over eight and a half hours. After completing the formalities of debriefing, the losses to the squadron that night started to become apparent. Bomber Command had lost a total of eight Lancasters and four Halifaxes on the raid. As the time passed by which the aircraft would have run out of fuel and with no notification from another station of any diversionary landings, the men knew who was not going to make it back. Yet again Stuttgart had taken a significant toll on 166 Squadron with the loss not only of Flying Officer Singleton's crew but also the squadrons most experienced crew, that of Flying Officer R.J.B. Cann in Lancaster JB649. With every man aboard having completed at least 28 missions they were perilously close to finishing their tour and the rest of 166 Squadron could only hope that they had bailed out safely somewhere. While the men who had made it back to base began to take to their beds, in the French countryside all seven of Lancaster JB649's crew had indeed managed to bail out safely and were holed up for the night in places they hoped would keep them from the Germans clutches. Astonishingly all seven successfully evaded capture and managed to make their way safely back home.

After a hearty breakfast and a well deserved sleep, the majority of the day had already passed by the time the crews emerged from their beds. The night of the 26th July would see 166 Squadron send six crews to lay sea mines in the Heligoland Bight, off the coast of Wilhelmshaven, but Bernard's crew was not amongst those chosen so they decided to head off with several other crews to the village of Kirmington and more specifically, 'The Chopper'. 'The Chopper' was the colloquialism for the local pub which was, and still is, more correctly known as the Marrowbone and Cleaver. The pub was a squat building with two separate bars, one to either side of a central doorway and had an air of being cramped even when half empty. Luckily, as the weather was warm, the men could congregate outside in the garden when the thick, smoky atmosphere became too much of a fug. With so many of the stations crews being stood down for the night, even the garden was busy and the evening soon became rowdy as more warm ale was consumed and the men, interspersed with a few W.A.A.F.'s, celebrated the fact that for tonight at least they were still alive. By the time the landlord called a halt to proceedings, Bernard found himself separated from most of his crew and amongst a group of mixed aircrew and three W.A.A.F.'s whose sober occupation was as some of the bases air traffic controllers. As the group polished off their drinks a couple of the airmen headed off to stagger back to their Nissen huts while the three W.A.A.F.'s headed back down the village's only street to their barracks which were nestled some 500 yards away in a farmers field opposite the church.

That left just Bernard and Sammy Small gently swaying on unsteady legs as they drained their glasses. Sammy's crew had arrived at Kirmington just a fortnight before Bernard's and the two crews were both billeted in the same dispersed site and as a result the fourteen men had struck up a good friendship. Sammy was a wireless operator holding the rank of Pilot Officer in an experienced crew piloted by Flight Lieutenant, soon to be Squadron Leader, Rippon and had a similar mischievous air to him as Bernard had.

"Better get off then, it's a bloody long stagger from here". Said Bernard.

"Not for us old boy". Corrected Sammy "I've got the old steed parked up over there, hop on and I'll give you a pillion." Sammy explained, as he vaguely waved a pointed finger across the car park to his motorbike which leant against the side wall of the pub.

Bernard downed the last dregs of his pint and with a broad grin spreading across his face accepted the offer of a lift with a single word "Splendid!"

Sammy was equally as drunk as Bernard and their first attempt at climbing aboard resulted in both men, along with the motorbike, lying in a giggling heap on the floor. After several more abortive attempts, all of which had resulted in them losing their balance and ending up in a similar heap, they finally managed to get the bike started with Bernard clinging to one of the pubs downpipes while straddling the bike to stabilise it as Sammy operated the kick start. Eventually they managed to wobble off out of the village at an extremely slow speed. With no street lights and only a slit for a headlight, due to blackout precautions, the two men could barely see their hand in front of their face let alone the road and before they managed to get to the junction of the main road, which took them back to the bases main gate, Sammy lost control and they bumped down into the drainage ditch to the side of the road. The ditch still had some water in it despite it being late July and there was a layer of mud although the underlying ground was reasonably firm. Sloshing about for a few minutes the two men found their situation increasingly hilarious and eventually realised there was no way they could lift the heavy bike back out of the ditch.

"Oh well, back to plan A then Sammy. We'd better start walking; we'll come and pick it up tomorrow." Said Bernard.

"Hold on a minute. This ditch runs all the way along the road, we'll just ride down this instead. Of course it has the added benefit of preventing us getting lost and should help to keep us upright too!" Replied Sammy, as he was struck by what at the time seemed a splendid idea.

"OK, Skipper, take us home." Agreed Bernard, as he climbed back on the pillion and Sammy kicked the bike back into life.

As they sped down the ditch with increasing confidence, they howled with laughter as huge sprays of mud and brackish water flew up behind them covering their once pristine uniforms as they went. The intrepid pair's unofficial sortie came to an abrupt end as the sight of the bases main entrance loomed before them. A guard, alerted by the bikes engine and the howls coming from its passengers, had ventured to the middle of the road and could just make out the speck of light that was the bikes headlight coming towards him. Then suddenly the noise stopped and was replaced by two thuds followed by a short silence. Fifty yards from the main gate was a crossroads and the bike had met with a ninety degree turn in the ditch, throwing both men off the bike yet again and onto the grassy bank. After a momentary pause while their drunken brains checked that they were uninjured and realising that they were, they began screeching with laughter again as they helped each other to their feet and staggered towards the stunned guard.

Forgetting his protocol he shouted at the mud spattered and sodden drunks who lurched towards him "Who the bloody hell are you two?"

"I'm Adolf Hitler and this is Herman Goering; we've come to look at your lovely base, so be a good chap and show us where the bar is would you?" Quipped Bernard.

"I should shoot you two; bloody pilots." Grumbled the guard as he watched them stagger off down the road towards their Nissen huts to sleep it off.

Bernard felt a little delicate the following day and was delighted to hear that the operation set for that night had been cancelled, but he had managed to make a full recovery by lunchtime and took 'Hircleberry' aloft for a 45 minute air test that afternoon after having previously helped Sammy recover his filthy bike from the ditch.

At 1115 hours on 28th July, the daylight operation that had been planned was cancelled and a night raid, for which twenty aircraft were required, replaced it. Bernard's crew were now the fifth most experienced crew on the squadron and as usual were listed alongside 'Hircleberry' who had performed well during the previous days air test having undergone some routine repairs and maintenance.

As the target map was revealed at the start of the briefing there was an audible groan from the assembled crews and Jack MacDonald summed it up with three words. "Oh, bloody hell!" It was Stuttgart again.

LM176 began to rumble along the Kirmington runway at 2135 hours and hauled herself, along with 2,154 gallons of petrol and 9,000 lbs of bombs, off the ground and into the air. As was more often the case than not, their first point of navigation was to be in the skies above Reading. What the people of that particular town had done to upset the Air Ministry is not known but night after night aircraft gathered there before heading off to their various targets, sleep must have been a rare commodity for Readingites. Their route for the night took a more southerly course than the south-eastern one they had used two nights before and saw them rendezvous with the rest of the force at 12,000 feet as they crossed the coast at Selsey Bill. Maintaining their heading, the bomber stream, which by then numbered some 494 Lancasters and two Mosquitoes, continued to climb until they crossed the French coast above the Canadian invasion beach of Juno at a height of 17,000 feet. Still maintaining their southerly heading, they crossed Normandy but could see none of the French countryside as it was blanketed in nine to 10/10ths cloud, although at their height, way above the tops of the cloud, the moon was bright and the other aircraft of the stream were clearly visible.

Some seventy miles inland of the French coast, Jack MacDonald barked out his first course change of the night over occupied territory and Bernard, as instructed, turned to port and onto a south-easterly heading which would take them just to the north of Le Mans. Almost immediately after making their turn, the aircraft began throwing out their bundles of foil strips; the 'Window', which helped to confuse the German radar. So far the trip had been quiet and uneventful. There had been a couple of flashes of ground fire as they passed Le Mans but they were well out of the guns range and so far the German night fighters had failed to show up. The massive force thundered through the gap to the north of Le Mans and to the south of Orleans, until at a position to the south west of Orleans, they turned again to port and on to a bearing of 085 degrees which put them on a track parallel to, and south of, the one they had flown two nights before. Almost immediately, as if from nowhere, the relative peace of the trip so far was shattered as the dark, unmistakeable shapes of night fighters began to jink and weave amongst the bomber stream. With the visibility still extremely good above the cloud, the men of LM176 could clearly see bursts of gunfire both from the attacking Germans and from the Lancasters defensive Browning machine guns and for the next 180 miles, every so often they could see another Lancaster drop away in its slow death slide from the bomber stream, sometimes in flame and sometimes in sombre darkness.

With every available eye scanning the night sky 'Hircleberry' pushed on, all the time with another Lancaster above and slightly in front of her. For mile after mile they sped on across France, helplessly watching their colleagues take a battering while miraculously being left alone themselves. Surely it was only a matter of time before some Nazi pilot spotted them and it would be their turn to fight for their lives. Eventually Jack called through another course change and Bernard turned to port and onto a north-easterly heading which would take them to the west of Strasbourg. Maintaining the same heading for just over 100 miles they reached their next navigation point above the small town of Bouxwillen just inside the French border with Germany. Still around them the fighters were doing their worst as Bernard turned to starboard back onto a heading of 085 degrees which took them eastward towards the River Rhine. Somewhere beneath the cloud cover lay the river which described the German border with France and as they crossed it they were truly within the Reich. Just ten miles inside Germany, and a few miles south of Karlsruhe, Jack called up again. "100 degrees, Skipper. This is the bomb run."

"Looks like the fighters have had enough, I haven't seen any for a few minutes." Reported Les Bignell from the mid upper turret.

"Great, just in time to be replaced by flak." Said Gordon Cardew wryly. Bernard didn't reply but nodded and raised his eyebrows in agreement.

At 0138 hours the first Pathfinders began to mark the target with red target indicators and Wanganui sky markers which illuminated as green and yellow stars. Wanganui markers hung in the air and provided a method of marking the target when it was obscured by cloud. Initially the marking was a little scattered but with subsequent re-marking it became more concentrated. The aircraft of 166 Squadron were part of the first wave of attacking aircraft and just a few minutes after 'H' hour, which was 0145 hours, 'Hircleberry' found herself directly above Stuttgart at 17,500 feet. Down below, through the bulbous, Perspex nose and his bomb sight, Jock Walker could see nothing but the cloud which blanketed the target. As he prepared to release his bombs there was a huge explosion on the ground and he noted that his watch read 0147 hours. At 0149 hours, with the H2S ground reading radar telling them they were over the target, he released his 4,000 lb cookie along with ten 500 lb medium capacity, high explosive bombs and as far as weapons delivery was concerned their job was done. As always with a bombing mission, from that moment on they were flying for themselves and it was all about staying alive.

Bernard kept 'Hircleberry' straight and level for long enough to allow the photoflash to do its work then, under the instruction of his trusty navigator, banked to starboard and onto a new heading of 190 degrees to begin their escape from the target area. Flak bursts had begun several miles before they reached the target and were continuing as they left it but for once it didn't seem to be quite so intense, perhaps they had neutralized it on their previous raids, but all that mattered to them was that it wasn't as heavy as they had expected, after all, the fighters had been enough for one night and they still had to get back across France.

Twenty miles south-east of Stuttgart Bernard turned the Lancaster again to starboard above the small town of Metzingen and began the long journey out of Germany and across France. Heading north-west they crossed back over the Rhine and as had happened two nights before, 'Doc' Boyd reported that he could still see the glow of the fires from the heavily stricken target. In less than half an hour, between 0144 and 0212 hours, the force had dropped over 1,286 tons of bombs and 330 tons of incendiaries on the city.

Not far inside France they turned to port onto a south-westerly heading and followed the same route home they had taken on their last visit to Stuttgart. Every man aboard was expecting the night fighters to re-appear for a second go at the remaining bombers but for now the skies were quiet except for the surviving Lancasters, each intent on getting back home.

Still high up at 17,000 feet, they passed to the south of the towns of Nancy and Troyes. While passing Troyes Jack informed Bernard that he could start to lose height and gain speed down as low as 4,000 feet. Happy to try and get out of France as soon as possible, he pushed the nose forward and went into a shallow dive bringing his speed up to around 220 mph. By the time they were directly south of Paris he had taken 'Hircleberry' right down to 4,000 feet and kept his air speed as high as he dared without risking his engines which were being carefully monitored by the ever efficient Gordon Cardew. Fifteen miles to the south-west of Chartres they turned to starboard and onto a north-westerly track for the run to the French coast until, forty miles short of the coast, Jack instructed Bernard to begin to climb again to avoid ground fire from the coastal batteries and he managed to get 'Hircleberry' up to 9,000 feet as they crossed the coast at Villers-sur-mer. With France behind them the entire crew was amazed not to have seen any night fighters on the return journey but they were by then sufficiently experienced to know that it wasn't over yet and you weren't truly safe until you were back in the sparse confines of your Nissen hut.

The Channel was still cloud covered, as it had been on the outward journey, and they had to take Jack's word for it when he instructed them that they had just crossed the English coast at Bognor. As was almost customary the force continued on until they disturbed the good people of Reading for a second time that night before dispersing for their home bases. At 0550 hours Bernard deftly touched down back at Kirmington, once again amazed at how they had managed to come through unscathed. The next horror they had to face was to find out just who hadn't been quite so lucky.

Within a relatively short space of time it became evident that 166 Squadron had had an exceptional night as all the crews landed back at Kirmington safely. However, the story for bomber command as a whole was not a pretty one. As well as the raid on Stuttgart there had been another on Hamburg that night with 187 Halifaxes and 106 Lancasters making up that particular attack. The mystery of the missing night fighters on the return journey from Stuttgart was solved as they had hit the aircraft returning from Hamburg instead, shooting down some seven Lancasters and nineteen Halifaxes. However, the aircraft of the Stuttgart raid, who had been hit on the way out, had suffered even greater losses with forty Lancasters being shot down. In total Bomber Command lost 345 men killed and a further 79 taken prisoner; it was nothing less than a miracle that 166 Squadron had come through the night unscathed.

The crews of 166 Squadron would not have known the true extent of the losses of the night of 28th/29th July as Bomber Command didn't advertise such things, but they would have known just by looking out of their own aircraft windows that the losses had been heavy and that they had been most fortunate to come through untouched. Bernard's crew were stood down for the raid on 30th July as 21 aircraft of 166 Squadron joined a force of 692 aircraft that attacked German positions in Normandy in support of the advancing American ground troops. The final day of July saw the squadron, including Bernard's crew, readied for an attack on the docks of Le Havre with the Squadron's lead aircraft and its crew, piloted by Flying Officer Hutchinson, due to fly the last mission of their tour and to mark the occasion they were to be accompanied on the raid by the base commander, Wing Commander Garner.

The raid on Le Havre was to be a daylight one and at 1800 hours 'Hircleberry' took off, one of the first of the seventeen relieved crews of 166 Squadron, who were much happier with the day's choice of target. Once again the first navigation point was over Reading where the force of fifty 1 Group aircraft turned towards the coast at Bognor Regis. Out over the Channel the Lancasters turned to port onto a south-easterly course which would take them direct to their target some forty miles away. As they made their turn onto the bomb run Les Bignell called up on the intercom. "Our friends have arrived, Skipper. Spitfires above us." For the rest of the run in to the target the Spitfires held their station providing protection from above the bombing force. The weather all the way to the target was good with only 3/10ths cloud up to about 6,000 feet and even that had dissipated by the time the aircraft arrived over the target. At 1956 hours the first Pathfinders dropped their red markers but the Master Bomber called up almost immediately. Len Symmons was straight on the intercom to his bomb aimer. "We're to aim slightly to port of the markers, Jock."

Jock Walker confirmed the instruction and settled down to his bomb sight. As they neared the port the barrage of heavy flak grew in intensity, buffeting the aircraft as they made their way ever closer to their target and several aircraft were hit. Lancaster JB746 of 103 Squadron, piloted by Canadian Flying Officer J.L.G. Avon, had a wing blown clean off with five of the crew being killed and the remaining two managing to bale out and be taken as prisoners of war. Below, Jock could at last see the aiming point which was already beginning to become obscured by the smoke of the bomb bursts. From 14,000 feet and satisfied with his position as he identified the red target indicators, he dropped his load of eleven 1,000 lb and four 500 lb bombs into the port area at 1949 hours.

Maintaining his course, Bernard stayed straight and level through the continuing flak barrage to take the bombing photograph and then, three miles south-east of the target, banked sharply to starboard flying above the sea and parallel to the coast for the next eight miles which carried them out of the range of the flak barrage. Then, on the instructions of Jack MacDonald, Bernard threw the Lancaster into an even sharper 107 degree turn to starboard and onto a new bearing of 343 degrees, setting them on a north-westerly course back to England and the familiar landmarks of Bognor Regis and then Reading.

As 'Hircleberry's' wheels touched down at Kirmington at 2135 hours, the crew couldn't help but feel as if the mission had passed incredibly quickly. With their previous two raids having lasted for over eight hours apiece, this one had been completed in just three and a half and they were back in time to go to bed at a relatively normal hour. The attack had been highly accurate, with one crew claiming to have hit a submarine, and all the bombing being closely grouped with the only loss to Bomber Command being the unfortunate Lancaster JB746 of 103 squadron.

The raid on Le Havre counted as the crews nineteenth of their tour of thirty but it almost felt like cheating when they compared it with the likes of Stuttgart. However, they would happily take Le Havre another eleven times if they could.

The first day of August saw nineteen aircraft of 166 Squadron set to join a daylight raid on various separate V1 sites. The raid totalled some 777 aircraft spread across thirteen launching sites, with fifty Lancasters from One Group being allocated the target of Bellecroix/ Les Bruyers. The fifty Lancasters were made up of eight from 103 Squadron, nineteen from 166, twelve from 576 and eleven from 550, backed up by five Mosquitoes and two Lancasters as Pathfinders from Eight Group.

At 1840 hours Bernard eased 'Hircleberry' from the ground and climbed into the thick cloud which provided 10/10ths cover with its tops at just 3,000 feet. The aircraft slavishly headed south-east climbing towards the rendezvous at Orford Ness on the Suffolk Coast, and by the time they reached it they were at 12,000 feet. Up above the cloud the skies were of course clear and the fifty aircraft joined up and continued towards the target on a heading of 165 degrees which took them south-east across the North Sea and direct to their target located on the outskirts of St. Omer.

Maintaining height and position, Bernard felt as happy as it was possible to do so on a mission, as this was a relatively short run with a minimum time being spent over occupied territory. The thick cloud cover would help to protect them from ground fire and their only real fear was the appearance of German fighters. Although he knew that experience could not guarantee safety, he felt confident in his crew who had proved themselves to be efficient and professional many times over already. He had 'Hircleberry' in his favoured position; just below and just behind; and so far all was well.

At 2021 hours Jack called up from his navigators table. "That's the enemy coast, Skipper." Bernard looked down and realised he would have to take Jack's word for it as below him the cloud was still as thick as it had been when they took off and there was nothing to be seen of land or sea. The aircraft had crossed the French coast at Gravelines, ten miles to the west of Dunkirk, and they received some buffeting from the predicted heavy flak which was sent up from both towns and resulted in two of the Lancasters receiving some minor flak damage. A few minutes later, at 2024 hours, as the flak from Dunkirk and Gravelines subsided and was replaced with more from St. Omer; Len Symmons received a message on his wireless set and relayed it immediately to Bernard.

"Rembrandt has called Sultana, Skipper! Repeat Sultana, Skipper."

The entire crew instantly knew that Sultana meant abandon the mission and Jack immediately set about calculating a new course which saw them turn sharply to port onto a bearing of 090 degrees (due east) taking them to the north of their intended target and the town of St. Omer. Over the village of Cassel, Jack turned them northward back onto their intended course home which this time saw them cross the coast ten miles to the east of Dunkirk, just inside the French border with Belgium. All the time Les Bignell and 'Doc' Boyd scanned the sky for fighters with Les turning his mid-upper turret first one way and then the other making full 360 degree sweeps of the sky. In the nose, Jock Walker, with his primary role having been made redundant, took up permanent station in the front turret, adding another set of beady eyes to the defence of "Hircleberry" and her crew.

Over the sea they jettisoned enough of their bomb load to bring them below the safe landing weight and with still no sign of any German fighters, they turned once again to port and onto a new heading of 340 degrees taking them most of the way back across the North Sea. Eight miles off the coast of Southwold in Suffolk, they made their final course adjustment for home and at 2135 hours, two hours and 55 minutes after take off, they descended through the cloud to land safely back at Kirmington full of disappointment at having been so close to the target and yet unable to bomb. With St. Omer just a couple of miles from the target area the master bomber had no choice but to call off the attack, as to have gone ahead without visual confirmation would have almost certainly resulted in the town being bombed and the slaughter of many innocent French civilians. As it turned out, the cloud blanket extended right across northern France that day and of the 777 aircraft sent to attack, only 79 actually dropped their bombs with thankfully no aircraft lost.

With the disappointment of the previous nights raid behind them, 166 Squadron were required to put up 25 aircraft for another daylight raid on the French port of Le Havre on 2nd August. At 1645 hours 'Hircleberry' began her run down the Kirmington runway and into the air. Heading south-east, they climbed steadily towards their first navigation point which was off the north Kent coast near Whitstable. On Jack's instructions, Bernard turned the Lancaster to starboard and onto a new heading to the south-west which took them across the Kent Downs and over the southern English coast at Rye. Once above the Channel, the main force began to form up into its two waves, the first consisting of twenty aircraft with the best crews, especially bomb aimers, followed by the remaining 31 Lancasters from 1 Group; the Pathfinders who led them consisted of three Lancasters and five Mosquitoes from 8 Group. The crew of 'Hircleberry' were amongst those deemed to be the best crews and Jock Walker had proved himself to be a highly competent bomb aimer and so LM176 took up a position towards the front of the formation.

The fully formed force crossed the Channel at 12,000 feet, turning midway across onto their bomb run. At 1854 hours the first Pathfinders began to drop their red target indicators and were then backed up by the rest dropping yellow target indicators which burst at 4,000 feet and cascaded to the ground leaving trails of white smoke behind them. The first twenty Lancasters of the main force were only minutes behind and were already on their bomb run when the master bomber called up and informed them to bomb 200 yards short of the markers as the Pathfinders had slightly overshot. The accuracy that Bomber Command was now able to achieve was truly remarkable considering how they had struggled even to find the right town just a couple of years before.

Looking down through the Perspex nose, Jock Walker could see Le Havre laid out clearly below him with no cloud to obscure his view. Ahead, the first aircraft began bombing at 1859 hours with moderate levels of heavy flak rising up to meet them. Luckily, although the height of the flak was accurate, the direction was not, and only minor damage was suffered by just one aircraft. At 1902 the Bassin de la Barre area of the port, which was the aiming point, loomed into Jock's bomb site. Taking into account the 200 yard adjustment, he dropped his bomb load of eleven 1,000 lb and four 500 lb general purpose bombs from a height of 13,000 feet. Below he could clearly see the yellow markers although the target was already becoming obscured by smoke from the well aimed bombing to which they had just added. It was apparent that the attack had been accurate and well concentrated with the vast majority of the bombs falling on the harbour works and in the vicinity of the aiming point, causing several large fires which sent thick smoke rising to a considerable height. As soon as the bombing photograph had been taken they banked to port and away from the target area and then, five miles further on, turned ninety degrees to starboard taking them onto a course above the Channel and parallel with the coast. After another eight miles they turned again to starboard onto a north-westerly track which they maintained all the way back across the Channel to the English coast at Wittering and onto the Berkshire Downs. Looking down to his port side, Bernard knew that somewhere just beneath him his young son would now be preparing for bed and he smiled to himself at the thought and longed to be there to tuck him in. His moment of sentimentality was soon shattered as Jack MacDonald called up a course change and Bernard turned the Lancaster away from his son and wife and headed back to Kirmington where they landed at 2030 hours satisfied at a job well and safely done.

At 2232 hours, just a couple of hours after the crews had returned safely from Le Havre, the teleprinter buzzed into life with a request from headquarters for aircraft for the following day. All the message said was that 166 Squadron was requested to ready 23 aircraft for an operation early on 3rd August. It looked like the crews prospects for a lie in had all but vanished.

Sure enough the details of yet another daylight raid were received on the teleprinter at 0300 hours on the morning of 3rd August. By 1100 hours all 23 aircraft detailed to attack from 166 Squadron were running up their engines having been bombed up, repaired and armed with their crews briefed and breakfasted.

The rapid turn around of the aircraft was a testament to the hard working and superbly professional ground crews who worked tirelessly, often in difficult conditions and with very little recognition. The target for the day was to be a V1 storage and launching site at Trossy-St-Maximin, about 25 miles north of Paris and just south of the town of Creil. At 1120 hours the green light winked at Bernard from the signal van and he accelerated down the runway and into the air. Their first navigation point lay to the south-west; the town of Northampton, where they made a minor course adjustment onto the familiar heading which took them towards Reading. The force comprised some 180 Lancasters of 1 Group which was split into three sections. The first wave, which was to maintain a height of 13,000 feet, consisted of 55 aircraft led by two formations of three aircraft flying in vics (V shapes) who were designated the 'lead formations' and were distinguished by white painted stripes on the fins and upper and lower surfaces of the tail. They were to be the first aircraft to bomb the Pathfinders markers and on no account were any other aircraft of the main force allowed to overtake them. Following them was a wave of 66, which included the aircraft of 166 Squadron, who were instructed to maintain 12,000 feet and then finally came a third wave of 59 at 11,000 feet. The 1 Group attack was then to be followed up fifteen minutes later by a further 150 aircraft of 5 Group.

By the time the force gathered over Northampton they had reached their prescribed heights and below them the English countryside was blanketed in eight to 10/10ths cloud. Over Reading the force turned to port and onto a south-easterly heading that took them over the coast at Bognor Regis where, as they did so, the cloud below them cleared to reveal the wave tops of the Channel. Midway across Britain's protective belt of water they turned again to port and headed for the French coast which they crossed fifteen miles west of Dieppe. The formation maintained their course until they reached a point 45 miles inland from the French coast and above the village of Forges-les-Eaux where they turned to port again onto a due east course which took them thirty miles north of their final target. Their route was to take them initially beyond Trossy-et-Maximin so they would effectively be bombing the target on their way home. With the V1 site effectively behind them they turned to starboard to the south-east of Montdidier and then again above Compiegne and were by then on their bomb run which would take them over the town of Creil.

At 1411 hours, exactly on schedule, the ten 8 Group Mosquitoes of the Pathfinders dropped their red target indicators which were then backed up by yellow cascading indicators dropped by the supporting five Pathfinder Lancasters. At precisely 1415, which was the prescribed bombing hour, the first six aircraft of the 'lead formations' began to drop their bombs on the yellow markers that were cascading from 4,000 feet leaving their distinctive trails of white smoke behind.

As 'Hircleberry' ran into the target, the cloud below had thickened again and was providing 5/10ths cover which reached up to around 8,000 feet. The heavy flak batteries pumped their shells into the sky and although the level of flak was only moderate it was very accurate and 'Hircleberry' was buffeted by the shockwaves and surrounded by clouds of brown cordite. Len Symmons passed on a message from the master bomber to Bernard and Jock Walker that they should aim to the starboard of the yellow markers or on the red which were accurately placed. The flak was beginning to take its toll on the attacking force and Lancaster ME839 of 166 Squadron, piloted by Flying Officer H.A.L. Wagner, was fatally hit at a position to the north of the target where it crashed. While five of the crew were killed, Flying Officer Wagner survived and was taken prisoner while his Flight Engineer, Sergeant S. Witham, managed to evade capture and return home. Four other aircraft were lost on the raid and one of them was seen to be knocked from the sky when another aircraft bombed from above the prescribed height and hit the unfortunate Lancaster with its bomb load, cutting its port wing in half and sending it crashing to earth.

Having managed to avoid such dramas, Bernard's crew were under the direction of Jock Walker, their bomb aimer, who peered down through the cloud to the morass of smoke and target indicators below. At 1417 hours and at the correct height of 12,000 feet, Jock bombed as directed to the starboard of the yellow target indicators, sending eleven 1,000 lb and four 500 lb bombs towards the V1 site below. With the bombing photograph taken they banked sharply to starboard and headed back towards the coast on a north-westerly track which took them back home by the same route they had come in on.

As usual the crew maintained its vigilance all the way home, the clear skies above the cloud gave them perfect visibility but there were no German fighters around to be seen, just other Lancasters heading back the same way; five less than had headed out and 27 with flak damage. Bognor Regis was a welcome sight as 'Hircleberry' passed overhead and from there the route was almost second nature; north-west to Reading then turn to starboard for the final leg up the spine of England back to Lincolnshire. At 1600 hours, four hours and forty minutes after taking off, Bernard brought LM176 gently into Kirmington and had completed

22 missions; he dared not think it but just eight more and his tour would be over.

4th August saw 166 Squadron send nineteen aircraft to attack an oil refinery at Pauillac in western France. Bernard's crew were stood down for the day and spent the evening drinking beer in the garden of 'The Chopper' and were slightly drunk as well as delighted by 2200 hours as they counted back the nineteenth and last Lancaster.

With the Allies becoming increasingly desperate to wipe out the V-weapons production and storage sites, many of Bomber Commands operations had been targeted on them since the invasion. On 4th August, 291 aircraft attacked two of the sites, at Bois de Cassan and Trossy-St-Maxim. During the attack on Trossy-St-Maxim a Lancaster of 635 Squadron, piloted by Squadron Leader I. W. Bazalgette, was hit by flak and caught fire in the starboard wing and fuselage while on approach to the target. Despite the damage, Bazalgette continued onto the target and dropped his markers and bombs before turning for home. A short while later the Lancaster went into a steep dive but Bazalgette somehow managed to get the aircraft back under control in order to allow four of his crew to safely bale out. His bomb aimer and mid-upper gunner were both wounded and unable to jump, so Bazalgette decided to make a crash landing in order to try and save them. He managed to put the aircraft down successfully but before he could get his two stricken crew members out, the aircraft exploded and all three were killed. For his dedication and bravery, Squadron Leader Bazalgette was posthumously awarded the Victoria Cross.

The 5th August saw the briefing map showing the same target as it had the day before; it seemed the successful attack of the previous day was to be followed up in order to completely wipe the oil refinery from the face of the earth. It would not be the last target that the by then highly efficient and powerful Bomber Command would completely eradicate.

The 23 aircraft of 166 Squadron helped make up a force of 88 that were to attack Pauillac, while another 88 aircraft, also from 1 Group, were to attack another oil refinery just to the south at Blaye. In the afternoon sunshine, which was only disturbed by the odd fluffy cloud, the crews readied themselves for the long flight south to their target. At 1410 hours the wheels of 'Hircleberry' left the ground and headed for the initial navigation point to the south-west over Swindon where they turned slightly to starboard for their next point at Land's End.

Below them the beautiful countryside of Devon and Cornwall rolled past with the wheat fields beginning to turn golden ready for harvest and the crew peered down at the tranquil scene with a sense of longing. To head this far west was a rarity and almost a treat in the summer sunshine. At their relatively low height the crews were close enough to the ground to make out the smallest of details including the Land Girls working in the fields and to see the cows spooked by the throb of their engines.

At Land's End, above the angry Atlantic Ocean, they turned to port and headed out over the water and immediately began to drop height. Their briefing had called for them to drop down to just 1,000 feet for the majority of their time over the Atlantic, which meant that at such a low altitude Bernard would not be able to relax for a minute. Any problems or mistakes at that height, which subsequent events would prove, would give very little time for recovery. The wave tops sped by under the Lancaster and seemed almost close enough to touch, especially from the bomb aimer's position in the nose. Some ninety miles off the coast of Brest, Jack called a course change and Bernard turned to port onto a bearing of 138 degrees taking them onto a south-easterly course into the Bay of Biscay.

The need for constant vigilance became apparent as the aircraft neared a point six degrees west. Some of the aircraft had dropped too low and two of 166 Squadrons Lancasters collided. At a height of just 450 feet, PD227, flown by Pilot Officer Strath, hit the tail of NE806, flown by Flight Lieutenant Holman, and tore off the rear turret and tail section. NE806 then flipped onto its back and plunged into the sea disappearing from view beneath the water almost immediately, killing all aboard. PD227 was seriously damaged and had to turn back, later making a safe landing back at Kirmington. With the image of the collision fresh in their minds, they crossed the line of longitude at four degrees west and still 180 miles from the target they adjusted their course again to port and settled onto the bomb run. Approaching and then passing the three degrees longitude point, they began to climb again, leaving the wave tops below them and heading for their attack height of 8,000 feet. As they climbed they began to see the promised fighter cover, provided by 28 Mosquitoes of 100 Group, appear above and to either side of the main bomber stream.

The presence of the superb Mosquitoes boosted the crew's confidence as the target neared and they added to their defence by beginning to drop 'Window' as they crossed one degree west, just 120 miles from the target. The weather had been clear and bright all the way down over the Atlantic and as they approached the coast it showed no signs of changing. There was not a cloud to be seen and visibility was excellent as they crossed the coast to the south of Soulac-sur-mer, almost midway between La Rochelle and Bordeaux. Up ahead, at 1858 hours, the eight Pathfinding Lancasters from 8 Group began to drop their yellow target indicators but were initially wide of the mark. The master bomber quickly corrected the error and the first aircraft began to bomb at 1901 hours. Five minutes later Jock Walker was issuing his course corrections to Bernard; "Left, left, steady" until eventually he was satisfied as a group of as yet untouched petrol tanks came into view through his bombsight and at 1907 hours he released his load of nine 1,000 lb and three 500 lb general purpose bombs.

Below the target was a mass of fire and smoke and the bombing had been concentrated and effective with several large explosions and numerous large fires burning.

With their load accurately delivered, Bernard turned sharply to port as they left the target area and crossed the water of the Gironde inlet where, to the south-west of the town of Mirambeau, they turned hard to port again and headed back towards the Atlantic. Crossing the coast, Bernard finally began to climb again up to a height of 12,000 feet for the journey home. Out over the Atlantic Ocean and about eighty miles west of Rochefort, they turned to starboard and onto a bearing of 356 degrees (very nearly due north) which took them up across the Bay of Biscay, the French, Brittany peninsular and then across the Channel. The entire trip so far had been blessed with no enemy ground or air defence and apart from the tragic collision out over the Atlantic, had passed without incident. As the Channel disappeared behind them and they crossed the southern English coast at Bridport they began to feel safe again; as safe as they could before their wheels finally touched the ground. However, what should have been the simple part of the mission proved to be far from it as the weather closed in as they crossed England and they were forced to divert to Bernard's old O.T.U. base of Wymeswold in Leicestershire, where they touched down safely at 2305 hours, very nearly nine hours after taking off.

Having been diverted to Wymeswold the squadron returned to Kirmington on 6th August and were stood down from operations at 1039 hours. With no operation for that day Bernard was delighted to hear he had pulled a week's leave and so early on the morning of 7th he set off for Berkshire feeling like a schoolboy on his birthday at the prospect of being back with Ellen and little Doug.

With Bernard and his crew going their separate ways for seven days, 166 Squadron set about getting on with the war. That night they sent 23 Lancasters as part of a force of over 1,000 aircraft that bombed German positions in the Normandy battle area with all 23 returning safely. After a lot of cancellations and recalls a similar raid for the 8ᵗʰ was finally cancelled and the squadron got a well deserved night off.

The 9ᵗʰ August saw the squadron's raid cancelled yet again, although five aircraft were required for a 'Bullseye' raid which was a diversionary flight designed to draw the German fighters away from the main attacking force. All five returned safely despite one having to carry out a violent corkscrew manoeuvre in order to avoid a fighter that had taken the bait.

10ᵗʰ August saw 22 aircraft sent to attack the railway marshalling yards near Paris with all successfully attacking the primary target and returning safely and the day after, a further 22 aircraft were sent to attack another marshalling yard, this time at Douai in northern France, with the same successful results.

On 12ᵗʰ August 166 Squadron took part in three separate raids. The first involved eleven aircraft attacking the Bordeaux petrol dump with armour piercing bombs during daylight, with ten hitting the target and one aborting but all making it back safely. The second raid called for seven aircraft, equipped with H2S, to attack Brunswick. Taking off at 2120 hours, six attacked and returned successfully but PD260, piloted by Warrant Officer L.W. Davies R.C.A.F., failed to return with the entire crew being buried in Hanover Cemetery. The final raid of the day was a rush job to support the ground forces in France around the Falaise gap. The squadron had just four aircraft left and all were to be sent although one could not be readied in time but the final three managed to attack successfully.

With the chaos of the day before, the squadron welcomed the rest as they were stood down for 13ᵗʰ August. As Bernard and his crew were returning to base on 14ᵗʰ the squadron took part in two further raids from which, once again, they all returned safely. Six aircraft dropped mines around Bordeaux and eleven attacked northern France around the Falaise gap as the Germans tried to escape from the rapidly advancing Allies. Bernard's wonderful week with his family had been tempered slightly by a nagging thought he was unable to remove from the back of his mind. The hardest part, he had found, about being on leave was dealing with such large losses all in one go on return to his base. To lose crews one or two at a time while he was there was bad enough but to have lost eight or ten by the time he returned was a different kettle of fish. With that sense of loss he also hated the strange sense of guilt he felt as if things would have been different if his crew had been flying with them when they were lost. He knew the feeling was irrational and maybe even a little silly, but no matter what he couldn't help it being there, just as he knew he couldn't help men being shot down and killed. So it was with a sense of wonder that he saw so many familiar faces on his return with only the crew of Warrant Officer Davies to mourn.

At 1436 hours on 14th August 1944, the Order of Battle was posted for a daylight raid which was to be launched early the following morning. Bernard's crew decided a good night's sleep was more important than a reunion drink in 'The Chopper' so forfeited their revelry for an early night in their increasingly stuffy and midge ridden Nissen hut.

The raid for the 15th August was to be an attack on a Luftwaffe night fighter base named Le Culot in Belgium; the airfield is now called Beauvechain and is still a military airfield. 24 aircraft from 166 Squadron were detailed for the raid and they would be just a part of 101 1 Group aircraft to hit the base with the Pathfinding duties being carried out by six Mosquitoes and nine Lancasters from 8 Group. In total that day Bomber Command was to attack nine airfields using some 1,002 aircraft with a view to knocking out the Luftwaffe's resistance to their planned new offensive on German cities.

At 0940 hours the first aircraft began to leave the ground, with Bernard easing 'Hircleberry' off at 1000 hours, and heading south-east to Orford Ness on the Suffolk coast. Nestling in their bomb bay they carried nine 1,000 lb general purpose, four 1,000 lb semi armour piercing and four 500 lb general purpose bombs with a view to render the bases inoperable by cratering the runways and surrounding airfield as well as hopefully catching some aircraft on the ground and damaging the infrastructure of the base.

At Orford Ness Jack called a new bearing and Bernard turned slightly to port onto a south-east heading, all the time continuing to climb as he had to reach 16,000 feet by the rendezvous point which was mid way across the Channel. The weather was perfect with not a cloud to be seen and as a result the crew could gradually witness the force come together. At the rendezvous point Jack turned them onto a bearing of 116 degrees and Bernard edged the aircraft slightly to port until he settled on the correct heading. With 'Hircleberry's' heading correctly adjusted they headed for the Belgian coast which they crossed near the town of Breskens and maintaining their course, continued across Belgium passing to the south of Antwerp. The pressure was on the navigators for this particular raid as there were several airfields being attacked simultaneously which were very close together with separate forces flying very similar routes. Above 'Hircleberry's' particular group ranged a reassuring gaggle of 48 Spitfires, their beautiful shape exuding confidence in the skies they were now beginning to dominate, and all the crews felt much happier for their presence, especially on such a bright, clear day where the bomber stream was clearly visible for forty or fifty miles around. Seventeen miles south-east of Antwerp they turned to starboard onto a heading of 165 degrees which took them to a position south-east of Brussels where they made another turn to starboard, this time onto the bomb run.

Heading south-westward, they had just ten miles to their target when the flak started up but it never reached anything more than a moderate level, although it was accurate. Around them the other forces were breaking off to their individual airfield targets and ahead of them, at 1155 hours, the Mosquitoes, using the OBOE navigation system, dropped their yellow target indicators which were backed up two minutes later with red markers which fell inaccurately on the western edge of the airfield. The master bomber called up immediately and instructed the crews to bomb to the east of the red target indicators and on the yellows and the message was rapidly passed on to Bernard and Jock Walker by Len Symmons. At exactly 1200 hours, which was the prescribed 'H-hour', the first bombs began to fall on the airfield and one minute later, from 16,000 feet, Jock Walker found himself peering down on the perfect situation for a bomb aimer. He had the yellow target indicators bang over the aiming point just to the left of the runway with the wayward reds for reference off to his right, the visibility was perfect with no cloud and little smoke and he could perfectly see the concrete runways beneath him. With little chance of a target ever being better identified, he released his bombs and watched them fall away towards the target where to his delight 'Doc' Boyd in the rear turret saw them burst in a long line right across the centre of the runway.

"Bang on! Well done Jock." Called 'Doc' as he witnessed the bombs strike.

"We aim to please." Mocked Jock in reply, fully aware of the awfulness of his pun.

With the photograph taken, Bernard banked sharply away to starboard and onto a new bearing of 308 degrees taking them north-west back across Belgium. As they moved out of the target area the flak died away completely and the only fighters around were their protective umbrella of Spitfires and some American Mustangs, which were protecting another force off in the distance. Skirting the western suburbs of Brussels, they headed past Ghent and out to the coast, which they crossed a couple of miles east of Zeebrugge. With a slight course adjustment to port above the middle of the Channel, they crossed the English coast at Orford Ness and turned to head north-west along the spine of England and back to Kirmington, where they landed at 1330 hours.

There was very little good about any aspect of a bombing mission over occupied territory but the entire crew agreed that it really didn't get any better than that. The mission had been a complete success with no aircraft lost, although thirteen received some flak damage, several of those from 166 Squadron, but once again 'Hircleberry' had survived without a scratch. In total the force had dropped 1,238 x 1,000 lb bombs and 399 x 500 lb bombs on the one airfield.

With most of the afternoon and the evening to themselves, the majority of the crews made their way to 'The Chopper' for a few pints of flat, warm beer in celebration of their success earlier in the day and Bernard's crew were no exception, spending the evening swapping tales with other crews and flirting with the W.A.A.F.'s. At 1015 hours the following morning, two Orders of Battle were posted and showed ten aircraft on one and eight on the other. It didn't escape Bernard's notice that the eight, of which his crew was one, consisted of the most experienced crews on the squadron. That, he felt, could only mean one thing; trouble.

The briefing filled in the blanks and took away the need for any further conjecture as all eighteen aircrews were put out of their misery and informed that they would all be attacking Stettin, a port on the current German/Polish border lying at the head of a huge inlet at the western end of the Baltic Sea. The ten less experienced aircraft would be directly attacking the town itself as part of a main force which consisted of some 461 Lancasters, while the other eight would be part of a much smaller force of 89 aircraft who would be 'gardening' (code for mine laying) in the Baltic and Kiel Bay.

At 2045 hours the first of the 166 Squadron aircraft heading for the town of Stettin began to take off and with the last one away, the first of the minelaying aircraft began to leave at 2110 hours with Bernard finally getting airborne at 2115. Their target lay a long way off to the east across the North Sea and the first leg of their journey was a short hop in a south-easterly direction to the Lincolnshire coast at Mablethorpe. As they climbed away from Kirmington, keeping below the 2,000 feet maximum they had been set, and headed for the coast, the weather around them was good with clear visibility in the waning summer sun. Above Mablethorpe Jack gave Bernard a heading of 060 degrees and he banked to port taking 'Hircleberry' out over the North Sea in a north-easterly direction.

'Hircleberry' held her course and height for the next 230 miles across the grey, brown waters of the North Sea until they reached the line of longitude at 5 degrees east, where they made the most minor of course adjustments to port but more importantly began to climb. As they gained height they could no longer make out the individual waves as they crested; in the gathering gloom of fading daylight, the surface of the sea had merged to a singular, muddy, black colour. Out here, over the North Sea, there was obviously no threat from flak and Bernard felt less determined to gain his usual spot in the bomber stream. Having taken off after the main force, the 'gardeners' lagged a little behind and Bernard felt that maximising height was the best he could do for his aircraft and crew. So, with a briefed height of between ten and 12,000 feet, he pushed LM176 to the maximum permitted height by the time they reached longitude 8 degrees east, just eight miles off the Danish coast at Hvide Sande. At that point they turned to starboard onto a bearing of 090 degrees, exactly due east, and crossed the Danish coast heading inland. After a few, short minutes they turned again, following the route taken by the main force a few minutes earlier, onto a bearing of 112 degrees, which took them south-east across the Danish peninsular. Beneath them, slipping away unseen in the darkness, passed the multitude of islands and seaways that made up Denmark until eventually they crossed the island of Zealand and into the Baltic Sea.

As they headed out across the waters of the Baltic, above them at about 15,000 feet the cloud cover had built up to a full 10/10ths and the main force had climbed through it to clear skies above, but the 'gardeners' were to remain below it, still in clear air but perilously visible to any night fighters and flak batteries. Jack barked a new bearing of "144 degrees, Skipper." and Bernard turned again to starboard heading towards the German coast.

All too soon the first of the German Baltic islands were passing below them but so far there had been no sign of resistance from the Germans either in the air or on the ground. At 54 degrees north latitude, near the German town of Wolgast, Jack issued his instructions for the bomb run. "090 degrees, Skipper. Drop down to 11,000, that's your bomb height."

Bernard turned to port losing the required 1,000 feet as he did so and settled into his bomb run. From there on in he was under the control of Jock Walker, the bomb aimer, and the ground reading radar set known as H2S. The H2S could produce a picture on a cathode ray tube of the outline of the ground below and for this operation the identification point was the island of Gristow in the eastern channel which led from Stettin bay out into the Baltic Sea.

With the crew happy that they had the definitive outline of Gristow on the H2S set, at 0112 hours Jock released the six 1,500 lb Mark 4 mines into the sea from the prescribed 11,000 feet. Away to their starboard side they could see the glow of the fires from the main attack on the town of Stettin some thirty miles south of their position. The Lancaster jumped up as it was relieved of its burden and Bernard banked away to port and headed north-east, back out into the skies above the Baltic Sea. A couple of miles off the coast, Jack issued a new heading and Bernard made a sharp turn to port turning them onto a north-westerly heading which would take them all the way back across the Baltic and the island of Zealand until they were above the waters of the Kattegat, which separates Denmark from Sweden.

Throughout the attack, and on their route back to the Kattegat, once again 'Hircleberry' had avoided any real resistance with only light levels of heavy flak, but the marauding night fighters were still a threat as one of their number was about to find out.

Lancaster PD153 of 166 Squadron, piloted by Flight Lieutenant Dee, had successfully dropped their mines at 0118 hours and had followed Bernard's route out over the Baltic. With the dark water beneath them, Sergeant Schafer, in the mid-upper turret, saw the ominous outline of a Junkers Ju88 sweep in behind them as did their rear gunner Sergeant Fitzgerald. Fitzgerald opened fire and was delighted to see the German go into a downward spiral, heading towards the Baltic where it crashed and exploded on impact.

Blissfully unaware of the excitement unfolding behind them, 'Hircleberry's' crew turned to port above the Kattegat and crossed the Danish peninsular to the south of the town of Arhus. Maintaining their due west heading, they soon crossed the western coast of Denmark and were back above the North Sea where they turned to port and retraced their outward route, south-westward towards the English coast. The long haul across the completely black expanse of the North Sea was a dark and lonely affair; perfect as far as a returning bomber crew was concerned, a situation which could only have been improved by the presence of a fighter escort. As Bernard guided LM176 back across the 5 degree east line of longitude, he began to slowly lose height until eventually they turned to starboard in the skies above Mablethorpe for the last, short leg back to Kirmington where they landed at 0500 hours. After nearly eight hours in the air, the crew was exhausted but once again delighted at the fact that they could tick off another mission from the required thirty; Bernard had now completed 26 missions but dared not contemplate just how close he and his crew were getting to the end, just in case they tempted fate.

Bomber Command lost just five Lancasters during the raid on the town of Stettin that night and none during the minelaying around Stettin Bay. 166

Squadron again managed to come through the night unscathed although in all operations, which totalled some 1,188 sorties, Bomber Command lost sixteen aircraft.

17th August saw the squadron requested at 1115 hours to prepare eighteen aircraft for a raid on Ertvelde-Rieme oil refinery but the mission never materialized and at 1540 hours all operations were cancelled. So, more out of boredom than any need for it, the crew took 'Hircleberry' up for a stooge around the English countryside under the pretence of bombing practice. The following day saw the attack on the Ertvelde-Rieme oil refinery finally go ahead with 166 Squadron supplying eighteen aircraft but Bernard's crew was stood down for the night. Two days of inactivity seemed like an eternity on a bomber base with little else to do but visit the pub and with the end of their tour seemingly so close, all the crew wanted to get on with it, although none of them would actually say so out loud. Their frustration was about to grow to new levels and with it their consumption of flat beer from 'The Chopper'. On 19th and 20th the squadron was stood down from operations, 21st saw 25 aircraft detailed for an operation to Stettin, only for that to be downgraded to eleven aircraft to attack Bordeaux, which in turn was cancelled at 1516 hours. Finally, on 22nd August, 25 aircraft were readied and briefed for another raid on Stettin. At 1956 hours, with the four Merlin engines throbbing powerfully and finally relieved to get going again, Bernard received a message that the mission was cancelled. With just ten minutes to take off this was the cruellest blow so far.

Thinking that the tedium could get no worse, the crews once again headed off to the pub, both relieved and desperately disappointed at the same time. Tomorrow, they would get going again, tomorrow they all agreed, through slightly fuzzy heads and the bottom of a pint pot.

Tomorrow came and the wisdom borne from ale proved to be completely wrong as the squadron was stood down yet again. The waiting was bordering on becoming physically painful as the adrenaline levels built up then plummeted and the cycle repeated itself over and over as the plans were constantly changed. 24th August promised some relief at last as 23 aircraft were detailed once again to attack Stettin with the remaining five on 'gardening' operations where Bernard and his crew had dropped their mines on their last operation. With the briefings complete and the aircraft readied the operation was cancelled at 1936 hours. Not surprisingly there was a hail of frustrated swearing from the crew and the well worn path to the pub was trodden one more time.

The 25th August dawned with slightly blurry heads but with decent weather which promised some action at last. Finally, after eight days of interminable inactivity, they would resume their fight. At last their minds would have a little respite from the constant stress of uncertainty and their livers could have a break too.

The target for the night was to be the Opel motor works at Russelheim in eastern Germany. The force consisted of 412 Lancasters, 189 from 1 Group, 126 from 3 Group, 34 from 6 Group and 63 from the 8 Group Pathfinders. 166 Squadron supplied 26 aircraft for the raid which would take a long route southward through France before turning east across Europe to the target. With such a long route ahead of them, each Lancaster was loaded up with 2,040 gallons of fuel and carried a single 4,000 lb 'cookie' and thirteen clusters of 4 lb incendiaries. The attacking aircraft were split into three waves who would sweep in and complete the attack in just ten minutes with the aircraft of 166 Squadron helping to make up the 115 aircraft of the first wave. The first aircraft of 166 Squadron began to take off at just before 2000 hours and Bernard hauled LM176 off the Kirmington runway at 2015 hours heading south towards the usual navigation point of Reading.

Climbing steadily all the time, they turned to port over Reading and headed for the coast at Selsey Bill, the rendezvous point, which they reached at the prescribed height of 8,000 feet. Crossing the Channel in clear weather with only the odd patchy cloud and the slowly fading daylight, the other Lancasters of the formation were clearly visible as they all continued to gain height up to 14,000 feet before they crossed the Normandy coast. Eight miles off the French coast, to the north of Caen, Jack issued a new bearing of 143 degrees and Bernard banked to port taking 'Hircleberry' across the coast to the east of Caen. For the next eighty miles they headed south-east across the French countryside until, slightly to the north of Nogent-le-Rotrou, they turned again to port onto a new bearing of 102 degrees. Once again Bernard had managed to settle just behind and below another Lancaster, which was no mean feat considering there were only a handful of aircraft ahead of them in the main force. Soon after having made their turn the crew began throwing out the bundles of 'Window' to disrupt the German radar and passing some 45 miles south of Paris, they eventually reached the town of Courtenay where Jack turned them onto a track just to the north of east for the next leg of their flight. The route selected for the night was a test of the navigators' skill as it twisted and turned across occupied Europe in an effort to keep the force away from ground defences and so far it had been successful. "034 degrees, Skipper. You can climb to between sixteen and 18,000 feet" called Jack as they reached Mirecourt. Once again they banked to port and headed north-east towards the German border near Saarbrucken. Their next turn came just before the German border where this time Bernard banked to starboard and took them into Germany itself. The superbly plotted route had kept them away from ground fire and so far the Luftwaffe had been none existent as well; that luxurious state wasn't to last.

With the force to the south-east of Heidelburg, Bernard's intercom crackled into life. "329 degrees, Skipper. This is the bomb run, target fifty miles ahead." Informed Jack.

Bernard banked to port heading north-west through Germany when the first of the night fighters began to make their presence felt amongst the bomber stream. At 0053 hours the first of the Pathfinders began to drop their long sticks of flares, which were subsequently backed up by mixed red and green target indicators. As the force approached the target, the ground forces could only muster a token gesture of heavy flak, although it did increase to a moderate level as the raid developed. Two minutes before the intended bombing time of 0100 hours, the first aircraft began to bomb. Ahead of them the crew of 'Hircleberry' could see the first explosions on the ground and at 0101 hours there was a huge explosion which produced a bright yellow flame and large amounts of smoke. Just a minute later, at 0102 hours, Jock Walker lined his sights up over the centre of the red target indicators and from 18,000 feet dropped his bomb load.

Having remained straight and level long enough to take the bombing photograph, Bernard banked slightly to port and headed out of the target area and to the north of the town of Mainz. As the force began to make its way home the night fighters began to engage again. In total 38 Lancasters of 1 Group alone were engaged by fighters resulting in two Focke-Wulf F.W.190's, one Junkers Ju88 and one Messerschmitt Me410 being claimed as destroyed. The aircraft of 166 Squadron received their fair share of attention from the fighters with ten exchanges of fire. LM694, piloted by Flight Lieutenant Dee, was attacked no fewer than three times but managed to successfully beat off each attack with a JU88 being claimed as damaged in the first encounter and then in the second attack an unidentified Lancaster came to their assistance successfully shooting their attacker down in flames.

Once again Bernard's crew continued their good luck and had managed to avoid any attention from the fighters as they made a ninety degree turn to port just north of Mainz to begin the journey south-west back across Germany. They flew on for just over eighty miles above Germany before making another course adjustment, this time to starboard just inside the German border and crossing into France near Thionville. Once inside France's border they dropped their height down to 10,000 feet and settled on a new course which took them to the south-eastern outskirts of Reims. At Reims Jack turned them onto a new bearing of 218 degrees and a south-westerly track back to Courtenay from where they would retrace their steps back to base. As 'Hircleberry' approached Courtenay for the second time that night, they climbed back up to 14,000 feet where they would stay until they left occupied territory and crossed the Normandy coast. The journey westward to the south of Paris and then north-west up to Normandy passed without them sighting any fighters and the crew crossed the coast at the same point they had crossed on the way in. The welcome sight of the dark Channel soon passed as the even more welcome sight of the English coast at Selsey Bill slipped beneath them and they turned for Reading, gradually losing height from there all the way back to the safety of Kirmington where 'Hircleberry' landed at 0435 hours after over eight hours in the air.

The crew could hardly believe their luck in avoiding the fighters again, as they heard that ten of the 26 crews from 166 Squadron had reported fighter engagements and were even more surprised that all of 166 Squadrons aircraft had once again managed to return unharmed. In total Bomber Command lost fifteen Lancasters on the Russelheim raid but overall the attack was deemed successful with concentrated bombing causing considerable damage to the forge and gearbox works, although some parts of the Opel works, notably the assembly line, was up and running again within a few days.

The 26th August saw nineteen of the crews of 166 Squadron requested for a raid on Kiel while five more were to take the much longer trip for minelaying in the Gulf of Danzig (now Gdansk) on the Polish coast; Bernard's crew were to make the long trip.

With much further to travel to their target, the first minelayers set off at 2030 hours and 'Hircleberry' began her journey at 2035 hours with the main force beginning to leave half an hour later. As had been the case on their last minelaying trip to Stettin, the 'gardeners' headed for Mablethorpe on the Lincolnshire coast before turning to port on a bearing of 060 degrees and heading out across the North Sea in a north-easterly direction, all the time keeping their altitude below 2,000 feet to avoid German radar detection. The weather was good and the skies clear as the small force of 'gardeners', which consisted of twelve Lancasters, the other six of which came from 576 Squadron, formed up together for the long drag across the water. For the next 230 miles they ploughed on, maintaining the same course with the only reference point for navigation being the accuracy of their instruments above the featureless sea. Eventually they crossed the 5 degree east line of longitude, where they made a small adjustment to their course and began to steadily climb up to 14,000 feet heading towards the Danish peninsular. Still thirty miles off the Danish coast, the crews began to drop 'window' before turning to starboard and on to a due east heading which once again took them over the Danish coast at Hvide Sande, exactly where they had crossed on their way to Stettin ten days earlier. This time the trip across Denmark was accompanied with huge white flashes in the sky as a severe electrical storm raged and instead of being buffeted by flak, they were bounced around by turbulence instead. Given the choice they all much preferred mother natures fireworks than those of mans own making.

Continuing on their due east course, they soon crossed the narrow Danish peninsular and then, south of Arhus, crossed the coast out across the Kattegat. Within minutes they were above land again as the Danish island of Zealand appeared beneath them. Still heading east, they passed to the north of Copenhagen before leaving Denmark and crossing the thin channel of water which separates it from Sweden. Crossing the Swedish coast at Landskrona the weather was still clear as the southern tip of Sweden passed beneath them. Eventually they reached the eastern coast, just to the south of the town of Ahus, where Jack called up a new bearing of 114 degrees. Bernard banked to starboard and finally turned off the easterly heading and onto a south-easterly which would take them across the Baltic Sea.

With the electrical storm behind them, the conditions had returned to near perfect and visibility was good with their navigation being further aided by their H2S radar. The crew had no trouble in identifying the distinctive north-western tip of the Hel peninsular, which ran like a finger out into the bay and Bernard made a slight adjustment to starboard in order that they would fly along the length of the peninsular to their next turning point. As they began their run along the Hel peninsular, the heavy flak guns located on ships in the bay, backed up by fire from the nearby town of Gdynia, began to pound away, throwing up considerable amounts of accurate flak. Battling on through the ground fire, the tip of the Hel Peninsular came into view and with the assistance of the H2S they turned to starboard onto their bomb run which would take them not only into the mouth of the port of Danzig (Gdansk) but into the teeth of the ground fire as well. At 0129 hours from 14,000 feet, Jock Walker identified the correct 'garden' and released his 'vegetables' which consisted of three 1,800 lb Mark VI and two 1,500 lb Mark IV mines. The fire coming up from the ships continued to be accurate and heavy in concentration and the small force was taking hits although again 'Hircleberry' had suffered nothing more than a bumpy ride.

With the mines laid, Bernard turned again to starboard and headed north-west up the coast towards the town of Gdynia where even more flak batteries were intent on adding to the Lancasters troubles. 'Hircleberry' shook and bounced as shells exploded nearby but still she avoided being hit, until eventually the explosions began to fade and the crew knew they had broken free of the guns range. Arriving back at the northwest tip of the Hel peninsular they turned to port onto a bearing of 294 degrees which took them back out over the Baltic, gradually dropping down to 10,000 feet as they did so.

'Hircleberry's' miraculous run of good luck had not managed to rub off on the other aircraft of the force. Many had received severe flak damage and ME792 of 576 Squadron, piloted by Pilot Officer Murray, had already been downed in the Gulf of Danzig with no survivors. The six aircraft of 166 Squadron had not all been as lucky as 'Hircleberry' either and two were struggling to stay in the air. LM652, piloted by Flying Officer Bradley R.C.A.F., eventually crashed in the Baltic with only two of the bodies ever being recovered, while LM694, piloted by Flight Lieutenant Dee, struggled onward battling to overcome the serious damage it had received.

Flight Lieutenant Dee and his crew seemed to be the opposite of Bernard's crew as they seemed to get all the bad luck going. They had experienced a series of dramas and attacks and suffered damage on several occasions in what had been an eventful tour to date; none more so than the night before when they had been attacked on no less than three occasions. They had obviously survived the trials of the previous night's raid but unfortunately, they were not to survive this one. After battling valiantly to keep the aircraft in the air they managed to make it back across the Baltic but eventually crashed at Rye in Denmark killing all aboard.

The journey home was a long and lonely one for Bernard's crew. They retraced their steps back across the Baltic, Sweden and Denmark alone and out into the North Sea, where once again they began to lose height down to 6,000 feet, which they would maintain all the way back to base. With three of the twelve aircraft that had been sent to lay mines being shot down, there was little by way of other

Lancasters to be seen and the men manning 'Hircleberry's' gun turrets saw not hide nor hair of either friend or foe on the way back. As they crossed the English coast at Mablethorpe they found themselves diverted to R.A.F. Lossiemouth in Scotland and amid much disgruntled swearing from the crew, Jack calculated a new course.

After ten hours in the air, their longest mission so far, they finally touched down safely at Lossiemouth at 0635 hours; exhausted but relieved to have made it unscathed through the hail of flak. The loss rate of 25% for their minelaying mission had been huge and as news filtered back to Kirmington of their unscathed survival 'Hircleberry's' ground crew finally had all their fears about the x-ray jinx removed once and for all.

'Hircleberry's' crew, along with the other three 166 Squadron aircraft that had been diverted to Lossiemouth, returned to Kirmington on 7th August and underwent the usual interrogation by the intelligence officer where they learned for themselves of the squadrons losses. The raid on Kiel, which the rest of 166 Squadron had been involved in, had resulted in the loss of seventeen Lancasters but none of those had been from 166. The final line from the intelligence officer informed them that the squadron had been stood down for the rest of the day and that night as well, so the decision was made to head for 'The Chopper' and raise a glass to the crews of Flying Officers Bradley and Dee.

Bernard's crew received a 48 hour leave on 28th and headed off for Lincoln while the rest of the squadron was asked to prepare for an operation only to have it cancelled at 1603 hours and the crews once again stood down.

While the crew of 'Hircleberry' sampled the different pubs of Lincoln, 166 Squadron was back in the air on 29th August with nineteen aircraft bombing Stettin and a further five laying mines in Stettin Bay. Both missions were highly successful but the raid on Stettin itself took a large toll of bomber crews with 23 Lancasters lost including PD261 of 166 Squadron, piloted by Flight Lieutenant Dunton, with the loss of the entire crew. That night 166 Squadron also lost PD226, piloted by Pilot Officer Heath R.A.A.F., during the minelaying in Stettin Bay.

30th August saw the possibility of any operations that day finally cancelled at 1420 hours but at 1455 Bernard's and one other unlucky crew were called up for a radio countermeasures operation. For two hours in the early evening they stooged around the countryside of eastern England, dropping window to confuse the German radar in order to cover other surreptitious activities being carried out by more secretive branches of the R.A.F. It was probably just as well after a couple of days on the loose in Lincoln, but the worst effect of their 'window' operation, as far as the crew of 'Hircleberry' was concerned, was that it kept them away from 'The Chopper'.

At 1630 hours on 30th August, 166 Squadron was requested to supply 24 aircraft for an attack on the Konz marshalling yard in western Germany early the following morning. As a result the crews packed themselves off to bed early expecting an alarm call at the crack of dawn, but as they slept, at 0324 hours, the attack was put back for several hours and the crews were left to their slumbers. The attack on Konz was finally postponed at 0950 hours and the squadron informed that there would be no action for the day, but less than an hour later, at 1047 hours, just as the crews started to make preparations to keep themselves occupied for the day, they were requested to supply ten aircraft for an attack on a V2 site at Agenville and a further eight to attack a similar site at St. Riquier, both in northern France. As the Order of Battle was posted, Bernard found that his crew was to lead the ten aircraft on the Agenville target and with the briefing complete the crews found themselves at their dispersals by 1230 hours underneath leaden skies.

The met report at the briefing had suggested that the cloud should break up as they headed south but at 1310 hours Bernard took off into a thick blanket of 9/10ths cover. The target was a V2 storage site located in tunnels and the aim was to bring down the entrance to them so blocking the Germans access to their deadly rockets. In order to do so the bombing would have to be extremely accurate and the prospect of thick cloud would only make their job more difficult.

As usual the Lancasters of 166 Squadron initially headed south-westward towards the navigation point of Reading, climbing to 12,000 feet as they did so. There were nine raids on V weapons storage and supply dumps that day and three of them were to be carried out simultaneously by Lancasters solely of 1 Group. The first 1 Group raid consisted of 49 Lancasters attacking at Raimbert, the second, 'Hircleberry's' raid, by 52 aircraft on Agenville and the third, by 48 aircraft, eight of which were from 166 Squadron, attacking St. Riquier.

The 52 aircraft of the main force for the Agenville raid met up over Reading and turned to the south-east, en-route for the next navigation point above the Sussex town of Worthing. The only man aboard who had any certainty of their position was the navigator, Jack MacDonald, as the cloud prevented anyone else from seeing for themselves. "127 degrees, Skipper. That's Worthing below us." Called Jack.

Without even the most fleeting of a moments doubt about the accuracy of Jacks instruction, Bernard turned to port and onto the new heading that took them out over the Channel. As had become the norm amongst the entire crew, the trust in each and every one of them to do their job accurately and efficiently was now absolute. Halfway across the Channel Bernard noticed that 'Hircleberry' was feeling a little 'heavy' and Gordon Cardew identified the problem as ice forming on the leading edges; for the time being the problem wasn't too bad but if it worsened and the crew did nothing about it, it could bring them down. Gordon took it upon himself to monitor the situation and in consultation with his pilot decide when it was time to lose height to warmer air. The crew found themselves in 9/10ths strato-cumulus cloud which stretched from a height of 10,000 feet up to 13,000 feet and continued to obscure all views of the Channel below and the other aircraft around them, which always tended to put the nerves on edge.

"Enemy coast, Skipper. 073 degrees." Informed Jack, and once again, without question, Bernard turned to port onto what was the bomb run. The risk from the icing had passed as the air had warmed and having crossed the French coast about ten miles to the east of Dieppe, their course would take them over the southern outskirts of Abbeville and past St. Riquier, which would be bombed just a few minutes later, and on to Agenville.

Up ahead, the predicted break in the clouds was not materializing and the first effort at marking the target was not accurate with the Master Bomber ordering that it should be re-marked. As the crews came ever closer to the target, so the accuracy of the flak guns increased as did their intensity. Then came the radio message they didn't want to hear.

"Teacloth has been on, Skipper. We are to go round again as they are re-marking." Came the unwelcome news from Len Symmons.

"Bugger." Was the reply from the pilot's seat.

As they began their turn to port their worst fears were realized as the flak became even more intense and accurate. The Lancaster was being buffeted and jostled and then 'Doc' Boyd called up from the rear turret. "That's a bit close, Skipper. A lump of flak's just gone straight through the port fin!"

"How bad is it 'Doc'?" Inquired Bernard.

"Few inches square, not too bad." Confirmed 'Doc'.

Within moments Les Bignell had called up from the mid-upper turret to inform Bernard that another piece of flak had ripped through the fuselage and Bernard requested that they inform him if things got any worse.

"Teacloth says we are clear to bomb on the red target indicators, Skipper. We are to drop down to below 9,500 feet which is cloud base." Came the news from

Len Symmons as they were completing their circuit and coming back on to the bomb run. The flak continued to burst around them but so far had not caused any more damage. Jock Walker peered through his bombsight at the clouds below which stubbornly remained at 9/10ths cover and Bernard brought the Lancaster down through the cloud until they were clear of its base and at 8,500 feet. Despite the briefing having instructed the crews not to drop below the cloud base to bomb, the Master Bomber had obviously decided he wanted this target destroyed today and decided to take the risk. As they dropped below the cloud the flak guns could see the outline of the bombers against the grey sky and the attacking crews felt even more vulnerable.

Below him Jock could see the red target indicators but they appeared to be scattered, so he chose the biggest group he could find and at 1531 hours, pressed his bomb release button and let loose thirteen 1,000 lb and four 500 lb general purpose bombs. As he did so he felt disappointed as he knew the raid was not going to be the most accurate and he had no real idea if his bombs would fall anywhere near their intended target.

With the photograph taken and after what seemed to have been an eternity over the target, Bernard banked slightly to port and headed away from the target area and the flak, northward towards the town of Bethune. Despite having been hit several times by flak 'Hircleberry' had been one of the lucky ones. Lancaster LM243 of 103 Squadron had been shot down near Abbeville with all but one of her crew killed, the survivor suffering a broken pelvis. 166 Squadron also suffered losses as NE112, piloted by Flying Officer Tutty, on the crews seventeenth mission, was severely damaged in the target area and came down near St. Riquier which was due to be bombed a few minutes later, although the St. Riquier raid was cancelled by the Master Bomber due to the awful weather. Two of the crew were killed while Flying Officer Tutty and his Flight Engineer managed to escape capture and return to England with the remaining three being taken prisoner. One of those captured was the Wireless Operator, one Flying Officer Donald Pleasance, who would later become famous as a film actor, most notably playing the evil Ernst Blofeld in the 1967 James Bond film, You Only Live Twice and Colin Blyth (the forger) in The Great Escape.

Many of the other aircraft who had circled the target had been hit by flak and some were struggling to stay in the air as they made their escape across northern France towards the Pas-de-Calais. To the south-east of Bethune, under Jack's instructions, Bernard turned 'Hircleberry' onto a new bearing of 348 degrees, taking them almost due north to the French coast, which they crossed just inside the border with Belgium and to the east of Dunkirk. Once out over the water they turned to port, to cross the North Sea, back to the English coast at Orford Ness.

Two of the Lancasters that had suffered damage over the target would not manage to make the coast. Realising that they would not be able to stay in the air much longer, the 166 Squadron crew of NE170, piloted by Flying Officer F.E. Elliott R.C.A.F., turned for the shortest route back across the Channel but crashed near the town of Hesdin killing three of the crew with the other four managing to evade capture and return home. Suffering the same problems, the 550 Squadron crew of NF962, piloted by Pilot Officer Siddall R.N.Z.A.F., on just their second mission, crashed near L'etoile killing all aboard. Flying with them was Wing Commander Sissley who had been flying the fifth mission of his second tour in a mentoring role to the new crew.

The cloud persisted all the way back across the North Sea and Orford Ness was as invisible to the crew as Worthing had been on the way out. Turning to starboard from Orford Ness, 'Hircleberry' headed up the spine of England back to cloudy Kirmington where she landed her crew safely at 1645 hours. As they climbed out the rear door of the Lancaster to inspect the flak damage, there was an air of disappointment about the crew. They should have been happy at another mission completed and all being back safely in spite of being hit several times by flak, but somehow the raid had been 'messy' and their experience told them it had not been accurate. Their mood would only darken at their interrogation by the intelligence officer when they learned of the loss of two of 166 Squadrons crews into the bargain.

Of the ten aircraft from 166 Squadron to attack Agenville, two had been shot down and all but one hit by flak, while in the second attack on St. Riquier only four managed to bomb before the mission was cancelled by the Master Bomber and one suffered minor flak damage. It just went to prove that any target, no matter how close to home, or how soft it may have looked during the briefing, could still be fatal.

The end of Bernard and his crew's tour was coming tantalizingly close but none of them dared tempt fate by discussing it or being so foolish as to count how many sorties they had left, as that was bound to bring bad luck. All they could do was keep their heads down, do their jobs as best they could using all the tricks experience had taught them and most importantly pray that their luck held.

The first day of September saw the squadron required to supply fifteen aircraft for an attack on the Ehrang marshalling yards in Germany, near the border with Luxembourg, but the mission was cancelled at 1317 hours and at 1810 the crews received the welcome news that they were allowed out for the night. Having once again drunk their fill at 'The Chopper' they returned to base to find that while they had been enjoying themselves in the pub they had been requested for an early morning raid on Gilze Rijen airfield. Thankfully the attack time had been pushed back at 2230 hours which gave them time to sleep off the effects of the beer. When they woke they were not too disappointed to find that the raid had been cancelled altogether and that there would be no raids for the day.

The morning of 3rd September dawned and with it the Second World War entered its sixth year and Bernard his fifth in R.A.F. blue. The occasion looked like it would be marked with the promised raid on the Gilze Rijen airfield but the raid was cancelled again at 1047 hours, so in order to relieve the tedium of the day, Bernard volunteered to take Lancaster NF986 up for an air test. No sooner had he been granted his request than the squadron was stood up again at 1100 hours and so fifteen aircraft headed off to Germany while Bernard headed to R.A.F. Ludford Magna, which wasn't even outside the county. The raid was successful but due to the continuing poor weather nine of them had to divert to another Lincolnshire base at Sandtoft on their return.

The squadron was stood down again from operations on 4th September, as those diverted the day before made their way home, and then on 5th September Bernard and his crew finally re-appeared at the top of the Order of Battle and were delighted to find out at the briefing that it was for a relatively short trip to Le Havre for which 166 Squadron was to supply 21 aircraft.

The raid on Le Havre was intended to destroy the pocket of resistance left in the port by taking out the remaining German headquarters and troop concentrations. That would assist the Canadian ground troops, who were by that point within striking distance being just two miles from the outskirts of the port. The attack was to be in daylight and to consist of three waves, totalling 294 main force aircraft from 1 and 3 Groups, with the marking carried out by thirty Mosquitoes and 24 Lancasters of 8 Group. The aircraft of 166 Squadron were to be in the first wave and each wave was to be separated by fifteen minutes in order to allow each one time to bomb accurately as the Canadian ground troops were so close to the aiming point. The briefing had been incredibly detailed with heavy emphasis being put on the importance of the various bombing instructions.

With all their checks completed and the myriad of bombing instructions duly noted, the crew of LM176, being the first in the line of 21 waiting aircraft, received the green light from the chequered van and accelerated down the Kirmington runway, their wheels leaving the concrete at 1550 hours which Jack dutifully recorded in his logbook.

'Hircleberry' climbed away towards the south-west, heading for the navigation point just west of Slough, over what is now junction 7 of the M4 motorway, before turning onto an almost due south course towards the south coast.

The crews of Kirmington took off into 9/10ths cloud which did not bode well for their bombing instructions which required a definite visual identification. But, as they headed ever closer to the rendezvous point, which was one mile east of Bognor Regis, they climbed up through the Strato-cumulus, which topped out at about 9,000 feet, and entered the clear skies above. Having reached, and then maintained, the required height of 12,000 feet by the rendezvous point, the gathered first wave could see that the cloud below them was steadily breaking up as they moved ever southward. Heading across the waters of the Channel they could see the occasional glimpse of the silvery surface of the water through the ever diminishing cloud as Jack called up from the Navigators position with a course change. "138 degrees, Skipper. This is the bomb run." He instructed.

Bernard acknowledged and banked to port onto a south-easterly heading, which put Le Havre less than fifty miles away and dead ahead. With no fighter cover for the operation and the ever improving visibility, the air gunners' eyes were out on stalks, almost not daring to blink as they searched for the Luftwaffe, but so far all had been quiet on the fighter front. As the target grew ever closer the first of the specific bombing instructions came into effect. With twenty miles to go, and still out over the Channel, Bernard opened the bomb bay doors and the Master Bomb Switch was turned on. This course of action would allow any malfunctioning bomb release mechanism to drop its bombs harmlessly into the Channel and not onto the Canadian troops on the outskirts of Le Havre. Once they were satisfied that all was well, the Master Bomb Switch was turned off again until one minute before the moment of bombing, but the bay doors were left open.

Up ahead of the main force, at 1755 hours, the expected green markers from the OBOE guided Mosquitoes became lost in a narrow bank of cloud that had drifted over the target and as a result the back up red markers could not be accurately dropped. With the first wave of the main force due over the target between 1800 and 1806 hours there was no time to accurately mark before their arrival and the bank of cloud would not have passed in time for them to bomb visually. The mission planning had been excellent and the fifteen minute gap gave them time to order the first wave to orbit the target and make the bomb run again while the Pathfinders remarked and the cloud bank slipped out of the way. Len Symmons broke the bad news. "Hambone has been on, Skipper. He says Bigboy is to go round again."

Bigboy was the code for the entire first wave and almost as one they began the bank round to starboard in order to perform a circling manoeuvre which would put them back on the bomb run and on the correct heading. Again, due to the proximity of the Canadians, the crews had received strict instructions that on no account were they to bomb on any other heading than the one they had been given.

As they made their turn, the familiar puffs of heavy flak burst in the skies around them but the concentration was thankfully moderate and the more experienced crews, while always wary of it, took little notice.

By the time the aircraft had settled back on their correct heading, the Pathfinders had accurately dropped their red target indicators which characteristically cascaded down from about 4,000 feet trailing white smoke behind them. The cloud bank had also moved away sufficiently for the bomb aimers to get good visual fixes through the continually thinning cloud, which was by then less than 3/10ths cover and topped out at 7,000 feet. Peering down, Jock Walker identified the breakwater, which they were instructed to ensure their cross hairs had passed before bombing, and then seeing the markers and satisfying himself they were accurate, at 1810 hours he pressed the bomb release button from the prescribed 12,000 feet making 'Hircleberry' one of the first aircraft to bomb.

'Hircleberry' jumped as the thirteen 1,000 lb and four 500 lb general purpose bombs fell away, Bernard maintained his course, as usual, for his photoflash to operate but instead of turning abruptly away from the target once it had operated he maintained his south-easterly course, as instructed, for another five miles. Above the waters of the Seine estuary they eventually banked away to starboard onto a new bearing of 223 degrees, taking them south-west along the French coast towards Villers-sur-Mer, which was all safely under Allied control and so provided no threat from flak.

The French coast was clearly visible in the late summer sunlight but just before they reached land, Jock turned them north-west on to a new bearing of 317 degrees to take them back across the Channel. As they headed for home the mood aboard 'Hircleberry' seemed a little lighter than it had been on previous raids. While the men were still alert to the dangers they knew had not yet passed, the combination of the late summer sun, the accuracy of their attack, the lack, so far, of fighters and ground defences and the witnessing first hand of the gains being made by the Allies on the ground, all combined to lift spirits which over the previous months had been constantly strained by the twin evils of fear and stress.

With the other returning aircraft scattered around them, the remainder of the journey back across the Channel, crossing the English coast above the Naval port of Portsmouth and back to Reading, passed without incident, as did the final leg back to Kirmington where they landed at 1928 hours. After taxiing back to their dispersal and applying the brakes Bernard dutifully opened the bomb bay doors in order to help the armourers get 'Hircleberry' ready for the next operation, as to open them by hand took considerable effort, before finally shutting down the last two Merlin engines. For five of the seven men aboard there was just one more mission to complete and their tour would officially be over; the end was becoming tantalisingly close.

The raid on Le Havre had been a huge success with 335 of the 348 aircraft sent successfully attacking the target and not a single loss. In total they managed to drop some 1,821 tons of high explosive and a further 62 tons of incendiaries; unfortunately for Le Havre there would be more to come.

As 'Hircleberry's' crew entered the debriefing, Bernard was quickly pulled aside by Wing Commander Donald Garner and told to report to his office afterwards; Bernard already knew what the conversation would be about and had prepared his answer already.

With the Intelligence Officer's work done, Bernard parted ways from the rest of the crew and while they headed off for a bite to eat and a freshen up; he headed straight to Wing Commander Garner's office. Garner was held in high esteem by the men of 166 Squadron as a man who understood the stresses and strains on the crews and took everything in to account in his decision making. He was no pushover and imposed just the right balance of carrot and stick in motivating his men. As a result of his fair handedness there was little the men would not do for him. "Hello, Steel. Another successful 'op' then, eh?" He queried, without waiting for a reply, as he knew he was right, he got straight to the point. "You must be aware that the next trip is the last in the tour for most of your crew and I'd like to join you aboard your aircraft to mark the occasion." His statement was a carefully worded one within which lay an unasked question, which gave Bernard the choice to answer it or not as he deemed fit.

"I've spoken to the others who've done 29 Sir, and they've all agreed that we would like to finish our tour as a crew. Boyd's got one extra to do and Symmons two, Sir. Perhaps we could delay it until then?" Explained Bernard.

"Splendid, Steel. I'll arrange it. Have a good evening." Replied Garner, delighted that Bernard had spotted the hidden question and had responded to it just as he thought he would. Garner knew his men well and had no doubt that the outcome would have been any different.

The following day saw a virtual repeat of the raid the day before with Le Havre again being hit by three waves of aircraft. In total 344 aircraft would be attacking the target with 160 Lancasters of 1 Group, 127 more from 3 group, along with a token force of three ageing Stirlings and thirty Mosquitoes and 24 Lancasters from the Pathfinders of 8 Group.

166 Squadron was again providing 21 aircraft with Bernard's crew, as the most experienced on the squadron, again at the head of the Order of Battle. This time the aircraft of 166 would be spread between the three waves with Bernard's crew in the second wave and each wave was to attack twenty minutes apart.

Once again the briefing was full of safeguards and processes that had to be followed by the crews to prevent the accidental bombing of the Canadian troops who were still within just two miles of the various aiming points. The only difference from the previous day's raid was that the Canadians may mark their forward positions with yellow flares and therefore under no circumstances should any bombing of yellow markers take place. With the details of the raid noted, both in mind and notebooks, the crews made their way to their dispersals during the late afternoon. Once again the skies were overcast and the forecast for the target was even less encouraging than it had been the day before.

Bernard lifted 'Hircleberry' off the Kirmington concrete at 1720 hours and headed for the same navigation point as the day before to the west of Slough. However, this time, instead of turning due south they turned slightly further to port and headed towards the gap between Bognor Regis and Littlehampton which was to be the rendezvous point. Once again they climbed up towards 12,000 feet and quickly entered thick cloud as they crossed the Channel. Len Symmons soon piped up having received a radio message from the Master Bomber. "Leper has given basement as 10,000, Skipper." Having been instructed at the briefing to drop below the cloud base in order to make visual target identification, the coded message from the Master Bomber had given the estimated cloud base as 10,000 feet. Having dropped down to that height they soon found it wasn't the base and the figure was rapidly revised downward again, firstly to 8,000 feet and then to 6,000 feet. By the time they had broken through the base of the cloud they had already made the final turn to port for the target and were heading south-east directly to Le Havre. Once again there was no fighter cover and despite the heavy cloud, Les Bignell and 'Doc' Boyd still scanned the skies constantly and diligently; no one wanted to take any chances this close to the end of their tour.

As had been the case the day before, the aircraft had to open their bomb doors above the Channel while still some twenty miles short of the target and test their Master Bomb Switch. Ahead of them, the first wave of attacking aircraft had already bombed and the Master Bomber had been pleased with the outcome despite the murky weather conditions.

Unlike the previous days raid this one saw a slightly different aiming point for each of the waves and with the first wave successfully completed, the Pathfinders set about marking for the second wave. The cloud base was down as low as 6,000 feet and dropping all the time, above that height it was 10/10ths thick and impenetrable and all the aircraft had dropped below it. The lack of height was of concern to the crews as they would be more vulnerable to flak but ground resistance was minimal with only very slight concentrations of heavy flak, possibly due to the success of the attack the day before.

At 1915 hours the OBOE Mosquitoes began to drop their green target indicators which again were backed up by cascading reds, as had been the case for the previous raid. The main force of the second wave began to arrive at just after 1920 hours but the aircraft of 166 Squadron were towards the back of the group and found themselves amongst the last to bomb in the wave. Their relatively late arrival made the bomb aimers job all the more difficult as the smoke from the attack was making visual identification even more tricky. They were under express instructions not to bomb unless they had definite identification of the aiming point or had been instructed by the Master Bomber to use the target indicators once he was satisfied their position was correct; under no circumstances were they to bomb the smoke.

Jock Walker found himself at 6,700 feet as 'Hircleberry' made her bomb run and just a minute before he dropped his bombs he saw the Pathfinders lay down their red cascading markers. However, the markers fell just short of the aiming point and Jock delayed his release until he found his cross hairs over the right spot. At 1922 hours he dropped nine 1,000 lb general purpose, four 1,000 lb semi armour piercing and four 500 lb general purpose bombs into the chaos below.

With the bombs gone and the photograph taken, Bernard banked to port away from the target area and along the northern banks of the Seine estuary before making a sharp turn to starboard onto a new bearing of 210 degrees which took them south-west across the waters of the estuary itself. One final turn over French territory saw them bank to starboard again onto a north-westerly route taking them back above the brown murky waters of the Channel and heading for home. One final course adjustment in mid Channel put them on a path to cross the English coast at East Wittering and then onto the usual navigation point of Reading.

With five of the airmen aboard 'Hircleberry' having completed their thirtieth and what should have been the final mission of their tour, they landed safely back at Kirmington at 2050 hours in the gathering gloom. Their loyalty to each other was evident in that nobody mentioned the fact; as far as each one of them was concerned, if any one of them still had another mission to complete; then they all did.

The third wave of the attack on Le Havre had to be abandoned by the Master Bomber as the cloud base had dropped too low for visual identification and the target indicators could no longer be seen. As a result the raid had not been anywhere near as accurate or effective as the day before but the German troops inside Le Havre had still suffered under two waves of attacks while once again Bomber Command escaped without loss.

With the sight and sound of the V1 becoming commonplace over southern England, on 8th September the Germans launched their V2 for the first time. Unlike the V1, the population would never get used to the sight and sound of the V2, as there was none. Stavely Road, Chiswick was the first to be hit by a V2 that September morning but many more would suffer under the silent killer. The V2 was the first ballistic missile which was fired into the lower reaches of space before re-entering at supersonic speed in free fall (no engine power) to its target, where the 1 ton warhead detonated without warning as the missile hit at a speed well in excess of the speed of sound.

The V2 was a liquid fuelled rocket powered by an Ethyl and liquid Oxygen mix which produced a thrust force of over 55,000 lbs (25,000 kg) at lift off. The fully fuelled launch weight was 28,500 lbs (13,000 kg) and the engine burn, which lasted for just over a minute, propelled the missile to a height of up to sixty miles and a speed of 3,300 mph (5,300 km/h). The V2 stood 14 meters tall and carried a one ton, Amatol warhead over a range of up to 250 miles which brought London ominously within its reach. The missile was guided by a preset gyroscopic system but was only accurate to within ten miles and was therefore not suitable as a precision weapon but against cities, where accuracy was not necessary, it was devastating. The V2 was launched at many cities both in Britain and mainland Europe with some 3,000 being launched in total and over 7,000 people killed before the Allies could finally overrun their production centres and put a stop to their menace. After the war the V2's designer, Werner Von Braun, was smuggled to America and ultimately designed the Saturn V rocket which put Neil Armstrong on the moon in 1969, the fact that thousands of slave labourers died in the production of his V2 programme was conveniently forgotten.

V2 rocket with cutaway sections to show the internal workings

The 7th September saw 166 Squadron ready 23 aircraft for operations but no instructions to take off were received and the raid was delayed until the following morning. The briefing took place in the early hours of the 8th and the crews were delighted to find that their target for the day was once again to be Le Havre, although they wondered just how much of it was left to bomb. At 0650 hours, laden with thirteen 1,000 lb and four 500 lb general purpose bombs, Bernard and his crew once again took off from Kirmington and headed south-west to the navigation point to the west of Slough. The route for the day was exactly the same as that they had taken two days before and the force was once again to attack in waves. The force totalled some 333 aircraft from 1, 3 and 8 Groups, including four Stirlings in what would turn out to be the last bombing mission for the type.

The aircraft of 3 Group would attack in three waves at different aiming points and then be followed fifteen minutes later by the 1 Group aircraft who would again attack in three waves at another three aiming points. The 23 aircraft of 166 Squadron were split up amongst the three 1 Group waves with Bernard's crew being in the last wave and therefore right at the back of the bomber stream.

With the Canadians still extremely close to the aiming points, all the same safeguards were in place and the briefing had seemed very much like a case of déjà vu; had all the crews flying that day been on the raid of two days earlier, the briefing itself would have been all but redundant.

The cloud cover as they headed south was a solid 10/10ths but by the time they reached Slough it was showing signs of breaking up. Yet again they turned onto their southerly heading at Slough and crossed the English coast at 10,000 feet between Bognor Regis and Littlehampton. As the aircraft pushed on across the Channel the cloud cover, which had been showing promising signs of dissipating, began to close in again and was soon back at a full 10/10ths. Turning to port and on to their heading for the target out over the Channel, the cloud was still showing no sign of letting up and ahead of them the first wave of 1 Group aircraft, with their allotted fifteen minutes over the target having expired, were ordered to abandon the mission and return home with only three of the 49 aircraft in the wave having bombed.

The second wave fared no better as the cloud seemed, if possible, to be getting worse and only five of the sixty bombed before they too were sent home. At 0840 hours the aircraft of the third wave were instructed to drop down as low as 6,000 feet by the Master Bomber in an attempt to get under the cloud. As they reached what should have been the target area, Len Symmons picked up a further radio message at 0845 hours. "Anthill 1's been on, Skipper. He wants us to orbit."

With groans from the crew, Bernard began to bank round to port in order to complete a wide circle to bring them back in to the target on the correct heading. The ground fire was not heavy in concentration, with just an estimated ten heavy and five light flak guns firing, but it was accurate and two aircraft in the first wave had suffered hits. Every moment over the target, and therefore above the flak guns, increased the chances of 'Hircleberry' being hit herself and there wasn't a crew in Bomber Command, either past or present, who didn't dread having to go round again as many had perished in the attempt.

The Master Bomber was desperately trying to get a visual fix on the aiming point in order that he could lay down his green markers but eventually he had to concede that the cloud was too thick and at 0850 hours, just as the main force was back above what should have been the target, he issued his final message; Len

Symmons picked it up loud and clear. "Samson from Anthill 1; Marmalade." He repeated it a couple more times and the entire force of 51 Lancasters knew its meaning as being 'Main force from Master Bomber; abandon mission.' Len passed on the message to his Skipper and with Jack MacDonald calling out the next bearing, they began the journey home.

The route home, which was the same as that of the 6th September, was shrouded in cloud and once again the Luftwaffe was nowhere to be seen; partly because of the awful weather but mainly because they were rapidly becoming a spent force as the combined air forces of Britain and America increasingly dominated the skies over Europe. Eventually, after what had been an extremely frustrating trip and a tiring one with the concentration required to fly almost entirely on instruments, the crew landed back at Kirmington at 1040 hours.

Wing Commander Garner was an extremely fair minded commanding officer and unlike some counted the mission towards the crews' totals. He reasoned that it wasn't their fault they could not bomb and most of them had been over the target not once but twice; that showed determination enough for him and the least he could do was allow it to count. So finally, after more than three months at 166 Squadron, Bernard's crew was just one mission away from joining the elite club that had completed their tour; they had to be lucky just one more time.

The crew were itching to get into the air for what they hoped and prayed would be their final, successful mission but the powers that be decided that the squadron was to be rested for the next two days. Finally, on 10th September 1944, the Order of Battle was posted with Bernard's crew listed to take part in yet another daylight raid and as the map was revealed in the smoky briefing room they were relieved to see that so far their luck was holding and yet again the target was to be Le Havre.

The ongoing pounding of Le Havre was to provide Bernard and his crew with what would be, one way or another, the final target of their tour. 10th September would have one of just two outcomes, success in the form of a safe return, which would see them rested for at least six months from operational flying and would probably mean they safely saw out what was left of the war, or failure, which meant being shot down and either taken as a P.O.W. or killed. This close to the end failure was unthinkable, so they didn't think about it.

Much to the crew's disappointment their popular Wing Commander, Donald Garner, was not to accompany them on their final trip as he had been outranked by Group Captain Gerald Carter who had decided he would fly with them instead.

Carter was 44 years old and had been a career R.A.F. officer, gaining his wings as far back as February 1920. He had seen immense changes in his quarter of a century's service and was highly experienced but his rank now distanced himself from the crews more than he would have liked. The crew too would have preferred the presence of the more familiar Donald Garner but none the less they were honoured by the presence of such a high ranking officer and just hoped he didn't bring with him a change in their fortunes.

For their last trip 'Hircleberry' was loaded up with thirteen 1,000 lb and four 500 lb general purpose bombs all fused for instantaneous detonation as it was expected the Allied troops would soon be entering the port. The assumption was correct as Le Havre, in no small part due to the efforts of Bomber Command, would finally fall into Allied hands the following day. The raid had been designed as the final knockout blow to the German troops left in Le Havre and the full weight of Bomber Command was put to the task. The raid had eight separate aiming points spread throughout the area with a total, including the Pathfinders, of 993 aircraft attacking, all of them Halifaxes or Lancasters with the exception of 45 Mosquitoes of the Pathfinders.

The level of organisation in getting so many aircraft in the right position, over eight separate aiming points, above the same town was immense and the Pathfinders would have to be at their best for the mission to succeed. The briefing was highly detailed and in a rare move the crews were informed of the aiming points and bombing times of all the other attacking aircraft as well as their own in order that they had the most complete picture of what was going on as possible.

With all the detailed instructions noted, the crew arrived at their dispersal at just after 1600 hours and despite the significance of the occasion went through the same ritual they had completed, with the exception of just one, at least thirty times before. Group Captain Carter knew better than to get in their way and hung back, watching as the last of the crew stood next to the starboard undercarriage and lit a cigarette. The smoke curled upwards and spread out on the underside of the huge wing and then, after just a couple of puffs, he threw it to the floor and ground it out with his left foot. Carter smiled to himself as the airman tenderly stroked and then patted the tyre as if saying goodnight to a sweetheart before, unspeaking, he climbed aboard. Allowing a few seconds for Bernard to make his way to the cockpit and get himself settled, Carter too clambered aboard and headed forward to take up his place in the temporary seat alongside Bernard and Gordon Cardew.

Having flown several times with crews on their last mission, Carter was always impressed by the slick effectiveness of an experienced crew and this one was no exception. Nothing was missed or skipped over, yet it all seemed effortless and efficient. With no mention from any of the crew of the fact that this was the last trip, or in fact anything other than just another raid, at 1655 hours, Bernard eased 'Hircleberry' off the Kirmington runway and headed away to the south-west towards the familiar navigation point to the west of Slough. 166 Squadron had put up 25 aircraft for the days raid which was maximum effort and all the personnel on the base had had to work extremely hard to ensure they were all ready in time.

Arriving at their navigation point near Slough, Jack called up a course change onto a bearing of 177 degrees and Bernard turned to port and headed south towards the coast. The briefing had prescribed a height of between eight and 10,000 feet for the rendezvous at the south coast and by the time he had completed his turn at Slough, Bernard was already at 10,000 feet and just below and behind the tail of another Lancaster; no point in changing things now he thought. The 200 Lancasters of 1 Group who were taking part in the days raid had been equally split between two aiming points, codenamed Bentley 1 and 2, and would bomb just minutes apart with Bentley 1 going in first; Bernard's crew were to make up part of Bentley 2.

The weather for the previous raids on Le Havre had been abysmal but that day the clouds over England amounted to no more than thin, broken Cumulus and the visibility was good. The wind was light and from the north-east and posed no real problem for a navigator as good as Jack MacDonald. Crossing the coast, once again between Littlehampton and Bognor Regis, the cloud, that had been thin from the outset, began to thin even more and by the time they reached their target it would have disappeared altogether. Halfway across the Channel, with the sunlight glinting on the top of the water, Jack called up. "134 degrees Skipper. This is the bomb run." Every action and every radio message began to take on a new significance. Once again none of the crew said anything as to tempt fate was the worst crime imaginable, but they all new that each little landmark was steadily being ticked off; they all knew for example that Jack had just called the bomb run for the last time but knew they were not safe until Bernard issued his congratulations message which he always did as he shut 'Hircleberry's' engines down on return to base.

As had been the case with the previous three raids on Le Havre, all the safety precautions to try and prevent bombing of the Allied troops had been put in place and again the bomb bay doors were opened twenty miles short of the target while still out over the Channel and the Master Bombing Switch tested. Once again all worked as it should and 'Hircleberry' continued on to her target.

At 1845 hours the first of the five OBOE fitted Mosquitoes began to mark the target with their green target indicators and they were subsequently backed up by red cascading markers dropped by the five Pathfinder Lancasters of 8 Group. However, for once the red target indicators overshot the mark by some 700 yards, and with accuracy vital to protect the Allied troops below, the Master Bomber made a radio transmission which Len Symmons relayed to Bernard and Jock Walker. "Toolkit 1 has called the reds as an overshoot, Skipper. He says to undershoot by 700 yards but they are remarking."

'Hircleberry' was still some way short of the aiming point and 'Toolkit 1' had called up again by the time they arrived informing them that the target had been accurately remarked and that the first set of markers they came to on their bearing were in the correct place. So far the mission had been unopposed either from ground fire or by the Luftwaffe and that, coupled with the clear visibility, was making for a good operation. With the target accurately marked, 'Hircleberry' was in the final stages of her bomb run and Jock could clearly see both the target indicators, which he confirmed were accurately placed, as well as the aiming point itself. At 1858 hours from 10,000 feet Jock pressed his Bakelite bomb release button for the last time and sent their bomb load into the carnage below. The crew had all completed their required thirty bombing missions; all they had to do now was get home.

The first stage in their escape to safety began with the bombing photograph which, once taken, allowed them to bank away to port and out of the target area. Thankfully there was still no resistance from the Germans and the lack of flak was a rare treat. Ten miles inland of Le Havre, Bernard banked hard round to starboard until he was on a new bearing of 210 degrees and heading south-west, which took them over the town of Honfleur, before turning again sharply to starboard onto a bearing of 298 degrees. That course took them across the French coast at Trouville-sur-mer and back out over the Channel heading north-west. Still the skies were clear and bright and 'Doc' Boyd and Les Bignell scanned the blue skies diligently for any fighters but still the Luftwaffe failed to appear. Out over the Channel, by then some 25 miles north of Omaha beach, where the invasion of France had begun in such bloody fashion for the Americans, Jack MacDonald informed Bernard of another course change. "358 degrees, Skipper. That takes us back to Reading." Bernard banked gently to starboard as smoothly as if the Lancaster was a passenger paying airliner instead of a weapon of destruction and headed back to the English coast.

Soon the welcoming land mass of southern England loomed into view resplendent and welcoming in the bright weather and for the first time a member of the crew alluded to the fact that this wasn't just another mission. Bernard broke the radio silence with an uncharacteristic message. "Friendly coast ahead, chaps."

There was a ripple of approval from around the aircraft and those who could, strained to get a quick view of the very welcome sight before settling back to their jobs. In the rear turret 'Doc' could see nothing and just had to take his Skippers word for it; he never doubted him for a moment. Within seconds the efficient air of the crew had been restored and Bernard knew he didn't have to remind them not to get carried away. The turrets were still manoeuvring, still untrusting of the Germans, still fully aware that it could all still go horribly wrong, despite the fact they were nearly home.

Within a few minutes, 'Doc' Boyd too got his sight of the English coast as 'Hircleberry' slipped over it above West Wittering and over the radio he quipped; "Confirmed, Skipper. That's definitely a friendly coast!" Once again the men managed a smile and a chuckle to themselves as the stress and fear began to fall away and they began to accept the fact that they might just make it.

Continuing north, the Hampshire countryside never looked so beautiful and the sight of Reading was a surprisingly welcome one too. They turned above the town for the last time and headed north-east back to Kirmington and soon had the familiar sight of the village church ahead of them. The W.A.A.F.'s on the radio congratulated them on their return, fully aware that this was their last 'op', and instructed them to land which they did in a text book manner at 2020 hours. Bernard taxied 'Hircleberry' to her dispersal point where a group of ground staff and a couple of the crews who had already arrived back had gathered to greet them. Bernard and Gordon shut down 'Hircleberry's' engines and systems and when everything was complete Bernard leant across the front of Group Captain Carter to Gordon and shook him firmly by the hand before accepting Carter's heartfelt congratulations. With the handshakes completed Bernard called the rest of the crew on the intercom. "Well done men; a tour well done!" With that the cheers rang out and the celebrations could begin. The crew, which their ground staff had believed were doomed when they received X-X-ray, had proved to be a rare beast indeed, a good one and a lucky one.

The following morning the men of 'Hircleberry's' ex-crew woke with powdery mouths and sore heads having consumed a huge amount of beer and gin at 'The Chopper', most of which they hadn't had to pay for. The sobering up process began with breakfast and appeared as if it would be a slow one, but the processes of the R.A.F. were not so slow and Bernard was told that his crew were to leave the base over the next two days and begin their post operational leave as their billets would be required for their replacements; war was no time for sentimentality.

Having sobered up enough by the afternoon, Bernard took to the skies in the bases Airspeed Oxford to transport Jock Walker and Len Symmons to the R.A.F. base at Wroughton in Wiltshire from where they would head off on their well deserved leave. Unsure of when or if they would ever meet again, they shared a hearty farewell before Bernard took off with a lump in his throat and headed back to Kirmington, being waved away by his two crewmates as he went. The following day he volunteered to take 'Doc' Boyd to R.A.F. Snitterfield in Warwickshire, which was a relief landing ground for Bernard's old posting at Church Lawford, as the first leg of 'Doc's' long journey back to Canada. Bernard himself left Kirmington a couple of days later, followed over the next few days by the rest of the crew, and headed to the Berkshire countryside to spend a long desired week with Ellen and the now nearly two year old Douglas. The relief to the entire family that Bernard had survived what so many didn't was almost palpable and when his weeks leave finished, for the first time since he had joined up, Ellen didn't experience that feeling of dread she usually felt when he went away. Now she was beginning to believe that Bernard would actually make it through the war unscathed.

227 Lancasters and ten Mosquitoes attacked Monchengladbach on the night of 19th/20th September 1944 with Wing Commander Guy Gibson V.C. acting as the master bomber. Gibson, who had won his Victoria Cross for his actions in leading the famous Dambusters raid, was flying a Mosquito from 627 Squadron and could be heard issuing instructions throughout the raid. Without giving any indications of problems, Gibson headed for home after the raid was finished, but crashed in flames before he reached the Dutch coast. There were no reports or claims from night fighters so the cause of the crash is still unknown, but Gibson and his navigator, Squadron Leader J. B. Warwick, were both killed and subsequently buried at Steenbergen-en-Kruisland.

Bernard arrived at his new posting of 1656 Heavy Conversion Unit at Lindholme in Yorkshire on 25th September 1944 and a few days later he was handed his Form 414a, Summary of Flying Assessment, from 166 Squadron, which had been completed by Wing Commander Garner in his absence. Bernard was delighted that the man for whom he had so much respect had deemed him to have performed above the average. High praise indeed in the language of the day; unknown to Bernard there would be more praise to come.

Although Bernard's time at 166 Squadron had come to an end, the squadron itself continued to find itself in the thick of the action for the remainder of the war before being disbanded at the end of hostilities. Along with many other squadrons, once the fighting was over most of the huge force of Bomber Command found itself surplus to requirements. By the time it was disbanded in November 1945, the squadron had flown on 291 separate raids, 76 while equipped with Wellingtons and the remaining 215 with Lancasters. The Wellingtons had flown 789 sorties, in which they lost 39 aircraft (4.9%), while the Lancasters flew 4,279 sorties losing 114 aircraft at a loss rate of 2.7%.

FORM 414 (A)

SUMMARY of FLYING and ASSESSMENTS FOR YEAR COMMENCING 1st .... *19 ......

[* For Officer, insert " JUNE " ; For Airman Pilot, insert " AUGUST."]

| | S.E. AIRCRAFT | | M.E. AIRCRAFT | | TOTAL for year | GRAND TOTAL All Service Flying |
	Day	Night	Day	Night		
DUAL						
PILOT			89.36	130.26		
PASSENGER	—	—	—	—		

ASSESSMENT of ABILITY

(To be assessed as :—Exceptional, Above the Average, Average)

(i) AS A .....HB..... † PILOT.................. *Above the Average*

(ii) AS PILOT-NAVIGATOR/NAVIGATOR......................................

(iii) IN BOMBING...

(iv) IN AIR GUNNERY...

(v) IN S.B.A..

† Insert :—" F.", " L.B.", " G.R.", " F.B.", " Instructor ", etc.

ANY POINTS IN FLYING OR AIRMANSHIP WHICH SHOULD BE WATCHED

Date.... 25.9.44 ....

Signature .... W/Cdr

Officer Commanding.... 166 SQUADRON R.A.F.

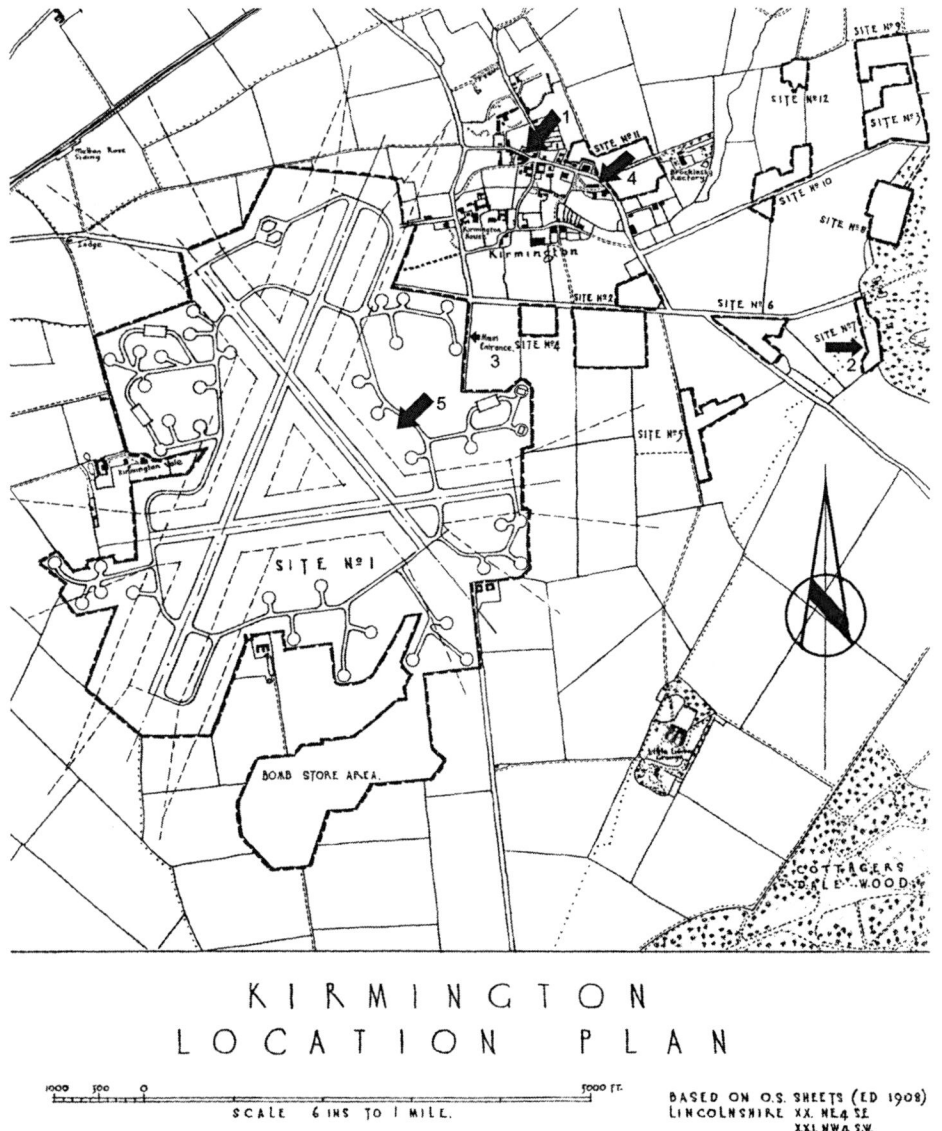

K I R M I N G T O N
L O C A T I O N   P L A N

SCALE   6 INS TO 1 MILE.

BASED ON O.S. SHEETS (ED 1908)
LINCOLNSHIRE XX. NE4 SE
XXI. N.W.4 S.W.

1)   The Chopper (Marrowbone and Cleaver Pub)

2)   Dispersed site 7. Bernard's billet

3)   Main site entrance

4)   St. Helen's church, Kirmington

5) Control tower

Maps adapted from originals by kind permission of the Trustees of the RAF
Museum Hendon. Crown copyright.

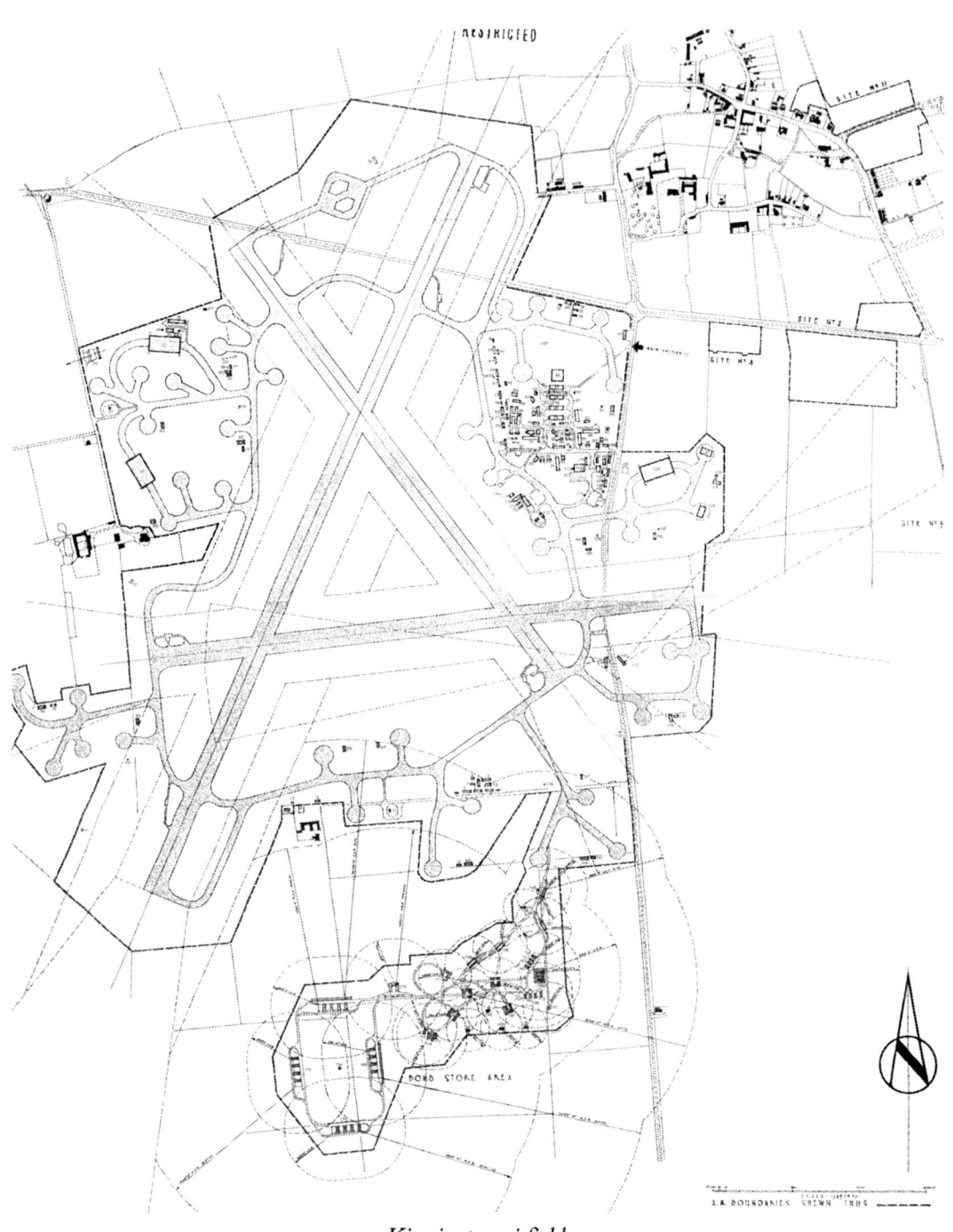

Kirmington airfield

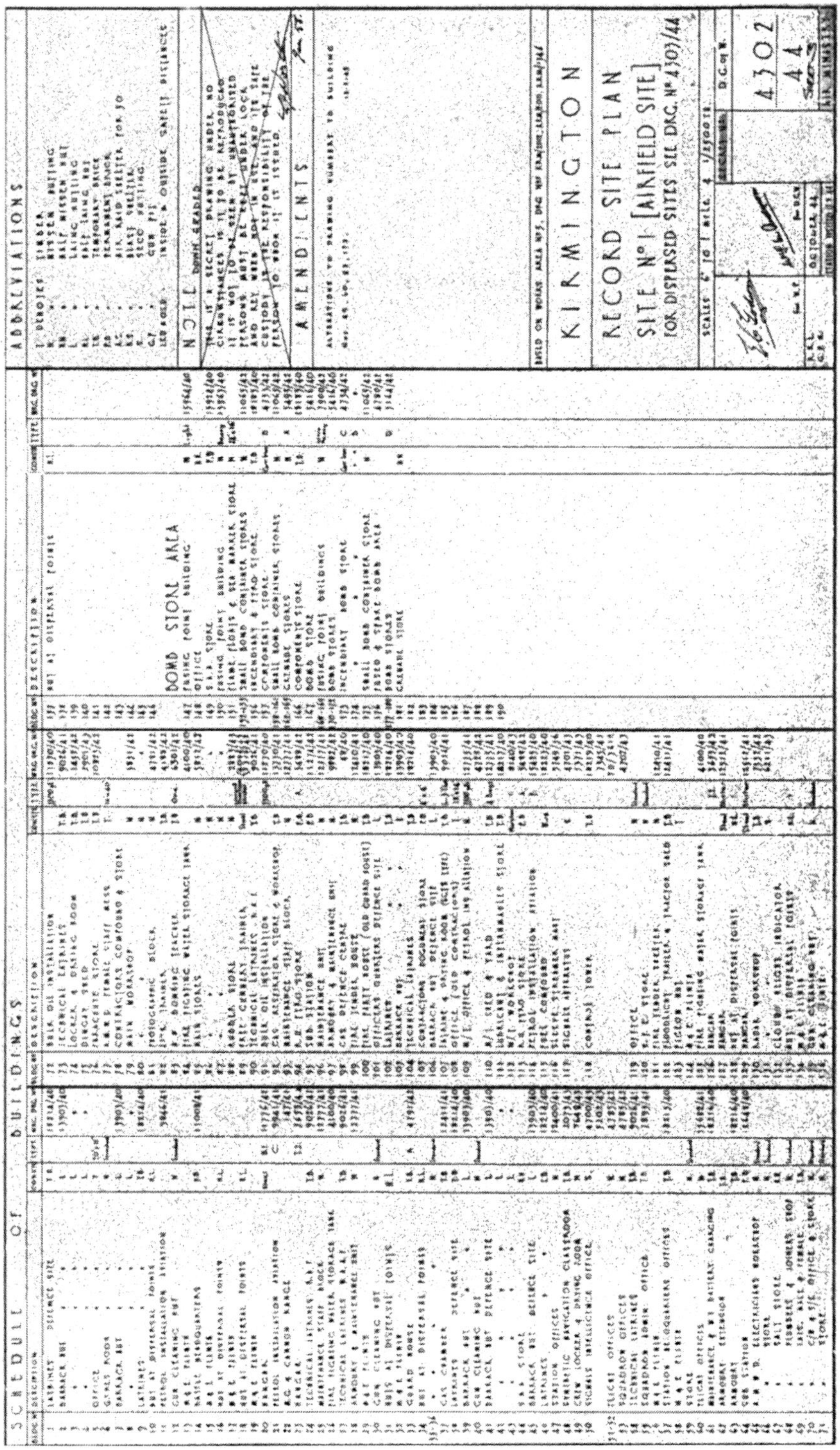
SCHEDULE OF BUILDINGS
ABBREVIATIONS
BOMB STORE AREA
NOTE
AMENDMENTS
KIRMINGTON
RECORD SITE PLAN
SITE No 1 [AIRFIELD SITE]
FOR DISPERSED SITES SEE DRG. No 4307/44
4302
44

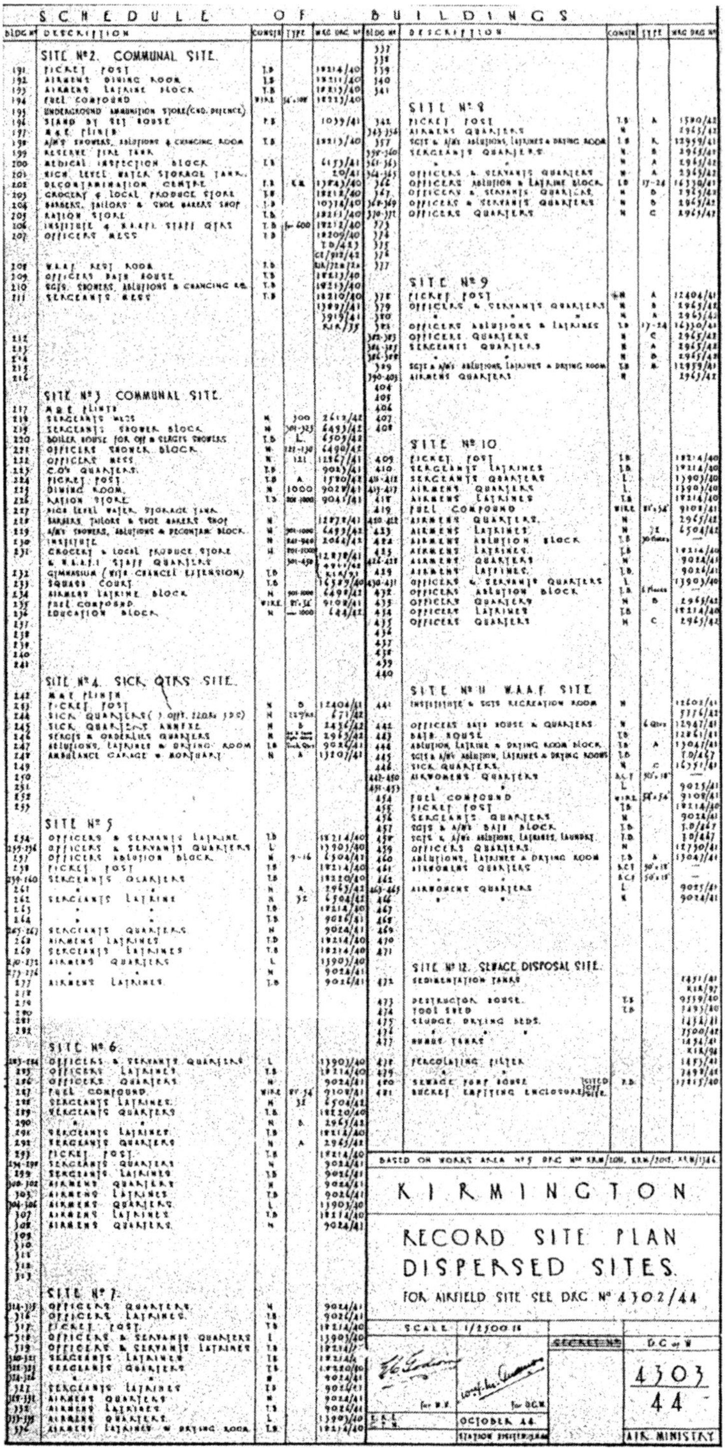

SCHEDULE OF BUILDINGS

KIRMINGTON

RECORD SITE PLAN
DISPERSED SITES.

FOR AIRFIELD SITE SEE DRG No 4302/44

SCALE 1/2500

4303
44

OCTOBER 44

AIR MINISTRY

CHAPTER THIRTEEN

Cool courage

1656 Heavy Conversion Unit. R.A.F. Lindholme, Yorkshire.
26ᵗʰ September 1944 to 25ᵗʰ November 1945.

As Bernard left Kirmington for Berkshire with two weeks leave to look forward to, he was given his next posting which was to be as an instructor at 1656 Heavy Conversion Unit based at R.A.F. Lindholme in Yorkshire, where he and his crew had undergone their own conversion training. For Bernard, his arrival back at the windswept, desolate Lindholme base on 26ᵗʰ September 1944 was like travelling back in time. He had entered the gates there as a 'pupil' less than six months before and it was here that he had received the last two men of his crew. Those six months seemed like a different lifetime as so much had happened since, but here he was again, this time without his crew and as an instructor and instead of flying his beloved Lancasters, he would be back on Halifaxes as 1656 Heavy Conversion Unit had not yet been upgraded. The two weeks leave he had enjoyed in the Berkshire countryside with Ellen and Douglas had been idyllic, enjoying the last remnants of summer as the farmers brought in the end of the harvest from the fields and he was able to start the process of putting the pressures and strains of operational flying behind him. The news from the front also helped soothe Ellen's fears as it seemed increasingly likely that the war would be over before Bernard would be recalled to an operational squadron, which would usually be after a period of six months. Little did he and the rest of the world know just how much fight the Germans had left in them.

As usual there was little time allocated to settling in and on 27ᵗʰ September Bernard found himself allocated to 'C' Flight and back in the air in Halifax BB267 with two other instructors, Flying Officer Berry and Pilot Officer Bate, undergoing an air test to check that he was still up to standard on the aircraft he had not flown for six months. After just 35 minutes they had been suitably impressed and passed him over to Flight Lieutenant Holmes and Squadron Leader Brooks in JP192 who were equally satisfied, this time in just 25 minutes. With no flying possible the following day, Bernard was again taken up by Squadron Leader Brooks on 29ᵗʰ

September to check on his ability to land the aircraft and then following a three hour 35 minute cross country the next day, he was deemed fit and competent to begin instructing.

On 2nd October Bernard's first pupils were Flying Officer Armstrong, who as yet had no crew, and Flying Officer Firth who brought his crew along for a familiarization flight which lasted for one hour forty minutes. That was followed up with a slightly more stressful flight with a Flight Lieutenant Playford, who spent seventy minutes practicing landing on three and then two engines. Throughout the rest of the month Bernard took up eighteen separate pilots, mainly without their crews, carrying out such exercises as landing on a reduced number of engines, circuits and landings, bombing practice, corkscrewing, night circuits and air tests with the only respite coming from the poor weather which dogged the month, especially towards the end when fog and low cloud covered most of the eastern part of the country for long periods. Despite interruptions from the weather, he still managed to get airborne on 32 occasions and racked up over 29 hours in the air.

Bomber Command were determined to show the German public the level of overwhelming aerial power they could wield and so launched Operation Hurricane. The unlucky recipient of Bomber Commands attentions was to be Duisburg and shortly after dawn on 14th October, they launched 519 Lancasters, 474 Halifaxes and twenty Mosquitoes against the city with a protective escort of R.A.F. fighters. In total 957 of the aircraft managed to bomb, dropping 3,600 tons of high explosive and a further 820 tons of incendiaries with thirteen Lancasters and a solitary Halifax being lost. Not satisfied that the display of strength had been effective enough, they returned that night by sending a further 498 Lancasters, 468 Halifaxes and 39 Mosquitoes, spread over two waves and separated by a two hour break. This second attack totalled 4,040 tons of high explosive and another 500 tons of incendiaries bringing the total dropped on Duisburg to almost 9,000 tons in just 24 hours; the damage was so intense that there are no reliable casualty reports available. As well as the huge Duisburg raid, 5 Group also sent a further 233 Lancasters and seven Mosquitoes to attack Brunswick. The total tonnage dropped for the 24 hour period was 10,050 tons; a total that would remain a record for the entire war.

As well as the flying and lectures at Lindholme there were plenty of activities, both compulsory and voluntary, that the personnel could get themselves involved in to while away the fog covered hours, with sport playing a huge part. During

October all personnel had to undergo firearms training in the use of a Rifle and a Sten gun on the 25 yard range and 130 personnel received fire training from the National Fire Service with a further 543 receiving anti-gas training. The variety of sports available for the personnel to participate in was exhaustive with boxing, badminton, fencing, tennis, swimming, soft ball, net ball, squash, football, hockey, rugby, weight lifting, P.T. and cycling all on offer. In addition to that there were 22 cinema showings, three dances and three E.N.S.A. concerts; it's a wonder they ever got into the air at all.

However, it wasn't all sport and cinema and as Bernard had witnessed at other training units, the possibility of being killed was still a very real one. One of the problems both H.C.U.'s and O.T.U.'s had was that they tended to operate old aircraft, many of which had suffered from battle damage or rough treatment from the trainee crews flying them. 1656 H.C.U. was no exception and suffered three crashes during October, two of which were caused by engine failure and the other through swinging on landing. One of the Halifaxes that crashed through engine trouble was BB284 which came down on 23rd October at Little Stretton in Shropshire after the starboard outer engine failed. Five members of the crew managed to bale out suffering minor injuries but the pilot, Warrant Officer T.A. Ellison, and bomb aimer, Sergeant J.F.C. Wheeler, were killed. As well as the loss of the three aircraft due to crashes, the unit lost four others just through wear and tear, three were to be used for ground instruction only and a fourth, BB267 was declared written off due to deterioration beyond repair by Bernard himself following an air test on 19th October.

Following the success of Operation Hurricane against Duisburg just ten days before, Bomber Command launched another huge attack, this time against Essen, on the night of 23/24th October. 1,055 aircraft, consisting of 561 Lancasters, 463 Halifaxes and 31 Mosquitoes, dropped 4,538 tons of bombs including 509 x 4,000lb 'Cookies'. Five Lancasters and three Halifaxes were lost on the raid and huge levels of damage were inflicted but that did not stop the force returning on 25th October when a further 508 Lancasters, 251 Halifaxes and twelve Mosquitoes attacked in daylight through heavy cloud. The raid was a success with the vital Krupps steelworks being seriously damaged and the towns electrical supply system being virtually wiped out; two Halifaxes and two Lancasters were lost.

The change of month brought with it considerable changes to Lindholme too as No.1 Aircrew School was moved away to R.A.F. Sturgate in Lincolnshire on the 1st and 1656 H.C.U. was re-equipped to operate using a 50/50 split of Halifaxes and Lancasters; a change that Bernard wholly supported. However, not all the changes were to his liking as he had been under the umbrella of 1 Group for almost his entire time in the R.A.F. but Lindholme was transferred to the control of 7 Group with effect from the 3rd. In reality the changes barely impacted on the staff at the unit but for some strange reason it felt to Bernard as if he had been ordered to start supporting a different football team.

The weather for the first four days of November was good enough not to interfere with the unit's activities but on 5th it took a turn for the worse. Heavy rain set in and serious icing conditions above 25,000 feet called a halt to all the cross country exercises planned, although Bernard still managed to get airborne for a ninety minute familiarization flight in one of the old Halifaxes with two Flying Officers. The weather improved the next day and despite the upheavals caused by the changes going on around them, the instructors ploughed on. For the next few days everything went well until the first accident of the month occurred on the night of 8/9th. It was a sign of things to come. Having completed a night time cross country exercise, Halifax JP192 inexplicably came into land at Lindholme with its undercarriage retracted and was damaged beyond repair although, luckily, the crew escaped unhurt apart from the ear bashing they must have received and their dented pride.

The following night the crew of another Halifax, HR796, had an equally lucky escape as they lost control of the aircraft during a night cross country over Sussex but all managed to bale out safely. Two days later Halifax LW226 taxied into Lancaster LM741 resulting in considerable damage for which the Lancaster had to be repaired off site, although the Halifax was patched up at Lindholme. The accidents continued on 12th November as Halifax BB362 was the next 1656 H.C.U. aircraft to be totally written off, as it swung on landing at R.A.F. Carnaby, but once again there were no injuries. With the carnage going on around him seeming to be worse than on an operational squadron, Bernard headed off to R.A.F. Sandtoft to attend a flying instructor's familiarization course on Lancasters; which seemed an incredible waste of time considering he had just completed a full tour of operations on them.

A huge blow was struck by Bomber Command against the German Navy on 12th November as the Battleship Tirpitz, sister ship of the Bismarck, was attacked by thirty Lancasters from 9 and 617 Squadrons. The weather over Tromso fjord in Norway was clear and the huge ship was hit by at least two massive Tallboy bombs. The ship then exploded and capsized, killing or injuring 1,000 of the 1,900 crew and with it took the last remaining credible threat from a German surface vessel.

While Bernard was away at Sandtoft the accidents not only continued at Lindholme but increased in severity as well. Three aircraft were seriously damaged on the 15th and had to be repaired off site, Halifax W7860 swung on take off and collided with Lancaster LM175 and then Halifax W7771 belly landed on two engines but there were no serious casualties. All that changed on the night of 18th November when an instructor, Pilot Officer Marsh, walked into a spinning propeller of Lancaster W4995 and suffered a compound fracture of the skull. He was transferred to Doncaster Royal Infirmary where he later died. As tragic as Pilot Officer Marsh's loss was, even worse was to come. On the night of 20/21st November there were three crashes. The first involved Halifax BB254 at 2055 hours, which took off with its bomb bay doors open and came down three miles north-west of the airfield while carrying out night time circuits and landings. The pilot, flight engineer, wireless operator and navigator were all killed. Halifax W7875 was the second crash of the night as it also came down to the north-west of the airfield at 2200 hours during a night cross country. Five of the crew, four of them Canadians, were killed with just the rear gunner surviving with minor injuries. The third and final accident of the night came as Halifax W7875 also crashed on take off just outside the airfields perimeter but luckily, this time, all the crew escaped with minor injuries.

Having completed his familiarization course on 16th November, Bernard was delighted to receive two weeks leave, which meant he avoided the carnage of late November at Lindholme, although once again the bad news was waiting for him as he returned to the base on 30th November, but soon there would be news of a loss that would be of a more personal nature.

December began with the continued change over from Halifaxes to Lancasters and all the associated problems that brought. The change was not as simple as just flying away the Halifaxes and bringing in Lancasters, although that too was an ongoing operation. In addition the staff had to change all the demonstration equipment layouts, prepare the new Lancaster instructional fuselages, which were usually old aircraft which were no longer fit to fly, re-organise gunnery training and arrange for new day and night fighter affiliation exercises. Despite the work load, the complete transfer of all flights to Lancasters had been completed by the end of the first week of the month with just a last few Halifaxes remaining to be flown off the base.

Even getting those last few Halifaxes away was proving a problem as the weather during the month was the worst of the year with heavy fog persisting for days at a time. Even so by the end of the month the instructors managed to complete their commitment to put out thirty fully trained crews and completed 1,055 hours of flying.

4th December was no exception to all the other tragic days of the brutal Second World War in that it brought more death and destruction, but on that night Bernard lost an old friend as 'Hircleberry' flew for the last time. With Bernard and his crew leaving Kirmington back in September, 'Hircleberry' had been used by a variety of crews on operations since, and on the night of 4/5th December 1944 she was flown by Flying Officer S.R. Hanna R.C.A.F. and his crew of five other Canadians and a single Briton on a raid to Karlsruhe. The raid had been made up of 369 Lancasters, 154 Halifaxes and twelve Mosquitoes and had been extremely accurate causing severe damage. Only one Lancaster had been lost in the raid, also from 166 Squadron, and the crew of 'Hircleberry' had safely made it back to Kirmington arriving over the airfield on the Beam Approach system at 2310 hours heading eastward. As instructed, they flew over the east/west runway in order to make their 'S' turn and land in a westerly direction. About three miles to the east of the airfield, with everything running smoothly and happy to be safely home, they began to bank round to starboard above Brocklesby Park in order to line up with the runway. Then, at 2314 hours, the starboard wing suddenly dropped followed by the nose which caused the aircraft to go into a flat spin. At their low altitude it was impossible for the pilot to regain control and 'Hircleberry' crashed into the ground and burst into flames killing the entire crew.

The subsequent investigation revealed the simple tragedy of the accident. The fire, which had broken out after the crash, had caused little actual damage to the wreckage and from the remains of the aircraft the investigators were able to piece together what had happened. As the aircraft was beginning what would have been her final turn of the night, the Flight Engineer realised the fuel was getting a little low and so switched tanks, but unfortunately he had made a miscalculation and had used the wrong fuel cocks, switching to empty tanks. From that moment 'Hircleberry' and her crew were doomed as her fuel starved starboard engines stopped abruptly, causing loss of control and the subsequent crash. At a reasonable height, Flying Officer Hanna and his Flight Engineer may well have been able to regain control, but so close to the ground such an elementary mistake was fatal. Proof if any aircrew ever needed it that you were only safe when you were in front of the Intelligence Officer with a mug of tea in your hand.

Two photographs of the wreckage of Lancaster LM176 'Hircleberry'. In the bottom photo the fuselage around the cockpit has been cut away to remove the crew and immediately behind the cut area 'Hircleberry' can still be seen as painted by Jack MacDonald

Bernard's first three days of December were taken up with air tests on the ageing Halifaxes and it wasn't until the 6th that he began instructing on the Lancasters, a position in which he felt very much at home. The weather was good enough to allow some flying every day up to 12th and then the thick fog and low cloud set in, preventing any flying at all until 17th when the fog finally lifted again.

Although Bernard had been aware of it for a while, some much appreciated good news was made public on 12th December 1944, as the London Gazette announced that he had been awarded the Distinguished Flying Cross, which was, and still is, awarded for 'an act or acts of valour, courage or devotion to duty while flying in active operations against the enemy'. Wing Commander Garner, Bernard's commanding officer at 166 Squadron, had first applied for the award on his behalf in early September, before Bernard had completed his operational tour, and the application was endorsed by Group Captain Carter immediately after his tour had finished. The officers' recommendation forms are shown below and the testimonies speak volumes. With the decoration also came a wave of congratulations from family members and even from the Base Commander (that is 13 Base which was made up of three airfields, Elsham Wolds, Kirmington and North Killingholme) Air Commodore Swain; the second telegram was from Wally, Bernard's older brother.

Wt. 25617/P1434 100,000 Pads 9/43 H.P. 51–7341

R.A.F. Form 1924 ·   **POSTAGRAM.** Originator's Reference Number:—
13B/S.490&/6/P.1.

To F/O. B.F. Steel, D.F.C., Date :—
No. 1656 C.U.,   16th December, 1944.
R.A.F. Lindholme.   CONFIDENTIAL.

From :   Base Commander, H.Q., No. 13 Base.

     I am very pleased to see your award of the Distinguished

Flying Cross in the London Gazette dated 12th December, 1944.

     Hearty congratulations on this well deserved

recognition of your good work.

Originator's Signature		A/Cdre.	Time of Origin

The officers DFC recommendations read as follows; Wing Commander Garner wrote;

This Officer, as Captain of aircraft, has now completed 33 sorties on targets ranging from Germany to enemy occupied territory, including the pre-invasion period and

RECOMMENDATIONS FOR HONOURS & AWARDS

Confidential

NON-IMMEDIATE

352

Christian Names: Bernard Frank   Surname: STEEL

Rank: Pilot Officer (Acting F/O.)   Official Number: 174798

Command or Group: No.1 Group   Unit: No.166 Squadron

Total hours flown on operations 169

Number of sorties 33

Total hours flown on operations
since receipt of previous award .... N/A

Number of sorties since receipt
of previous award .... N/A

Recognition for which recommended .... D.F.C.

Appointment held .... Pilot/Captain of Aircraft

Particulars of Meritorious Service

This Officer, as Captain of Aircraft, has now completed 33 sorties on targets ranging from Germany to enemy occupied territory, including the pre-invasion period, and operations in support of the land forces. He has consistently shown himself to have great determination and has proved himself to be a good leader of his crew. He always seeks out the target with a total disregard for enemy opposition and has never failed to press home a successful attack. He cheerfully accepts any hazard, either of weather or enemy defences, and on occasions when an engine has failed to deliver the required power, he has carried on with his task. His crew is regarded as one of the most successful on the Squadron and there is no doubt that their discipline and devotion to duty has been inspired by his example. He is painstaking in his efforts to improve his own flying and to reach the optimum of operational efficiency, and for his great devotion to duty, the skill which he has consistently displayed and his cool courage, he is recommended for the award of the Distinguished Flying Cross.

Date: 5th. September, 1944.   Wing Commander, Commanding,
166, Squadron,   R.A.F.

REMARKS BY STATION COMMANDER.

This Officer has now completed his tour of operations. Throughout he has shown that, under a quiet manner, he possesses a fine offensive spirit and that he can always be relied upon to reach his target, and to press his attacks right home regardless of the strength of enemy opposition. I have no hesitation in recommending him for the award of the Distinguished Flying Cross.

Date: 13th September, 1944.   Group Captain, Commanding,
R.A.F. Station, Kirmington.

Crown copyright. National Archives, Kew.

operations in support of the land forces. He has consistently shown himself to have great determination and has proved himself to be a good leader of his crew. He always seeks out the target with a total disregard for enemy opposition and has never failed to press home a successful attack. He cheerfully accepts any hazard, either of weather or enemy defences, and on occasions when an engine has failed to deliver the required power, he has carried on with his task. His crew is regarded as one of the most successful on the squadron and there is no doubt that their discipline and devotion to duty has been inspired by his example. He is painstaking in his efforts to improve his own flying and to reach the optimum of operational efficiency and for his great devotion to duty, the skill which he has consistently displayed and his cool courage, he is recommended for the award of the Distinguished Flying Cross.

Group Captain Carter added;

This officer has now completed his tour of operations. Throughout he has shown that, under a quiet manner, he posseses a fine offensive spirit and that he can always be relied upon to reach his target, and to press his attacks right home regardless of the strength of enemy opposition. I have no hesitation in recommending him for the award of the Distinguished Flying Cross.

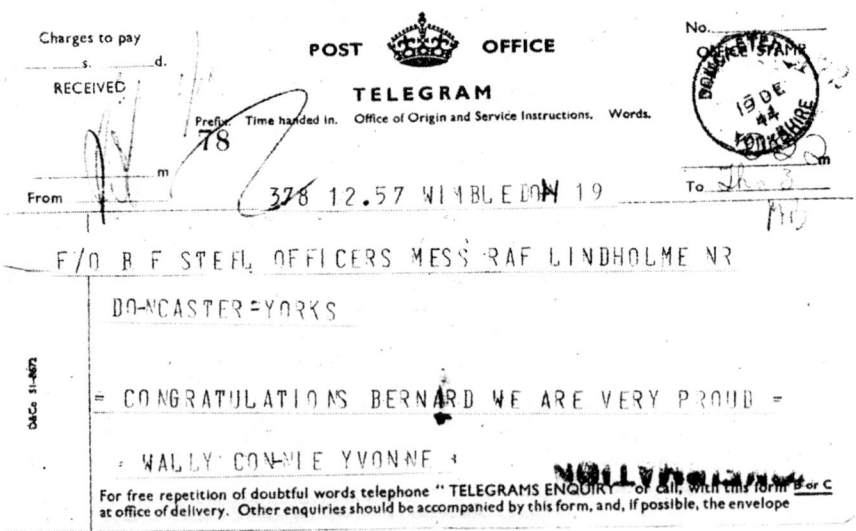

Having lost so much time to the weather, the instructors had to make up for lost time and as a result Bernard took four flights on 17th December before the weather closed in again the next day. The weather continued its determined attempt to stop all training right up to and including the Christmas period which passed with Bernard and the other officers serving traditional Christmas dinner to some 800 airmen.

On 23rd December Bomber Command launched a daylight raid on Cologne with 27 Lancasters and three Mosquitoes using the OBOE system which required a long, straight course to be flown to the target with the predicted cloud cover providing protection for the attacking aircraft from the German defences. However, the cloud had cleared on approach to the target and the crews were instructed to break formation and attack visually in order to make it harder for the defences to lock onto them. Unfortunately the instruction did not reach the lead Lancaster, piloted by Squadron Leader Robert Anthony Palmer of 582 Squadron who was flying his 111th mission. Palmer, unaware of the change of plan, continued on his straight and steady course and was hit by heavy anti-aircraft fire which caused fires in two of his engines and filled the fuselage with smoke. The aircraft was also attacked by fighters but Palmer knew he had to maintain his straight and steady course and refused to take evasive action, managing to reach and accurately bomb the target before he finally lost control with only the rear gunner escaping by parachute. For his determination Squadron Leader Palmer was posthumously awarded the Victoria Cross.

The passing of Christmas still did not bring a break in the weather until 30th when Bernard made what would be one of his last flights in a Halifax as he took JD469 to 61 Maintenance Unit (M.U.'s either stored aircraft or passed them on to approved dismantlers as the aircraft were struck off charge) based at Hooton Park in Cheshire to await its fate.

The first day of 1945 saw Bomber Command launch a daylight raid involving 102 Lancasters and two Mosquitoes from 5 Group which were sent to attack a stretch of the Dortmund-Ems Canal near Ladbergen, which was once again successfully breached. During the raid a Lancaster from 9 Squadron, piloted by Flying Officer R.F.H. Denton, while flying through heavy flak during its bombing run, was badly hit and caught fire. The crews' wireless operator, Flight Sergeant George Thompson, managed to rescue the mid upper gunner who was unconscious in his burning turret and put out his burning clothes with his bare hands. Having noticed that the rear gunner was also trapped in his turret by fire, despite the pain from his own burns, he battled his way through the still burning fuselage to rescue his rear gunner as well, before once again extinguishing the man's clothing with his already severely burnt hands. He then made his way to the cockpit to inform his pilot of the severity of the damage to the aircraft and its crew, but his wounds were so severe that his pilot didn't even recognise him. Flying Officer Denton managed to crash land the aircraft near Brussels with Thompson being taken to a local hospital where one of the gunners died almost immediately and Thompson died three weeks later. For his courage in rescuing his crew mates, George Thompson was posthumously awarded the Victoria Cross.

The year may have changed but as usual the awful British weather didn't and January 1945 began the way 1944 had ended, with thick fog and poor visibility. With the New Years hangovers confined to history, Bernard took to the skies for the first time in 1945 during the evening of 2nd for a marathon two hour forty minute session of night circuits and landings with one Warrant Officer Robinson in Lancaster ED625. The following day was a complete wash out as far as flying went, and then, on the 4th, he once again made the mournful trip in Halifax BB255 to the maintenance unit at Hooton Park in what was probably its last flight; Bernard himself took his last ever flight in a Halifax on 7th during an air test in LL487.

The weather continued to wreak havoc throughout the month with gales, fog and snow all preventing flying. At 1539 hours on 12th January, Lancaster L4889 caught fire in Hangar 4. The fire spread to the roof of the hangar and the Lancaster was completely destroyed before the fire service managed to extinguish the flames at 1745 hours. The improved standard of aircraft and the reduced flying hours, due to the weather, resulted in a minimal number of accidents during January with just two. The first, at 1620 hours on 15th, resulted in the writing off of Lancaster ND757 as it ran off the end of the runway on landing and crashed to the north-west of the airfield; the second, on 22nd, saw Lancaster JB646 have to divert to Carnaby after losing its starboard main wheel during a night time undershot landing at Lindholme; no aircrew were seriously injured in either incident. By the end of the month 1656 H.C.U. had, despite the weather, managed 1,006 flying hours with nineteen crews completing their training and being posted to squadrons.

The weather began to improve through February and as a result 1656 H.C.U. was able to exceed their planned training figures with each crew managing to get more 'air time' than the syllabus required. Bernard too was busy in the air, carrying out 32 different flights which varied in content from taxi trips in the station flights Airspeed Oxford, to night time fighter affiliation exercises in Lancasters; in February alone he spent over 42 hours in the air. The unit too exceeded its recent figures, as in the previous few months they had just about scraped over 1,000 hours 'air time' but February saw them achieve 1,727 hours in putting out thirty crews, averaging 49 hours flight time each.

The improved weather also seemed to help keep the accident rate low with just three incidents in the month. The first, and most mysterious incident, occurred on 6th February during a cross-country flight. Lancaster LM175, the Lancaster registered immediately before 'Hircleberry', was last contacted near Shrewsbury before vanishing without trace. It is likely that the aircraft either crashed in the Welsh mountains or continued on westward and ran out of fuel over the Irish Sea. Bearing in mind that some 70 years later no trace of the aircraft has been found, it is more likely that the latter scenario was the aircraft and crews ultimate fate.

The other two accidents were slightly more mundane in nature as at 1407 hours on 13th February, Lancaster JA868 swung on take off from Lindholme and belly landed on the main road at the end of the runway. There were no casualties but the aircraft had to be taken away to a maintenance unit for repair. Five days later, at 2155 hours, Lancaster EE139 overshot the runway on landing which caused the starboard undercarriage to collapse, but thankfully, once again the crew escaped unharmed with the aircraft being repaired on site by specialist contractors who were brought in from elsewhere.

During the night of 13th/14th February 1945 Bomber Command launched an attack against the German city of Dresden. The city was by that time just behind the Eastern Front and was a communications centre where German troops could be brought forward and supplied by rail to join the fight against the Russians. Winston Churchill took a direct hand in the planning of the raid which was needed in the face of the war situation at the time but in typically duplicitous politician style, when the raid came in for serious criticism after the war Churchill tried to distance himself from the whole episode and left 'Bomber' Harris to bear the brunt of the criticism. The plan was for the Americans to carry out the first stage of the raid on Dresden but due to poor weather they had to postpone their raid which should have taken place during daylight on 13th February and as a result Bomber Command went in first that night and lost six Lancasters during the attack.

In total 796 Lancasters and nine Mosquitoes attacked Dresden in two waves dropping 1,478 tons of high explosive and 1,182 tons of incendiaries which created a firestorm of unprecedented magnitude that burned for four whole days. During the afternoon of 14th February the city was attacked again, this time by

311 B-17's of the U.S.A.F. who dropped a further 771 tons of bombs. The horrific power available to Bomber Command was evident in the casualty statistics; it is impossible to determine exactly how many were killed as the city was flooded with refugees fleeing from the advancing Russian Army, but estimates place the number at between 40,000 and 50,000 although wildly exaggerated figures of 200,000 were claimed by the German propaganda minister, Josef Goebbels, a figure which is still claimed as accurate by some today; it would appear that despite his many shortcomings, Goebbels was very good at his propaganda job.

During the night of 23/24th February 1945 Bomber Command sent 367 Lancasters and thirteen Mosquitoes to attack the German town of Pforzheim just to the west of Stuttgart. The raid, in which Bomber Command lost ten Lancasters, was the only one of the war on the town but created huge levels of destruction. It is estimated that 83% of the towns built up area was destroyed by the 1,825 tons of bombs that fell in just a 22 minute period and which resulted once again in a horrific fire storm. The death toll was put at 17,600 with an area of 4.5 square kilometres completely engulfed by flames. The raid would turn out to have the third highest casualty rate of the war, only eclipsed by the raids on Hamburg and Dresden.

The Master Bomber for the raid on Pforzheim was Captain Edwin Swales, a South African serving with 582 Squadron. During the raid his aircraft was attacked twice by night fighters and severely damaged with two engines and the rear turret being put out of commission. Swales had been unable to react to the evasion instruction coming from his crew as he was issuing bombing instructions to the main force at the time and despite the damage to his aircraft, he continued to direct the bombing operations until the end of the raid. Swales began the homeward journey but soon realised the aircraft would not make it and ordered his crew to bale out, which they all did successfully, but Swales could not get out himself and died in the subsequent crash. For his bravery, dedication to duty and for saving his crew at his own cost, Captain Edwin Swales was posthumously awarded the Victoria Cross; the last Bomber Command V.C. of the war.

The weather continued to improve through the month of March and as a direct result so did the performance of the conversion unit. The conditions were sufficiently stable in the first half of the month for Bernard to get airborne at least once every day up to and including the 13th. after which he took a very welcome weeks leave and headed back south to Ellen and little Doug, who was by now a robust two and a half year old toddler.

Bomber Command set their final record of the war on 12th March 1945 as they sent their largest number of aircraft ever to attack a single target against the city of Dortmund. In total 1,108 aircraft, 748 Lancasters, 292 Halifaxes and 68 Mosquitoes, dropped a record tonnage of 4,851 tons on the beleaguered city and caused such utter destruction that no reports of the raid survive, although it is known that all production and industry was completely halted. The casualty figures, although not known for certain, were relatively light as by the time the bombers arrived most of the residents had fled the city for the safety of the countryside, just two Lancasters were lost in the raid.

Despite the undeniable aerial superiority that the Allies had in the skies over Europe, the inside of a heavy bomber was still an extremely dangerous place to be as the raid of 16/17th March proved. That night 277 Lancasters and sixteen Mosquitoes attacked the Nazi stronghold of Nuremburg for the final time. The raid was a success with huge damage and fires being created and over 500 people on the ground killed but in the air many were dying as well. A considerable force of German night fighters, in what seemed to be the Luftwaffe's last throw of the dice, got amongst the bomber stream and wrought havoc, bringing down 24 Lancasters, a huge loss rate for that period of the war of 8.7%

While Bernard was away on leave the first mishap of the month befell Lancaster R5730 in an unavoidable accident caused by a tyre bursting on landing. The burst resulted in the aircraft crashing to the north-east of the airfield causing repairable damage to the aircraft and none to the crew. Having enjoyed a relaxing week at home Bernard was back in the air on 24th March in Lancaster PD291, carrying out a familiarization exercise and circuits and landings with Flight Sergeant Kowald in a two and a half hour flight.

With the weather remaining reasonably good, the unit continued to fly whenever possible and as a considerable amount of hours mounted up it became increasingly inevitable there would be another accident at some point. That point finally came on 25th March as Lancaster NN815 crashed to the west of the airfield, while practising three engine landings, and was written off; although once again the crew managed to walk away unhurt. The weather finally let the unit down on 29th as low cloud covered the airfield, but with that exception 1656 H.C.U. managed to keep getting airborne and by the end of the month had clocked up 2,110 hours in the air and successfully passed out forty fully trained crews.

As a direct effect of the Allies successes on the Western Front, the German V weapons attacks ended on 27ᵗʰ March as the last V2 fell on Orpington in Kent. Their six month reign of terror was finally over after some 1,050 V2s had struck south-east England killing 2,754 people and injuring 6,523 more.

Once again the weather managed to behave itself for the month of April with only a handful of days where flying was not possible and Bernard managed to get airborne at least once a day from the 2ⁿᵈ to the 20ᵗʰ with bombing practice and fighter affiliation exercises taking up the majority of his time, regularly interspersed with the monotony of circuits and landings. As an example of just how accurate bomber command was becoming, bearing in mind that these results were achieved by inexperienced crews, the average range of the bombs dropped from above 10,000 feet for the unit that month was just 172 yards from the target.

The accidents for the month came in a rush during the first two days. At 1545 hours on 1ˢᵗ April, Lancaster HK755 crashed to the north-east of the airfield after losing control while practising a three engine landing and Lancaster NG227 landed heavily causing the undercarriage to collapse at 0120 hours the following morning. HK755 was repaired off site but NG227 was written off with all the crews escaping without serious injury. The rest of the month was accident free and on 26ᵗʰ April Bernard happily accepted another week of leave and once again headed back to Berkshire. 1656 H.C.U. had yet another successful month with 45 crews and two additional pilots successfully completing their training with 2,170 hours of flying time; for Bernard and the other instructors their success was not measured by such statistics but by the fact that they had managed to complete another month without anyone being killed.

The night of 14/15ᵗʰ April saw the final raid of the war by a large Bomber Command force against a German city, as they attacked Potsdam to the west of Berlin. A force of 500 Lancasters and twelve Mosquitoes attacked but due mainly to the fact that most of the route was above territory which had been recently taken by Allied ground troops, only one Lancaster was shot down by a roving night fighter. The attack was aimed at the railway junction and German barracks of the Guards regiments and was reasonably successful, with severe damage being caused in the city. A high ground casualty figure of around 5,000 has been attributed to the raid, mainly because the residents, quite reasonably, believed the approaching aircraft were en-route to Berlin, just a few miles to the east, and failed to take shelter in time.

With the war on the ground reaching its end in Europe the Russians were preparing for yet another major assault on 15th April, this time on the main prize; Berlin. After a long and bitter struggle which had seen them at one point pushed back to the outskirts of Moscow and so close to defeat at Stalingrad, the Russians finally found themselves amassing a huge force on three sides of the German capital. The Red Army could boast around 1.6 million men, backed up by 4,000 tanks, 2,500 self propelled guns, 15,500 artillery pieces and 7,000 aircraft. At 0500 hours the very next day, the assault on Berlin began with a huge artillery bombardment followed up, at 0700 hours, by tanks and infantry; the German Reich was rapidly approaching its death throes.

Bomber Command launched a major raid against Hitler's 'Eagle Nest' and the surrounding S.S. barracks on 25th April as they sent a force of 359 Lancasters and sixteen Mosquitoes on the attack during which Lancasters of 617 Squadron dropped the last of the huge 'Tallboy' bombs of the war. The raid was accurate, despite weather problems and the Mosquitoes having to operate at over 30,000 feet due to the mountains interfering with their OBOE equipment; two Lancasters were lost.

That night, with the end of the war in Europe in sight, 107 Lancasters and 12 Mosquitoes attacked an oil refinery at Tonsberg in southern Norway in what would turn out to be the last raid carried out by the heavy Bombers of Bomber Command. The attack was accurate and the target severely damaged with one Lancaster, piloted by Flying Officer A. Cox, coming down in Sweden with all the crew surviving and being interned until the end of the war. They would turn out to be the crew of the last of the more than 3,300 Lancasters to be lost during the war.

With April approaching its end it was becoming increasingly obvious to the men of 1656 H.C.U. that the end of the war, in Europe at least, was only a matter of weeks away. They were kept well informed of the situation on all battlefronts by means of the intelligence information boards which were kept updated with maps and photographs as well as written articles. Despite what seemed to be the end, the unit was still under pressure to keep producing crews as the war in the Pacific was showing no signs of ending anytime soon and it was believed that a large force of Bomber Command aircraft, up to 1,000, would be sent to assist the Americans under the code name of Tiger Force, once the European war had been wrapped up.

Amongst the trainee crews there was a general air of despondency settling over many of them as they felt with the war rapidly coming to an end they would never get their chance to see some action and to 'do their bit'. They didn't know how lucky they were, but some of the more pragmatic amongst them hoped they would never have to. Little did any of them know of Churchill's plans for Tiger Force and unless there was a rapid change in the situation in the Pacific, these men would be doing 'their bit' a very long way from home.

30th April was to be a momentous day in the long and bitter Second World War and it began with the Americans taking the city of Munich while in Italy they took Turin and the British reached Trieste. However, all those events were overshadowed, and almost forgotten, under the news that at 1530 hours Hitler and his new wife, Eva Braun, had committed suicide in his bunker. The bitter fighting continued to rage just outside the bunker and the Reichstag until, at 2250 hours, the Russians took the Reichstag building and planted their flag on its roof in triumph. Later that night the German, General Krebs, began to negotiate the surrender of Berlin to the Russian General Zhukov. The only fight left for the German troops was to fight their way back westward in order to be able to surrender to the British and Americans rather than the Russians, who they were rightly fearful of.

1ˢᵗ May saw General Krebs approach General Zhukov of the Red Army seeking a ceasefire. Zhukov demanded unconditional surrender which was agreed by the German command, despite resistance from notable senior Nazi's such as Goebbels. Realising that total defeat was now upon them, Joseph Goebbels, the German propaganda minister, had his wife kill their six children before he and his wife killed themselves. What remained of the German High Command issued an order to cease all resistance in Berlin but some die-hards continued to fight rather than fall into the hands of the Russians. Berlin was totally occupied on 2ⁿᵈ May after seventeen days of vicious fighting and by the evening over 70,000 Germans had been taken prisoner but despite the surrender of Berlin, the Germans were still fighting in other areas of both the Western and Eastern fronts although their counterparts in Italy finally surrendered on 2ⁿᵈ May.

The final action of the war for Bomber Command was to take place on the night of 2/3ʳᵈ May 1945 as a force of Mosquitoes was sent to attack targets around Kiel to prevent German troops fleeing to Norway, where it was believed they would try to put up a final stand. Initially 53 Mosquitoes attacked airfields in the area, with one being brought down during a Napalm (petrol based chemical which explodes in flames on impact) attack on Jagel airfield killing its crew of Flying Officer R. Catterall, D.F.C. and Flight Sergeant D.J. Beadle. The initial attack was then followed up by a raid in two waves by 126 Mosquitoes using H2S and OBOE navigating devices, which caused considerable damage and ended German resistance in the town which was subsequently declared an open city. The final tragedy for Bomber Command came that night amongst a force of 89 Radio countermeasure aircraft that were sent out in support of the Kiel raid. Two Halifaxes from 199 Squadron collided and crashed near Meimersdorf, to the south of Kiel, killing thirteen of the sixteen men aboard; they were to be the tragic last of many thousands of aircrew that Bomber Command had lost during six years of relentless fighting.

By 3rd May the Russians had finished the mopping up of resistance in Berlin and the British took the town of Hamburg as the Western and Eastern fronts began to join up all along the line. General Montgomery, in charge of the British forces in the north of Germany, received the unconditional surrender of all the German forces in Holland, Denmark and north-west Germany on 4th May while both Innsbruck and Salzburg fell to the Americans and the only Germans left fighting in and around Berlin were not fighting for the Nazi cause but still attempting to fight their way westward to surrender to the Americans and British rather than to fall into the hands of the Russians.

Early in the morning of 7th May 1945, at General Eisenhower's headquarters in Rheims, the Germans, represented by General Jodl, finally signed the unconditional surrender of all their forces to the Allies which was due to take effect on the first minute of 9th May and then, on the 8th May, the Germans signed the surrender to the Russians in a town near Berlin. As the prescribed time for the cessation of hostilities in Europe came around, German forces all over Europe laid down their arms and surrendered to the Allies and the Russians. Only a few small groups defiantly continued to hold out while all across Europe thousands of people gathered on the streets to celebrate the end of the war in a day of celebration that has become known as VE-Day, Victory in Europe. With the defeat of the main protagonist in Europe, the last remaining enemy to be defeated was the Japanese in the east, and they too were sliding inexorably to defeat, but would continue to fight bitterly for every inch of ground.

Bernard returned from his leave in the early days of May to a base affected by poor weather with heavy rain and thundery showers preventing flying on numerous occasions. He finally got airborne again on 7th May with two flights totalling nearly three hours airtime. As he returned to the 'ops' room that afternoon the place was buzzing with excitement and everyone seemed to have a beaming smile on their faces. The drawn and tired looks, which had been a seemingly constant feature of people's faces for the last few years, seemed to have magically gone and then the reason for the change was announced to Bernard by an un-named voice. "They've only bloody surrendered, Bailey." Came the most welcome five words Bernard had heard in a long time and at that point his face began to beam as well.

The following day, 8th May, was declared as VE-day and all work was suspended in order for a proper celebration to take place. In the morning all ranks assembled opposite the control tower for a thanksgiving service and while everyone was assembled the Station Commander announced that transport had been laid on so that anyone who wished to could leave the station to celebrate. Not surprisingly nearly everyone did and Bernard and the other instructors leapt into the back of a lorry whose driver was determined only to take them to nearby Doncaster, but they insisted he took them to Lincoln, the heart of bomber country and the only place any self respecting bomber air crew could spend such a momentous day. The streets of Lincoln were packed with revellers dancing, singing and drinking and Bernard and the other instructors headed for the centre of it which was focused around the Saracens Head pub, a favourite haunt of aircrew throughout the war. The Saracens Head was packed with revellers and bedecked with bunting and the flags of all the Allied nations. There were so many people celebrating that the entire width of the street outside was a sea of people all intent on making the most of the historic moment. Not surprisingly the instructors did not make it back to Lindholme until sometime the following day and a little the worse for wear, but for once, due to the extreme nature of the circumstances, the Station Commander turned a blind eye and after a two day break from flying the unit eventually got back to work.

Due to the combination of poor weather, the VE celebrations and his leave period, Bernard only made twelve flights that month although, somehow, the unit as a whole still managed to achieve its target and put out 45 fully trained crews and fitted in some 1,715 flying hours.

The news of the German surrender wasn't the only good news to come Bernard's way that month as his temporary rank of Flying Officer was confirmed and made substantive on 11th May. The only concern left for him was Tiger Force and the thought that he may well have to be redeployed, he reasoned with himself that the powers that be would send all these freshly trained crews first but as we all know, with British bureaucracy, you never can be sure.

The month was also good news again on the accident front with just one accident which occurred at 1535 hours on 16th as, during a well executed landing, the starboard wheel of Lancaster W4995 came off causing the undercarriage to collapse and the aircraft to crash to the north-east of the airfield; once again the crew managed to escape with nothing more than minor injuries.

Away to the east the Japanese were continuing to put up stiff resistance against the Americans on Okinawa and in the Philippines as they had on countless other islands across the Pacific over the previous three years. The U.S.A.A.F. continued to launch large scale bombing missions over mainland Japan with a force of over 500 aircraft attacking the centre of Tokyo on 24th May. All the while the American commanders continued to make plans for the invasion of mainland Japan, which was set to begin on 1st November. The tenacity the Japanese had displayed while defending the Pacific islands had been exceptional and that example filled the American high command with dread as they considered how many men they would lose in an invasion; their estimates put the potential losses at over one million men.

Despite the cessation of hostilities in Europe, the conveyor belt of training crews continued into June 1945 in the face of the unseasonably poor weather, with heavy rain and thundery conditions regularly interrupting flying. However, signs of a slackening of pace were beginning to become evident as Saturday afternoons and all day on Sundays had been allocated as stand-down periods during which there was no flying and only the barest of essential duties were carried out to maintain the operation of the station.

In spite of the weather, Bernard was airborne on all but one of the first seven days of the month after which he took a weeks leave where he could finally celebrate the victory in Europe with Ellen, although his fears about Japan he kept to himself. By the time he returned, the feel of the base had changed considerably as it no longer felt like a restricted wartime base and the luxury of the Saturday/Sunday stand-down had been introduced on the 9th which contributed hugely to the more relaxed atmosphere.

The steady wind down of the wartime R.A.F. had begun almost straight away following the cessation of hostilities in Europe. Many base staff were being de-mobbed even as early as June and 240 staff took up places on courses in vocational training and re-settlement courses that month, which had begun in earnest in an attempt to prepare people for their return to or, in many cases, their first taste of civilian life.

Yet again the month passed without serious injury to any of the unit's aircrew but several Lancasters weren't quite so lucky. On 9th June at 0513 hours, Lancaster PD443 caught fire while a flash bomb was being removed from the aircraft and was subsequently reduced to little more than scrap by the ensuing fire. The only aircraft to be involved in a crash was Lancaster LL811, which swung on take off at 2330 hours on 20th June and crashed to the north of the airfield and was also written off. Two other Lancasters, JA922 and ED623 were deemed beyond repair on site due to general deterioration.

Bernard returned to the air on 18th June in Lancaster ME583 taking up Flying Officer Marriott for an air test but a more unusual duty was about to come his way. Towards the latter half of the month the air ministry allowed 'Lindy' flights, which were effectively sightseeing tours of the bomb ravaged areas of Germany for ground based staff to be able to witness what they had been able to achieve through their support of the aircrews. 1656 H.C.U. carried out eleven flights in June and on 24th Bernard piloted one of them himself. Flying with just a flight engineer and navigator as crew, he took five passengers on an extensive six hour tour of the Ruhr area on a route that started from Lindholme to Skegness, across the North Sea to Rotterdam, south to Arnhem, along the River Rhine until they joined the Dortmund-Ems Canal, which they followed north to Munster. At Munster they turned around and headed south to Gelsenkirchen, then to Essen and even further south to the shattered remains of Cologne. They then turned westward to pass over the remains of Duren and Aachen, which had both been ravaged by ground fighting as well as aerial attack, before turning north-west to fly over Antwerp then Walcheren Island before crossing the North Sea back to Southwold on the Suffolk coast and finally back to Lindholme. Despite the interruptions, stand-down days and Lindy tours, 1656 H.C.U. still managed to reach their required target of fully trained crews by 25th June and by months end had put out 38 fully trained crews, achieving 1,747 hours of instructional flying in the process.

The island of Okinawa finally came under complete American control on 22nd June but at a tremendous cost and a fearful example of how expensive an operation against mainland Japan would be. In taking the island the Americans had lost around 50,000 dead, wounded and missing and had lost nearly 40 ships, mainly to Kamikaze attacks, while the Japanese had lost a massive 110,000 dead and 7,500 taken prisoner. Despite continuing to suffer heavy defeats on all fronts, such as the Philippines on 5th July, and huge losses of life both military and civilian, the Japanese had still shown no sign of surrender forcing the Allies to issue a chilling proclamation which demanded that Japan surrender unconditionally or face complete destruction. The Japanese ignored the warning, unaware of the subtle clue as to what was to come, and so on 6th August 1945 a new and horrific phase of warfare began.

With the war in Europe over, the number of crews arriving at the unit for training was steadily falling and so the instructors in turn were flying less and less. For the whole of the month of July Bernard only made eleven training flights and two more 'taxi' trips in the stations Oxford. Across the unit, staff were beginning to be de-mobbed and three officers and sixteen other ranks were released during the month. As well as those actually being released, many more were preparing themselves as best they could for life in civvy street by taking up the opportunity to participate in one or more of the educational and vocational training courses which had been set up. The choice of subjects was wide with English, maths, general knowledge, French, German, science, Economics, history, geography, shorthand or book-keeping all available with plans to introduce courses on pharmacy, electrical engineering and physiology. The students could then take examinations in their chosen subject and during July over 300 people had taken up the chance to get involved in at least one of the classes. Bernard had been lucky enough to receive an excellent education at Rutlish School and felt little need for any further education, but back then most people received only the most basic schooling and the chance to better themselves was not to be spurned, hence the high take-up rate.

In the air Bernard had undergone the usual routine of circuits and landings, bombing practice and fighter affiliations but sometimes days passed in between flights and towards the end of the month he went for thirteen days without getting airborne. With the war in Europe over and the likelihood of being re-deployed to the Japanese theatre seeming to diminish all the time, he was beginning to long for the time when he too would be released from the service. The flying was the only thing which was making his time at Lindholme bearable and as that tailed off so he became increasingly restless and desperate to get home; Bernard had finally had enough.

1656 H.C.U. still managed to put out another 36 fully trained crews in July 1945 and managed it in just 1,425 hours of flying time. The accidents too were minimal with just one for the month when, on 13th Lancaster W4994 suffered a collapsed undercarriage as the pilot tried to turn off the runway at too high a speed following a landing.

From Tinian Island in the Marianas chain on 6th August 1945, a B-29 Superfortress, named Enola Gay, after pilot Colonel Paul Tibbets mother, took off at 0210 hours heading for the town of Hiroshima. Just over six hours later, at 0815 hours, they dropped their single bomb on the awakening town below and the world witnessed the explosion of the first atomic bomb. The huge explosion instantly killed over 92,000 people with a further 30,000 dying later from the effects of the nuclear fallout; still the Japanese refused to surrender.

With three days having passed since the bombing of Hiroshima and still no sign of surrender, the U.S.A.A.F. dropped a second atomic weapon, this time on the town of Nagasaki. The B-29, named 'Great Artist', was piloted by Major Charles Sweeney and the casualty count was around 24,000 killed and another 45,000 injured, many of whom, over time, succumbed to the effects of radiation. Despite this second use of America's new found awesome power the Japanese military still refused to surrender even in the face of pleading from the Emperor Hirohito. Finally, the following day, the Japanese accepted the terms of the surrender as long as the Emperor could maintain his position, a lone concession to which the Allies agreed.

The number of new crews arriving at Lindholme continued to fall as August arrived and as a result, in the words of the Air Commodore in charge of 71 Base, "Good instructors have been declared surplus to requirements, better ones have been retained to finish the job." It appeared Bernard was one of the better ones, as for now, he was going nowhere. The start of the month was promising for him as his disappointment at not yet being released was soothed by four training flights in the first two days followed by another epic 'Lindy' tour over the Ruhr area on 3rd which lasted for over five hours. However, the world changed as, on 6th August, the Americans dropped the first atomic bomb on Hiroshima and in a stroke virtually wiped out the need for large, heavy bomber forces. The news of the awesome new weapon caused considerable debate amongst the crews and instructors remaining at Lindholme and amongst the discussions were thoughts that they may be trained to drop a British version of the bomb. They were of course blissfully unaware that Britain did not, and would not have, such a capability for several years as the Americans refused to share their technology; a move that was particularly mean of them as the British had freely shared the equally world changing technology of the jet engine.

Within days the Americans had dropped the second atomic bomb and the war in the Pacific finally came to an end and with it the entire Second World War. The war had been long and bitter and had taken a huge toll of lives and had brought once great nations to their knees, both victors and defeated alike. For those who had survived it, the effects would last for the rest of their lives, but at that point all they wanted to do was to return to their families and begin to put the whole experience behind them, but for Bernard the waiting would go on for some time yet.

In total 1656 H.C.U. produced just fourteen crews and completed only 481 hours flying in August, an indication of just how much the training programme had been cut back. More and more of the bases personnel were taking part in the education programmes available and there was a definite air of finality beginning to set in, a feeling that was confirmed when the staff were told that the unit would be disbanded within three months. For Bernard, and probably for many others, the news came as a great relief as they could see the light beginning to emerge at the end of what had been a very long tunnel.

Following his 'Lindy' tour on 3rd August Bernard did not fly again for ten days until, on 13th, he took two training flights followed by another the following day before taking two weeks leave. He returned to Lindholme in the first days of September and next took to the skies in Lancaster ME377 on 3rd September; five years to the day since he joined the R.A.F. and six since the war had begun.

On the morning of 2nd September 1945 the U.S. battleship, Missouri, was at anchor in Tokyo Bay when, at 0800 hours, the Japanese Foreign Minister Mamoru Shigemitsu, representing the government, and the Chief of Staff General Yoshijiro Umezo, representing the military, signed the documents of surrender. As representative for the Allies the U.S. General MacArthur countersigned the document along with Admiral Sir Bruce Fraser representing the British as well as representatives from Australia, China, France, Russia, Holland, New Zealand and Canada.

Six years after the most devastating and all encompassing conflict the world has ever known had started, so it came to an end. The devastation around the globe in terms of material damage was and remains incalculable, as does the final death toll. The true figure for those who lost their lives, be it fighting on one of the many fronts, at sea, in the air or on the ground; those who died in air raids or from hunger and those who were massacred in the horrific Nazi death camps or Japanese prisoner of war camps, is equally incalculable but is reliably estimated at between 55 and 60,000,000 people. That is the equivalent of every man woman and child alive today in the U.K.

September saw the cessation of training for all foreign crews at Lindholme with five New Zealand and three Australian crews being withdrawn from the course midway through. On 6th September Bernard flew another 'Lindy' tour lasting nearly five hours and the sight of the complete devastation never failed to amaze him and made him wonder just how it would all be put back together again. He did not fly for the next twelve days but just as the tedium of ground schooling was beginning to become unbearable he got back in the air on 18th with nearly three hours of circuits and landings with Warrant Officer Hughes, followed by a much more enjoyable three hour cross country the following day with Warrant Officer Arden in Lancaster PB860. With only a few instructors left on the base, Bernard flew on most days until the end of the month and played a large part in the training of the ten crews to be passed out that month. In total the unit flew for some 744 hours, although many were wasted on the foreign crews who did not complete the course, but the crews who did complete managed to get their bombing margin of error down to a very credible 136 yards.

With 1656 H.C.U. due to be disbanded, the unit was on a gradual wind down of both its own staff and the crews being trained. With the arrival of October the number of training crews was at a minimum as the unit had not received any new crews since 30th August. Most of the ground instructors had also completed their work and had been either de-mobilised or transferred out leaving the last few flying instructors, such as Bernard, to finish off the job. However, the usual British weather wasn't helping with thick fog rolling in from the moors to the east of the station preventing flying, especially at night, which stopped the crews from completing their vital night-time cross country exercises.

Bernard still managed to get airborne four times in the first two days of the month with two Warrant Officers, Hughes and Atkins, each time in Lancaster PA965 carrying out 'Lucero' training. Lucero was the updated version of the Beam Approach System and incorporated the H2S ground reading radar and Identification Friend or Foe systems. The promising start to the flying month soon ground to a halt with the weather cancelling out most flying until he next got airborne on 8th October as he piloted another 'Lindy' tour over the Ruhr which lasted for five hours 35 minutes. Once again the weather closed in and prevented Bernard from flying for the next eight days until on 16th he took a full crew up for an 'Eric' exercise. Eric exercises were window dropping and countermeasures exercises and for nearly five hours they stooged around the countryside employing their new high tech' electronic wizardry while at the same time shovelling large amounts of the considerably low tech' window foil strips out of the aircraft.

The weather continued to fluctuate between short bursts of good weather and longer bursts of atrocious and as a result Bernard only got into the air twice more that month. On 19th he spent an hour and a half instructing night circuits and landings with Flying Officer Kerry in Lancaster LM741 and then the following day he undertook his last 'Lindy' tour spending four hours forty minutes over the shattered remains of Germany in Lancaster PB860.

Despite the small number of under training crews left at Lindholme there was still the odd accident and October produced one such event. At 1340 hours on 9th October, Lancaster PB857 was approaching to land when its port outer engine cut out causing the propeller to 'windmill'. A wind-milling propeller (one which slowly spins as it is forced round by wind resistance) effectively acts as a brake and prevented the pilot from maintaining height, which ultimately caused the Lancaster to crash on to the peat moors ¾ mile to the south east of the airfield. All the crew managed to escape the wreckage without serious injury but the fire service could not take their tender onto the peat moor and the aircraft caught fire and burnt out totally destroying it, as well as setting fire to the moor which was eventually extinguished five hours later.

The weather played a huge part in determining the amount of flying instruction carried out during October and although all the remaining crews had completed all the necessary dual flying they still had night cross countries to complete. In total just six crews completed their training and were posted away with a total flying hours tally for 1656 H.C.U. for the month of just 563 hours. By the end of October there were only 98 under training aircrew left on the base, that's just fourteen crews and then Bernard's job, he hoped, would be done.

Bernard was aware that his R.A.F. career had just weeks to run as November dawned and as far as instructional flights were concerned he had already finished, his circuits and landings lesson with Flying Officer Kerry on 19th October having been his last. November would indeed see the end of his flying days and although he didn't yet know it, he only had three flights left. The first came on 6th November with a flight to R.A.F. Silloth on the Solway Firth which was the site of a Maintenance unit. Flying Officer Lees had flown one Lancaster to the unit for its disposal and Bernard flew with him in Lancaster ND512 in order to ferry him back again.

The final few crews were finishing their training and all would have completed and left the unit by 10th November; but Bernard would not be there to see it. On 7th November he left Lindholme aboard Lancaster EK-J on a transportation mission and headed firstly for Sylt, a German town on an island off the western coast of the Danish peninsular. Having delivered his cargo at Sylt he then headed to Cambrai in eastern France for further deliveries before heading back north-east to Brussels, the Belgian capital. Amazingly, despite so many hours spent over enemy territory, this was the first time in his life Bernard had actually set foot on foreign soil and he had managed to visit Germany, France and Belgium all in one day and once he left Brussels he would never set foot on foreign soil again.

For reasons unfortunately unknown, Bernard managed to stay in Brussels for six days and with no duties to perform he found time to tour the capital and the surrounding areas seeing the damage caused by both the Allies and the Germans up close; it wasn't a sight he enjoyed and the experience affected his thoughts for many years to come. Trips to the shopping centre of the capital provided a relief from the sights of war and he was able to buy some handmade local lace as a present for Ellen, a sign of an age long past as the doilies he bought on that trip would grace the cake plates at every family gathering for years to come; a custom which has since, in turn, died a silent death.

Instructors and ground crew of 1656 H.C.U. just prior to its
disbandment in November 1945.
Bernard is seated to the left (as we look) of the officer
with the visible chair on the front row.

With his presents stowed neatly away, Bernard climbed into the pilot's seat of Lancaster EK-N on 13th November 1945 for what, unbeknown to him, would be the final time. His journey home once again required a diversion to Sylt to drop off some cargo before the final leg, and his final flight, back to Lindholme.

Having completed his return journey from Europe Bernard's career as a pilot had finally drawn to a close and made for impressive reading. In total he had flown on 33 operational missions, one of which had to be aborted, and two Nickel (leaflet dropping) raids over enemy territory. He had amassed 1,771 hours and 25 minutes of daylight flying, 443 hours and 55 minutes at night with 141 hours and five minutes of that time flying on instruments alone. In total he had made 1,982 individual flights totalling 2,215 hours and twenty minutes in eight different types of aircraft.

Just two days later, with all the training crews having already left, on 15th November 1945 1656 Heavy Conversion Unit was disbanded and R.A.F. Lindholme was returned to the control of 1 Group. With the Unit disbanded Bernard was sent home on leave on 16th November but he knew it was all over and that he would never have to return to another R.A.F. base. His leave period took him up to his actual release date, which was set as 28th November 1945, with his last day of service being set as 23rd January 1946 which gave him two months paid leave in order to settle himself back into civilian life. After five years and five months in the blue of the R.A.F. it was a life he was more than ready for.

CHAPTER FOURTEEN

Return to Westminster

Civvy Street. 29th November 1945 onward.

Bernard and Ellen had, once the war in Europe had come to an end, begun the search for a new home and had been informed of a house which had come up for rent in Epsom, Surrey. Ellen's parents lived just a few doors down from the three bedroom house at 140, East Street and after a cursory inspection of the property they decided to rent the house. Ellen had been swayed by the fact that her parents were on hand just a few doors away and Bernard was convinced by the fact that two doors in the opposite direction was the King Arms pub.

As soon as Bernard was able, he gathered up his family and their few remaining possessions and they moved in to begin their lives all over again. The house was relatively small but as is the case with all Victorian houses, well built, with two, square, downstairs rooms plus a kitchen with three bedrooms above, the smallest of which, at the back of the house, could only be accessed by walking through another bedroom. There was no bathroom and all washing had to be done in the kitchen sink and as was usual in most households of the time, a bath was no more than a tin tub in front of the open fire in the dining room; as for the toilet, that was outside.

Despite what we might consider today to be poor conditions, the house on East Street was a palace to the Steel family who had been effectively homeless since the V1 attack of June 1944 and Ellen busied herself in making it as homely and comfortable as possible, a task which she proved to be exceptionally good at.

By the time Christmas 1945 arrived they were well and truly settled in, although most of their furniture was of the utility type which was manufactured by the government and distributed to bombed out families. Christmas was a happy, family time with the clouds of war removed for the first time in six years and Bernard could barely believe he and his entire family was still around to see it.

Although his time in the R.A.F. was over and he would never again wear the uniform, it would continue to play a significant part in his life for some time to come. On 1st January 1946 he was awarded the Air Force Cross for exceptional services as a flying instructor whilst serving with 1656 Heavy Conversion Unit. The award brought Bernard's haul of medals to five as he had already received the D.F.C. and three campaign medals in the form of the 1939-45 Star, The France and Germany Star and the Defence Medal and he would also receive a sixth medal in the shape of the British War Medal a little later, but shamefully there would be no campaign medal for the men of Bomber Command.

The contribution made by Bomber Command to the outcome of the war has, astoundingly, come under criticism from some people over the years, as usual the politically correct and ill informed who seem to be given exposure due to their sensationalist views, over those furnished with the facts. The beginnings of this shameful treatment however fall squarely on the shoulders of Winston Churchill who, for political reasons, omitted any mention of Bomber Command and its efforts in his victory speech as he tried to distance himself from the Dresden raid which had already become sensationalised. The popular press had seized upon Josef Goebbels propaganda figures of 200,000 deaths instead of the actual 25 to 40,000 and had been claiming that Dresden was of no military importance. The actual fact is that Dresden was a town well supplied with transport links which was allowing German forces to be moved up towards the Russian front and was a strategically important target. The Russians requested that the city should be attacked and Churchill issued the order, although due to his political manoeuvrings it would be Bomber Harris who would bear the burden of responsibility.

Although each and every branch of the military played a vital and heroic role, it can be argued that Bomber Command did more to make the winning of the Second World War possible than any other single branch of the services or individual organisation. All the organisations were essential from the Land Girls to the men of the Atlantic convoys, both in the Merchant and regular Navy, who played a huge part in managing to keep the nation fed and supplied throughout the entire war, but they could not take the war to the Germans. Similarly the vital code-breakers based at Bletchley Park allowed the military to concentrate on the most important targets and gave warnings of all kinds of German activities, but they too could not attack the Germans. The British Army fought many heroic battles in theatres around the world such as North Africa and Burma while the Navy too fought hard right across the globe throughout the war, but once again these actions had little effect on the populace of Germany itself and it was there that the war would ultimately have to be won. Of course the Army would ultimately 'win' the war by occupying German territory, but since the outbreak of war nearly six years earlier the only method of taking the war directly to the German people in their homeland was via Bomber Command. They had been the very first force to attack a German target on the very first day of the war and continued to do so to its very end.

Bernard's medals from left to right, Distinguished Flying Cross, Air Force Cross, 1939-45 Star, France & Germany Star, Defence Medal and the British War Medal.

Many of those who have aimed their criticism at the actions of Bomber Command also claim that the war was over by summer 1944 as the Allies advanced across France towards Germany itself, and with hindsight they may well be right, but at the time, as the Germans launched their huge Ardennes offensive, which became known as The Battle of the Bulge, they didn't look like a defeated nation and had they managed to reach the coast and cut off the Allied armies, the war could still have been lost. Having come so close to victory, late 1944 would have been no time to let up; the pressure had to be kept up or the Allies risked allowing the Germans time to recover.

Critics have also claimed that the attacks by Bomber Command did little to affect German output of war materials, stating quite correctly that in many cases production increased as the war went on. That is true, but had those industries gone unmolested throughout the war, the German industrial output capacity would have been many times greater than it actually was and would also have enabled them to spend even more time in research and development work which would have given them even greater weapons. As it was they were well ahead of the Allies in many aspects, such as with the V1 and V2 rocket, which if they had managed to develop even a small nuclear warhead capable of being carried by the V2, would have resulted in the Allies losing the war. In the field of conventional weapons their tanks were far superior to those available to the Allies but were more technical and took longer to produce, a fact that would not have been important had their factories and those that worked in them been left alone by Bomber Command. The tank situation was echoed by the introduction of the Messerschmitt ME262 jet fighter which, even in relatively small numbers, was beginning to wreak havoc amongst the bomber streams in the last days of the war. Untouched by Bomber Command, the German war machine would have had many more of these lethal aircraft available to them.

Without the actions of Bomber Command and the U.S.A.A.F., the landings on D-Day would have been an impossible achievement. The constant threat of attack to German cities tied up thousands of men to man searchlights and anti-aircraft guns, most importantly the deadly 88mm. Without the aerial attacks those men and their weapons would have been deployed all along the Atlantic Wall and the Allies would have been blown off the beaches back into the sea.

The constant sleepless nights, hardship, homelessness, hunger and fear that Bomber Command brought to the German civilian worker also ground down their ability to help the German war effort, a fact admitted to by Albert Speer, the German minister for production. During interviews after the war he made it quite clear that it was his belief that the difference between a German victory and defeat had been the overwhelming Allied airpower.

As a result of the critical voices, Bomber Command were the only branch of the services not to receive a specific campaign medal and there was no memorial to the men who fought and died until as late as 2012, whereas Fighter Command, and rightly so, has the Battle of Britain Memorial on the south coast, overlooking the white cliffs of Dover, which honours every man who took part in the Battle of Britain, whether he lived or died. Only now, seventy years after the fact, it has taken later generations who have seen through the critics' bluff, to raise the funds for a Bomber Command Memorial, which now stands in London's Green Park. Unfortunately it arrived too late for many of the survivors and the loved ones of those lost in the battles to visit and pay their respects. The reasons for the validity of the memorial are evident in the statistics which are described later in this chapter.

The men and women of Bomber Command were asked to achieve the impossible by the politicians and once they achieved it the cowards of Whitehall, whose own failings led to the war in the first place, shamefully abandoned them. Whether you believe Bomber Commands actions were right or not, the policies of the Government and the Command were not made by the airmen involved. It is impossible to look at the individual aircrews with anything other than admiration as they spent long hours above enemy territory in what can only be described by today's standards as awful aircraft, surrounded with fuel and bombs while being shot at by fighters and ground fire and with statistically little chance of survival. Yet they went, night after night, scared stiff most of the time, but they still went and they did it for all of us. A brave man is not one who has no fear; he is a fearful man who presses on in the face of that fear.

A statistical summary of the efforts of Bomber Command is a huge undertaking but the most accurate account is found in The Bomber Command War Diaries by Martin Middlebrook and Chris Everitt, which gives an account of every day's operations and several statistical summaries. All the statistics used in this chapter come from their comprehensive work.

Their assessment covers the period from the 3rd September 1939, the first day of war, to 7/8th May 1945, the last day of war, a total of 2,074 days. In that time Bomber Command managed to launch operations on 71.4% of all nights, and 52.5% of all days, completing a massive total of 387,416 individual sorties during which they dropped a total bomb tonnage of 955,044 tons. While the statistics relating to their achievements are impressive, those relating to their losses are horrific. The casualty rate for bomber crew was higher than any other individual branch of the British armed forces, which is not altogether surprising as they were in the front line for every day of the entire war. In total around 125,000 men served as aircrew in Bomber Command throughout the war and nearly 60% of those became casualties. Obviously the overwhelming majority of the casualties were suffered on operations (85%) but as we have seen in the earlier chapters the training units were also a dangerous place to be and were responsible for the vast majority of the remaining 15%. A total of 47,268 men were killed in action or while as prisoners of war with a further 8,195 killed in flying or ground accidents and 37 killed in ground fighting. In addition 9,838 were taken prisoner, many of those wounded, with a further 8,403 injured on operations who returned to England or were wounded in flying or ground accidents in the U.K. The total casualties for Bomber Command add up to 73,741 or 59% of those who served.

Bomber Command was not of course just made up by personnel from the R.A.F. but from many nations and the casualties were spread between them all. Aircrew of the R.A.F. obviously lost the most men, as they were proportionately the largest group, and suffered 38,462 fatalities (69.2% of all fatalities) but alongside that the Canadians lost 9,919 (17.8%), the Australians 4,050 (7.3%), New Zealand 1,679 (3%), Poland 929 (1.7%) with the remaining 1% spread across several other nations.

Of course not all the aircrew shot down were killed and many were taken as prisoners of war but a considerable number managed to escape the clutches of the Germans and often, assisted by resistance movements, managed to return to England. In total 1,975 evaded capture and returned home while a further 156 R.A.F. men of all commands managed to escape from German P.O.W. camps and make it all the way back home.

The men and women of the ground staff were not immune to the dangers of war either and although the total numbers of ground staff serving with Bomber Command is unknown as it was so huge, their casualty numbers are known; 1,479 men and 91 W.A.A.F's lost their lives while on active duty and a further 52 male ground staff became prisoners of war.

Bernard too had not come through the war unscathed. Like many other ex-servicemen, he would carry the legacy of his time in battle for the rest of his life. Today we are all well aware of combat stress or post traumatic stress disorder as it is known, but back then it was still little understood and many men suffered without ever knowing what was happening to them. Like so many men Bernard spoke little of his experiences, especially during the years immediately after the end of the war, preferring to try and forget it all in the hope that it would go away; the truth of the matter is that it doesn't. Mentally he appeared to be unaffected by his experiences but there were small signs if you looked and listened carefully enough. Many times as a young boy I heard him mutter the words, "Bloody death machines" to himself as an aircraft passed overhead carrying holidaymakers to sunnier climes. At first I didn't understand why he made the comment but as I grew older and began to understand the war and his role in it, it became more obvious. Initially I felt he was lamenting the loss of so many of his colleagues killed aboard similar craft, but as time has passed I have come to realise it was both that and the death they rained down on the people below. The physical effects of the war were more obvious as, soon after the end of hostilities, he developed a stomach ulcer which would occasionally flare up and confine him to bed for a few days, but compared to a lot of people Bernard seemed to get off quite lightly.

Despite the incredibly high level of skill and experience Bernard had gained as a pilot, he showed no desire to continue his flying career or to ever return to it. He never again piloted an aircraft, in fact he only ever took to the air twice more in his life and that was for a return trip for a holiday in Jersey and he never again set foot on foreign soil either. He was happy to put his R.A.F. career behind him and get back to the peace and tranquillity of his pre-war life, becoming the family man he often thought he would not live long enough to become. The second step on that road, after having settled in their new home, was to return to work. Bernard was lucky enough that, unlike today, employers showed considerable loyalty to their employees in those days and Cluttons were good enough to re-employ him in his old job. So, in early 1946, he returned to his old office and so completed his round trip from Westminster.

In mid February 1957 a letter dropped through the letter box of 140, East Street from the Air Ministry. Unsure what news it would bring, Bernard was relieved to see that the letter confirmed that, having reached the age of 45, he was no longer liable to be recalled to service and that he was to relinquish his commission while retaining the rank of Flying Officer; seventeen years after it had begun, Bernard's service with the R.A.F. was finally over.

He remained an employee of Cluttons until his retirement at the age of 65 in 1977. In the intervening 31 years he and Ellen brought up Douglas but had no more children and he retired to the same house they had moved into in late 1945. In the meantime Douglas had married and had two boys of his own bringing grandchildren to Bernard and Ellen upon whom they doted and lavished their affection, especially in the years after Douglas divorced in 1975. Two more grandchildren would come their way fifteen years later, a boy and a girl from Douglas' later marriage but there would be little time for Bernard to enjoy them.

In the summer of 1990 he suffered a serious stroke which affected his left side, and which being left handed, seriously affected his quality of life. At first he could barely speak and could not write, but gradually he battled through and regained his speech, although with a recognisable slur, and was even able to begin to write again. By summer 1991 he was much more mobile and had regained his sense of humour, which was never far from the surface even if his condition did, understandably, get him down occasionally. On 17th June 1991 Bernard had his lunch with Ellen and then went for his afternoon nap in his favourite chair in the front room of the house on East Street; peacefully he settled in and dozed off never to wake up.

Bernard and Ellen in retirement in the garden at 140 East Street. Epsom

Six years later Ellen passed away in much the same way, suffering a huge stroke from which she never regained consciousness and died on 17th January 1997 at the age of 86. With her passing went another of a generation that did so much to shape the world we live in today and had a profound effect on the family members they left behind and who were lucky enough to be a part of their lives. The story of Bernard and Ellen's war makes up the vast majority of this book but the war makes up just a tiny part of who they were. The war undoubtedly had a huge and deep effect on them, as it did on all those of their generation who were touched by it. Like countless others they played their part in the defeat of the Nazis and they are a prime example of the many good hearted and brave souls around the world who ultimately came together to defeat the evil and hatred of Hitler and his allies. The Second World War shows us that in desperate times, not only how the people of Britain rise to the challenge and excel themselves, but how the people of the world, despite their differences of race and religion, can come together to overcome huge odds. Perhaps now more than ever we would do well to remember that.

★★★

The association of the Steel family with the Lancaster bomber was not over with the death of Bernard. Despite the fact that there are very few Lancasters left in the world, and only one flying in Britain with the Battle of Britain Memorial Flight, a circumstance arose in 2007 when the surviving Steels managed to get their hands on the controls of one of those mighty beasts one more time.

Douglas in the cockpit of the 'City of Lincoln'

While researching this book the officer in charge of my Fire Service watch, Paul Crowther, contacted the Battle of Britain Memorial Flight who were good enough to invite myself and Douglas (my father) up to R.A.F. Coningsby to spend the day with them. The visit had to be hastily arranged as the Lancaster was due to go away for a major overhaul and to be painted in new colours as the Phantom of the Ruhr; we were lucky enough to be the last people to experience her in the guise of Mickey the Moocher. Having been shown around the hanger holding the various and equally impressive Spitfires and Hurricanes belonging to the flight, we were then taken aboard the cramped Lancaster. Barely believing our luck we occupied each of the crew positions and settled in the cockpit to chat with our guide. To be able to experience the environment in which Bernard had fought and in which so many men lost their lives was a truly humbling experience and brought home just what a difficult environment to operate in a Lancaster was.

To all those who served aboard those aircraft and other bombers like them, I can have nothing but admiration and respect; and to you all I give my deepest thanks.

APPENDIX

Operational histories of aircraft flown by Bernard Steel

No. 22 Elementary Flying Training School (Cambridge) 16/3/1941 to 17/5/1941.

Aircraft type: DeHavilland DH82 'Tigermoth'

N6545 5 Maintenance Unit 9/1/39, **to 22 Elementary Flying Training School 3/7/40,** to 6 Maintenance Unit 2/8/43, to 21 Elementary Flying Training School 22/8/43, to 20 Maintenance Unit 27/11/43, Struck off charge January 1947, sold to private buyer.

N6595 5 Maintenance Unit, to 43 Elementary & Reserve Flying Training School 23/5/39, to 43 Group 25/6/41, to 17 Elementary Flying Training School 19/8/41, to 43 Group 17/9/41, abandoned after wing lost & Struck off charge 30/9/41. ★

N6609 5 Maintenance Unit 2/3/39, to 43 Elementary & Reserve Flying Training School 10/7/39, **to 22 Elementary Flying Training School 31/12/41,** 10 Maintenance Unit 9/7/42, to 222 Maintenance Unit 28/2/43, lost at sea while en-route to South African Air Force 1/4/43.★

N6630 10 Maintenance Unit 10/3/39, 30 Elementary & Reserve Flying Training School, **22 Elementary Flying Training School 31/12/41,** Struck off charge 22/8/45. ★

N6927 6 Maintenance Unit 29/6/39, **to 22 Elementary Flying Training School 15/10/39,** to 24 Elementary Flying Training School 12/6/44, to 24 Reserve Flying School 26/6/47, hit by Gloster Meteor on navigation exercise at Runcton damaged beyond repair 24/9/48, Struck off charge 30/9/48.

N9276 5 Maintenance Unit 4/10/39, **to 22 Elementary Flying Training School 3/7/40,** to 202 Advanced Flying School, to 20 Maintenance Unit 27/4/50, sold to Wiltshire School of Flying 31/10/50.

R4855 20 Maintenance Unit 27/2/40, **to 22 Elementary Flying Training School 21/10/40,** to 10 Maintenance Unit 28/2/43, to 21 Elementary Flying Training School 10/3/43, to 29 Elementary Flying Training School 22/3/43, to 8 Maintenance Unit 26/11/47, sold for scrap to International Alloys Ltd. Aylesbury 30/3/50.

R4903 5 Maintenance Unit 12/1/40, **to 22 Elementary Flying Training School 9/1/41,** to 43 Group 12/5/41, damaged beyond repair after hitting fire tender at Bottisham 10/5/41, Struck off charge 19/5/41.

R5196 5 Maintenance Unit 18/4/40, **to 22 Elementary Flying Training School 12/11/40,** to 46 Maintenance Unit 14/4/42, to 15 Elementary Flying Training School 24/6/42, to 12 Maintenance Unit 24/7/45, sold for scrap to W.F. Lamont Ltd 29/12/49.

T5369 20 Maintenance Unit 3/5/40, **to 22 Elementary Flying Training School 22/1/41,** to Empire Central Flying School 2/6/43, to 20 Maintenance Unit 11/11/43, to 38 Maintenance Unit 8/1/44, to 65 Squadron 14/12/45, to 315 Squadron (Polish) 1/3/45, to 10 Maintenance Unit 19/4/45, to Station Flight Hullavington Wiltshire, to Station Flight Horsham St. Faith 11/2/53, sold privately re licensed as D-EDIN destroyed 1/8/61.

T5636 15 Maintenance Unit 17/6/40, **to 22 Elementary Flying Training School 5/10/40,** to 4 Elementary Flying School 20/6/43, to 33 Maintenance Unit 24/9/46, sold to Hampshire & Sussex Aviation 31/3/54.

T5637 15 Maintenance Unit 17/6/40, **to 22 Elementary Flying Training School 25/10/40,** 20 Maintenance Unit 25/7/45, to Aston Down, sold to Roldean Ltd 9/3/50.

★ Both N6609 and N6630 are showing as having moved to 22 EFTS after Bernard Steel's service with the unit. The reason for this is that the AM78 (movement card) was not filled out on the actual date they moved to the unit and the error was only discovered during the RAF census of December 1941, hence the date being shown as 31/12/41. N6595 had already left 22EFTS by the time of the census and as the AM78 had also been neglected when it moved to 22 EFTS it does not show as ever having served with 22 EFTS. Trust me, it did.

No.2 Service Flying Training School (Brize Norton) 1/6/1941 to 7/8/1941.

Aircraft type: Airspeed Oxford.

NB. (unc) denotes a unit name change.

L4576 3 Flying Training School 24/6/38, to Central Flying School 16/6/39, **to 2 Service Flying Training School 12/9/40 (unc) 2 (Pilots) Advanced Flying Unit,** 13/7/42 Sold for scrap Enfield rolling mills (Bradford) 14/2/49.

L4586 RAF College 18/7/38, storage 20/7/40, **to 2 Service Flying Training School 2/9/40,** to 1 Signals School at RAF College as 2838M 22/12/41 (airframe used for instructional non flying purposes), Struck off charge 9/9/44.

L9646 RAF College 27/1/39, **to 2 Service Flying Training School 8/2/40,** to 6 (Pilots) Advanced Flying Unit 18/5/42, engine cut out, crashed during forced landing at Holt Castle, Worcester. 9/6/42.

L9650 RAF College 31/1/39, storage 26/6/40, to 3 Service Flying Training School 7/8/40, **to 2 Service Flying Training School 31/7/41 (unc) 2 (Pilots) Advanced Flying Unit,** to 3 (Pilots) Advanced Flying Unit 4/9/42, storage 27/10/43, to 14 (Pilots) Advanced Flying Unit 11/2/44, Struck off charge 10/9/44.

L9657 8 Flying Training School 7/2/39, (unc) 8 Service Flying Training School, **to 2 Service Flying Training School 21/9/40,** hit trees on take off at night from Akeman Street landing ground and destroyed by fire, 9/1/42.

N4588 14 Flying Training School 20/5/39, (unc) 14 Service Flying Training

School, storage 30/4/40, **to 2 Service Flying Training School 30/8/40, (unc) 2 (Pilots) Advanced Flying Unit,** to 21 (Pilots) Advanced Flying Unit 31/5/44, engine cut out, hit HT wires on low level navigation exercise, crashed and overturned at Norton in Hales 14/8/44.

N6250 2 Flying Training School 13/3/39, (unc) 2 Service Flying Training School, (unc) 2 (Pilots) Advanced Flying Unit, storage 19/6/42, to 1624 (Anti-aircraft co-operation) Flight 23/7/43, Struck off charge 18/10/43.

N6255 2 Flying Training School 16/3/39, (unc) 2 Service Flying Training School, (unc) 2 (Pilots) Advanced Flying Unit, storage 27/8/42, to 21 (Pilots) Advanced Flying Unit 5/5/44, storage 18/1/46, sold for scrap to S.B. Lunzer & Co. Ltd 8/9/47.

N6261 5 Flying Training School 22/3/39, (unc) 5 Service Flying Training School, to Station Flight Aldergrove 2/11/39, storage 25/1/40, **to 2 Service Flying Training School 30/8/40,** storage 24/12/41, to 2 Flying Instructors School 26/3/43, to RAF College 30/7/43, to 14 (Pilots) Advanced Flying Unit 1/12/43, storage 6/9/44, Struck off charge 9/10/44.

N6262 5 Flying Training School 22/3/39, (unc) 5 Service Flying Training School, to 3 Service Flying Training School 21/8/40, **to 2 Service Flying Training School 14/5/41, (unc) 2 (Pilots) Advanced Flying Unit,** to 6 (Pilots) Advanced Flying Unit 14/7/42, storage 21/4/43, to 21 (Pilots) Advanced Flying Unit 21/3/44, Struck off charge 18/1/45.

N6268 2 Service Flying Training School 15/8/40, (unc) 2 (Pilots) Advanced Flying Unit, storage 6/8/42, to 7 Anti-Aircraft Co-operation Unit 22/6/43, storage 24/10/43, to 21 (Pilots) Advanced Flying Unit 14/11/43, Struck off charge 2/6/44.

N6382 13 Flying Training School 1/8/39, to 5 Service Flying Training School 6/10/39, to 11 Flying Training School 3/7/40, **to 2 Flying Training School 5/7/41,** storage 18/2/42, to 15 (Pilots) Advanced Flying Unit 6/7/42, to Lichfield 30/9/43, Struck off charge 2/6/44.

N6404 2 Flying Training School 17/8/39, (unc) 2 SFTS, (unc) 2 (Pilots) Advanced Flying Unit, to 3 (Pilots) Advanced Flying Unit 1/8/42, storage 29/2/43, to 271 Squadron 23/2/44, hit building on approach in bad visibility during night navigation exercise, Little Rissington 27/3/44.

P1923 14 Service Flying Training School 13/12/39, storage 11/8/40, **to 2 Service Flying Training School 29/8/40, (unc) 2 (Pilots) Advanced Flying Unit,** storage 28/5/42, to 6 Anti-Aircraft Co-operation Unit 22/10/42, (unc) 577 Squadron, to 21 (Pilots) Advanced Flying Unit 5/5/44, to 12 (Pilots) Advanced Flying Unit, Struck off charge 29/6/45.

P8905 Allocated to Royal New Zealand Air Force as NZ1279 but kept in UK as P8905. **2 Service Flying Training School 21/8/40, (unc) 2 (Pilots) Advanced Flying Unit,** to 15 (Pilots) Advanced Flying Unit 9/7/42, to 18 (Pilots) Advanced Flying Unit 30/7/43, storage 14/4/44, to 14 (Pilots) Advanced Flying Unit 12/6/44, to 7 (Pilots) Advanced Flying Unit 15/9/44, (unc) 7 Service Flying Training School, Struck off charge 14/2/46.

P8906 Allocated to Royal New Zealand Air Force as NZ1280 but kept in UK as P8906. **2 Service Flying Training School 2/9/40, (unc) 2 (Pilots) Advanced Flying Unit,** storage 13/7/42, to 15 (Pilots) Advanced Flying Unit 26/7/42, storage 14/12/43, to 21 (Pilots) Advanced Flying Unit 31/1/44, Struck off charge 3/7/45.

P8910 Allocated to Royal New Zealand Air Force as NZ1284 but kept in UK as P8910. **2 Service Flying Training School 29/8/40,** storage 30/5/42, to 6 Anti-Aircraft Co-operation Unit 20/10/42, storage 10/7/43, sold to KLM (Dutch Airline) 12/1/46, transferred to Royal Netherlands Air Force as C-10.

P9025 2 Service Flying Training School 30/6/40, Struck off charge 4/3/42.

R6145 2 Service Flying Training School 4/12/40, to 1 Flying Instructors School 3/3/42, (unc) 18 (Pilots) Advanced Flying Unit, dived into ground at Bretford, near Rugby while overshooting 22/11/42.

R6242 2 Service Flying Training School 20/5/40, to RAF College 4/9/41, to 15 (Pilots) Advanced Flying Unit 13/4/42, to 20 (Pilots) Advanced Flying Unit 16/4/43, Struck off charge 14/3/44.

R6335 14 Service Flying Training School 27/8/40, storage 10/2/41, to **2 Service Flying Training School 3/1/42 ★,** storage 15/2/42, to 8 Anti-Aircraft Co-operation Unit 11/10/42, storage 1/12/43, to 587 Squadron 12/12/43, Struck off charge 19/5/44.

R6337 2 Service Flying Training School 17/8/40, (unc) 2 (Pilots) Advanced Flying Unit, storage 11/9/42, to 7 Flying Instructors School 8/11/42, Sold for scrap W.F. Lamont 23/6/49.

T1384 2 Service Flying Training School 11/4/41, lost control during circuit in low cloud at night, flew into the ground 1mile South-east of Akeman Street landing ground 16/7/41.

V3211 2 Service Flying Training School 20/8/40, storage 11/11/41, to 3 (Pilots) Advanced Flying Unit November 44, storage April 45, Struck off charge 19/11/45.

V3244 RAF College 6/9/40, to 2 Flying Instructors School 30/9/40, (unc) 2 Central Flying School, **to 2 Service Flying Training School 28/5/41,** flew into the ground at night in bad visibility 1.25 miles south of Chipping Norton 3/8/41.

V3349 2 Service Flying Training School 27/4/41, (unc) 2 (Pilots) Advanced Flying Unit, to 5 Glider Training School 15/8/42, to 14 (Pilots) Advanced Flying Unit 7/2/43, storage 10/2/44, to 21 (Pilots) Advanced Flying Unit 8/5/44, Struck off charge 30/5/46.

V3535 2 Service Flying Training School 7/5/41, (unc) 2 (Pilots) Advanced Flying Unit, to 6 (Pilots) Advanced Flying Unit 14/7/42, to 1692 (Bomber support training) Flight 29/6/44, crashed on overshoot at Croydon 13/12/44.

V3585 2 Service Flying Training School 16/5/41, (unc) 2 (Pilots) Advanced Flying Unit, collided with R6075 on approach to Akeman Street landing ground 23/6/42.

V3687 2 Service Flying Training School 7/2/41, (unc) 2 (Pilots) Advanced Flying Unit, storage 20/6/42, to 1481 (Target Towing) Flight 21/7/42, to United States Army Air Force 19/4/44.

* R6335 is shown as joining 2SFTS on 3/1/42, after Bernard Steel served with the unit. This is because the AM78 (movement card) was not completed when it moved to the unit and the error discovered during the RAF census of December 1941, hence the date of 3/1/42.

No.2 Central Flying School (Church Lawford) 19/8/1941 to 15/10/1941

Aircraft types: Avro 621 Tutor; Airspeed Oxford;

Avro Tutor

K3231 Station Flight Hendon 22/3/33, to 5 Flying Training School 28/9/33, to 2 Aircraft Storage Unit 21/8/35, to Station Flight Cranwell 12/10/35, to **2 Central Flying School 23/11/40,** to 18 (Pilots) Advanced Flying School 27/10/42, Category B damage (repairable but off-site) 4/11/42, Struck off charge 8/1/43.

K3355 2 Aircraft Storage Unit Cardington Bedfordshire 8/2/34, to Station Flight Halton Buckinghamshire 23/7/34, to 1 Squadron Northolt 8/7/36, to 5 Maintenance unit 14/8/39, **to 2 Central Flying School (date unknown)** (unc) 2 Flying Instructors School, to18 Maintenance unit 23/8/42, Category E (damaged beyond repair) and Struck off charge 4/6/43.

K3384 1 Aircraft Storage Unit Peterborough 18/4/34, 6 Armament Training Station 12/4/35, to 1 Aircraft Storage Unit 6/4/36, London University Air Squadron 6/7/36, to 600 Squadron 5/10/36, to 22 Maintenance Unit 9/4/40, to 3 Flying Training School 28/7/41, **to 2Central Flying School 2/8/41,** to 8 (Pilots) Advanced Flying Unit, to 15 (Pilots) Advanced Flying Unit, to 18 Maintenance Unit 23/3/43, Category E (damaged beyond repair) and Struck off charge 4/6/43.

K3390 1 Aircraft Storage Unit Peterborough 24/4/34, to 6 Armament Training

Station 3/4/35, to 609 Squadron 15/5/36, to 502 Squadron 22/4/37, to 12 Maintenance Unit 1/1/40, to 18 Maintenance Unit 16/7/40, **to 2 Central Flying School 2/3/41,** to 18 (Pilots) Advanced Flying Unit 27/10/42, 1 Flying Instructors School 14/11/42, Category E (damaged beyond repair) 20/5/43.

K3428 Station Flight Kenley 17/7/34, to 6 Armament Training Station 18/4/35, to 502 Squadron 9/11/37, to 12 Maintenance Unit 5/8/40, **to 2 Central Flying School 15/3/41,** to 18 (Pilots) Advanced Flying Unit 27/10/42, Category E (damaged beyond repair) 20/5/43.

K3450 Unknown Station Flight 23/2/35, to London University Air Squadron 1/4/36, to 604 Squadron 5/9/36, to 22 Maintenance Unit 7/4/40, **to 2 Central Flying School 26/7/41,** Category E (damaged beyond repair) 23/7/42, Struck off charge 1/1/47.

K3470 1 Aircraft Storage Unit Peterborough 2/5/35, to Cambridge University Air Squadron 17/6/36, to 8 Maintenance Unit 27/8/39 to 30 Maintenance Unit 14/8/40, to 18 Maintenance Unit 28/10/40, **to 2 Central Flying School 17/5/41,** Category E (damaged beyond repair) 15/10/42.

K4810 1 Aircraft Storage Unit Peterborough, 2 OTS (unknown Unit), to 1 Flying Training School 10/11/36, to 1 Aircraft Storage Unit 3/8/38, to 23 Elementary & Reserve Flying Training School 16/9/38, to 8 Maintenance Unit 31/8/39, to 30 Maintenance Unit 2/9/40, to 20 Maintenance Unit 21/11/40, **to 2 Flying Instructors School 27/11/40, (unc) 2 Central Flying School,** to 18 (Pilots) Advanced Flying Unit 27/10/42, to 18 Maintenance Unit 31/1/43, to 92 Group Communications Flight 25/6/43, Category E (damaged beyond repair) & Struck off charge 27/11/43.

K6104 2 Aircraft Storage Unit Cardington 9/7/35, to 614 Squadron 15/6/37, to 20 Maintenance Unit 30/11/39, **to 2 Flying Instructors School 5/1/41, (unc) 2 Central Flying School,** to 1 Flying Instructors School 31/8/42, to 2 Flying Instructors School 24/9/42, to 2 Air Gunners School 25/9/42, to 18 Maintenance Unit 17/11/42, to 15 (Pilots) Advanced Flying Unit 31/12/42, Category E (damaged beyond repair) 20/7/43.

K6121 2 Aircraft Storage Unit Cardington 30/9/35, to Oxford University Air Squadron 25/6/36, to 500 Squadron 16/10/37, to 12 Maintenance Unit 23/4/40, to 18 Maintenance Unit 16/7/40, **to 2 Central Flying School 2/3/41,** 18 Maintenance Unit 23/8/42, Category E (damaged beyond repair) & Struck off charge 14/10/43.

Airspeed Oxford

N4733 Central Flying School 10/8/39, **to 2 Central Flying School 15/5/41,** to 18 (Pilots) Advanced Flying Unit 27/10/42, stalled and dived into ground 1m South-South-East of Wythall, Warwickshire, destroyed by fire, 28/8/43.

N4768 14 Service Flying Training School 13/9/39, **to 2 Flying Instructors School 29/10/40, (unc) 2 Central Flying School,** to 1 Flying Instructors School 15/5/42, engine cut out, lost height and stalled while avoiding trees at Warwick relief landing ground, 12/7/42.

N4791 15 Service Flying Training School 26/9/39, storage 5/10/40, **to 2 Flying Instructors School 3/11/40, (unc) 2 Central Flying school,** to 18(Pilots) Advanced Flying Unit 27/10/42, storage 31/7/43, to Admiralty 789B Squadron 24/10/40, to 762 Squadron 15/3/44, Struck off charge 5/12/45.

N4797 2 Service Flying Training School 2/10/39, storage 21/9/40, **to 2 Central Flying School 28/11/40,** to 18 (Pilots) Advanced Flying Unit 27/10/42, to 1 Beam Approach School 24/8/43, to 15 (Pilots) Advanced Flying Unit 22/12/43, storage 30/3/44, to 526 Squadron 23/11/44, to North Weald 26/4/45, Struck off charge 13/12/46.

N6369 2 Flying Training School 17/7/39, (unc) 2 Service Flying Training School, **to 2 Central Flying School 31/12/41,** (unc) 1 Flying Instructors School, (unc) 18 (Pilots) Advanced Flying Unit, to Dunsfold 20/8/43, to 2 Group Communication Flight 27/11/43, struck off charge 15/5/44.

N6401 600 Squadron 15/8/39, to Blenheim Conversion Flight 30/11/39, to Central Flying School 23/3/40, storage 28/7/40, **to 2 Central Flying School 6/1/41,** (unc) 1 Flying Instructors School, storage 3/4/42, to 286 Squadron

4/6/42, engine caught fire in the air, crash landed at Carew Cheriton, 25/7/42.

N6426 13 Flying Training School 15/9/39, to 3 Service Flying Training School 20/10/39, storage 29/10/40, **to 2 Flying Instructors School 2/11/40, (unc) 2 Central Flying School,** (unc) 1 Flying Instructors School 10/3/42, (unc) 18 (Pilots) Advanced Flying Unit, to 105 Squadron 6/7/44, to Station Flight Bourn 2/9/44, re-designated 5511M (Airframe used for instruction) 12 School of Technical Training, Melksham, 27/7/45.

P1070 Aircraft & Armament Experimental Establishment Nov/39, storage 29/1/40, to 2 Service Flying Training School 25/10/40, **to 2 Flying Instructors School, (unc) 2 Central Flying School,** (unc) 1 Flying Instructors School, storage 30/5/42, to 4 Group Communication Flight 6/8/42, Struck off charge 20/9/44.

P8995 2 Flying Instructors School 11/9/40, (unc) 2 Central Flying School, storage 25/6/42, to 1 Flying Instructors School (date unknown), to 8 Advance Flying Training School 17/7/51, storage Oct/53, Sold for scrap to Enfield Rolling Mills Ltd. Bradford, 21/2/56.

P9030 2 Flying Instructors School 10/9/40, (unc) 2 Central Flying School, to 18 (Pilots) Advanced Flying Unit 27/12/42 storage 1/4/44, to 14 (Pilots) Advanced Flying Unit 1/6/44, Struck off charge 30/8/44.

R6022 2 Flying Instructors School 28/10/40, (unc) 2 Central Flying School, collided on take off with N4766 at Church Lawford, damaged beyond repair, 4/1/42.

R6024 2 Flying Instructors School 28/12/40, (unc) 2Central Flying School, storage 30/5/42, to 1 Flying Instructors School, (unc) 18 (Pilots) Advanced Flying Unit 27/10/42, storage 8/3/44, to Ground Controlled Approach Wing Yatesbury 25/8/44, to 488 Squadron 10/10/44, to 604 Squadron 28/12/44, to 264 Squadron 4/1/45, to 410 Squadron 29/3/45, storage 9/6/45, Struck off charge 17/9/45.

R6029 2 Flying Instructors School 15/1/41, (unc) 2 Central Flying

School, to 18 (Pilots) Advanced Flying Unit 27/10/42, storage 28/2/44, sold back to Airspeed 18/2/47 became private aircraft G–AJLR.

R6034 2 Flying Instructors School 3/1/41, (unc) 2 Central Flying School, to 1 Flying Instructors School 30/6/42, storage 8/11/42, to 18 (Pilots) Advanced Flying Unit, storage 13/3/43, to United States Army Air Force 27/5/43.

R6059 2 Flying Instructors School 5/11/40, (unc) 2 Central Flying School, (unc) 1 Flying Instructors School, bounced on landing at Warwick relief landing ground and crashed on attempted overshoot, 4/8/42.

R6074 2 Flying Instructors School 25/4/41, (unc) 2 Central Flying School, (unc) 1 Flying Instructors School to 18 (Pilots) Advanced Flying Unit 27/10/42, to Lissett 19/7/44, Damaged beyond repair 12/11/45.

R6076 2 Flying Instructors School 2/11/40, (unc) 2 Central Flying School, (unc) 1 Flying Instructors School, to 6 (Pilots) Advanced Flying Unit 9/7/42, storage 27/1/43, Struck off charge 14/3/45.

R6091 2 Flying Instructors School, (unc) 2 Central Flying School, to Air Transport Auxiliary 17/2/42, storage 29/11/42, sold back to Airspeed 26/3/47, to Royal Danish Air Force as 21–242, 8/4/47.

R6295 11 Service Flying Training School 11/6/40, **to 2 Central Flying School 31/12/41,** (unc) 1 Flying Instructors School, (unc) 18 (Pilots) Advanced Flying Unit, Struck off charge 3/3/44. ★

V3225 2 Flying Instructors School 26/9/40, (unc) 2 Central Flying School, to 6 (Pilots) Advanced Flying Unit 6/8/42, storage 20/11/42, to 20 (Pilots) Advanced Flying Unit 14/8/43, Struck off charge 8/6/50.

V3226 2 Flying Instructors School 26/9/40, (unc) 2 Central Flying School, (unc) 1 Flying Instructors School, (unc) 18 (Pilots) Advanced Flying Unit, re-designated 3833M (airframe used for ground instruction for flight mechanics and riggers) 5 School of Technical Training, Locking, Jan/43.

V3227 2 Flying Instructors School 26/9/40, (unc) 2 Central Flying School, (unc) 1 Flying Instructors School, to 6 (Pilots) Advanced Flying Unit 6/9/42, storage 18/11/42, to 20 (Pilots) Advanced Flying Unit 6/4/43, bounced on landing at Weston-on-the Green 22/2/45, not repaired and Struck off charge18/4/45.

V3436 2 Central Flying School 28/2/41, (unc) 1 Flying Instructors School, (unc) 18 (Pilots) Advanced Flying Unit, storage 8/4/44, to 20 (Pilots) Advanced Flying Unit 30/6/44, lost height and crash-landed at Simonsbath, Devon damaged beyond repair 8/1/45.

V3504 2 Central Flying School 18/3/41, (unc) 1 Flying Instructors School, (unc) 18 (Pilots) Advanced Flying Unit, storage 6/3/44, to 21 (Pilots) Advanced Flying Unit 21/2/46, storage 8/5/47, to 23 Reserve Flying School 10/8/53 however unit had already been disbanded, to Durham University Air Squadron 31/8/53, storage 23/4/56, Sold for scrap Hants & Sussex Aviation Ltd, Portsmouth 30/7/56.

V3581 2 Central Flying School 10/3/41, (unc) 1 Flying Instructors School, (unc) 18 (Pilots) Advanced Flying Unit, lost control after attempted overshoot at night, hit hedge and crashed at Lawford Lodge Farm, Church Lawford 2/12/42.

V3870 3 Service Flying Training School 2/3/41, **to 2 Central Flying School 31/12/41,** (unc) 1 Flying Instructors School, (unc) 18 (Pilots) Advanced Flying Unit, storage 16/7/43, sold to Holmwood motors, Swansea becoming private aircraft G-AHXA 21/5/46. ★★

W6549 2 Flying Instructors School 13/1/41**, (unc) 2 Central Flying School,** (unc) 1 Flying Instructors School, (unc) 18 (Pilots) Advanced Flying Unit, re-designated 3835M (airframe used for ground instruction for flight mechanics and riggers) 5 School of Technical Training, Locking Apr/45.

AB701 2 Central Flying School 12/7/41, (unc) 1 Flying Instructors School, (unc) 18 (Pilots) Advanced Flying Unit, Struck off charge 3/7/44.

AB703 2 Central Flying School 12/7/41, (unc) 1 Flying Instructors School, (unc) 18 (Pilots) Advanced Flying Unit, storage 26/7/43, to Cosford 7/4/44, to 5 School of Technical training 21/3/46, to 10 Advanced Flying Training School 30/7/52, Struck off charge 25/2/54.

★ R6295 is not shown as being allocated to 2 CFS until after Bernard Steel had left the unit. He flew it on two occasions, on 8/10/1941 and again on 13/10/1941. This would indicate an error in the date of transfer to 2CFS from 11SFTS.

★★V3870 is shown as joining 2CFS on 31/12/41, after Bernard Steel served with the unit. This is because the AM78 (movement card) was not completed when it moved to the unit and the error was only discovered during the RAF census of December 1941, hence the date of 31/12/41.

No. 3 Service Flying Training School (Watchfield) 20/10/1941 to 25/10/1942 Unit name changed to 3 (Pilots) Advanced Flying Unit on 1/3/42. (Incorporating No1 Beam Approach School, Course no 56 (Watchfield) 4/11/1941 to 15/11/1941.)

Aircraft type: Airspeed Oxford MK1, Avro Anson.

Airspeed Oxford

L4579 3 Flying Training School 1/7/38, **(unc) 3 Service Flying Training School, (unc) 3 (Pilots) Advanced Flying Unit,** storage 14/8/42, to 8 Anti-Aircraft Co-operation Unit 8/1/43, 290 Squadron 12/12/43, storage 7/6/44, to 7 Flying Instructors School 15/7/44, storage 9/8/45, Sold for scrap 23/7/47.

L4614 5 Flying Training School 22/9/38, (unc) 5 Service Flying Training School, **to 3 Service Flying Training School 10/8/40,** hit hanger during overshoot, stalled and crashed Boscombe Down 22/2/42.

L9697 3 Flying Training School 1/3/39, **(unc) 3 Service Flying Training School, (unc) 3 (Pilots) Advanced Flying Unit,** storage 30/6/43, to 6 (Pilots) Advanced Flying Unit 5/9/43, Struck off charge 19/5/44.

L9699 3 Flying Training School 7/3/39, **(unc) 3 Service Flying Training**

School, lost control in turn and dived into the ground at Shorncote, Gloucestershire 3/1/42.

N4560 Aircraft & Armament Experimental Establishment 14/2/39, to Royal Aircraft Establishment 13/7/39, storage 6/6/40, to 12 Service Flying Training School 4/11/41, **to 3 Service Flying Training School 26/12/41, (unc) 3 (Pilots) Advanced Flying Unit,** storage 13/12/43, to 15 (Pilots) Advanced Flying Unit 13/2/44, storage 30/5/45, Struck off charge 23/5/46.

N4565 7 Flying Training School 6/3/39, (unc) 7 Service Flying Training School, to 11 Service Flying Training School 14/9/39, storage 25/1/40, **to 3 Service Flying Training School 7/8/42, (unc) 3 (Pilots) Advanced Flying Unit,** re-designated 3658M (airframe used for ground instruction of flight mechanics and riggers) 3 School of Technical Training Blackpool (Squires Gate) 22/4/43.

N6251 2 Flying Training School 13/3/39, (unc) 2 Service Flying Training School, **to 3 Service Flying Training School 7/6/40, (unc) 3 (Pilots) Advanced Flying Unit,** storage 14/2/42, to 21 (Pilots) Advanced Flying Unit 24/3/44, Struck off charge 3/7/45.

N6266 5 Flying Training School 30/3/39, (unc) 5 Service Flying Training School, **to 3 Service Flying Training School 25/9/40, (unc) 3 (Pilots) Advanced Flying Unit,** storage 12/12/42, to 3 Flying Instructors School 3/5/44, Struck off charge 23/11/44.

N6287 14 Flying Training School 16/5/39, (unc) 14 Service Flying Training School, storage 25/7/40, to RAF College 4/8/40, storage 22/5/41, **to 3 (Pilots) Advanced Flying Unit 30/5/42,** Struck off charge 8/2/43.

N6296 11 Flying Training School 28/6/39, to 3 Flying Training School 23/8/39, **(unc) 3 Service Flying Training School, storage 7/8/42,** to 7 Anti-Aircraft Co-operation Unit 21/10/42, engine failed and dived into the sea on approach to North Coates, 13/5/43.

N6299 15 Flying Training School 3/6/39, (unc) 15 Service Flying Training School, storage 5/12/40, **to 3 Service Flying Training School 10/1/41,** to 2 Service

Flying Training School 7/3/42, (unc) 2 (Pilots) Advanced Flying Unit, to 6 (Pilots) Advanced Flying Unit 19/5/42, to 3 Flying Instructors School 25/11/43, to 17 Service Flying Training School, engine cut out on take off and belly landed 1 mile south-south-west of Cranwell 26/11/44.

N6422 11 Service Flying Training School 11/9/39, storage 11/7/40, **to 3 Service Flying Training School 3/10/40, (unc) 3 (Pilots) Advanced Flying Unit,** storage 16/10/42, to 138 Squadron, to 3 Group Communication Flight 17/12/43, Struck off charge 31/8/44.

N6435 15 Service Flying Training School 26/9/39, to 2 Service Flying Training School, **to 3 Service Flying Training School 13/5/41,** storage 23/10/42, 116 Squadron 29/11/42, storage 31/1/44, to Ground Controlled Approach Wing Honiley 24/8/44, to Navigation Training Unit (Pathfinder Force) 4/1/45, storage 18/6/45, Struck off charge 15/6/50.

P1932 2 Service Flying Training School 21/12/39, **to 3 Service Flying Training School 23/8/41, (unc) 3 (Pilots) Advanced Flying Unit,** storage 24/6/42, to 15 (Pilots) Advanced Flying Unit 12/7/42, to 14 (Pilots) Advanced Flying Unit 15/9/42, Struck off charge 30/3/45.

P1935 8 Service Flying Training School 6/1/40, storage 19/11/40, to 2 Service Flying Training School 2/3/41, **to 3 Service Flying Training School 23/5/41, (unc) 3 (Pilots) Advanced Flying Unit,** storage 18/2/43, to 20 (Pilots) Advanced Flying Unit 18/2/44, to 15 (Pilots) Advanced Flying Unit 4/1/45, Struck off charge 18/10/45.

P1962 8 Service Flying Training School 24/1/40, to 14 Flying Training School 26/5/40, to 2 Service Flying Training School 10/2/41, **to 3 Service Flying Training School 9/5/41, (unc) 3 (Pilots) Advanced Flying Unit,** storage 9/8/42, to Empire Central Flying School 15/7/42, to 16 (Polish) Flying Training School 14/7/44, Struck off charge 6/10/44.

P1988 3 Service Flying Training School 15/2/40, (unc) 3 (Pilots) Advanced Flying Unit, failed to take off from South Cerney and undercarriage raised to stop 19/3/42.

P8825 RAF College 1/4/40, to 5 Service Flying Training School 4/4/40, **to 3 Service Flying Training School 5/9/40, (unc) 3 (Pilots) Advanced Flying Unit,** storage 6/11/42, to 21 (Pilots) Advanced Flying Unit 21/1/44, Struck off charge 25/11/44.

P8898 Allocated to Royal New Zealand Air Force as NZ1272 but kept in UK as P8898. 2 Service Flying Training School 29/8/40, to 12 Service Flying Training School 15/11/41, **to 3 Service Flying Training School 10/1/42, (unc) 3(Pilots) Advanced Flying Unit,** storage 16/2/43, to 21 (Pilots) Advanced Flying Unit 24/3/44, Struck off charge 22/7/46.

P8931 11 Service Flying Training School 3/6/40, **to 3 Service Flying Training School 19/10/41, (unc) 3 (Pilots) Advanced Flying Unit,** to Melton Mowbray 2/1/44, to United States Army Air Force 7/7/44, Struck off charge 21/6/47.

P8992 RAF College 20/6/40, **to 3 (Pilots) Advanced Flying Unit 10/6/42,** storage 3/3/43, to United States Army Air Force 1/12/43.

P9023 3 Service Flying Training School 19/9/40, (unc) 3 (Pilots) Advanced Flying Unit, storage 2/12/42, to 21 (Pilots) Advanced Flying Unit 24/3/44, propellers hit ground on take off from Seighford 15/3/45.

P9031 14 Service Flying Training School 30/8/40, to 2 Central Flying School 23/10/41, to 12 Service Flying Training School 10/11/41, **to 3 Service Flying Training School 28/1/42, (unc) 3 (Pilots) Advanced Flying Unit,** storage 21/12/42, to 16 (Polish) Flying Training School 7/9/43, storage 30/6/44, to Mepal (Cambridgeshire) 19/7/44, storage 11/4/47, to 16 Reserve Flying School 18/5/51, to 5 Reserve Flying School 23/5/52, storage 10/3/54, Struck off charge 24/3/54.

R5972 15 Service Flying Training School 24/11/40, **to 3 Service Flying Training School 12/5/41, (unc) 3 (Pilots) Advanced Flying Unit,** storage 9/4/44, to 150 Wing 28/11/44, to 116 Squadron, to Fighter Command Communications Squadron 22/3/45, Struck off charge 19/4/45.

R6032 2 Service Flying Training School 30/12/40, to **3 Service Flying Training School 28/6/41, (unc) 3 (Pilots) Advanced Flying Unit,** storage 2/10/42, to 3 Flying Instructors School 18/10/42, Struck off charge 12/5/44.

R6086 3 Service Flying Training School 10/2/41, (unc) 3 (Pilots) Advanced Flying Unit, to 5 Operational Training Unit 15/11/43, to 131 Operational Training Unit 26/6/44, to 544 Squadron 15/7/44, Struck off charge 25/9/45.

R6098 3 Service Flying Training School 20/3/41, (unc) 3 (Pilots) Advanced Flying Unit, to Air Training Corps Flight Halton 2/1/43, to 3 Flying Instructors School 3/8/43, to 1 School of Technical Training Linton-on-Ouse 22/8/43, undercarriage collapsed while starting engines, Linton-on-Ouse 10/8/44.

R6237 14 Service Flying Training School 15/5/40, **to 3 Flying Training School 17/4/41, (unc) 3 (Pilots) Advanced Flying Unit,** storage 24/4/42, to Admiralty 30/7/43, to 781 Squadron 12/8/43, to 762 Squadron Apr/44, storage Nov/45, to Station Flight Belfast Dec/45, storage May/46, to Lossiemouth Jan/49, storage Jul/49, Struck off charge 27/3/50.

R6247 15 Service Flying Training School 21/5/40, to RAF College 18/9/40, to 6 Flying Training School 20/6/41, **to 3 Service Flying Training School 10/1/42, (unc) 3 (Pilots) Advanced Flying Unit,** storage 20/12/42, to 14 (Pilots) Advanced Flying Unit 10/11/43, Damaged beyond repair 30/8/44.

R6294 11 Service Flying Training School 11/6/40, (unc) 11 (Pilots) Advanced Flying Unit, **to 3 (Pilots) Advanced Flying Unit 9/5/42,** storage 11/10/43, to 20 (Pilots) Advanced Flying Unit 31/3/44, to 3 (Pilots) Advanced Flying Unit 4/1/45, Struck off charge 25/4/45.

R6319 3 Service Flying Training School 11/6/40, (unc) 3 (Pilots) Advanced Flying Unit, storage 4/6/42, to 6 Anti-Aircraft Co-operation Unit 15/10/42, to 14 (Pilots) Advanced Flying Unit 8/10/43, Struck off charge 19/5/44.

R6330 3 Service Flying Training School 20/6/40, (unc) 3 (Pilots) Advanced Flying Unit, storage 18/9/42, to 3 Glider Training School 27/9/42, to 2 Flying Instructors School 12/3/43, to 14 (Pilots) Advanced Flying Unit 13/2/44, Struck off charge 18/10/45.

T1011 2 Service Flying Training School 28/5/41, to 12 Service Flying Training School 20/8/41, **to 3 Service Flying Training School 12/1/42, (unc) 3 (Pilots) Advanced Flying Unit,** collided with P8931 on landing at South Cerney damaged beyond repair 18/3/42.

T1047 15 Service Flying Training School 7/3/41, **to 3 Service Flying Training School 3/10/41, (unc) 3 (Pilots) Advanced Flying Unit,** storage 18/5/43, to 11 (Pilots) Advanced Flying Unit 27/9/43, to 21 (Pilots) Advanced Flying Unit 26/12/44, storage 8/5/46, sold for scrap to Hendron, Belfast 5/5/50.

T1107 3 Service Flying Training School 20/3/41, (unc) 3 (Pilots) Advanced Flying Unit, storage 17/12/42, to 3 School of General Reconnaissance 4/5/43, to Admiralty 21/2/44, to 782 Squadron Apr/44, Cat E (damaged beyond repair) 21/9/44.

T1108 3 Service Flying Training School 20/3/41, (unc) 3 (Pilots) Advanced Flying Unit, storage 1/4/43, to 233 Squadron 12/3/44, to 107 Operational Training Unit 17/5/44, Struck off charge 12/3/45.

V3148 12 Service Flying Training School 18/5/41, (unc) 12 (Pilots) Advanced Flying Unit, **to 3 (Pilots) Advanced Flying Unit 28/7/42,** storage 26/8/43, to 6 (Pilots) Advanced Flying Unit 3/10/43, storage 23/8/45, Struck off charge 15/1/47.

V3530 RAF College 12/4/41, **to 3 Service Flying Training School 28/12/41, (unc) 3 (Pilots) Advanced Flying Unit,** storage 26/3/43, to 510 Squadron 4/6/43, (unc) Metropolitan Communication Squadron, to 139 Wing 3/11/44, to 98 Squadron 18/6/45, storage 27/8/45, sold for scrap to W.F. Lamont 28/6/49.

V3557 15 Service Flying Training School 16/1/41, to 14 Service Flying Training School 10/12/41, **to 3 Service Flying Training School 23/12/41, (unc) 3 (Pilots) Advanced Flying Unit,** storage 22/1/43, to 16 (Polish) Flying Training

School 27/4/43, storage 21/11/43, to Fairford 30/5/44, to 85 Squadron 1/9/44, to Fairford 28/9/44, to Great Dunmow 19/10/44, Struck off charge 18/12/44.

V3569 3 Service Flying Training School 13/1/41, (unc) 3 (Pilots) Advanced Flying Unit, storage 30/12/42, to Handley Page 25/1/43, Struck off charge 25/5/45.

V3583 3 Service Flying Training School 11/5/41, (unc) 3 (Pilots) Advanced Flying Unit, to 20 (Pilots) Advanced Flying Unit 7/4/43, Struck off charge 2/10/44.

V3589 3 Service Flying Training School 6/5/41, (unc) 3 (Pilots) Advanced Flying Unit, to Admiralty 8/6/44, to 740 Squadron Jun/44, storage Nov/44, to Station Flight Belfast Dec/44, No further trace.

V3628 3 Service Flying Training School 25/2/41, (unc) 3 (Pilots) Advanced Flying Unit, to United States Army Air Force 2/3/44, returned to RAF 9/6/44, No further trace.

V3642 3 Service Flying Training School 28/9/41, (unc) 3 (Pilots) Advanced Flying Unit, storage 19/7/42, to 406 Squadron 30/1/43, Struck off charge 27/5/44.

V3644 3 Service Flying Training School 12/1/41, hit tree while low flying, Oldbury-on-Severn Gloucestershire 27/10/41.

V3784 6 Service Flying Training School 23/2/41, (unc) 6 (Pilots) Advanced Flying Unit, storage 3/4/42, **to 3 (Pilots) Advanced Flying Unit 7/6/42,** storage 26/7/43, to United States Army Air Force 18/5/44.

V3869 3 Service Flying Training School 2/3/41, (unc) 3 (Pilots) Advanced Flying Unit, spun and hit the ground while recovering from a dive near Lechlade Gloucestershire, 5/4/42.

V3908 3 Service Flying Training School 8/5/41, (unc) 3 (Pilots) Advanced Flying Unit, overshot landing at Southrop and hit a hedge, damaged beyond repair 5/5/43.

V3909 3 Service Flying Training School 8/5/41, (unc) 3 (Pilots) Advanced Flying Unit, storage 24/11/42, to 1530 Beam Approach Training Flight 25/8/43, Struck off charge 12/5/44.

V3937 3 Service Flying Training School 21/5/41, (unc) 3 (Pilots) Advanced Flying Unit, storage 6/11/42, to 14 (Pilots) Advanced Flying Unit 26/7/44, storage 17/9/44, Struck off charge 2/11/44.

V4050 2 Air Observers School 30/8/41**, to 1 Beam Approach School 16/9/41,** to 3 (Pilots) Advanced Flying Unit 5/6/44, re-designated 5489M (airframe used for ground instruction of flight mechanics and riggers) 4 School of Technical Training St. Athan 24/7/45, Struck off charge 18/10/46.

V4051 2 Air Observers School 30/8/41**, to 1 Beam Approach School 17/9/41,** dived into the ground 1 mile North-West of Watchfield after night take off 7/12/42.

V4052 2 Air Observers School 30/8/41**, to 1 Beam Approach School 17/9/41,** storage 9/5/44, sold as scrap to J. Dale & Co. London Colney 29/3/49.

V4053 2 Air Observers School 4/9/41**, to 1 Beam Approach School 26/9/41,** bounced on landing at Kelmscott and stalled on attempted overshoot 28/5/43.

V4054 2 Air Observers School 30/8/41**, to 1 Beam Approach School 17/9/41,** to 3 (Pilots) Advanced Flying Unit 8/3/44, re-designated 5490M (airframe used for ground instruction of flight mechanics and riggers) 4 School of Technical Training St. Athan 26/7/45, Struck off charge 25/7/46.

W6551 14 Service Flying Training School 1/1/41, to **3 Service Flying Training School 19/10/41,** crashed after mid-air collision location unknown 4/1/42.

W6570 3 Service Flying Training School 24/3/41, (unc) 3 (Pilots) Advanced Flying Unit, to United States Army Air Force 13/12/43.

W6571 3 Service Flying Training School 24/3/41, (unc) 3 (Pilots)

Advanced Flying Unit, storage 26/3/43, to York 16/7/43, to Rufforth 5/9/43, to East Kirkby 6/6/44, crashed location unknown 24/8/44.

W6576 12 Service Flying Training School 18/4/41, **to 3 Service Flying Training School 10/1/42, (unc) 3 (Pilots) Advanced Flying Unit,** storage 30/9/43, to 239 Squadron 29/3/45, storage (date unknown), to 1335 (Meteor) Conversion Unit 6/9/45, storage (date unknown), Struck off charge 18/8/50.

W6634 3 Service Flying Training School 30/4/41, (unc) 3 (Pilots) Advanced Flying Unit, storage 8/8/43, to 233 Squadron 12/3/44, to 107 (Transport) Operational Training Unit 17/5/44, (unc) 1333 Transport Support Conversion Unit, School of Air Transport 2/11/45, to 1508 (Radio Aids Training) Flight 14/11/45, to School of Air Transport 19/12/45, Struck off charge 30/5/46.

X6647 3 Service Flying Training School 19/10/41, (unc) 3 (Pilots) Advanced Flying Unit, to 21 (Pilots) Advanced Flying Unit 17/1/46, storage 15/2/46, Struck off charge 3/9/47.

X6653 14 Service Flying Training School 24/10/41, **to 3 Service Flying Training School 23/12/41, (unc) 3 (Pilots) Advanced Flying Unit,** storage 16/6/42, to 16 (Polish) Flying Training School 10/11/43, to 1524 Flight 2/6/44, storage 4/1/45, to Pocklington 21/3/46, to 1513 Flight 7/5/46, storage (date unknown), sold for scrap to Enfield Rolling Mills Ltd. Bradford 3/11/49.

X6739 3 Service Flying Training School 23/2/42, (unc) 3 (Pilots) Advanced Flying Unit, storage 21/3/44, sold back to Airspeed 2/7/47, no further trace.

X6838 3 (Pilots) Advanced Flying Unit 24/9/42, storage 22/5/43, to Admiralty 21/8/43, to 758 Squadron Aug/43, storage Apr/45, to 762 Squadron Aug/45, storage Nov/45, to Station Flight Dale Sept/46, storage Mar/47, Struck off charge 6/9/50.

X6876 3 (Pilots) Advanced Flying Unit 11/9/42, flew into the ground on overshoot at South Cerney and destroyed by fire 28/10/42.

X7068 14 Service Flying Training School 26/11/41, **to 3 Service Flying Training School 23/12/41, (unc) 3 (Pilots) Advanced Flying Unit,** storage 21/2/44, to Station Flight Burn (Yorkshire) 30/8/44, to 4 Group Communication Flight 22/3/45, storage (date unknown), sold for scrap to Hendron, Belfast 5/5/50.

X7184 3 (Pilots) Advanced Flying Unit 10/7/42, Struck off charge 12/5/44.

X7247 3 (Pilots) Advanced Flying Unit 22/5/42, suffered a flying accident and Struck off charge 9/10/44.

AB649 12 Service Flying Training School 9/6/41, **to 3 Service Flying Training School 6/11/41, (unc) 3 (Pilots) Advanced Flying Unit,** to Supermarine (comms) 5/9/42, Struck off charge 19/5/44.

AB727 3 Service Flying Training School 3/8/41, (unc) 3 (Pilots) Advanced Flying Unit, storage 20/8/45, Struck off charge 31/1/47.

AB728 3 Service Flying Training School 3/8/41, (unc) 3 (Pilots) Advanced Flying Unit, hit blister hanger on night take-off from South Cerney 27/11/42.

AB769 2 Service Flying Training School 28/8/41, (unc) 2 (Pilots) Advanced Flying Unit, **to 3 (Pilots) Advanced Flying Unit 10/8/42,** (unc) 3 Service Flying Training School, Struck off charge 31/12/46.

AP390 3 Service Flying Training School 31/8/41, (unc) 3 (Pilots) Advanced Flying Unit, storage 17/11/43, to 15 Maintenance Unit Communication Flight 6/12/43, to 233 Squadron 9/3/44, to 107 Operational Training Unit 17/5/44, storage (date unknown), Struck off charge 15/6/45.

AP391 3 Service Flying Training School 31/8/41, (unc) 3 (Pilots) Advanced Flying Unit, to Allied Expeditionary Air Forces Controller of Supplies 13/12/43, to Signals Flying Unit 1/9/44, to Foulsham 12/10/44, storage 3/9/45, Struck off charge 7/8/47.

AP398 3 Service Flying Training School 11/9/41, (unc) 3 (Pilots)

Advanced Flying Unit, to 14 (Pilots) Advanced Flying Unit 10/5/43, Struck off charge 21/6/44.

AP400 3 Service Flying Training School 11/9/41, (unc) 3 (Pilots) Advanced Flying Unit, Struck off charge 9/11/43.

AP401 3 Service Flying Training School 12/9/41, (unc) 3 (Pilots) Advanced Flying Unit, lost control on night overshoot at Bibury and hit the ground destroyed by fire 13/10/42.

AP402 3 Service Flying Training School 12/9/41, (unc) 3 (Pilots) Advanced Flying Unit, Struck off charge 22/10/44.

AP403 3 Service Flying Training School 13/9/41, (unc) 3 (Pilots) Advanced Flying Unit, engine cut out on approach to Long Newnton, undershot and hit a hedge damaged beyond repair 5/7/43.

AP468 3 Service Flying Training School 21/10/41, (unc) 3 (Pilots) Advanced Flying Unit, to United States Army Air Force 9/1/44.

AP469 3 Service Flying Training School 21/10/41, (unc) 3 (Pilots) Advanced Flying Unit, both engines cut out attempted to belly land at night and flew into the ground 1 mile south of Cirencester Gloucestershire 30/9/42.

AP470 3 Service Flying Training School 22/10/41, (unc) 3 (Pilots) Advanced Flying Unit, swung on take-off from Lulsgate Bottom and hit obstruction destroyed by fire 7/5/43.

AP471 3 Service Flying Training School 24/10/41, (unc) 3 (Pilots) Advanced Flying Unit, storage 25/12/43, to 16 Operational Training Unit 4/1/45, storage 5/9/45, Struck off charge 31/5/46.

AS147 6 Blind Approach Training Flight 2/6/41, to 16 Operational Training Unit 10/9/41, **to 3 (Pilots) Advanced Flying Unit 16/4/42,** Struck off charge 26/6/46.

AS477 3 Service Flying Training School 30/4/41, (unc) 3 (Pilots) Advanced Flying Unit, hit tree while low flying and destroyed by fire White House Farm, Brinkworth, Wiltshire 18/4/42.

AT674 3 Service Flying Training School 26/10/41, (unc) 3 (Pilots) Advanced Flying Unit, engine cut out on overshoot at night, crash landed 1 mile North of Bibury 19/7/42.

AT738 2 Service Flying Training School 20/11/41, (unc) 2 (Pilots) Advanced Flying Unit, **to 3 (Pilots) Advanced Flying Unit 18/3/42,** hit house and destroyed by fire on night take off from South Cerney 12/8/42.

AT769 1 Beam Approach School 8/2/42, Struck off charge 25/5/44.

BF947 3 Service Flying Training School 26/2/42, (unc) 3 (Pilots) Advanced Flying Unit, Struck off charge 19/4/45.

BG158 3 (Pilots) Advanced Flying Unit 3/6/42, hit HT cables during night navigation exercise crashed and destroyed by fire 2 miles North of Cirencester Gloucestershire 8/1/43.

BG172 3 (Pilots) Advanced Flying Unit 20/4/42, Struck off charge 20/5/44.

BG544 3 (Pilots) Advanced Flying Unit 11/6/42, Struck off charge 11/5/44.

BG599 3 (Pilots) Advanced Flying Unit 3/7/42, undercarriage collapsed in heavy landing damaged beyond repair Southrop 4/6/44.

BG600 3 (Pilots) Advanced Flying Unit 6/7/42, storage 31/12/42, sold back to Airspeed 10/10/46 no further trace.

BM671 3 Service Flying Training School 15/11/41, (unc) 3 (Pilots) Advanced Flying Unit, to United States Army Air Force 30/4/44, returned to RAF 17/9/45, to Bomber Command Communication Flight 6/1/53, to 61 Group Communication Flight 5/5/55, storage 30/9/55, sold for scrap to J.G. Williamson 22/3/56.

BM844 3 (Pilots) Advanced Flying Unit 6/6/42, to Biggin Hill 28/4/44, to Croydon 12/6/44, to 277 Squadron 9/11/44, re-designated as 5056M to 1023 Squadron Air Training Corps 24/2/45, Struck off charge 3/3/45.

EB861 3 (Pilots) Advanced Flying Unit 13/9/42, lost propeller and crashed near Upton Wiltshire 21/8/43.

EB909 3 (Pilots) Advanced Flying Unit 1/10/42, Struck off charge 17/5/46.

ED115 3 (Pilots) Advanced Flying Unit 14/6/42, hit obstruction while low flying 1 mile East of Aston Gloucestershire 15/7/42.

ED120 3 (Pilots) Advanced Flying Unit 22/5/42, storage 11/8/43, to Royal Norwegian Air Force 2/5/47 as V-AB.

ED122 3 (Pilots) Advanced Flying Unit 22/5/42, re-designated as 5515M (airframe used in ground construction of WAAFs as well as men as electricians, instrument makers and armourers) at 12 School of Technical Training Melksham 27/7/45.

ED123 3 (Pilots) Advanced Flying Unit 9/5/42, hit HT cables while low flying near Brinkworth Wiltshire 11/5/43.

ED125 3 (Pilots) Advanced Flying Unit 9/5/42, Struck off charge 19/4/45.

ED132 3 (Pilots) Advanced Flying Unit 9/5/42, storage 12/11/43, to Skipton-on-Swale 31/7/44, to Heston 25/8/45, storage 9/4/46, sold for scrap 3/9/47.

ED234 3 (Pilots) Advanced Flying Unit 13/8/42, Struck off charge 2/1/45.

Avro Anson

R3584 Wireless Intelligence Development Unit, to 109 Squadron, **to 1 Beam Approach School,** to 3 Air Observers School, 7 Operational Training unit, Struck off charge 19/4/45.

R3586 Wireless Intelligence Development Unit, to 109 Squadron, **to 1 Beam Approach School,** to 3 Air Observers School, to 3 (Observers) Advanced Flying Unit, to 16 (Polish) Service Flying Training School, Struck off charge 30/8/44.

R9830 Beam Approach Training and Development Unit, **to1 Beam Approach School,** to 3 Air Observers School, to 3 (Observers) Advanced Flying Unit, to School of Flying Control, to Beam Approach School, Struck off charge 1/1/45.

1525 Beam Approach Training Flight (Docking/Bircham Newton) 27/10/42 to 11/9/43

Aircraft Type: Airspeed Oxford

AT728 2 (Pilots) Advanced Flying Unit 14/3/42, **to Bircham Newton 1525 Beam Approach Training Flight 15/7/42,** to 18 (Pilots) Advanced Flying Unit 6/2/44, undercarriage collapsed on landing at Warwick damaged beyond repair 5/4/45.

AT729 2 Service Flying Training School for 1525 Beam Approach Training Flight 9/3/42, storage 7/2/44, to Thorney Island 15/4/48, to School of Land/Air Warfare 30/3/51, to Waterbeach 3/2/53, struck off charge 28/5/56.

AT742 2 Service Flying Training School for 1525 Beam Approach Training Flight 10/3/42, storage 29/8/43, to 1539 Beam Approach Flight 29/9/43, to 3 (Pilot) Advanced Flying Unit 5/10/43, caught fire at dispersal and damaged beyond repair Bibury 19/8/44.

DF212 Definite log entries for this code number and logged as an Oxford, however no Oxford of this number ever existed! Could well be DF282.

DF278 1525 Beam Approach Training Flight 13/2/42, to 2 (Pilots) Advanced Flying Unit 5/7/42, to 11 (Pilots) Advanced Flying Unit 6/10/43, to 20 (Pilots) Advanced Flying Unit 23/12/43, storage 21/6/45, struck off charge 22/5/46.

DF279 1525 Beam Approach Training Flight 13/3/42, to 2 (Pilots) Advanced Flying Unit 15/7/42, storage 25/9/43, to 14 (Pilots) Advanced Flying Unit

9/10/43, hit by L4540 while parked at Dallachy damaged beyond repair 13/5/44.

DF280 1525 Beam Approach Training Flight 13/3/42, storage 17/11/43, to 1527 Beam Approach/Radio Aids Training Flight 6/7/45, storage 28/2/46 to Pocklington 27/3/46, struck off charge 8/6/50.

DF281 2 Service Flying Training School 9/3/42, (unc) 2 (Pilots) Advanced Flying Unit, **to 1525 Beam Approach Training Flight 15/7/42,** storage 31/1/43, **returned to 1525 Beam Approach Training Flight,** struck off charge 2/7/43.

DF282 1525 Beam Approach Training Flight 13/3/42, storage 31/1/43, to 14 (Pilots) Advanced Flying Unit 9/10/43, to 15 (Pilots) Advanced Flying Unit 29/2/44, storage 10/6/45, struck off charge 15/6/50.

DF455 1525 Beam Approach Training Flight between Jan and Sep/42, storage 17/7/44, to 1655 Mosquito Training Unit 1/12/44, (unc) 16 Operational Training Unit, storage 30/8/45, to 2 Transport Aircraft Modification Unit 24/10/45, to 1552 Radio Aids Training Flight 29/12/45, to 1 Ferry Unit 2/9/46, struck off charge 8/6/50.

HN123 1525 Beam Approach Training Flight 28/5/43, to 3 (Pilots) Advanced Flying Unit 30/5/44, (unc) 3 Service Flying Training School, Storage 18/6/46, to Rhodesian Air Force 27/2/47.

HN469 1525 Beam Approach Training Flight 4/7/43, hit trees on approach to Docking in fog 16/1/44.

HN697 1525 Beam Approach Training Flight 30/7/43, to 3 (Pilots) Advanced Flying Unit 30/5/44, storage 22/5/46, to 1 Ferry Unit, 18/4/47, to Glosters Aircraft Manufacturer 21/7/47, storage 23/9/47, struck off charge 8/6/50.

LB461 1525 Beam Approach Training Flight 26/5/43, to 3 (Pilots) Advanced Flying Unit 30/6/44, to 16 (Polish) Flying Training School 11/1/46, storage 7/8/46, to 104 Flying Refresher School 1/8/51, to 9 Advance Flying Training School 31/3/52, storage 8/7/53, sold for scrap to Hants & Sussex Aviation Ltd Portsmouth 13/12/55.

No 6 (Pilots) Advanced Flying Unit (Little Rissington, Gloucestershire) 12/9/1943 to 16/11/1943.

Aircraft Type: Airspeed Oxford.

T1209 6 (Pilots) Advanced Flying Unit 27/6/43, storage 16/12/45, Struck off charge 9/5/46.

V3209 Central Flying School 26/8/40, to 11 (Pilots) Advanced Flying Unit 30/12/42, **to 6 (Pilots) Advanced Flying Unit 20/8/43,** Struck off charge 28/6/44.

V3847 6 Service Flying Training School 13/3/41, **(unc) 6 (Pilots) Advanced Flying Unit,** to Communications Flight Woodley 16/6/44, to 3 Flying Instructors School 22/6/44, Struck off charge 28/1/45.

V3857 6 Service Flying Training School 13/3/41, **(unc) 6 (Pilots) Advanced Flying Unit,** Struck off charge 30/5/46.

V4227 6 (Pilots) Advanced Flying Unit 28/7/43, storage 8/10/45, Struck off charge 28/5/46.

W6578 6 Service Flying Training School 4/3/41, **(unc) 6 (Pilots) Advanced Flying Unit,** storage 17/7/44, to Croft 2/8/44, to Binbrook 28/3/46, to Burmese Air Force 19/12/48.

X6645 2 Service Flying Training School 19/10/41, **to 6 (Pilots) Advanced Flying Unit Unknown date,** to 12 (Pilots) Advanced Flying Unit 29/7/44, storage 15/6/45, to 1555 Radio Aids Training Flight 7/3/46, to 1513 Beam Approach/Radio Aids Training Flight 6/5/46, sold back to Airspeed 10/1/47, no further trace.

X6649 6 Service Flying Training School 21/10/41, **(unc) 6 (Pilots) Advanced Flying Unit,** Struck off charge 26/6/44.

BF942 6 Service Flying Training School 22/2/42, **(unc) 6 (Pilots) Advanced**

Flying Unit, (unc) 6 Service Flying Training School, storage 1/2/46, Struck off charge 12/4/46.

BG548 6 (Pilots) Advanced Flying Unit 26/6/42, to 12 (Pilots) Advanced Flying Unit 27/7/44, storage 21/6/45, Struck off charge 29/11/45.

BG629 6 (Pilots) Advanced Flying Unit 9/7/42, Struck off charge 26/10/44.

DF246 6 (Pilots) Advanced Flying Unit 21/6/42, Struck off charge 14/7/44.

DF288 6 (Pilots) Advanced Flying Unit 30/4/42, storage 14/8/45, struck off charge 15/6/50.

EB701 6 (Pilots) Advanced Flying Unit 17/8/42, storage 26/8/45, Struck off charge 15/1/47.

EB857 6 (Pilots) Advanced Flying Unit 12/8/42, storage 14/8/45, Struck off charge 20/6/46.

EB858 6 (Pilots) Advanced Flying Unit 24/9/42, Struck off charge 12/5/44.

HM732 6 (Pilots) Advanced Flying Unit 21/4/43, (unc) 6 Service Flying Training School, to 17 Service Flying Training School 5/1/46, Struck off charge 12/6/46.

HN643 6 (Pilots) Advanced Flying Unit 4/6/43, to 15 (Pilots) Advanced Flying Unit 1/2/44, storage 3/6/45, to Coningsby 21/5/49, to Hemswell 31/3/50, to 230 Operational Conversion Unit 2/2/51, to Station Flight Scampton 15/10/52, to Station Flight Waddington 3/6/55, storage 28/6/56, sold for scrap 23/10/56.

HN649 285 Squadron 15/3/43, **to 6 (Pilots) Advanced Flying Unit 2/4/43,** storage 5/2/46, sold for scrap to W.F. Lamont 23/6/49.

HN712 6 (Pilots) Advanced Flying Unit unknown arrival date but between Sep/42 and May/43, storage Dec/43, struck off charge 18/5/46.

HN723 6 (Pilots) Advanced Flying Unit 13/4/43, to 15 (Pilots) Advanced Flying Unit 1/12/44, engine cut out and belly landed in field in Wiltshire 28/2/45.

LW773 6 (Pilots) Advanced Flying Unit 23/5/43, hit a tree while low flying at Lower Slaughter Gloucestershire 10/4/45.

LX159 6 (Pilots) Advanced Flying Unit 20/5/43, hit by LX526 while parked at Windrush (relief Landing ground for Little Rissington) damaged beyond repair 13/12/44.

LX160 6 (Pilots) Advanced Flying Unit 21/5/43, (unc) 6 Service Flying Training School, storage 17/1/46, Struck off charge 16/5/46.

LX178 6 (Pilots) Advanced Flying Unit 28/5/43, collided with W6586 crashed and destroyed by fire at Windrush (relief landing ground for Little Rissington) 20/10/43.

MP358 6 (Pilots) Advanced Flying Unit 15/2/43, (unc) 6 Service Flying Training School, Struck off charge 28/1/46.

No. 81 Operational Training Unit (R.A.F. Tilstock, Shropshire) 13/12/1943 to 30/12/1943.

Aircraft Type: Armstrong Whitworth Whitley Mk 5.

P5003 Delivered between 3/5/40 and 10/6/40 to 58 Squadron, to 19 Operational Training Unit, **to 81 Operational Training Unit,** struck off charge 28/6/45.

T4177 Delivered between 30/7/40 and 30/8/40 to 10 Operational Training Unit, to 3 Operational Training Unit, **to 81 Operational Training Unit,** struck off charge 9/8/45.

Z6962 Delivered between 7/8/41 and 31/8/41 to 3 Operational Training Unit, **to 81 Operational Training Unit,** struck off charge 22/2/45.

BD274 Delivered between 26/3/42 and 24/4/42 to 10 Operational Training Unit, **to 81 Operational Training Unit,** struck off charge 14/12/45.

EB340 Delivered between 22/9/42 and 15/10/42 **to 81 Operational Training Unit,** struck off charge 22/3/45.

EB364 Delivered between 22/9/42 and 15/10/42 **to 81 Operational Training Unit,** struck off charge 29/3/45.

LA924 Delivered between 24/3/43 and 13/6/43 **to 81 Operational Training Unit,** struck off charge 20/2/45.

28 Operational Training Unit (Wymeswold, Leicestershire) 21/1/44 to 18/3/44.

Aircraft Type: Vickers Armstrong Wellington

R1727 45 Maintenance Unit 10/4/41, to 22 Operational Training Unit 11/5/41, to 26 Operational Training Unit 12/12/42, **to 28 Operational Training Unit 27/5/43,** category E damage (damaged beyond repair) 18/4/44.

T2741 9 Maintenance Unit 11/8/40, to 75 Squadron 26/9/40, to Brooklands (probably for repair or upgrade) 19/11/40, to 45 Maintenance Unit 10/2/41, to 15 Operational Training Unit 27/4/41, to 12 Operational Training Unit 19/6/41, to 25 Operational Training Unit 26/7/42, **to 28 Operational Training Unit 4/7/43,** to 18 Maintenance Unit 10/4/44, struck off charge and scrapped 31/8/46.

T2922 22 Maintenance Unit 2/12/40, to 12 Operational Training Unit 23/12/40, to 43 Group unknown date, to 12 Operational Training Unit 17/5/41, **to 28 Operational Training Unit 11/8/42,** category E damage (damaged beyond repair) 26/3/44.

X9936 46 Maintenance Unit 3/9/41, to 22 Operational Training Unit 9/9/41, to 20 Operational Training Unit 24/12/42, **to 28 Operational Training Unit 16/7/43,** category E damage (damaged beyond repair) 8/4/47.

Z1049 46 Maintenance Unit 30/9/41, to 20 Operational Training Unit 7/10/41, to 15 Operational Training Unit 24/7/43, **to 28 Operational Training Unit 27/10/43,** reduced to spares 5/7/44.

Z1162 45 Maintenance Unit 7/11/41, to 109 Squadron 23/11/41, to 1474 Wireless Interception Flight 10/7/42, **to 28 Operational Training Unit 29/1/43,** category E damage (damaged beyond repair) 8/4/44.

DV805 44 Maintenance Unit 11/4/42, to 12 Operational Training Unit 20/4/42, to 23 Operational Training Unit 25/4/42, to 28 Operational Training Unit 29/8/42, to 12 Maintenance Unit 3/4/43, **to 28 Operational Training Unit 18/10/43,** category E damage (damaged beyond repair) 25/4/44.

LN591 ★ 84 Operational Training Unit 4/10/43, to 48 Maintenance Unit 30/3/44, to 24 Operational Training Unit 2/5/44, to 27 Maintenance Unit 18/7/45, Struck off charge 11/3/48.

LN593 ★ 84 Operational Training Unit 4/10 43, to 8 Maintenance Unit 21/6/45, Struck off charge 31/1/46.

★ Neither LN591 or LN593 are shown as being attached to 28 OTU, however both 28 and 84 OTU were part of 92 Group and were based only 24 miles apart. It is therefore likely that there may have been some overlapping of aircraft use.

1656 Heavy Conversion Unit (Lindholme, Yorkshire) 16/4/44 to 11/5/44.

Aircraft Type: Handley Page Halifax.

W7860 103 Squadron 21/9/42, to 51 Squadron 3/11/42, to 12 Maintenance Unit 12/6/43, to 1668 Heavy Conversion Unit 11/11/43, **to 1656 Heavy Conversion Unit 28/11/43,** struck off charge 8/2/45.

BB267 1656 Heavy Conversion Unit 14/12/42, category E damage (damaged beyond repair) 14/10/44, struck off charge 20/10/44.

BB269 1656 Heavy Conversion Unit 20/12/42, to 48 Maintenance Unit 10/12/44, struck off charge 14/12/44.

DT552 70 Squadron 8/10/42, to 51 Squadron 20/3/43, to 1658 Heavy Conversion Unit 6/4/43, **to 1656 Heavy Conversion Unit 14/4/44,** to 1662 Heavy Conversion Unit 13/5/44, category E damage 27/6/44, struck off charge 30/6/44.

JP188 1656 Heavy Conversion Unit 3/1/44, to 48 Maintenance Unit 30/12/44, Struck off charge 11/1/45.

No.1 Lancaster Finishing School (Hemswell, Lincolnshire) 11/5/44 to 25/5/44.

Aircraft Type: Avro Lancaster.

R5500 207 Squadron between Feb and Jul 1942, to 460 Squadron, to 1656 Heavy Conversion Unit, to 1667 Heavy Conversion Unit, **to 1 Lancaster Finishing School,** re-designated 4902M at 4 School of Technical Training St. Athan (airframe used to train flight engineers, flight mechanics and riggers) Oct/44.

W4264 1656 Heavy Conversion Unit between Jul and Nov 1942, to 1662 Heavy Conversion Unit, **to 1 Lancaster Finishing School,** to 1662 Heavy Conversion Unit, to 1668 Heavy Conversion Unit, re-designated 5289M Jul/45

W4845 103 Squadron between Sep/42 and May/43, to 1656 Heavy Conversion Unit, to 1662 Heavy Conversion Unit, to 1656 Heavy Conversion Unit, **to 1 Lancaster Finishing School,** to 1662 Heavy Conversion Unit, re-designated 5219M (instructional airframe) Jul/45.

W4859 1656 Heavy Conversion Unit between Sep/42 and May/43, to 1662 Heavy Conversion Unit, **to 1 Lancaster Finishing School,** to 1662 Heavy Conversion Unit, category E (damaged beyond repair) after hitting barn on overshoot at Blyton, Lincolnshire 12/12/44.

166 Squadron (Kirmington, Lincolnshire) 26/5/44 to 26/9/44.

Aircraft Types: Avro Lancaster, Airspeed Oxford.

Airspeed Oxford.

AB712 11 Service Flying Training School 24/7/41, to Dalcross Station Flight 22/10/41, storage 30/6/43, to 6 (Pilots) Advanced Flying Unit 21/9/43, **to Kirmington Station Flight 8/7/44,** to 1 Ferry Unit 17/4/47, to Royal Hellenic (Greece) Air Force 21/4/47.

Avro Lancaster.

JB649 460 Squadron 10/11/43, to 626 Squadron 13/11/43, **to 166 Squadron Jan/44, category A damage (minor but beyond unit capacity) 23/1/44, returned to 166 Squadron 29/1/44, category B damage (repairable but off site) 16/3/44 repaired by A.V.Roe, returned to 166 Squadron 22/4/44, lost during raid on Stuttgart 26/7/44. (393 flying hours). ***

LL896 166 Squadron Mar/44, lost during raid on Revigny 13/7/44. (216 flying hours).

LM176 166 Squadron 16/6/44, crashed in Brocklesby Park near Kirmington returning from raid on Karlsruhe crew killed morning of 5/12/44. *

LM289 166 Squadron Jul/44, crashed at Barnetby-le-wold returning from raid on Lutzkendorf 5/4/45.

LM386 166 Squadron 15/11/43, lost during raid on Stuttgart 26/7/44. (413 flying hours).

LM388 166 Squadron 15/11/43, lost during raid on Revigny night of 12-13/7/44. (335 flying hours).

LM581 166 Squadron May/44, shot down near Epe, Holland following

raid on Gelsenkirchen 13/7/44. (83 flying hours). *

ND635 166 Squadron 21/2/44, lost during a raid on Agenville 31/8/44.

ME647 460 Squadron 20/2/44, to 166 Squadron 21/2/44, category A damage (minor but beyond unit capacity) 14/7/44, returned to 166 Squadron 28/7/44, lost during raid on Osterfeld night of 31/12/44 to 1/1/45. *

ME835 166 Squadron 7/1/44, lost during raid on Bochum night of 4–5/11/44. (389 flying hours).

ND628 32 Maintenance Unit 15/2/44, to 166 Squadron 21/2/44, category A damage (minor but beyond unit capacity) 24/3/44, returned to 166 Squadron 1/4/44, lost during raid on Stuttgart 24/7/44. (256 flying hours). *

ND635 166 Squadron 21/2/44, Lost during raid on Agenville 31/8/44.

NF986 166 Squadron between Jul and Sep 1944, undershot and hit trees, crash landed and burnt out near Croxley, Lincolnshire 4/11/44. (143 flying hours).

Aircraft marked with * were flown by Bernard Steel on operations.

1656 Heavy Conversion Unit (Lindholme, South Yorkshire) 26/9/44 to 23/11/45.

Aircraft type: Avro Lancaster
Handley Page Halifax
Airspeed Oxford.

Airspeed Oxford.

T1343 Station Flight Lindholme 29/12/43, storage 25/9/47, sold for scrap J. Dale & Co., London Colney1/7/48.

DF415 1503 Beam Approach Training Flight 31/5/42, **to Station Flight Lindholme 28/10/43,** to Station Flight Tibenham 11/8/45, storage 2/5/46, sold 5/5/50.

Handley Page Halifax.

W7771 Controller of Research and Development 5/7/42, Station Flight Netheravon 25/10/42, to 1656 Heavy Conversion Unit 29/1/44, to 60 Maintenance Unit 29/4/44, **to 1656 Heavy Conversion Unit 29/4/44,** category E damage (damaged beyond repair) 15/11/44, Struck off Charge 30/11/44. (483 flying hours).

BB254 18 Maintenance Unit 6/11/42, **to 1656 Heavy Conversion Unit 21/12/42,** category E (damaged beyond repair) burnt out 23/11/44, Struck off charge 24/11/44. (593 flying hours).

BB255 18 Maintenance Unit 9/11/42, **to 1656 Heavy Conversion Unit 29/12/42,** to 48 Maintenance Unit 4/1/45, Struck off charge 1/11/45.

BB267 1656 Heavy Conversion Unit 14/12/42, category E damage (damaged beyond repair) 14/10/44, Struck off charge 20/10/44.

BB269 1656 Heavy Conversion Unit 20/12/42, to 48 Maintenance Unit 10/12/44, Struck off Charge 14/12/44.

BB270 1656 Heavy Conversion Unit 20/12/42, Struck off charge 1/11/44 to 1662 Heavy Conversion Unit as instructional airframe, reduced to spares 6/2/45. (782 flying hours).

EB158

JD268 408 Squadron 23/6/43, to 429 Squadron 12/8/43, to 1659 Heavy Conversion Unit 31/1/44, to 1666 Heavy Conversion Unit 23/3/44, **to 1656 Heavy Conversion Unit 7/3/44,** Struck off Charge 8/2/45. (749 flying hours).

JD313 77 Squadron 7/7/43, recalled to Handley Page 23/9/43, to 48 Maintenance

Unit 24/12/43, to 1662 Heavy Conversion Unit 7/3/44, **to 1656 Heavy Conversion Unit unknown date,** to 48 Maintenance Unit 17/1/45, Struck off charge 1/11/45.

JD469 102 Squadron 21/8/43, to 1662 Heavy Conversion Unit 28/3/44, **to 1656 Heavy Conversion Unit 21/6/44,** Struck off charge at 48 Maintenance Unit 14/12/44.

JN965 45 Maintenance Unit 8/10/43, to 1 Overseas Aircraft Preparation 15/10/43, to 310 Ferry Training Unit 5/11/43, to 32 Maintenance Unit, to Bombing Development Unit 16/11/43, **to 1656 Heavy Conversion Unit 26/2/44,** to 48 Maintenance Unit 17/1/45, Struck off charge (deteriorated beyond repair) 25/1/45.

JN975 48 Maintenance Unit 22/10/43, **to 1656 Heavy Conversion Unit 9/1/44,** to 48 Maintenance Unit 30/12/44, Struck off charge 11/1/45.

JP192 1656 Heavy Conversion Unit 21/6/44, to 44 Maintenance Unit 17/4/44, to 1652 Heavy Conversion Unit 23/6/44, **to 1656 Heavy Conversion Unit date unknown,** category E damage (damaged beyond repair) 9/11/44, Struck off charge 16/11/44.

LL487 1667 Heavy Conversion Unit 10/6/44, to 48 Maintenance Unit 17/1/45, Struck off charge 1/11/45. ★

LL537 1667 Heavy Conversion Unit 29/7/44, to 48 Maintenance Unit 10/1/45, Struck off charge 1/11/45. ★

LW244 151 Squadron 5/9/43, to 158 Squadron 2/11/43, to 48 Maintenance Unit 19/2/44, **to 1656 Heavy Conversion Unit 9/5/44,** to 48 Maintenance Unit 20/1/45, Struck off charge 1/11/45.

Avro Lancaster.

R5730 1654 Heavy Conversion Unit between Feb and Jul/42, to 5 Lancaster Finishing School, **to 1656 Heavy Conversion Unit,** crashed 15/3/45 taken to a Maintenance Unit, Struck off Charge 29/1/47.

R5853 97 Communication Flight between Jan and Sep/42, to 61 Communication Flight, to 1660 Heavy Conversion Unit, to 576 Squadron, to 1 Lancaster Finishing School, to 1667 Heavy Conversion Unit, to 1651 Heavy Conversion Unit, Struck off charge 4/10/45. ★

W4995 101 Squadron between Sep/42 and May/43, to 625 Squadron, to 1 Lancaster Finishing School, **to 1656 Heavy Conversion Unit,** crashed at Lindholme 16/5/45, Struck off charge 25/3/48.

DV165 1667 Heavy Conversion Unit between May and Nov/43, to 300 Squadron, to 1 Lancaster Finishing School, to 1662 Heavy Conversion Unit, to 1667 Heavy Conversion Unit, swung on take off and undercarriage collapsed and burnt out at Sandtoft 9/4/45. ★

ED585 1656 Heavy Conversion Unit 11/2/43, to 1 Lancaster Finishing School, to 50 Squadron, Struck off charge 10/4/45.

ED623 207 Squadron between Nov/42 and Jun/43, to 626 Squadron, to 101 Squadron, to 1 Lancaster Finishing School, to 1667 Heavy Conversion Unit, **to 1656 Heavy Conversion Unit,** Struck off charge and scrapped 4/10/46.

ED749 100 Squadron between Nov/42 and Jun/43, to 300 Squadron, to 1 Lancaster Finishing School, to 1667 Heavy Conversion Unit, **to 1656 Heavy Conversion Unit,** to 1660 Heavy Conversion Unit, struck off charge 19/10/45.

ED905 103 Squadron between Nov/42 and Jun/43, to 166 Squadron, to 550 Squadron, to 1 Lancaster Finishing School, **to 1656 Heavy Conversion Unit,** swung on landing and undercarriage collapsed at Lindholme 20/8/45. (628 flying hours).

HK755 1667 Heavy Conversion Unit between Oct/43 and Feb/44**, to 1656 Heavy Conversion Unit,** to 10 Maintenance Unit following crash 1/4/45, scrapped 13/2/47.

JA673 156 Squadron between Jun and Sep/43, to 582 Squadron Apr/44, to 1669 Heavy Conversion Unit, **to 1656 Heavy Conversion Unit,** to 22 Maintenance Unit, sold for scrap 8/8/46.

JA868 103 Squadron between Jun and Dec/43, to 576 Squadron, **to 1656 Heavy Conversion Unit Nov/44,** to 46 Maintenance Unit, to 45 Maintenance Unit, Struck off charge 7/8/47.

LL748 476 Squadron between Oct/43 and Mar/44, to 550 Squadron, to 1 Lancaster Finishing School, to 1656 Heavy Conversion Unit, to 1662 Heavy Conversion Unit, **to 1656 Heavy Conversion Unit,** suffered damage in accident 21/11/45, Struck off charge 6/12/45.

LL804 115 Squadron between Nov/43 and Aug/44, to 300 Squadron, **to 1656 Heavy Conversion Unit,** to 1660 Heavy Conversion Unit, Struck off charge 28/3/46.

LL811 550 Squadron between Nov/43 and Aug/44, to 1 Lancaster Finishing School, to 1662 Heavy Conversion Unit, **to 1656 Heavy Conversion Unit,** swung on take-off and undercarriage collapsed at Lindholme 20/6/45.

LM369 101 Squadron between Oct/43 and Oct/44, **to 1656 Heavy Conversion Unit,** to 1653 Heavy Conversion Unit, Struck off charge 24/1/47.

LM741 100 Squadron Sep/44, **to 1656 Heavy Conversion Unit Nov/44,** to 1653 Heavy Conversion Unit Nov/45, Struck off charge 5/3/46.

ME377 32 Maintenance Unit between Oct/44 and Mar/45, to156 Squadron, **to 1656 Heavy Conversion Unit,** to 1653 Heavy Conversion Unit, to Royal Aircraft Establishment Farnborough, to 45 Maintenance Unit, Struck off charge 7/11/47.

ME583 576 Squadron between Nov/43 and Jan/44, to 550 Squadron, to 1 Lancaster Finishing School, **to 1656 Heavy Conversion Unit,** sold for scrap 8/8/46.

ND392 100 Squadron Dec/43, to 460 Squadron Dec/42, **to 1656 Heavy Conversion Unit Nov/44,** to 1660 Heavy Conversion Unit Nov/45, Struck off charge 26/3/46.

ND512 49 Squadron between Dec/43 and May/44, to 1653 Heavy Conversion Unit Nov/44, **to 1656 Heavy Conversion Unit,** to 22 Maintenance Unit, Struck off charge 2/6/47.

ND615 32 Maintenance Unit between Dec/43 and Mar/44, to 460 Squadron Mar/44, **to 1656 Heavy Conversion Unit Dec/44,** to 20 Maintenance Unit, struck off charge 30/4/46.

ND639 625 Squadron between Dec/43 and May/44, to 100 Squadron, **to 1656 Heavy Conversion Unit,** to 1667 Heavy Conversion Unit, crashed and burnt out on exercise after losing control in cloud at Crowle, Lincolnshire. Crew Killed 5/4/45.

ND747 75 Squadron Mar/44, to 3 Lancaster Finishing School, to Gee-H Training Flight, **to 1656 Heavy Conversion Unit,** to 1668 Heavy Conversion Unit, crashed 13/10/45 damaged beyond repair, Struck off charge 2/11/45.

NG436 35 Squadron between Jul/44 and Feb/45, **to 1656 Heavy Conversion Unit Aug/45,** to 12 Squadron, to 15 Maintenance Unit, Struck off Charge 27/11/46.

PA965 405 Squadron Jun/44, to 1660 Heavy Conversion Unit, **to 1656 Heavy Conversion Unit,** to 12 Squadron, to 9 Squadron, Struck off charge 15/11/46.

PB282 635 Squadron between May/44 and Mar/45, to 405 Squadron, **to 1656 Heavy Conversion Unit,** to 39 Maintenance Unit, to 12 Squadron, to 9 Squadron, Struck off charge 17/12/46.

PB577 115 Squadron between May/44 and Mar/45, to Gee-H Training Flight, **to 1656 Heavy Conversion Unit,** to 1668 Heavy Conversion Unit, Struck off charge 27/12/45.

PB857 1656 Heavy Conversion Unit Dec/44, crashed near to Lindholme Lake on approach to Lindholme 9/10/45.

PB860 1656 Heavy Conversion Unit 2/12/44, Struck off charge 20/12/45.

PB866 1667 Heavy Conversion Unit Dec/44, to 22 Maintenance Unit Sep/45, Struck off charge 2/6/47.★

PB868 1667 Heavy Conversion Unit between Oct/44 and Feb/45, **to 1656 Heavy Conversion Unit,** Struck off charge 16/11/45.

PB870 1667 Heavy Conversion Unit Dec/44, to 20 Maintenance Unit Oct/45, Struck off charge 10/10/46. ★

PD291 50 Squadron Aug/44, **to 1656 Heavy Conversion Unit Feb/45,** to 1660 Heavy Conversion Unit Jan/46, Struck off charge 25/7/46.

1667 HCU was based at Lindholme alongside 1656 HCU. This explains how Bernard Steel came to fly them even though they were never officially at 1656 HCU.

BIBLIOGRAPHY

Bomber Command Losses (1944). W.R. Chorley. Midland Publishing 2005.

The Bomber Command War Diaries. Martin Middlebrook & Chris Everitt. Viking 1985.

Elementary Flying Training. Air Ministry 1943.

Instructors Handbook of Elementary Flying Training. Air Ministry 1942.

The Oxford, Consul & Envoy File. John F. Hamlin. Air Britain 2001.

The Lancaster File. J.J. Halley. Air Britain 1985.

Pilot's and Flight Engineer's Notes Lancaster. Air Ministry 1944.

Pilot's Notes for Oxford I & II. Air Ministry 1944.

Pilot's Notes for Tiger Moth. R.A.A.F. 1944.

R.A.F. Handbook 1939-1945. David Wragg. Sutton 2007.

Royal Air Force Flying Training and Support Units. Ray Sturtivant, John Hamlin & J.J. Halley. Air Britain 1997.

Selected for Aircrew. James Hampton. Air Research 2003.

Tail End Charlies. John Nichol & Tony Rennell. Penguin 2005.

The Whitley File. R.N. Roberts. Air Britain 1986.

And with thanks to the following organisations.

Battle of Britain Memorial Flight.

The National Archives.

R.A.F. Museum Hendon.